MEXICO'S INDIGENOUS COMMUNITIES

Mexico's Indigenous Communities
Their Lands and Histories, 1500–2010

Ethelia Ruiz Medrano

TRANSLATED BY *Russ Davidson*

University Press of Colorado

Published by the University Press of Colorado
5589 Arapahoe Avenue, Suite 206C
Boulder, Colorado 80303

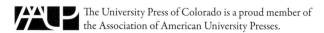 The University Press of Colorado is a proud member of
the Association of American University Presses.

The University Press of Colorado is a cooperative publishing enterprise supported, in part, by
Adams State College, Colorado State University, Fort Lewis College, Mesa State College, Metro-
politan State College of Denver, University of Colorado, University of Northern Colorado, and
Western State College of Colorado.

∞ The paper used in this publication meets the minimum requirements of the American
National Standard for Information Sciences—Permanence of Paper for Printed Library Materials.
ANSI Z39.48-1992

Library of Congress Cataloging-in-Publication Data

Ruiz Medrano, Ethelia.
 Mexico's indigenous communities : their lands and histories, 1500–2010 / Ethelia Ruiz Medrano.
  p. cm.
 Includes bibliographical references and index.
  ISBN 978-1-60732-016-6 (hardcover : alk. paper) — ISBN 978-1-60732-017-3 (e-book : alk.
paper) — ISBN 978-1-60732-133-0 (pbk : alk. paper) 1. Indians of Mexico—Land tenure—
History. 2. Indians of Mexico—Legal status, laws, etc.—History. 3. Indians of Mexico—Claims.
4. Indians of Mexico—Ethnic identity. 5. Land tenure—Law and legislation—Mexico—History.
6. Ethnohistory—Mexico. I. Title.
 F1219.3.L34R85 2010
 333.2—dc22
                            2010029945

Design by Daniel Pratt

20 19 18 17 16 15 14 13 12 11   10 9 8 7 6 5 4 3 2 1

Contents

Contents

Illustrations

Tables

Acknowledgments

My work on this book would not have been possible without the generous support of the John Simon Guggenheim Memorial Foundation, which awarded me a Latin American–Caribbean area research grant in 2006; Consejo Nacional de Ciencia y Tecnología, which provided research assistance in 2001; and my excellent History Office Directors—Professor Ruth Arboleyda (2002–2008) and Professor Arturo Soberón (2008–2010)—both of whom gave me much-needed support and friendship.

I likewise thank the archivists and librarians at Seville's Archivo General de Indias and Mexico's Archivo General de la Nación (AGN), also in Seville. At the AGN, I am especially indebted to Soledad Villafuerte for the benefit of her vast experience as head of the Archivo de Buscas. I also thank these AGN staff who ably helped me locate documents and obtain publication permissions: Roberto Beristian, Gabriel Damián Enríquez, Armando Santiago Sánchez, and Jorge Nacif Mina. The ongoing assistance I received from the librarians at the National Library of France in Paris, in particular that of Zoubida Zerkane with respect to obtaining permissions to publish documents, was extremely helpful. I also acknowledge the assistance of archivists at the Archivo General Agrario in

Acknowledgments

Mexico City, the Archivo General Agrario in Puebla, and the Archivo Municipal of Tlaxiaco. The director of the Archivo Municipal, Roberto Santos Pérez, was unstinting in his efforts to help. The time I spent at the Archivo de la Sacristía de Santa Inés Zacatelco and the Archivo de la Sacristía de Acuitlapilco, both in Tlaxcala, was especially rewarding, and I will long remember my pleasant conversations with the director of the former, Toribio Morales Carvente. Equally important was the kind and capable assistance I received from staff members at the outstanding U.S. Library of Congress in Washington, D.C. I also extend special thanks for their stellar dedication to Miguel Angel Gasca of the Biblioteca del Museo de Antropología, INAH, and Ixchel Cervantes Ruiz of the Biblioteca Manuel Orozco, INAH, who invariably turned up manuscripts, copies, books, and articles I needed.

On an individual level, the opportunity I had to discuss my ideas and research with a wide circle of scholars benefited me immeasurably. I am tremendously grateful to William Taylor, Muriel McKevitt Sonne Professor Emeritus at the University of California at Berkeley, who read the manuscript and gave me sage and sensible insights. New York University anthropology professor Thomas Abercrombie, with his deep understanding of the indigenous world and keen critical temperament, was a special source of inspiration. My husband and I had the good fortune of traveling with him to the state of Guerrero, and I have no doubt that his incisive observations helped me improve this work. I am also grateful to him as well as to Elizabeth Hill Boone, who holds the Martha and Donald Robertson Chair in Latin American Art at Tulane University; Susan Kellogg, professor of history at the University of Houston; and Eleanor Wake of the School of Languages at the University of London for having reviewed my proposal to the Guggenheim Foundation.

Others who deserve gratitude are my dear Professor Antonio Acosta from the University of Sevilla, Spain, who opened the world of archives to me twenty-five years ago, and Professor Guilhem Olivier of the Instituto de Investigaciones Históricas at UNAM, for helping me understand more clearly the importance of ethnology. I am grateful to Professor Frank Salomon, John V. Murra Professor of Anthropology at the University of Wisconsin-Madison, Professor Kevin Terraciano of UCLA, and Professor Gerardo Gutiérrez of the University of Colorado, all of whom offered comments on the text. In addition, Gerardo Gutiérrez kindly used the facilities of his cartographic laboratory to produce the detailed maps that appear in this book. For his excellent work and considerable patience, I am grateful to Russ Davidson, Curator Emeritus of Latin American and Iberian Collections at the University of New Mexico in Albuquerque, who translated the manuscript and has become a good friend.

My interest in learning more about the nature and affairs of contemporary indigenous society has not only filled up my in-box with a new set of intellectual problems and questions; it has also given me a host of wonderful new friends. Among these, I am particularly grateful to Professor Adolfo de Paz of the Universidad de Guerrero, who served as a guide and introduced me to different pueblos in the state. In Atliaca I was fortunate to gain the trust of Maestro Modesto Vázquez Salgado, a humanist par excellence, who shared the story of his exemplary life. In Santa María Cuquila I made a number of warm friendships and am grateful to everyone in the pueblo for their welcoming ways and willingness to let me join in the routine of daily life, disclose their plans for the future, and accept my admiration for their long and rich history. Among these Cuquilan associations, I am especially grateful to my compadre, Emiliano Melchor Ayala, and to Germán Ortiz Coronel and Don Camilo Coronel Sánchez, as well as to Cecilia Melchor, Misael Melchor, and Olivia and Elia Melchor.

Moreover, to have enjoyed the friendship of two greatly gifted anthropologists, John Murra and Luis Reyes García, both now deceased, was very important. Their experience and understanding of the indigenous world of Peru and Mexico remain an inspiration. The memory of these two beloved scholars will be with me forever.

Over the years, many other individuals—colleagues and friends alike—have given me much encouragement and support. I am grateful to Christopher Boyer, Jose Contel, Helios Figuerola, Soledad Figuerola, Maria de Gutiérrez, René Marneau, Zuanilda Mendoza, John Monaghan, Aurore Monod, Johannes Neurath, Enrique Omaña, Lorraine Orlandi and family, Mónica Palma, Carlos San Juan, Ignacio Silva, David Wright, and Yanna Yannakakis. My many pleasant conversations with all these colleagues and dear friends have helped me in writing this book more than they can imagine.

I express special thanks to Darrin Pratt, editor at the University Press of Colorado, for his interest in, and splendid work with, this book.

For their love and affection and their example of academic integrity, I am also grateful to my father, Professor José Ruiz Herrera, my brothers Carlos and Francisco, and my sister Carmiña. I particularly appreciate the many Saturdays spent in the company of my brother, Professor Roberto Ruiz, and his lovely family.

Whatever merits this work possesses are a result of the contributions of all those mentioned thus far; any errors or mistakes are mine alone. Finally, and most important, for all the joy they have given me I express my gratitude to the two most cherished persons in my life: my husband, Guilhem Olivier, and our daughter, Aurora Olivier Ruiz. With my husband I share not only many happy moments and common academic interests but also our love for our beautiful Aurora, whose birth occurred the same year (2002) I began this project. It is to her that I dedicate this work, with profound love—for she is the future.

MEXICO'S INDIGENOUS COMMUNITIES

Introduction

The pueblo of San Miguel Ecatepec, Tequiscistlán, located in the Oaxacan district of Tehuantepec, presented a "faithful copy" of a colonial codex to the agrarian authorities. The copy, done in black and white on paper and certified by the municipality's agent, was produced in "San Miguel Yautepec, Oaxaca, on 5 November 1941." This document clearly incorporates aspects of an important local oral tradition as well as information gleaned from what seems to be a colonial codex. The pueblo's authorities presented it to an agrarian tribunal to verify their community's long history. The fact that Indian pueblos would still copy the codex in the mid-twentieth century is interesting enough, but giving these exercises—undertaken over matters of land—even greater interest was their recovery and recounting of ancestral myths and stories.[1]

In Mexico, numerous Indian pueblos zealously guard ancient documents for a variety of purposes, among which the issue of land and its rightful ownership looms large. Indeed, the practice of drawing up and preserving historical documents has been a determining factor in the history of Mexico's Indian communities, especially since the beginning of the sixteenth century. In this work, I examine the historical documents of Indian communities in both the state of Oaxaca and the central part of Mexico from the sixteenth century to the present, focusing in particular on the genres of painted manuscripts, maps, and oral accounts.

In Chapter 1, I review the ways the principles informing and underlying royal power created the legal foundation on which conquered vassals of the Castilian king could bring charges in court against powerful men who represented him in his overseas colony. The king's legitimacy resided in offering justice to his vassals, which necessarily involves a consideration of both the rights those vassals possessed and the different political mechanisms such rights engendered for the purposes of commanding and negotiating power.

I also demonstrate that only through the presence of cultural intermediaries were the Indian pueblos capable—soon after they were conquered—of understanding and employing the Spanish system of justice to their own advantage, albeit with all the cultural problems and difficulties of legal terminology inherent in the situation. These intermediaries (missionary priests, royal functionaries and officeholders, lawyers, legal representatives, interpreters, and persons of mixed race) opened a path to the courts and legal authorities that enabled the Indian communities, and members of the native nobility in particular, to bring lawsuits and argue claims before the colonial powers. At the same time, however, the Indians' capacity to engage and steer through the complicated apparatus of the colonial legal system implied a certain measure of autonomy on their part. Since at least 1531, they had possessed the right, when bringing lawsuits before the courts and tribunals, to employ some of their own customs and traditions. The evidence in every such legal proceeding, for example, was presented in the form of codices or pictorial documents (which enjoyed the same legal status as notarial deeds and records); furthermore, their oral testimony was given in the Indians' language. A large number of translators or interpreters were invariably used in all judicial cases.

This autonomy was exercised within a system of delicate balances or constraints. Clearly, it was essential to recognize that, as part of a complex system of legitimacy, it was the king who ultimately dispensed justice—a condition that applied even to those who had become his vassals through conquest in faraway lands—and that in the case of New Spain, the incorporation of the native population into the colonial judicial system was accomplished in part through the aid of cultural intermediaries. Yet it also followed, as a consequence, that judicial practices had to be comprehensible to the Indians. For that to happen, it was necessary that such practices make sense within their own cultural frame of reference.

The context and circumstances that prevailed at the end of the sixteenth century have led me to believe even more strongly that it was the Indians who managed to negotiate the introduction of evidence in a manner that coincided with their own practices and customs. I argue that, operating in a decidedly complex economic and political environment, the Crown chose in general to distance itself ideologically from the political need to legitimate its power. This development entailed a series of changes with respect to the social condition of the Indians. The Crown and the colonial regime sought (with all its consequences) to assimilate the Indians into the kingdom without evidencing an interest in, and even prohibiting the use of, their native practices and customs, especially insofar as they involved recounting the Indians' history prior to the conquest. What is more, in this environment, those who played the role of cultural intermediary—the missionaries and native nobility in particular—lost political influence and force.

In Chapter 2, I deal with a related problem—that of the presentation of historical evidence, or proof, by the Indians—within an evolving historical context that showed little favor toward Indian communities in the seventeenth and eighteenth centuries. During an initial stage of research, I assumed that if indigenous practices and customs were forgotten and, moreover, were assigned no "legal" meaning within the colonial administrative structure, I would fail to encounter any codices or pictorial representations the Indians presented before the colonial courts.

Fortunately, however, this proved not to be the case. Notably in the central part of New Spain and in what today constitutes the state of Oaxaca, various Indian communities continued (by utilizing different negotiation strategies) to present judicial arguments pictorially, with recourse to maps in particular. What is more, in the mid-seventeenth century some pueblos began to advance a new type of legal argument while pleading their cases. The novelty took the form of narrating their local histories, especially as they concerned disputes and litigation over issues of land and property. In cases of this nature, representatives of the pueblo would describe, both orally and in writing (on some occasions using Nahuatl), the story of their arrival at or migration to their community and the various rites by which they took "possession" of their lands. To reinforce their position and give their arguments greater force, they also presented pictorial documents, or painted manuscripts, whose antiquity—a condition asserted by the Indians in many instances—presumably verified the early history of the pueblo.[2]

To my way of thinking, making sense of the concept of indigenous-inspired negotiation, accounting for its workings and success in the colonial context, calls for a particular type of analysis that I undertake in Chapter 2 by examining actual cases as I came across them in the archives. Such a study of specific cases allows one to gain insight into the different negotiation strategies the pueblos employed, a process that might be termed "the presentation of culturally complex evidence before the colonial courts."

In Chapter 3, I extend the time frame and endeavor to learn whether the process of indigenous negotiation with state power, based on the Indians' use of old, long-held records, continued into the postcolonial period. The fact that Mexico's nineteenth-century governments took a particularly hard line toward the Indian pueblos is common knowledge.[3] The idea that the Crown's Indian vassals required special protection[4] disappeared with the advent of the Mexican national state (a development that repeated itself in Spain's other former New World colonies).[5] In rapid order after independence was achieved, the native population—to a person—was granted the status of citizen. Thus, the transition the Indians abruptly experienced—from being protected vassals of the king to becoming citizens of the state, with specific rights and obligations—forced upon them a new reality and a new set of problems. How were they to assert their newfound rights outside the boundaries maintained by the protector state? The legislation enacted to break up communal property[6] was especially destructive of the collective rights to land the Indian pueblos had long enjoyed,[7] and the laws passed later during the 1890s, under Porfirio Díaz's rule, continued the process of privatizing the ownership of land.[8] In the face of these developments, the pueblos' margins for negotiation became ever narrower, although as more studies are done of the political agendas the Indian pueblos crafted during these years, the seeming inevitability of this conclusion may be called into question.[9] This situation, although generally the case, did not hold true everywhere. Recent research has shown that the laws of *desamortización* (disentailment) enabled some pueblos to preserve their land. The present-day state of Oaxaca stands out in this regard. There, by taking legal steps sanctioned in the agrarian legislation, pueblos that lacked productive, arable land—such as those in the Mixteca Alta and Mixteca Baja—could apparently stave off the loss of their land and consolidate its communal status.

Under such circumstances, it stretches the imagination to think that Indian communities would maintain the practice of introducing pictorial documents in the national courts, let alone the custom of recounting the history of how they came to take possession of particular lands, as a way of validating their claim to those lands. Against all such assumptions, however, cases exist of the Indians doing precisely that. I particularly encountered these examples in the section called *Buscas*, in the Archivo General de la Nación.[10] It suffices to note here that this section of the archive begins with documents produced shortly before passage of the Leyes de Reforma[11] and is composed of requests by Indian pueblos that searches be undertaken for the primordial titles and other historical documents that guaranteed their claims of landownership, along with the related request that the archive certify the authenticity of these documents so they could be submitted as evidence in court cases. In short, during the nineteenth century a substantial number of Indian pueblos continued to negotiate with judicial offi-cials for the use of both pictorial maps and historical narrative as legal arguments in conflicts over land.

Even more remarkable, a department *ex profeso* of paleography was created at the Archivo General de la Nación in 1854 for this express purpose, so that copies—exquisitely produced and hand-colored—could be made (and rendered in translation, when necessary) of original Nahuatl and Spanish pictorial maps, codices, and other historical documents. Those who carried out the department's work were excellent copyists who succeeded in locating numerous manuscripts of this sort. Some even undertook the copy work in their homes, a form of arti-san labor that has continued to the present day and is motivated by the same purpose—to deliver copies of documents to the pueblos that bear a certificate of historical authenticity, that identify and furnish evidence of their lands. Of the hundreds of Indian pueblos whose existence is officially recorded in Mexico, a small number have failed to discover the historical documents that would uphold their claim to have possessed certain lands. The majority, however, have been suc-cessful in this endeavor.

In light of this record, I began to ask whether the process might not have continued after the revolution, likely spurred on by Mexico's agrarian reform pro-gram.[12] The agrarian legislation enacted in 1917 had specifically mandated that Indian pueblos, to be legally granted *ejidos* (common or communal lands), estab-lish the date of their founding. Paralleling this directive are indications that reveal exactly how the pueblos' primordial titles served as privileged documents in fur-thering the process by which ejidos were granted or restituted.[13] In this manner, throughout the twentieth century some pueblos continued to present pictorial material (maps) and historical accounts that attested to the fact that their posses-sion of certain lands dated back centuries.

In Chapter 4, I offer modern-day case studies related to the overall theme of this book. In 2003, in the Nahua pueblo of Atliaca, state of Guerrero, I met Maestro Modesto Vázquez Salgado, a village schoolteacher and lawyer who, together with the people of his pueblo, fought for several years to recuperate land illegally occupied by a rich mestizo rancher. One of the strongest arguments that enabled them to win the case before the court was their ability to prove that the state had recognized Atliaca as a pueblo for more than half a century, under the communal lands system. I recount this experience for the people of Atliaca, showing the continuing importance for Mexican pueblos of the search for his-torical documents—in this case, those concerning their more recent history. I particularly trace Modesto's role in the dispute over Atliaca's land.

Also in Chapter 4, I follow the case of a pueblo in the Mixteca Alta of Oaxaca named Santa María Cuquila. I got to know the people of this village in 2004 because of their interest in obtaining a paleographic transcription of a document dated near the end of the sixteenth century, lodged in their community museum. Over the years I have also collaborated with the residents in the search for other historical documents that belong to them, held by different archives. As a result of this contact, I have gained insight into Cuquilans' perception of their local history, the reasons they are interested in tracing it, and especially the emphasis they place on the age and prestige of their pueblo. Cuquila has an agrarian history closely tied to its primordial titles, of which it has a special understanding. I try to show what such a perception is and how, in recuperating their history, they are recuperating themselves, thereby ensuring a better future for their families and the community as a whole.

In sum, my intention in this work is to demonstrate how, over a long period, Indian pueblos have pursued a complex process of political negotiation through the introduction of historical evidence—both written and pictorial—and to underscore that in some cases the history of the pueblos, as appropriated by the pueblos themselves, serves as an important marker of identity as well as a political weapon by which the pueblos can improve their present condition and gain hope for the future.

NOTES

1. See Chapter 3 of this work. Similar cases occur in other parts of Latin America. The Aymara people of Coroma, in the southern Altiplano of Bolivia, have developed a very moving and picturesque custom. Inside the folds of traditional textiles, some of which date to pre-Hispanic times, they wrap up old documents that tell the story of their lands, and, with these bundles draped over their backs, they begin to dance. For these Aymara the woven fabrics of dazzling color guard the souls of their ancestors and—as the swaddled documents recount—the history of their community as well. Cristina Bubba, "Los rituals a los vestidos de María Titiqhawa, Juana Palla y otros fundadores de los Ayllu de Coroma," in Thérèse Bouysse-Cassagne, ed., *Saberes y memorias en los Andes. In Memoriam Thierry Saignes,* 377–400 (Lima: Institut des Hautes Études de l'Amérique Latine, Institut Français d' Études Andines, 1997).

2. Kevin Terraciano and Lisa Sousa, "The 'Original Conquest' of Oaxaca: Late Colonial Nahuatl and Mixtec Accounts of the Spanish Conquest," *Ethnohistory* 50, 2 (2003): 349–400; Roskamp Hans, *La historiografía indígena de Michoacán: El lienzo de Jucutácato y los títulos de Carapan* (Leiden: Research School of Asian, African, and Amerindian Studies [CNWS], Universiteit Leiden, 1998); Michel Oudijk, *Historiography of the Bènizáa: The Postclassic and Early Colonial Periods [1000–1600 A.D.]* (Leiden: CNWS, Universiteit Leiden, 2000); Stephanie Wood, "Don Diego García de Mendoza Moctezuma: A Techialoyan Mastermind?" *Estudios de Cultura Náhuatl* 19 (1989): 215–259; Wood, "The Cosmic Conquest: Late Colonial Views of the Sword and the Cross in Central Mexican Títulos," *Ethnohistory* 38, 29 (1991): 176–195; Wood, "El problema de

la historicidad de los títulos y los códices Techialoyan," in *De tlacuilos a escribanos*, Xavier Noguez and Stephanie Wood, eds., 167–211 (Mexico City: El Colegio de Michoacán and El Colegio Mexiquense, 1998); Wood, *Transcending Conquest: Nahua Views of Spanish Colonial Mexico* (Norman: University of Oklahoma Press, 2003); Paula López Caballero, ed., *Los títulos primordiales del Centro de México* (Mexico City: Consejo Nacional para la Cultura y las Artes [CONACULTA], Colección Cien de México, 2003); Robert Haskett, *Visions of Paradise: Primordial Titles and Mesoamerican History in Cuernavaca* (Norman: University of Oklahoma Press, 2005); Ethelia Ruiz Medrano, "El espejo y su reflejo: Títulos primordiales de los pueblos indios utilizados por españoles en Tlaxcala, siglo XVIII," in Danna Levin and Federico Navarrete, eds., *Indios, mestizos y españoles interculturalidad e historiografía en la Nueva España*, 167–202 (México: Universidad Autónoma Metropolitana, Instituto de Investigaciones Históricas, and Universidad Nacional Autónoma de México, 2007).

3. Antonio Escobar O., ed., *Indio, nación, y comunidad: En el México del siglo XIX* (Mexico City: Centro Francés de Estudios Mexicanos Centroamericanos [CEMCA] and Centro de Investigaciones y Estudios Superiores en Antropología Social [CIESAS], 1993); Victoria Chenaut, *Aquellos que vuelan. Los totonacops en el siglo XIX*, Colection Historia de los Pueblos Indígenas de México (Mexico City: CIESAS and Instituto Nacional Indigenista, 1995); Leticia Reina Ayoma, *Caminos de luz y sombra: Historia indígena de Oaxaca en el siglo XIX*, Colection Historia de los Pueblos Indígenas de México (Mexico City: CIESAS and Comision para el Desarrollo de los Pueblos Indigenas, 2004).

4. Juan de Solórzano y Pereyra, *Política Indiana. Edición facsimilar tomada de la de 1776 (Madrid)*, 2 vols. (Mexico City: Secretaría de Programación y Presupuesto, 1979), chap. 28, 206–213: "*Que los indios son y deben ser contados entre las personas, que el derecho llama* miserables: *Y de que privilegios temporales gocen por esta causa, y de sus protectores.*" [That the Indians are and must be considered as among those people whom the law deems *wretched:* and what temporal privileges do they therefore enjoy by virtue of this condition and from their protectors.]

5. More on this development is found in Brooke Larson, *Trials of Nation Making: Liberalism, Race and Ethnicity in the Andes, 1810–1910* (Cambridge: Cambridge University Press, 2004).

6. "On 25 June 1856, the federal government passed the 'Law of *desamortización*,' better known as the Ley Lerdo, breaking up both rural plots of land and urban property belonging to religious and civil corporations. This piece of legislation, by calling for the disentailment of lands held by civil and religious entities, hastened the dissolution of the indigenous communities which had been established by the colonial regime. Lands ceased to belong to communities, or to the town or village councils which depended on them. Instead, they were split up, their ownership handed over to individuals—tenants or *comuneros*—who now possessed them outright or in usufruct" (241) "or they became the property of persons from entirely outside the community, who sued to obtain them" (238). Daniela Marino, "La modernidad a juicio: Pleitos por la tierra y la identidad comunal en el Estado de México (Municipalidad de Huixquilucan, 1856–1900), in Romana Falcón, ed., *Culturas de pobreza y resistencia: Estudios de marginados, proscritos y descontentos México,*

1804–1910, 237–264 (Mexico City: El Colegio de México and Universidad Autónoma de Querétaro, 2005).

7. Edgar Mendoza García, "Distrito político y desamortización: Resistencia y reparto de la propiedad comunal en los pueblos de Cuicatlán y Coixtlahuaca, 1856–1900," 209–235, and Marino, "La modernidad a juicio," both chapters in Romana Falcón, ed., *Culturas de pobreza y resistencia: Estudios de marginados, proscritos y descontentos México, 1804–1910* (México: El Colegio de México and Universidad Autónoma de Querétaro, 2005).

8. "Historians and contemporary observers are in agreement that in Mexico, during the regime of Porfirio Díaz, the ownership of land became concentrated to a degree heretofore unknown," in John H. Coatsworth, *El impacto económico de los ferrocarriles en el porfiriato, II,* 2 vols. (Mexico City: Sep-Setentas, 1976), 2: 42. Reina Ayoma, *Caminos de luz y sombra*: "Between 1881 and 1906, the alienation of empty or uncultivated lands [*terrenos baldíos*] in Mexico amounted to 49 million hectares, equivalent to a quarter of the country's land surface, of which 81 per cent was owned by North Americans" (141–142). Without question, as the author notes, the Porfirian laws affecting such lands, and the companion laws of colonization constitute a new version of the Leyes de Reforma. Reina Ayoma likewise concludes that in the case of the state of Oaxaca, this complex of Porfirian laws left the Indian pueblos landless (142).

9. Florencia E. Mallon, *Peasant and Nation: The Making of Postcolonial Mexico and Peru* (Berkeley: University of California Press, 1995); John Monaghan, "Mixtec Caciques in the Nineteenth and Twentieth Centuries," *Cuadernos de Historia Latinoamericana* (Special number of Códices, Caciques and Communities 5) (1997): 265–281; Chris Kyle, "Land, Labor and the Chilapa Market: A New Look at the 1840s' Peasant Wars in Central Guerrero," *Ethnohistory* 50, 1 (Winter 2003): 89–130; John Monaghan, Arthur Joyce, and Ronald Spores, "Transformations of the Indigenous Cacicazgo in the Nineteenth Century," *Ethnohistory* 50, 1 (Winter 2003): 131–150.

10. In 2003, in an effort to understand the origin and operation of this section of the national archive, I carried out a series of detailed interviews with its director, Soledad Villafuerte. She informed me that in her twenty years as head of the department, I was the first researcher to voice such an interest. One of the director's key responsibilities was to assist campesinos who had made their way to the office from different parts of the country to locate their "primordial titles." With Villafuerte's special approval, I had the opportunity to observe several of her interviews with campesinos engaged in this task. In addition, she spelled out how in many instances the lawyers the Indians retained, who were specialists in agrarian law, deceived their clients—for example, by collecting up to 10,000 pesos from them for certified maps for which, by law, the archive charged fewer than 100 pesos. For that and other such reasons, Villafuerte explained, she preferred to deal directly with the campesinos and not with their lawyers in all matters pertaining to the search for relevant historical materials.

11. Manuel Fabila, *Cinco siglos de legislación agraria [1493–1940],* 2 vols. (Mexico City: Secretaría de la Reforma Agraria, Centro de Estudios Históricos del Agrarismo en México, 1981), vol. 1, book 5, 159–168; José Blas Gutiérrez, *Leyes de Reforma: Colección de las disposiciones que se conocen con este nombre, publicadas desde el año de 1855 al 1868.*

Formada y anotada por el Lic . . . catedrático de procedimientos jurídicos en la Nacional Escuela de Jurisprudencia (Mexico City: Imprenta de El Constitucional, 1869); Juan N. Rodríguez de San Miguel, *Pandectas hispano-megicanas* [Estudio introductoria de María del Refugio González], 3 vols. (Mexico City: Universidad Nacional Autónoma de México [UNAM], 1991); "Decreto de Maximiliano de Habsburgo publicado en español y en náhuatl, sobre el fundo legal de los pueblos," in Ascensión H. de León-Portilla, *Tepuztlahcuilolli. Impresos en náhuatl. Historia y bibliografía* (Mexico City: UNAM, 1988), vol. 1, 289–291.

12. Guillermo Palacios, "Las restituciones de la Revolución," in *Estudios campesinos en el Archivo General Agrario,* Ismael Maldonado Salazar, Guillermo Palacios, and Reyna María Silva Chacón, eds. (Mexico City: Registro Agrario Nacional and CIESAS [Colección Agraria], 2001), vol. 3, 119–161.

13. Fabila, *Cinco siglos de legislación agraria [1493–1940],* vol. 1, circular no. 15: "Concerning the separate data that must be collected in the proceedings for granting ejidos. I. Population census. II. Agrarian census. III. Classification of the lands which the pueblo seeks to be granted. IV. Area of land that should correspond to each family head who possesses the status of farmer, as part of the final distribution as determined in accordance with the enabling law. V. The climate of the location. VI. Pattern of rainfall, if known. VII. Physical qualities of the land and native vegetation. VIII. The type of crops cultivated, or that could be cultivated, on the land in question. IX. Distance to and from the immediate surrounding pueblos. X. List of properties to be affected by the grant, stating, when possible, the total area comprised by the farms involved and the type of land on which they sit. XI. *Date on which the pueblo was established accompanied by a copy of the founding document . . .* México, 24 January 1917," 301 [emphasis added]; vol. 1, circular no. 18: "Resolving particular cases pertaining to either the restitution of ejidos or the concession of new grants, when the primordial titles do not indicate whether the land had been legally granted, México, 21 March 1917," 313–314; vol. 1, circular no. 30: "Giving notice to the Local Agrarian Commissions that during the processing of files pertaining to the restitution or granting of ejidos, evidence and summary statements may be admitted on the part of the owners of land . . . Mexico, 3 October 1917," 331.

1 | Historical Background

INDIAN ACCESS TO COLONIAL JUSTICE
IN THE SIXTEENTH CENTURY

A few years after the conquest of Mexico, a Spanish judge, Don Alonso de Zuazo, heard and pronounced judgment in a dispute concerning matters of land that arose among members of the native nobility. The conflict was apparently serious enough that it not only dragged on for some time but also resulted in the deaths of antagonists on both sides. In the course of the dispute, the Indian nobles presented several codices to the judge ("paintings" was the term used during the colonial period to describe these manuscripts). After he had examined the codices, the judge noted in laudatory fashion that the numerous details and fine points they contained allowed them to be treated like any other comprehensible and admissible legal document: "they provide evidence as much as any other writings provide it." The parties involved in the litigation took a different line, however, maintaining that the codices neither reflected their problem nor offered a possible solution. Consequently, the judge ordered that the *tlacuilo* (the person who painted the manuscripts, also indigenous scribe), whom he referred to as "amantecas" (artisan), repaint the codex, but this remedy failed to placate the Indian litigants. The judge then decided to bring in an enormous dog (*lebrel*) he had previously let loose on more than 200 criminals and Indians convicted of idolatry. The dog had been fattened on human flesh. With the terrifying sight of the ferocious animal as a backdrop, the judge informed the Indians that if they did not "paint the truth denoting the markers and boundaries of that controversy," the dog would be unleashed to kill them. Instantly, as if by magic, the artist painted a manuscript that was "altogether certain, and the parties approved it." The legal dispute was thus fully resolved, and the litigants on both sides emerged satisfied. Indeed, so content were they with the Spanish magistrate's clear judgment that the Indians decided to convert to Christianity.[1]

The evidence and proceedings in this case illustrate several points that merit our attention. First, they indicate that the native population was drawn into the judicial system in New Spain at an early date; second, that traditional indigenous codices (pictorial manuscripts) and maps were important evidence in trials; and third, that protocols existed—at least at this juncture—that enabled Indians to obtain justice in a manner they could comprehend, although on occasion this entailed the use of threats and other devices by the sovereign power whose final authority could not be questioned. Clearly, this third option does not seem to have unsettled the Indians or struck them as peculiar; in fact, to resolve matters on the basis of doctrine, authoritarian pronouncements may have accorded with their own view of the world.

JUSTICE IN ANCIENT MESOAMERICA

To understand how the justice system worked in Mesoamerica prior to the Spanish conquest is a very complex undertaking, made even more difficult by the fact that the application of the system undoubtedly varied from region to region. I do not intend to plunge into an extended discussion of this issue, yet I think it is important to cover certain points briefly. Thanks to the work of Fray Bernardino de Sahagún, we know that a special court called *tlacxitlan* (beneath, or at the foot of something) existed in the royal sanctum to hear testimony regarding "criminal activities,"[2] perhaps signifying in this context that those who were asking for justice were reaching up to a higher power from a lower position. In this court were "the *oidores*, or lord judges, and chief nobles" who had the responsibility of judging criminals and—should they choose—of sentencing them to death, which could be carried out in a number of ways. Or, by their verdict the guilty might instead be banished or imprisoned; the court decisions the nobles made apparently also included granting freedom to slaves.[3]

The Indian judges in this description were nobles who possessed the authority to hand down harsh judgments, including imposing public death by stoning, against persons who belonged to the same class; in this court, evidently, the only people who were tried and faced judgment were those who belonged to the nobility.[4] Further, these judges from the native nobility tried to fulfill their duties and exercise justice honestly and impartially.

Sahagún also observed that complaints against commoners (*macehual*) were heard by "senators, and elders" in different quarters of the royal palace, called *tecalli* or *teccalco*. He further mentioned that in this latter court the judges quickly asked that the Indians produce "the manuscript, on which was written or painted the charges or grounds for the suit: such as possessions, or houses or corn fields," and witnesses were called to provide evidence. In the chambers of the court of Texcoco, a "scribe or artist" was employed to record findings through specific reference to the codices, a practice also noted by the oidor Alonso de Zorita.[5] The judges' work was characterized by its honesty, or fidelity to the truth, since if they acted otherwise the king (*tlatoani*) would have them put to death for malfeasance and abuse of duty.[6] The Nahuatl section of Sahagún's work conveys the impression that the judges of the tecalli took down testimony and evidence, after which—because of their noble status—it was given to the judges of the other court, the tlacxitlan, to render verdicts and pronounce sentences.[7] Another manuscript, the *Codex Mendoza*, noted that judicial officials learned the skills of their office by practicing them from a young age and that the final appeal in any trial was decided by the powerful ruler Moctezuma.[8]

Similarly, Sahagún, Fray Toribio de Benavente Motolinía, Fray Diego Durán, and Zorita all placed great emphasis—in keeping with what their sources told them—on the high ethical standards with which judges in pre-conquest Mexico discharged their responsibilities, as they did on the summary deaths these same judges would suffer if they failed to act honestly.[9] To act as judges, then, the tlatoani appointed nobles, non-nobles who had distinguished themselves in war and in capturing slaves, and people who had been educated in the schools run by priests and who had acquired learning, displayed the ability to listen and to express themselves intelligently, possessed good memories, were not given to drunkenness, and upheld the honor of their family line.[10] Only in exceptional cases, involving complicated disputes that were difficult to resolve, did the tlatoani review the testimony and—in consultation with some of the judges—render the verdict himself.[11]

Thus, from the foregoing an interesting fact or distinction emerges; namely, that members of the nobility were tried in a different venue from the rest of native society and in all judicial affairs were judged solely by other nobles. In contrast, disputes among commoners were resolved by judges of lesser rank. In this world, apparently, justice was differentiated on the basis of social class, a state of affairs that, as we shall see, would change during the colonial period.

Further insight into the nature of justice in pre-Hispanic Mexico is provided in a learned study by Jerome Offner, whose examination of the topic is based on early indigenous sources involving the community of Texcoco. Offner points out that in the case of Texcoco, the system of justice was centralized in the figure of the tlatoani who ruled over that political domain, or *altepetl*.[12] The tlatoani relied on a pair of tribunals to administer justice. The first, known as Teoicpalpan (divine tribunal), heard cases that involved serious crimes and disputes; the second, called *tlatocaicpalpan* (the king's tribunal), dealt with less important cases.[13] In addition, the system included twelve judges who represented the six principal administrative districts that made up the territory of Texcoco. Each district was thus represented by two judges. All twelve judges heard cases and handed down sentences in the palace of Texcoco's tlatoani. They became judges only after being carefully vetted, and some were blood relatives of the ruler. In carrying out their duties, they were assisted by a large number of subalterns and were supported by the yields of agricultural lands designated specifically for that purpose.[14] Motolinía emphasizes how quickly the Texcoco judges pronounced sentences; they attempted to resolve all disputes, even the most complicated, in a period—to which the name *nappualtlatulli* was given—not to exceed eighty days.[15]

The Texcocan justice system enabled its authorities to maintain control over both a diverse range of ethnic groups and a considerable number of local rulers who governed smaller political units. The system had been carefully constructed, it seems, to serve as an instrument of social control for the *tlatoque* (high lords) of Texcoco and thus acted as a brake on certain types of antisocial behavior—such as alcoholism, murder, treasonous actions against the nobility, robbery, and adultery—all of which were seen to weaken and undermine the family, the broader society, and the altepetl itself.[16]

In this context, Motolinía provides further information with respect to Texcoco's judges and judicial system, noting that both Nezahualcoyotl and his son, Nezahualpilli, enjoyed sufficient political strength to issue a great number of laws designed to ensure that order prevailed within their domain. Indeed, the administration of justice was so successful in Texcoco that the tlatoani of the neighboring territory of Tenochtitlan referred "numerous disputes there so that they could be settled."[17] Another interesting fact, noted by both Motolinía and Zorita, involves a ritual practiced in the judicial proceedings not only of Texcoco but of other places as well. When a verdict was declared, it was the custom to swear it by the "earth goddess" or the gods in general. This practice is clearly very similar to that found in colonial judicial proceedings, in which God and the holy cross were invoked in the pronouncement of judgments. It is not entirely clear whether this practice among the indigenous population was truly their own or was projected back on them by later authors.[18] On balance, the ritual of pronouncing judgment or declaring truth in the name of the gods was, in fact, probably native to the Indian justice system. A similar practice was followed in another part of the Spanish empire. In the mid-sixteenth century, in the viceroyalty of Peru, the *corregidor* (Spanish official in charge of indigenous settlements) of Yucay made Indians involved in disputes swear in the name of their own gods, not those of the Christian religion, that they would state the truth.[19]

From the chronicles and other sources of the colonial period, we can infer that the Texcocan system of justice stood as a model and was emulated by other important altepetl in the region. Texcoco's centralized system required that its judges meet with the tlatoani every twelve days to discuss disputes that did not lend themselves to simple, straightforward resolution.[20] In Zorita's opinion, the way justice was administered varied little within and across the territory of the three most important altepetl—México-Tenochtitlan, Texcoco, and Tlacopan. To understand the form of justice practiced in one of these altepetl, he observed, was to understand its equivalent in the other two.[21]

Motolinía likewise explained that Texcoco's twelve judges enjoyed the services of twelve *alguaciles mayores* (chief constables), whose function was to place persons of privileged class (nobles) under arrest. To advertise their charge and office, they wore specially decorated blankets, "and wherever they went they met with compliance, as high-level agents of the ruler and his greater justice." The alguaciles, Motolinía mentioned, were called *achcauhtli* and the judges *Tecuytlatoque*.[22] In the outlying districts of Texcoco there were other judges who deliberated minor cases, but the bulk of judicial cases were reviewed and handled in the royal palace by the twelve high judges, in consultation with the tlatoani.[23]

Nevertheless, as Susan Kellogg has pointed out, for all the similarities between the Spanish colonial justice system and its pre-Hispanic counterpart in central Mexico—that of the Nahuas in particular—the two systems still differed in important respects. The Nahua system was only one element within a wider system of penalties—which rested to a considerable degree on supernatural sanctions—in addition to those imposed by family members, neighbors, the quarter or local district in which the accused lived, and artisan groups. Rules and norms were thus reinforced, and conflicts resolved, through a variety of channels. The system also provided few opportunities for appealing a decision and operated on a much faster timescale in resolving problems than the Spanish colonial system. By contrast, despite being more bureaucratic, the colonial system of justice allowed for greater flexibility as well as frequent appeals.[24]

From the available evidence, then, it is clear that justice in pre-conquest Mesoamerica was administered through a complex system grounded in the organization of the various altepetl that controlled the greater part of this region (México-Tenochtitlan, Texcoco, and Tlaclopan). At the same time, local differences undoubtedly existed within the general scheme.

One central fact, however, deserves special emphasis; namely, that the system rested at bottom on the power of the ruling class, creating an arrangement in which justice was administered one way for the nobles and another way for the common people. As observed earlier, though, the system also operated horizontally, so that justice was also served across and within different groupings and divisions of indigenous society, such as the local ward of the community in which a person lived. Ultimately, the most important point is that the complexity and sophistication of state and society in pre-conquest Mesoamerica led inexorably to the development of a complex system for administering justice. Only on this basis can one account for the rapid and widespread acceptance with which the Indians eventually greeted the introduction of the colonial justice system.

We can thus observe that words such as "lawyer" and "justice," a standard feature of the colonial lexicon, have equivalents in various indigenous languages. In the sixteenth century, for example, the Nahua terms to convey the office and function of lawyer were *tepan tlatoani* (*gobernante*), *tlatoliquaniani*, and *tlatlatoliquaniani*.[25] The word for justice in Nahuatl was *tlamelauacachiualiztli* or *tlatlamelauhcachiualiztli*.[26] Similarly, in the sixteenth century the term for lawyer in the Mixtec language was *taycahandaandodzoha* or *taycahanino*,[27] and the words for justice were *yodzandoho, yod. Ananindi, yosanindi*, and *yocanidi*.[28] As remarkable as it may seem, among the Zapotec population in the sixteenth century there were several ways of saying lawyer: *huecuecheticha, coquilleticha, huechinoticha*, lawyer "like the saints, who are our lawyers," *connij, vuelàa*, and *vuecij*.[29] More than one term was also used to convey the idea of royal justice, which—as the expression has it—"is justice in the person of the magistrate and political authority": *peninoçòo, rey*, and *lohuàa rey*.[30] Similarly, by the seventeenth century, Matlazinca had long had a word for lawyer (*huehechoyaata*), as it had for the expression "to be charged in court" (*quihehevemita*).[31] As this linguistic richness indicates, the system for administering justice was diffused widely across the colonial indigenous world.

JUSTICE FOR THE INDIAN POPULATION: FROM CONQUEST TO THE BEGINNING OF THE VICEROYALTY

Nonetheless, it is difficult to construe that justice of any type would have been provided to the Indians, who were subjugated and brought under Crown rule in the wake of the conquest and into the early years of the colonial period. At that time, a great many natives and their leaders were killed by the Spanish colonizers, typically justified on the grounds of conquest and stamping out idolatry. Little is known about how exactly the conquistadors went about administering justice, although on the basis of the extensive source material that exists for the decade 1521–1531, it is logical to deduce that justice with respect to the Indians was nonexistent.[32] One exception, or attempted exception, to this pattern was the judicial brief Nuño de Guzmán submitted to show that he had clearly sought justice when he sentenced the Tarascan king Cazonzi to death. Still, as is known, he took this action only to avoid the possibility of later censure by the Crown. The brutal execution of the king, carried out on Guzmán's orders, occurred within the context of a violent conquest and subjugation of the native population.[33]

The fierce nature of the wars of conquest is conveyed, for example, in a painting—executed on a strip of cloth in the sixteenth or perhaps even the seventeenth century—depicting the fire that consumed the *templo mayor*. A traditional calendar is represented along the border of the piece, and both Indian warriors and Spaniards mounted on horseback are seen in the painting, as is Moctezuma—who is portrayed tied up, with a cord around his neck, on which a Spaniard opposite him is tightening his hold. Both figures are situated on top of the palace (*tecpan*) of Tenochtitlan. Numerous glosses surround the codex, one of which reads, sadly and mournfully, in Nahuatl: "[W]hen they arrived, when in the water the men of Castile, [were] next to us . . . in that way did death come forth."[34] This painted manuscript, which appears somewhat late from a stylistic vantage point, reveals not only particular events the Indians remembered from the conquest but, even more, that political circumstances already existed in the colonial period such that one Indian pueblo or another could call up memories of the conquest to ratify its participation in the event or to condemn some aspect of the European invasion of Mexico.

On this point, Stephanie Wood has studied a large number of images found in the codices. They reveal scenes of the conquest, of the process of evangelization, and of punishments inflicted on the Indians in general. Furthermore, the sheer quantity of images available underscores that the events of the conquest and of the initial years of life in the colony formed a central theme in numerous pictorial manuscripts the Indians produced, for various reasons, in this era.[35]

As a vanquished people, the Indians were viewed by their conquerors as part of the booty of war and conquest. Thus, while still living in Coyoacán, Hernán Cortés commanded that members of the native nobility submit themselves to Emperor Charles V. In addition, after the siege and downfall of the Mexica, so much destruction was wrought in the city of Tenochtitlan that the Spanish were forced to establish themselves in Coyoacan for a period.[36] From there, Cortés also ordered that all native lords, who were accustomed to exacting tribute from the pueblos of the Triple Alliance and from the Mexica especially, now pay obeisance to him. This jurisdictional action on his part, known as the "general summons,"[37] was implemented—in the judgment of some eyewitnesses—at the cost of tremendous violence against indigenous governing authorities who had survived the conquest. As of that moment, with Doña Marina (*Malintzin*) serving as his interpreter, Cortés evidently managed to instill in these native lords a belief that as his vassals, they must henceforth pay tribute to Emperor Charles V, since their allies and rulers, the Mexica, had been defeated by the Spanish.

The information that exists about this episode, while confusing, seems to indicate that not all of the Indian nobles and other high officials ordered to appear before Cortés were willing to obey the compulsory call to vassalage. Cortés apparently reacted to their resistance by ordering that his captains, who had a pack of huge dogs (mastiffs) with them, let the animals pounce upon a group of Indian nobles—some of whom died as the result of wounds and bites inflicted by the ravenous creatures. The Spanish often used these mastiffs, which served as valuable aids in the wars of conquest, to persecute and punish the Indians at the outset of the conquest on the island of Hispaniola. A codex still in existence today depicts this extremely violent occurrence in Coyoacán. According to the Nahuatl gloss, the document was produced around 1559, and, from the information recorded on it, it appears that seven of the Indians died after being attacked by dogs (Figure 1.1).[38]

What is more, during these years the ubiquitous system of *encomienda* (the grant to a conquistador of a particular community of Indians for the purposes of exacting tribute and labor) converted the Indians into an involuntary workforce and led to full-scale pillaging of their wealth. The institution of orderly government in the newly conquered land was also impeded for a time by the recurring battles the Spanish settlers fought to consolidate their own power.[39] To these factors must be added the devastating loss of population the Indians experienced in the sixteenth century, a phenomenon clearly documented many years ago by Woodrow Borah. While the scale of loss and the actual numbers can be debated, they nonetheless offer a full sense of what the demographic crisis brought on by European exploitation and the spread of disease signified for the post-conquest indigenous communities of Mesoamerica. Since the exploitation of the Indians was largely channeled through the encomienda system, it is useful to delineate the main lines of royal policy governing this institution during those years.

The beginnings of the encomienda system in New Spain date to 1523. At that time Hernán Cortés, in his capacity as governor of New Spain (1523–1526), received a ruling from Emperor Charles V that the indigenous population could not be subjected to encomienda. This decision was largely a result of the disastrous results the practice had caused earlier in the Antillean colonies. To prevent a similar experience from occurring in New Spain, the emperor declared that the Indians were free vassals of the Crown and, as such, must not be granted in encomienda to private individuals.[40]

I.I Reproduction, no. 374 (no. 9 in John B. Glass and Donald Robertson, "A Census of Native Middle American Pictorial Manuscripts," in Robert Wauchope, ed., *Handbook of Middle American Indians: Guide to Ethnohistorical Sources,* vol. 14, part 3, 81–252 [Austin: University of Texas Press, 1975]). Date: Mid-sixteenth century. Courtesy, National Library of France, Paris.

Cortés, however, disobeyed the order and began to divide up and allocate Indian pueblos among the members of his army. Cortés's action marked the first challenge mounted by encomendero interests against the Crown. In the colonizer's mind, a conquest lacking *asiento* (a contract, or a base for enterprise) was not a proper conquest. Furthermore, if the land was not conquered, the population could not be controlled, and without such control the road to wealth was blocked. For Hernán Cortés, this last objective was paramount and thus helped guide the first orders he issued as captain general and governor of the conquered territory (1523–1526). Thus, Cortés's careful approach was not an expression or a symptom of his loyalty to the Crown but, rather, vivid evidence of a clear understanding of the conditions that would be needed to produce wealth in a territory that had been politically well organized prior to its conquest and also possessed fertile land. This realization underlies Cortés's interest, in the immediate aftermath of conquest, in letting the tlatoque take charge of the collection of tribute and the organization of Indian labor, as well as his concern that the native population's conversion to Christianity had been entrusted not to the secular clergy but to missionary friars, which meant that elements of a reformed religious order with an overpowering interest in converting the Indians was also present in the colony.[41]

Taken together, these factors and conditions led inexorably to a more complete subjugation of the indigenous population. Cortés may or may not have consciously planned this trajectory in all its aspects, but he acted with great clarity in putting in place the organizational framework of what from that point on became known as New Spain. This is the clarity and vision of a man who not only observed and understood forms of human organization that were different from his own but also saw—intact and whole for the last time—an indigenous society with a remarkable degree of cohesion, a society that had evolved complex channels of exchange and distribution, with attendant mechanisms and institutions for synchronizing such activity. The possibility of acquiring riches by commanding an army of workers great in number and accustomed to disciplined labor could hardly be overlooked. Cortés grasped this condition and tried to mold and preserve it, with the intent of advancing his personal interests, rewarding his men, and providing a source of wealth for the Crown.[42]

The apparent gap between theory and practice did not endure for long. As of that moment, the voluminous number of *pareceres* (rationalizations and self-interested statements of opinion) with which the Crown was flooded, as well as the explanations Cortés sent to the king regarding the establishment of the encomienda in New Spain, transformed the short-lived imperial opposition into gathering political support for the institution.

The need to reward the settlers and ensure consolidation of the new colony, coupled with the recognition that the Crown's coffers would be enriched through the encomienda, underlay the king's decision to sanction the institution. By 1525 the Crown had modified its position; it made a show of seeking information but was already inclined to approve a system, designed to be hereditary in nature, for parceling out Indian labor. In 1526 this option inched further toward approval, winning acceptance in the royal court. Two years later, in 1528, the Crown's inclination in favor of the encomienda finally prevailed, as is evident in the instructions it delivered to the First Audiencia (court and governing body under a viceroy) of New Spain.[43]

In these instructions, both the First Audiencia and the religious establishment are requested to provide information on five major points: summary descriptions of both the Spanish and indigenous populations, the names of the soldiers and adventurers who had fought at Hernán Cortés's side during the conquest, reports concerning the fertility and richness of the land, the number of mines, and the number of encomiendas already granted. Armed with this information, the Crown—so it hoped—would be in a position to make grants of encomienda in perpetuity in New Spain, grants that would bestow upon the encomendero certain legally binding jurisdictional powers.

While this information was being compiled, the emperor allowed the members of the First Audiencia to award to those who they believed displayed sufficient merit existing encomiendas that had become vacant as a result of the death of the encomenderos who held them. Against this development, however, the Crown for the first time formulated ordinances designed to protect the Indians; yet by failing to specify either the number of Indians who could be required to render service or the type of tribute they would be obliged to pay, it had skirted around the most fundamental problem affecting the interests and well-being of the subjugated indigenous communities. The encomenderos were now free to assert their claims to tribute and labor in the most extreme manner possible. The radical drop in the native population, from 25.2 million to 6.3 million in the three decades between 1518 and 1548 (Table 1.1), strongly suggests that they did so without compunction.

The unlimited power both the encomenderos and the oidores (judges of the audiencia) possessed in the years 1527–1530 brought them into sharp conflict with the Franciscan missionaries and resulted in the dismissal of all the oidores who formed the colony's First Audiencia. In effect, the missionaries and Fray Juan de Zumárraga in particular represented the political order the Crown needed to implant to help legitimize its rights over America. The missionaries were the visible symbol and embodiment of the royal conscience and, as such, acted as protectors of the emperor's Indian vassals.

To better ensure that this condition was met, the Crown had named the bishop protector of the Indians. Yet to be a protector in more than name only,

Table 1.1. Sixteenth- and Early–Seventeenth-
Century Indian Population

Year	Indian Population (in millions)
1518	25.200
1532	16.800
1548	6.300
1568	2.650
1585	1.900
1595	1.375
1605	1.075
1622	0.750

Source: Woodrow Borah, *The Aboriginal Population of Central Mexico on the Eve of the Spanish Conquest* (Berkeley: University of California Press, 1963).

to be able effectively to monitor and sanction Spaniards who abused their power over the Indians—a situation that was already widespread—the bishop required jurisdictional authority. The oidores, however, especially the president of the audiencia, Nuño de Guzmán, resisted any thought of conceding such jurisdiction to Bishop Zumárraga. The confrontation between them, which subjected the Franciscans to violent actions by the audiencia, reached the emperor's ears. The situation inflamed the colony and was only resolved by the dismissal of all the oidores, followed by the appointment of a second governing audiencia in 1531. The Second Audiencia was presided over by Sebastián Ramírez de Fuenleal, who had been serving as bishop of the island of Santo Domingo (1531–1535).[44]

The root question of just how the native population should be treated, both in law and in practice, would not go away. In a 1529 meeting in Barcelona, the Royal Council reached the same conclusion the Spanish government had come to earlier—namely, that the Indians were free people and should therefore not be subject to encomienda. It was further decided, and conveyed in 1530 through a secret instruction to the Second Audiencia, that the Indians granted in encomienda by the First Audiencia should be placed directly under the Crown. As a practical matter, a corregidor would take charge of these Indians. These steps represented a transitional measure, through which the Crown planned to curtail the power the encomenderos had accumulated.

Within the colonial civil administration, the most notable supporter of this royal strategy was probably Ramírez de Fuenleal. Bearing in mind the economic needs of the Crown as well as the need to establish a system to ensure adequate protection of the Indians, the audiencia president designed a policy that would weaken and reduce the control the ecncomenderos maintained over the Indian population. Under this policy, the encomenderos' privileges would be restricted to the exaction of personal services and tribute; beyond that, the Indians would remain free vassals of the Crown. In this sense, the tribute collected would be controlled and regulated by the audiencia.[45]

Ramírez de Fuenleal's initiative was adopted; in 1532 the regulation of tribute was formalized and accomplished through the vehicle of taxation. In addition, the new regime expressly stated that the encomenderos possessed no direct power or dominion over the Indians who owed them service and tribute; rather, jurisdiction over the Indians belonged to the Crown. At the same time, however, the emperor recognized that collectively the encomenderos still had considerable power and could react to his plans unpredictably and violently. To tamp down this possibility and quiet their restiveness, the encomenderos were led to believe that the court was weighing the option of instituting a broad-scale distribution of the Indians that would pass down to one's heirs in perpetuity. In reality, this consideration was never taken up, but the rumor served its purpose—it nurtured hope among the encomenderos and pacified them politically.

As a further measure underlying this objective, the emperor instructed the audiencia to show favor toward settlers who performed services that were useful to the Crown and requested that it present a general report on New Spain with a view toward a possible colony-wide parceling out of the Indians. Along these same lines, prior to 1532 the Crown had issued a royal decree to audiencia president Ramírez de Fuenleal, in which he was given the authority to grant Indians encomienda on the condition that circumstances warranted doing so and that other solutions for maintaining political order in New Spain had been tried and found wanting. For the Crown, the exercise of direct juridical control within the Indian pueblos translated into controlling the surpluses their labor and land produced. Inevitably, the application of the Crown's policy in New Spain was destined to spark a direct confrontation with the encomenderos.

Up to this point, the encomenderos had been able to act autonomously with respect to the Indians, and the unrestrained oppression the native population suffered at their hands was part of a prolongation of the militaristic aspect of the conquest. Similarly, the encomenderos made no distinction between encomienda Indians and Indian slaves. For them, the bulk of the indigenous population had been subdued through war and combat; enslavement was merely another part of the spoils. In simplest terms, the first group of encomenderos saw their venture in the Indies as an invitation to unlimited exploitation. Furthermore, despite the restrictions the restructuring of the encomienda in the form of the *corregimiento* (a corregidor's jurisdiction) was meant to place on them, the encomenderos remained very powerful. Their reasoning—both economic and political—generally found a sympathetic audience with the Crown, as long as its own jurisdiction was not imperiled.

Indeed, the Crown—at precisely those moments when it attempted to carry through with political transformations that would help gain certain rights for, and ensure the survival of, the Indians—notoriously acted in a contradictory fashion. In a number of cases, the Crown was forced to reverse itself in the face of pressure exerted by the colonists and encomenderos. For example, after a period in which the Crown prohibited enslavement, a barrage of complaints lodged by settlers, together with the economic exigencies of the colony, caused it to revoke that order. Worse still, by 1534 it was once again allowing Indian slaves to be branded.[46]

The constancy with which the colonists voiced complaints in their attempts to get the Crown to revoke or modify unwanted rulings and decrees did not reduce their effectiveness. To some extent this success was a function of numbers, since the complaining settlers never constituted a minority. Within the colony, those who stood to lose the most were the encomenderos who had received a grant of Indian labor and tribute from the First Audiencia, only to be deprived of it by the Second Audiencia. The damage inflicted on encomendero interests by the Second Audiencia's policy, however, was not confined exclusively to this cohort. A case in point involved the Indians who remained *vacos* (lacking an encomendero) because their encomendero had died. In such instances they were placed under Crown authority, and a corregidor was appointed to ensure that the tribute that was owed found its way into the royal coffers.[47]

This was the environment in which, around 1531, the members of the Second Audiencia (which governed New Spain from 1531 to 1535) elected to establish for the first time in New Spain a system of justice that would apply specifically to the Indians. More particularly, the oidores, among whom Vasco de Quiroga stands out, decided to devote one day each week to resolving cases that involved Indians. They then branched out further by deciding that they would incorporate practices native to the Indians' own culture, such as the use of codices, in trials that involved the indigenous population. One critical departure from the pre-Hispanic justice system, however—a distinction maintained throughout the colonial period—was that justice was administered in the same manner to all Indians, regardless of the caste or class to which they belonged.

To give full expression to their official control over the administration of justice, the oidores also centralized the judicial process, allowing no remnant of the pre-Hispanic system to exist and operate within the Indian pueblos. They also made use of Indian interpreters; at a later date, Spaniards performed this function as well.

The oidor and future bishop of Michoacán Vasco de Quiroga embodied an interesting feature of these early efforts to devise a justice system for the Indians. In reviewing cases before him, Quiroga sought the counsel of Indian elders who had once served as judges. The oidor Francisco Ceynos did likewise, making a point of consulting with venerable Indian judges of Tlatelolco when considering cases that involved Indians. In carrying out judicial proceedings, the oidores received help from missionaries, the Franciscans in particular. The Second Audiencia made an effort to settle Indian-related cases rapidly, and its decisions could be appealed only to the Royal and Supreme Council of the Indies, located in the Spanish city of Valladolid. The Indians greeted this innovation—the introduction of a trial process and judicial system that would apply specifically to them—enthusiastically and were soon arriving from every area of New Spain to present their case before the audiencia and request justice from the oidores.[48]

On another level, the audiencia's wish to differentiate and customize the administration of justice undoubtedly formed part of a strategy to assert more effective control over the Indian population, a strategy whose purpose is revealed through other, less formal measures. For example, in 1533 the members of the Royal and Supreme Council of the Indies informed the king that Ramírez de Fuenleal and his fellow oidores had dispatched one of Moctezuma's sons (whose name was not specified), along with four other Indian nobles, to the monarch's court in Spain because "they were persons whose presence in New Spain was not currently in the colony's interests." Clearly, an heir to the Mexica empire could pose a serious threat to the rights the Castilian monarchy claimed, and it was therefore preferable to send him into exile. The council members notified the emperor that the Indian nobles had reached the court in February or March 1533 and proffered the advice that he should place them in some kind of service, such as the horse guards, because "it will resonate well there [in New Spain and] leave the impression that they are attended to in your court and residence."[49]

In general, the members of the Second Audiencia's use of certain indigenous practices and mores in resolving legal cases, as well as the decision to introduce the Indians to Spanish legal practice gradually, conformed to the Crown's interest in achieving dominion over the Indians but in doing so within a protective, paternalistic framework. This interest, in turn, flowed from and was based on the emperor's possession of rightful titles and claims over America. Such thinking was constantly reinforced by the many theologians and jurists who made up a circle of advisers that surrounded the Catholic monarchs.[50] Against this broad canvas, however, in the conquered lands of the New World the spoils of war continued to flow and to define the realities of daily life.

Since the Castilian Crown had initially underwritten the so-called discovery of America, it necessarily followed that the Indies were incorporated politically into its realm. What is more, in 1493 Pope Alexander VI issued a momentous bull in which Castile and Portugal were, on the basis of divine right as transmitted through the Roman pontiff, granted temporal dominion over America, a grant that carried with it the obligation that the inhabitants of the new continent be converted to Christianity.[51]

The process of incorporating the Indies into the kingdom of Castile passed through several juridical phases between the years 1492–1493 and 1516. As based on law grounded in the *Partidas*,[52] as of 1492 America belonged to the Catholic monarchs of Castile and Aragón, since in European eyes it had been discovered as part of an undertaking by these monarchs. Moreover, in the papal bulls of 1493 the lands had been granted to these sovereign rulers as a personal possession, with the further provision that upon their death the lands would be inherited by the thrones of Castile and León and not of Aragón. Thus, when Ferdinand the Catholic died in 1516, the Indies became the inherited patrimony of Princess Juana la Loca and her son, Charles V.[53] By virtue of this inheritance, Castile's right over the territory of America was deemed inalienable. When, for example, the high court attorneys of several cities in the Spanish American colony confirmed this inalienability through the adoption of a series of legal provisions in 1519, 1520, and 1523, the practical effect was simply to corroborate the cities' existing status as well as secure their ennoblement. When a Castilian city was able to call itself "free," it signified that the city belonged to the king, that it formed part of the royal patrimony and was not subject to the will of any other governing authority. At the time, such status was a sign of honor and a guarantee of freedom.[54]

This privilege and title of the Crown conferred the right of dominion and also gave the Indians of America the status of vassals of the Crown. The question of the Castilian monarchy's jurisdiction and rights over America was instrumental in determining the forms government assumed in the colonies throughout the sixteenth century. Indeed, the mother country displayed a unique preoccupation. It can be said that the great ideological theme of monarchy in the century was that of defining its role as the universal guardian of Christendom, a role the Castilian monarchy arrogated to itself. The politico-ethical precepts of Christianity became in an unfailing way an organizing principle for the Spanish Crown. The task that fell to prominent theologians and jurists was to identify those precepts and vigorously debate them.

In addition, this quest for ethical and political legitimacy sparked a wave of thinking directed at finding reasons to uphold the rights of the Crown over America and contributed to the debate concerning the native population's legal character and rights. The majority view was that the papal concession justified Castile's title to America; since the concession had been granted so the Indians could be converted to Christianity, it followed that the king should issue a series of specific orders to guarantee their conversion as well as their proper treatment.[55] In this period, naturally enough, those who raised the strongest challenges to the Castilian king's claim of just title over America were his French and English adversaries. A number of Spanish authorities defended Castile's rights throughout the sixteenth, seventeenth, and eighteenth centuries. Some inside the Castilian realm also questioned the king's titles, however, principally because of the devastation of the native population by the Spanish. The supreme representative of this countercurrent was without question Fray Bartolomé de Las Casas.

Beginning in 1514 and ending only with his death in 1566, Las Casas fought unceasingly to move the Crown to take steps to guarantee the political and physical survival of the Indians in America. Through his voluminous writings, he sought to demonstrate that it was the king's duty to defend and safeguard the indigenous population, since his central mission was to convert that population to the Catholic faith and to see, thereby, that no one would take possession of its people or lands. In 1542, as a result of his persistent political efforts at the royal court, Las Casas helped secure promulgation of the *Leyes Nuevas*, a compendium of laws that imposed limits on the encomienda and guaranteed protection of the Indians.

This was a matter of fundamental importance. Subsequently, in 1565, in his role as advocate (*procurador*) for and defender of the Indians, Bartolomé de Las Casas would try, using every available avenue—including appearing before the Royal and Supreme Council of the Indies—to block the tributary policy favored by King Philip II. Las Casas at this time supported the attempt by the Andean *kurakas* (*caciques*, or native chiefs) to purchase the rights to encomienda from Philip II, an action he took in his capacity as procurador in this matter as well. Furthermore, Las Casas developed a compelling argument on behalf of the notion of restitution. In his judgment, this policy would have two great benefits: it would not only restore to the Indian nobles the lands and domains seized from them but would also enable the king to avoid the pain he was destined to suffer in the next life because of his wrongful dominion over the Indies.[56]

In addition, Las Casas was the sole defender of the Archbishop of Toledo (the primate of Spain) and confessor to King Bartolomé Carranza de Miranda, who was brought down in disgrace before Philip II when charged with following the ideas of Erasmus of Rotterdam. Las Casas and Carranza were good friends, and thanks to the latter, Las Casas managed to dissuade a wavering Philip II from granting encomenderos the right to hold Indian communities in perpetuity.[57]

In this context, recall that in the *Paraclesis*, the preface to his Greek and Latin edition of the New Testament, Erasmus explains that in converting the enemies of the Christian faith, the most powerful weapons are "the heart itself and the example drawn from life," not "empty ceremonies or syllogistic propositions." This theme is one to which Erasmus frequently returned. For example, in his preface to the *Enchiridion*, he reasoned that the Turks could be won over to the great cause if Christians would only live in accordance with Christ's precepts.[58] Erasmus's opposition to the scholastic theories underpinning the notion of "just war" held that they were flawed because they sanctioned war for material reasons. Las Casas was strongly influenced by this line of reasoning, as is evident, for example, in his treatise *Apologética Historia Sumaria*, in which he explicitly refers to Erasmus's convictions concerning war.[59] The critical analysis of these issues contained a potential danger for the Crown; a debate over the legitimacy of the

Castilian king's right to claim the Indies necessarily implied that such legitimacy might not exist.

Against this backdrop, the formulation of a detailed plan aimed at protecting the indigenous population buffered the Crown, helping it in large measure to maintain its rights over the distant lands.[60] Ultimately, however, an even more insistent reality must be kept in mind: the monarchy had to establish that its exercise of dominion was not simply legitimate but also profitable.

The need to uphold the Crown's legitimacy thus helped motivate the king and royal authorities to grant the Indians "official" protection—although it was qualified and not absolute—and to respect their practices and customs, as long as they did not lapse into idolatry or threaten royal jurisdiction. In one of the chapters of the 1542 *New Laws*, for example, it is specified that disputes involving Indians "be resolved with recourse to their practices and customs, since these are clearly not unjust, and that said audiencias exercise care to see that subordinate judges do likewise."[61]

The plan also implied that high-level royal officials—audiencia members as well as the viceroy—would need to be carefully chosen to ensure that their outlook was consistent with the declared commitment to protect the Indians. A case in point was the oidor Vasco de Quiroga, who before taking up his duties in New Spain had served as a judge in the kingdom of Castile, specializing in handling cases involving Jews and Saracens "both of Spain and of Africa, all of whom were subjects of Emperor Charles V."[62]

Vasco de Quiroga's experience also included service in 1525 as *juez de residencia* (person charged with conducting an inquiry into a public functionary's term of office) in the North African Spanish colony of Orán. This was an important but delicate assignment because a disturbing gulf had apparently opened between the local population and royal officials, whose actions had stirred considerable discontent. Quiroga's task was to review and investigate complaints and, on the basis of his findings, reach a judgment concerning the ill-performing functionaries of the Crown. In addition, the emperor charged Quiroga with restoring good relations with the king of Tremecin, a task Quiroga successfully fulfilled.[63] Quiroga's previous experiences are interesting because they reveal a man practiced in the art of dealing with and judging, from a high official vantage point, people of a different ethnicity. His record of service undoubtedly prepared Quiroga to meet the challenge of governing in New Spain and, in particular, of integrating some of the Indians' customs and practices into the administration of colonial justice.

Quiroga's record was also indicative of a man interested in the teachings and philosophy of Christian humanism. The year in which Vasco de Quiroga set out for New Spain, 1529, was also the year Erasmus's Spanish followers began to experience extensive persecution by the Inquisition. From this point forward, Erasmus's ideas and writings were no longer tolerated. Quiroga, however, had already come under their influence, and one of the clearest features of his own thinking is his idea that the Indians could be converted through the effect of the "virtuous example." He did not believe in preaching by force, nor did he believe the Indians would benefit in any way from coming into contact with the laity. Rather, his ideas were based on his thoroughgoing belief in the power of human character and conduct to transform people. Lurking behind this idea of the "virtuous example" as the fulcrum for conversion, one detects the shadow of Erasmus of Rotterdam. In this connection, it is also instructive that Quiroga's closest friend and assistant for seven years (1538–1545), Cristóbal de Cabrera, was not only a man of great intelligence and the owner of a multifaceted library but also the translator, from Greek into Latin, of a portion of Erasmus's edition of the New Testament.[64]

This current of Christian humanist thought, which had sparked the interest of some advisers in Emperor Charles V's court, as well as that of the emperor himself, was also evident in the selection of many of the missionaries who were sent to New Spain. They came out of reformed monasteries and, in many cases, had been educated in the great European universities where Erasmus's ideas and those of the Reformation were fervently discussed. Erasmus's notable influence on various members of the religious orders that operated in Mexico has been well documented.[65]

Furthermore, for much of the sixteenth century, the missionaries' interest was focused not merely on converting the Indians to Christianity but also on devising complex and sophisticated ways of achieving their conversion, such as mastering the indigenous languages, publishing Indian vocabularies and grammars, translating sermons and religious works into the Indian languages, and authoring tomes and critical studies on the beliefs and early history of the native populations. No less impressive during that century was the success the missionaries enjoyed in teaching the sons of the Indian nobility to read and write in Spanish, Nahuatl, and other indigenous languages, as well as in Latin and Greek.[66]

In addition, the missionaries displayed considerable interest in discussing various aspects of religion and Spanish imperial policy with a segment of the Indian population. This tendency, along with the constant objections they registered to the colonial powers' denial of rights to the Indian pueblos, was in many respects a reaction to the prevailing ideology rationalizing the emperor's just titles and, conversely, formed an element of the contemporary interest in Christian humanism. Some missionaries also had a recurring fascination with, and admiration for, indigenous society—both the one they observed around them and attempted to convert to the new faith and the older pre-Hispanic Indian society that had been destroyed in the conquest. Thus, while the conversion of the Indians to Christianity was of vital importance to the missionary friars, they were also interested in the ancient native cultures, manifesting a keen desire to learn about the "other." Such a desire, for example, together with his own studiousness, motivated Fray Bernardino de Sahagún to undertake the writing of his celebrated work, the *Historia General*. This book, contrary to the way it has generally been perceived, is more a monument to Sahagún's passion for learning than it is a manual on the extirpation of indigenous idolatries.[67]

In light of these factors, when the system of colonial justice devised for the Indians was first implemented, the context was generally favorable for their protection: both judges and missionaries were in place who, in the first case, were experienced in dealing with people of different ethnic backgrounds and, in the second, personified the desire to evangelize the Indians in accordance with the teachings of both Christian humanism and their own religious preparation. At the same time, the form of justice the colonial authorities applied to the Indians could not be based exclusively on native custom and practice. Given the distinct contours of peninsular history, that justice was bound to be many-sided. Castilian law had been deeply influenced by both Roman law and the law of medieval Europe, as reflected in the *Siete Partidas* in particular. The Spanish had evolved a flexible judicial system, notable since before the conquest for incorporating alien cultural elements, especially those of the Moors and Jews who had lived in the territories that made up the kingdom of Castile.[68]

Furthermore, the missionaries and oidores who possessed a broad outlook were not the only people who surrounded the indigenous world in the sixteenth century; the interests of settlers, encomenderos, ambitious royal functionaries, and the Crown itself also pressed down on it. To blend and accommodate this spectrum of interests was a goal of the first colonial authorities. While the interests of the indigenous communities were typically marginalized, beginning in the mid-seventeenth century the Indians still managed to survive and maintain themselves, even enjoying a slight increase in population.

If the missionaries, as the cultural intermediaries they were—complemented in this respect by some high-ranking royal officials—enabled indigenous practices and customs to work their way into the colonial justice system, the native population also participated actively in shaping the apparatus of justice in the Indies. Indian communities displayed, and continue to display, a strong ability to negotiate with the "other" and with outside powers in particular. By marshaling clever cultural strategies and showing a remarkable openness to new experiences, the Indians found in the realm of legal argumentation and resolution a place in which to engage in dialogue, defend their point of view, and convince the authorities, when possible, about their own rights.

This process of mutual accommodation required certain things from the Indians. First, to engage civil and judicial authorities, they had to adopt a posture of respectfulness. In addition, they had to take an interest in learning how to use the technicalities of the Spanish legal system to their advantage and how to protect themselves from the weaknesses of their legal position. Clearly, this body of knowledge and experience was critically important when it came to negotiating justice for themselves before the dominant power. In the sixteenth century, apart from a small number of isolated cases, the Indian communities never openly rebelled against the colonial authority. The narrow spaces for negotiation that were open to them, with the courts a prime example, afforded the Indians some release from the psychological pressures and social tensions to which they were subjected by the oppressive conditions in which they lived as a result of Spanish domination. Understandably, they used every tactic possible to wring favors out of this legal space for negotiation.[69] The process brought permanent change. Through her analysis of numerous Indian trials, Susan Kellogg has demonstrated that the legal system served as an important mechanism for transforming Nahua society, which over time altered its concepts of gender, inheritance, genealogy, and more.[70]

In 1531, a number of pueblos as well as groups of both Indian nobles and commoners began to present to members of the audiencia—as they would later to the viceroys—maps and codices as evidence for a claim or lawsuit. Most of these documents, which I call juridical codices,[71] lack the complexity of the pre-Hispanic religious and historical codices.[72] Although this type of document—produced specifically for a trial or judicial proceeding—existed in both the pre-Hispanic and Spanish colonial eras, it varied considerably during the latter in style and complexity, ranging from manuscripts that were very simple and contained little color and few traditional indigenous elements to those with rich texture and content, as, for example, the *Historia tolteca-chichimeca*.[73]

In the colonial period and particularly in the sixteenth century, however, not all codices or pictorial manuscripts were produced to be used in trials and judicial hearings. While documents of this particular type constitute the majority of those known to us today, Indian communities also produced codices for internal use, especially in connection with matters of tradition and the observance of autochthonous customs and rituals. This is the case, for example, with the codex known as *Joyas de Martín Ocelotl*, on which a shaman known by that name painted images of gold, silver, and other objects presented to him as offerings in return for services he performed that the Spanish later condemned, in a 1536 trial, as idolatrous.[74] This beautifully executed codex, which existed for the exclusive use of the Indian Martín Ocelotl and was not to be seen by others, had gold figures painted on it in the form of eagles, as well as images of jewelry and other precious objects he had received.

Another example of a codex produced purely for internal Indian pueblo use is the *Mapa de Cuauhtinchan no. 2*. This impressive pictorial manuscript depicts in detail many traditional rituals of power, including several involving human sacrifice. Dating from the sixteenth century, the manuscript was designed to serve specific rituals of historical recollection, in which a pueblo's taking possession of certain lands was linked to long-held stories of its journey of migration.[75] Not surprisingly, the vicissitudes of time have left few examples of this class of document. Yet others might still be found, perhaps among the pueblos of Oaxaca. In that region, in the colonial period the Indians had the custom of producing genealogies of their kings on canvas or cloth (*lienzos*) for internal use by those in positions of power. This practice was followed among the Mixtec in particular.

As noted earlier, however, the juridical codices constitute the most numerous examples of native pictorial manuscripts about which information still exists. During the government of the Second Audiencia, a large number of Indian pueblos produced and presented codices—especially to bring complaints against the oidores of the First Audiencia, whose president, Nuño de Guzmán, had tyrannized the Indians unmercifully. In the *juicio de residencia* conducted in 1532, a host of communities—among them Tenochtitlan, Tlatelolco, Texcoco, Otumba, Chalco, Zumpango, Tepeapulco, Coyocan, Cuautitlan, Ecatepec, Teutenango, Cuernavaca, Tlaxcala, Izucar, and Huexotzinco—submitted testimony against the oidores of the First Audiencia in the form of hundreds of painted manuscripts—large and small—depicting and documenting that the oidores had ordered them into war and robbed them of hundreds of objects fabricated out of gold as well as of blankets, feathers, shields, and numerous other valuable items, including a feathered standard representing the Virgen.[76]

Regrettably, although some examples still exist, the majority of these codices have not been preserved. Various early records have survived, however, that attest to the introduction of codices, or "painted manuscripts," as evidence in a trial; the greatest number of these records reside in the section Justicia in the Archivo General de Indias in Seville. As part of these trials, we can observe the use of interpreters and on occasion of legal representatives, as well as witnesses who belonged to religious orders. One such example, from the early colonial period, is the case brought in 1532 by the tlatoque of Amecameca, Don Juan Tezoampan and Don Thomas Tenango, who requested that several pueblos of dependent status be divided between them. As can be seen in Figure 1.2, the manuscripts they offered the audiencia contain a list of the pueblos, with their place names represented by glyphs, and both tlatoque appear with their personal names in glyph, accompanied by their wives.

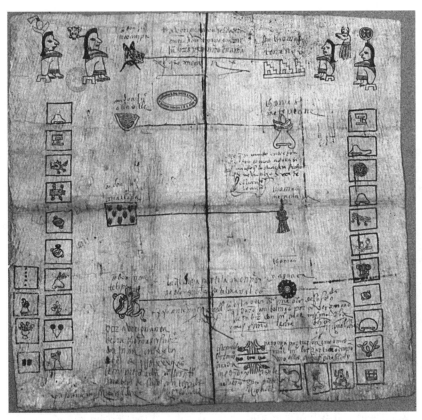

I.2 Reproduction, no. 26 (no. 5 in Glass and Robertson 1975). Date: 1532. Courtesy, National Library of France, Paris.

VICEROY ANTONIO DE MENDOZA AND INDIAN JUSTICE

Under the Second Audiencia, the justice system in the young colony continued to take shape and form during the sixteenth century. It was a system in which the most important decisions were made by the oidores. With the creation of the viceroyalty of New Spain in 1535 and the arrival of the first viceroy, Don Antonio de Mendoza (viceroy from 1535 to 1550), however, the central figure in the resolution of indigenous legal cases became the viceroy himself, although many of his decisions were made in consultation and agreement with the oidores.[77]

When he took up his duties in New Spain, Viceroy Mendoza was already experienced in dealing with people from different ethnic backgrounds, and he was matched in this regard by some members of the Second Audiencia. Part of this familiarity resulted from the viceroy's family circumstances. His father, Iñigo

López de Mendoza, the second Count of Tendilla, had served as captain general and magistrate of the Alhambra. He governed the city and province for eight years, ruling over both Muslims and Jews, and his governorship brought prosperity to the region. On one occasion the inhabitants of the Alhambra rebelled against the laws that mandated their prompt conversion to Christianity. The uproar was calmed only when the future viceroy's father stepped into the middle of the angry crowd, promising that the laws would be reformed. As a sign of good faith, he left his wife and two small children—one of whom was the future viceroy, Antonio de Mendoza—with the rebels.[78] The governor's offer of a truce was accepted immediately.

Antonio de Mendoza possessed both the intelligence and the power to develop a functioning administrative apparatus for New Spain, and his achievements in different areas of government allowed the colony to enjoy a period of relative stability.[79] With respect to the provision of justice, Viceroy Mendoza instituted a special jurisdictional authority to govern matters that affected the Indians. The prerogatives he enjoyed as viceroy, or the king's alter ego, and as president of the audiencia provided considerable leeway to pursue innovative measures in handling indigenous legal cases. More pointedly, the viceroy personally exercised jurisdiction over all Indian disputes and petitions and referred criminal cases involving Indians to the ordinary, or lower-level, courts. By personally reviewing and handling virtually all cases presented by the Indians, he was able to reach findings and resolve disputes nimbly and quickly.[80] If a case necessitated a judicial outcome, he passed it on to an oidor for final resolution. Whereas the cases of individual Indians could be settled administratively, in a more streamlined way, those that involved the native nobility or that concerned an Indian community in toto had to be dealt with through a full-scale legal proceeding.[81]

To gather as much information as he could about indigenous legal disputes, Mendoza commissioned the appointment of special judges who, as a rule, were Indians who belonged to the native nobility.[82] Similarly, both the viceroy and the audiencia employed interpreters to aid in trials, at times calling on missionaries to serve in this capacity. Circumstances led the viceroy to conclude that on many occasions the Indians sought to avail themselves of the court over matters of little importance, although he was also aware that at times they experienced terrible oppression without seeking any redress from the guilty parties. In light of this fact, he believed that any complaint lodged by the native population had to be investigated, however trivial it might appear, because "that which is little may conceal much."[83]

As a general rule, Mendoza, accompanied by his interpreters, devoted every Monday and Thursday morning to entertaining Indians' pleas and submissions over legal and judicial matters. If a case was simple and easily resolved, he settled it on the spot; he assigned problems that raised more difficult legal questions to one of the oidores. Following similar logic, minor, less difficult cases that originated outside Mexico City were entrusted to the political-judicial officials or the missionary priests in the place where the case arose to settle, thereby enabling the Indian plaintiffs to return to their pueblos without undue delay. As with the higher court, the colonial authorities who heard these provincial cases also used Indian judges to "probe into the differences" that had led the Indians to litigate an issue.[84] Unvaryingly, Viceroy Mendoza inquired into legal matters that affected the Indians in accordance with the information recorded in the codices, the heralded "painted manuscripts," the Indians put at his disposal. In fact, this and other colonial artistic forms flowered during Mendoza's time as viceroy. The religious orders were instrumental in this development, although no influence was more central than the founding of the Colegio de Santa Cruz in Tlatelolco. This institution for training and educating Indian nobles gave extraordinary impetus to the elaboration of codices during this period.[85]

In the final instance, disputes involving Indians that could not be resolved in New Spain were customarily sent to the Royal and Supreme Council of the Indies in Valladolid—a practice that endured throughout the entire colonial period. A case in point involved the Indians of Tepeucila who lived in the Oaxacan region of Cuicatlán. In 1543 they presented a codex in which numerous gold objects were depicted as evidence in a lawsuit they brought against their encomendero. The codex, a strip or length of paper 1 meter by 20 centimeters, contains drawings of gold objects such as crosses and the bases to which they were affixed, rosaries, pre-Hispanic figures, and flat rounded discs (*tejuelos*). Among the pre-Hispanic gold figures, the image of an anthropomorphized butterfly stands out, representing the goddess Itzpapálotl, the "Obsidian Butterfly," an aggressive or violent manifestation of the earth goddess. The goddess wears a band of feathers around her head and carries a fan in one hand and a rattle in the other. The traditional symbol for water (a rhombus with a point at the center), which is represented in many pre-Hispanic and colonial codices, appears at the base of the crosses.[86]

The Tepeucila Indians submitted that the gold objects depicted on the codex were only part of a much larger group of such objects their encomendero, Andrés de Tapia, had extracted from them without compensating them. In their testimony, the Indians made clear that whenever they complied with the encomendero's orders and handed the objects over to him, he had them locked up, beaten, and threatened with hanging if they complained to the viceroy and the audiencia. The Indians further charged that the encomendero, through his wife, Isabel de Tapia, saw to it that when the Tepeucila authorities (who were members of its nobility) came to pay the tribute the community owed, they were thrown into a dungeon. The other Indians of the pueblo were then informed that they had to pay a ransom if they wanted their leaders to be set free. Faced with this demand, the Indians—desperate to secure the release of their leaders—apparently visited indigenous merchants of México-Tenochtitlan and Texcoco, seeking to borrow money with which to pay the ransom.[87]

With the Indians present, the encomenderos also melted down the gold objects that were given to them and had the residue weighed to see if it equaled the total they were expecting. Clearly, it must have been painful for the Indians to witness their precious objects in the shape of butterflies, their earplugs, pitchers, and pots—all finely wrought—melted down without any feeling for their cosmological and spiritual symbolism. To the encomenderos, all that mattered was the material out of which they were made. On occasion, if the yield was small, the encomenderos would deceive the nobles of Tepeucila, telling them that part of the gold had been "burned" while being melted and that—to make up for this lost portion—they needed to give them even more of the precious metal.[88]

From the information contained in the lawsuit the Tepeucila Indians submitted, it emerged that over a five-year period they had handed over a large cache of objects of pure gold, including hundreds of rounded gold discs, six carved heads decorated with butterfly wings, five crosses, seven varied pieces of jewelry, and two earflaps. A cumulative payment of this magnitude was a tremendous loss for the community. Furthermore, the Indians also declared that the native merchants who had loaned them the money with which to ransom their leaders subsequently came to their pueblo to collect repayment of the loan but were so abusive that several nobles and hundreds of commoners fled from Tepeucila to Teutitlan, while others from the pueblo took refuge in the surrounding mountains. On top of these indignities was the violence practiced as a matter of course by the local encomendero, who would, for example, send either Indian *calpixque* (tribute collectors) or a Spanish mayordomo (steward) to deal with the residents of Tepeucila. This individual was no more sympathetic than his master and subjected the Indians to mistreatment. According to the testimony provided by Don Juan, the governor of Tepeucila, more than 1,500 members of the pueblo from more than 300 residences had abandoned the pueblo as a result of these unrelentingly harsh conditions.[89]

Ultimately, the complaint brought by the Indians of Tepeucila was resolved in their favor by the Royal and Supreme Council of the Indies. A section of the codex, however, was cut away (and has been lost ever since) because the council members decided that only part, not all, of the pictorial manuscript accorded with the truth.[90] It is thus clear, on the basis of the council's deliberations and actions in this case, that codices were considered a vital component of the testimony provided in disputes and trials involving the native population and were subject to thorough "examination," as legal evidence, at the highest judicial levels.

Consistent with his general posture, Viceroy Mendoza ordered that impor-tant rulings by the king concerning native customs be made known to the Indians in Nahuatl, to ensure that the pueblos understood them. This practice of translat-ing ordinances into Nahuatl indicates, in Susan Kellogg's view, that during this period a process was in place—not only within the royal audiencia but on the local level as well—within communities to educate Indians about the workings of the Spanish legal system and that as part of this process Indian functionaries served not just as interpreters but also as teachers. The practice further indicates that in New Spain, Spanish law and legislation were accommodated to meet local realities.[91]

In his writings, Viceroy Mendoza noted that when a case was heard involving one or more Indian communities, a large number of Indian nobles and common-ers would gather at the audiencia "because they all want to have notice of what the ruling and resolution is affecting the particular case." On occasion, the viceroy noted, he had been advised to receive fewer people because not only did they reek of a foul odor, but their large number created confusion and disturbed the pro-ceeding; he should, it was recommended, restrict entrance to one or perhaps two of the *principales* (nobles; upper-class Indians) from the pueblo involved in the liti-gation. Such advice notwithstanding, the viceroy held to the belief that "in com-munity and government matters, these Indians maintain the custom that everyone in the arriving party should receive direct notice of what is decided." Accordingly, Mendoza recommended to the succeeding viceroy, Luis de Velasco (1550–1564), that all the Indians who had come to help present a legal action or lawsuit be allowed to enter the audiencia chambers, without regard to their number, "because it is to their great satisfaction, in addition to being the advisable course."[92]

In executing the duties of his office, the viceroy undoubtedly examined a good number of painted manuscripts, many of which served as the basis for lawsuits brought by Indian pueblos against extremely powerful local settlers and encomen-deros. In 1549, for example, the pueblo of Tezoyuca (Morelos) presented—through the persons of Gaspar Tlapultecatl and Baltasar Atenpaneza, Indians native to an outlying part of Tezoyuca—one such document "in which they stated" that in 1543 Hernán Cortés, the Marqués del Valle, had robbed them of four "par-cels" of land located along the boundaries of the lands known as Atiquipaque and Suchitepeque, "which [the painted manuscript] they presented [documented] so that it may be officially recorded that they are of and belong to said settlement of Tezoyuca and its communal lands and so that the rightful actions be taken with regard to said lands" (Figure 1.3).[93] Various pueblos that fell within the marquisate filed suit against Cortés in 1549 on the grounds that he had seized lands from them and, as evidence for their claim, submitted several large-format painted manuscripts.[94]

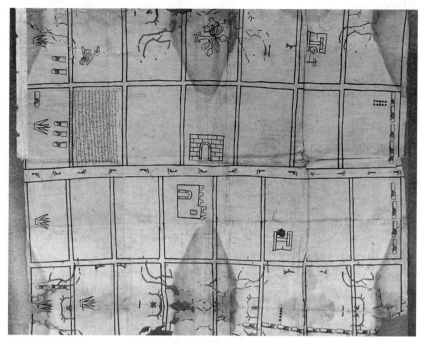

I.3 Reproduction, 3052.10 Codex no. 5. Date: 1549. Courtesy, Archivo General de la Nación, Mexico City.

VICEROY LUIS DE VELASCO AND INDIAN JUSTICE

This locally inspired and devised system of justice, described here in broad outline, continued to operate during the administration of Mendoza's successor, Viceroy Luis de Velasco (1550–1564). A telling instance occurred, for example, on August 18, 1554, when a large group of Indians from, among other places, Tlatelolco, Tacuba, Tlalmanalco, and Chalco planted themselves at the entrance of the Mexico City audiencia chambers, waiting to be received by the oidor, López de Montealegre.

The Indians carried—burdensome though it was—a series of painted manuscripts on which were depicted a variety of themes, including land boundaries, the outlay of labor contributed to different projects, tribute payments and accounts, and detailed renderings of physical mistreatment. In all these matters, they implicated a powerful member of the audiencia, the oidor Lorenzo de Tejada. In one group of codices alone, brought by the cabildo of Tacuba and members of the community's Indian nobility, they sought to demonstrate to the judge that in the space of a single day, nearly 24,000 Indians had been obliged to plant 12,000 grapevines in the orchard belonging to Tejada, in return for which he had paid them forty pesos.

As the hours and days elapsed, a stream of Indians from different parts of the Basin of Mexico showed other codices to the attentive Montealegre. The Indians explained the meaning of the paintings to the oidor, with their explanations translated from Nahuatl to Spanish by an audiencia interpreter. As this activity took place, a notary simultaneously recorded each declaration the Indian witnesses made and verified the content of the pictorial manuscripts.

This entire episode formed part of the juicio de residencia conducted from 1554 to 1556 when Tejada was oidor. Montealegre, following the process then in force, had in essence invited any Spaniards and Indians who had a complaint against Tejada to present it openly and publicly before the Audiencia of Mexico and to accompany the declaration with documentary evidence. The appearance in court by the representatives of various indigenous communities from the Basin of Mexico and their display of codices was a response to this official call and summons.[95]

Under Luis de Velasco's viceregal administration, the Indians lodged a large number of complaints in Nahuatl, many supported by codices or painted manuscripts. It is clear that in this period, codices were used for different purposes in a variety of situations. They were often employed, for example, in cases that involved one Indian community suing another or, as has been seen, in cases that pitted Indians against Spaniards—whether as part of a royal functionary's *residencia* (court or trial held at the end of a term in office) or some other incident or proceeding. Similarly, codices were used during official inspection tours of pueblos, in the exaction of tribute from Indian settlements, in producing and interpreting wills and genealogical documents, in the general submission of complaints by pueblos, in the awarding of grants and special favors, and in formalizing contracts between Spaniards and Indians.[96] The list goes on.

In their testimony, the Indians frequently employed language that is not only solemn but highly metaphorical, containing appeals and references to ancient customs. In some instances, for example, the viceroy or certain oidores are described as "wondrous" beings; in a similar vein, Indian litigants will exclaim that as the viceroy and oidores render justice, their "heart" is left satisfied.[97]

Thus, for example, the testimony given during a trial held in 1558 in the district of San Pablo (Mexico City) discloses that an Indian woman, Magdalena Teyacapa, bought land from an Indian named Acxotecatl for twenty strips of material that could be used to cover a hut. Her right to the land, however, was disputed by another Indian, Pablo Uitznauatl. One of the witnesses for Magdalena stated that he (the witness) was an "old one" (*tiueuetque*) and, as irrefutable proof of his authority, emphasized that the Indian woman had come before several "venerable" Indians "like myself," giving them some pulque she had taken from the maguey plants on her newly acquired land. She had said to the elders before her: "[T]ry this humble [gift] of wine which I've brought from some lands [of Tolpetlac] that I have purchased and I make known and declare to you, so it stays in your memory, should the one called Acxotecatl, native [of the district] of Tolpetlac, perhaps repent sometime of having sold them to me."[98] Thus, in a trial, the proof of ownership of land was simply contained in the rituals of a ceremony, through which the elders of a community, having received gifts, were made aware verbally of a particular state of affairs—in this case, of a transaction that occurred and the way a tract of land was acquired.

Another case that illustrates the Indians' reliance on metaphor and ancient custom was one involving Don Luis de Santamaría Cipac, the governor of Mexico and the last tlatoque in Tenochtitlan's line of rulers to occupy this position. In a dispute over certain lands, Santamaría Cipac defined what land signified for the indigenous population: it represented their "clothing" and their "patrimony" (*topatrimonio*).[99] These and similar expressions demonstrate that many of the disputes involving Indians in this period entailed the use of language and phrases derived from traditional indigenous culture, language, and terms that embodied ways of thinking that preceded the conquest.

In 1552, to cite an example, a number of Indians—all of whom belonged to the community of Tepozotlán (located in the present-day state of Mexico)— appeared before the viceroy in connection with complaints against the governor and principales of Tepozotlán they had presented a year earlier. These Indians were Francisco de Torrijos and Francisco del Águila, both of whom served as alcaldes; Rafael Damián, a principal in the pueblo and quarter of Cuautlapa; Don Mateo Nazayo and Martín Ribas, principales in the pueblo and quarter of Xolo; and Don Martín and Diego Vicente, principales in the pueblo of Tepuxaco. They explained to the viceroy that on the basis of his (the viceroy's) decision, Francisco Maldonado—an Indian noble and native of Chiconautla—had been appointed as a judge to resolve the difficulties. After spending a month inquiring into the situation, however, Maldonado had not only failed to carry out his charge but according to the Indians had spent all his time going about "well attended to and closely accompanied by the governor and principales" of Tepozotlán, "showing them much affection and good will." From the Indians who had brought the complaint, he asked for large gifts of both money and food. All of this—the full range of Maldonado's actions and conduct—was depicted in a "painting."

Furthermore, taking advantage of his position as judge, Maldonado threatened the Indians who had originated the complaint, telling them "he had been first lion, then tiger, then snake, who had been sleeping but would awaken and would eat and devour them." The judge, that is, revealed to the Indians the secret

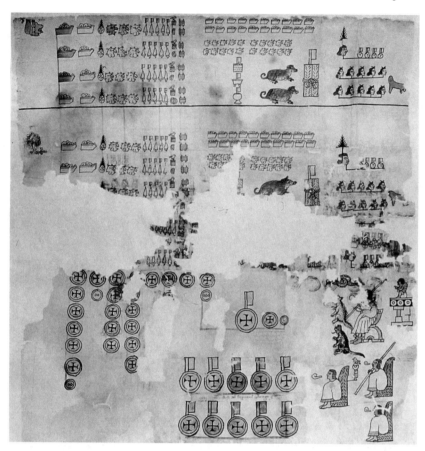

I.4 Reproduction, no. 1799. Date: 1552. Courtesy, Archivo General de la Nación, Mexico City.

that these powerful creatures were his double in animal form and that if they did not obey him, they would be served as food. The Indians, stricken with fear, begged the viceroy to appoint a different judge. The fact that the threats the Indian noble made were real to them is clear from the manuscript they presented. On its lower right-hand side, next to the place name of Tepozotlán, is a depiction of the Indian judge with his long staff of justice, accompanied by a lion, tiger, and serpent—his doubles. This imagery clearly expresses one element of the Indians' predicament (Figure 1.4).[100]

The viceroy also received numerous legal petitions in which the Indians furnished information pertaining to their past history. This practice was followed especially in the claims Indian nobles submitted to collect tribute and in the

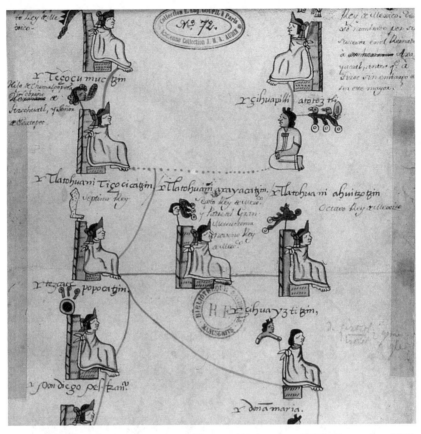

I.5 Reproduction, no. 72 (no. 258 in Glass and Robertson 1975). Date: after 1554. Courtesy, National Library of France, Paris.

complaints pueblos filed to repossess lost territory and the rights that went with it. In these instances, the Indians typically provided information about their lineage and kin by presenting genealogical data. This was done, for example, by the noble descendants of the Mexica tlatoque, as in the particular case of Don Pedro Dionisio, who declared that he was descended from the tlatoani Itzcohuatzin (Itzcoatl in reverential pose; Figure 1.5).

A similar case was brought by Don Juan de Mendoza, governor of the pueblo of Tecamachalco, who in 1560 claimed that its members were derelict in paying the tribute they owed him, in keeping with his status and that of his spouse. He reminded the authorities that this privileged position had been rightfully passed down to him from his parents and grandparents. He further claimed that his lineage went back through "eight hundred years" of direct ancestors, all of whom had been tlatoque of the pueblo. On that basis he requested that the Indians be ordered to pay him the tribute he was due, especially inasmuch as foodstuffs were so costly. Mendoza also recalled that he had come to Hernán Cortés's aid by providing him with food and *tamemes* (Indian bearers) for the conquest of Tenochtitlan, an argument many Indian nobles were accustomed to making whenever they sought to claim or reclaim certain rights.[101]

The community of Tacuba offers another example of a pueblo that during this period recalled its own history to enhance and substantiate its legal position. The tlatoque of Tacuba, Don Antonio Cortés Totoquihuaztli, was thoroughly wedded to tradition. To wit, in 1574 he ordered that his will be drawn up before Fray Pedro Horoz, the guardian of Tacuba's Franciscan monastery, dictating it in Nahuatl and also painting a codex to show the lands and sites he was leaving to his heirs. This testamentary codex is composed of two sheets, each of which shows several plots of land of different dimensions. What had been the palace (*tecpan*) of Tacuba is seen at the center of the first sheet. One of the pieces of land bears the glyph of *ahuizotl*, a strange and mythical Mesoamerican aquatic animal that carries a fan on its foot and has the glyph that represents water jutting out from the lower part of its body. There are also signs of a path and a Christian church. On the second sheet of the codex are various plots of land, each of which bears its name in the form of a glyph.[102]

In 1566 this same Indian, Don Antonio Cortés, petitioned the Crown to relieve Tacuba of having to exist under the encomendero system, requesting instead that the community be given the status of a pueblo under the jurisdiction of a corregidor, thus enabling it to pay tribute to the king alone. To support his petition, Cortés explained in considerable detail that Tacuba (Tlalcopan) was one of three capitals or political centers (altepetl) that had governed the region prior to the arrival of the Spaniards. He included a list of thirty Indian nobles who, because of their ancestral line, had never paid tribute to anyone—a privilege, he was careful to point out, that had also been enjoyed by the family members who preceded them. Items 3 and 4 of Cortés's report reveal the form under which the Triple Alliance was organized prior to the Spanish conquest:

> Item 3: Each of the three capitals was on its own and maintained a separate and distinct judicial system, such that one capital was not subjugated to another, nor did they interfere in the administration of justice, other than to have the native rulers join together in matters of war or when some pueblo or province rebelled and rose up against one of them, which pact was made for a period of eighty plus eighty days, one time by one capital, another time by the other, according to their turn [and term], in order to impart such order and coordination as seemed necessary, and [to carry out] the responsibilities of justice and government, and to grant the favors and mercies that [they desired],

each one within its own sphere of government and power and administration, as determined by its one third part of the government of this New Spain, so it is stated.

Item 4: Each one of the said three capitals forever had its provinces that were subject to it, each of the three according to its one third part, and each province came to its corresponding capital to deliver its tribute, services, and summons, with each capital assigning the people it thought necessary [to provide for them] and whatever else suited it, so it is stated.[103]

The information Cortés presented also included the fact that when the Spanish first arrived, the person governing Tlacopan had been his father, Xotoquihuazin. Cortés also explained that prior to the conquest, when the tlatoque of one of the three altepetl of Mexico, Texcoco, and Tlacopan died, "they pointed to the eldest son as the successor, placing a hand over his head." Moreover, when one of these rulers died, the two other tlatoque from the other two altepetl held a meeting in the altepetl of the deceased tlatoque, where they called upon the heir "and crowned him as king and ruler of that capital, each placing his crown on the heir's head followed by that capital's own crown."[104]

Thus, members of the indigenous nobility—both those from important pueblos and those from smaller outlying communities—attempted to come before the audiencia to present various claims and arguments with the purpose of obtaining justice. To bolster their evidence, they generally brought codices. This practice, in turn, invoked a special proceeding so the codices or paintings could be certified as legal documents. From the consideration of a minor legal complaint brought by a community in the Valle de Toluca, it is possible to reconstruct the way the process of certifying codices operated. The central persons involved in this complaint were two Indians, both natives of Tlacotepec, a pueblo in the southern part of Toluca. During the mid-sixteenth century, in the year 1565 specifically, this pueblo was adjacent to lands belonging to both the Marqués del Valle and another pueblo, Capultitlán.

The case has a number of interesting angles. First, it involves a dispute between Indians from different ethnic backgrounds, one—Alonso González—of Nahua origin and the other—Pablo Ocelotl—a Matlatzinca. The case was tried to determine which of the two Indians possessed the legal right to a substantial plot of land, some houses, and a field of maguey plants, whose collective value amounted to 1,000 pesos of standard gold. To establish the veracity of their claim, both individuals presented a codex. The documents were copied by two *tlacuiloque* (native artists), with the copies subsequently incorporated into the judicial record:

In the pueblo of Xiquipilco in the Valle del Matalçingo of this New Spain on the third day of the month of April in the year fifteen hundred and sixty five, I Gomez Davila, notary in service to His Majesty, prepared for copying this painting from an original that forms part of the case presented by Pablo Oçelutle and his sons, and Francisco Yquixitotol, otomite Indian from said pueblo of Xiquipilco and another Indian from Metepeque duly copied it, and Gaspar Borjes, interpreter for this Audiencia in the Mexican language and in Spanish, and Francisco, interpreter in the Mexican language and in otomite, took and received their oath by God and by Santa María and in lawful manner by a sign of the cross, and in discharge of their duty translated it and declared that said painting is true and certain and faithfully copied from the original which forms part of said case and that it contains no error in substance, by God and their consciences on which they rest, and this is the truth and is what transpired and is verified by the witnesses present, Luis de Leon and Diego Lopez, in said pueblo of Xiquipilco. Given before me, Gomez Davila His Majesty's notary.[105]

This activity, as set down in the record, suggests that a wide circle of tlacuiloque existed in the colony, functioning as notaries and executing copies of codices for inclusion in judicial proceedings. It is also apparent that a particular juridical ceremony existed to govern the production of these copies; the Spanish authorities had thus worked out a uniform process in which they employed artists who specialized in making copies of codices for those involved in court cases and litigation. This particular legal dispute will be considered again later.

Throughout the sixteenth century, moreover, the codices the Indians presented at a trial were literally "read" by the native witnesses, and on many occasions the Spanish judge's specific request to the Indians for such a "reading" is recorded in the trial record. An example of this practice is seen in a 1575 trial, when the Spanish authority asked the Indians of Texcoco if they had texts or "paintings" recording the fact that the Indians who belonged to the settlement of Tenango served as tenant farmers of the Texcoco tlatoque. Without delay, the Indians submitted as proof a codex on *amatl* (bark paper) from 1544 and also made clear that they had two more such codices, from 1560 and 1561, that were kept under the care of the principales of their pueblo. One of the Indian witnesses, a seventy-year-old man named Cebrian Chontatl, who could neither read nor write, was asked by the presiding judge to "read" the glyphs on the 1544 codex:

He stated that the first division, situated toward the left, signified the dependent community of Atenco. Asked what comes next, by the second division where there is a head he stated that what comes next is where you find the commoners of said community who number one hundred and forty one. Asked what the third division signified, he stated that it was the corn paid in tribute by these commoners to the said principales who were there. . . . [I]t came to one hundred forty measures, each one of the said commoners, in accordance with the accounts, gave one measure on the scale of that time, which would be more or less like three of today's measures, because this witness saw them and compared them to the ones we use today. . . . He was asked what the first sum in the fourth division signified, and he stated that it represents sixteen and a half blankets and two *huipiles* [Indian women's blouses]: He was asked what the fifth and final division signified, and he stated that it was one load and [460] cacaos.[106]

In light of this discussion, it seems reasonable to believe that the justice system as applied to the native population in this period took into account important characteristics of indigenous culture and adapted them to the workings of Spanish law. At the same time, of course, this flexibility was circumscribed by its context; the Spanish authorities saw the Indians as minors, as incapable of defending themselves juridically because of their inherent weakness of character and primitive, pre-Christian condition. Thus, as of 1563, the manner in which the Indians existed, their fundamental condition and natural juridical state, was defined as "wretched"; given their status as vassals of the Crown, it was considered the monarch's duty to protect, defend, and shield them. The Indians, in sum, "are considered wretched because of the gentile state in which they exist."[107] Nonetheless, an exception was made for the native lords, principales, and nobles (tlatoque and *pipiltin*). These Indians were not lumped into the category of *miserabilis* because for the Crown and royal officialdom the indigenous nobility possessed social and legal standing analogous to that enjoyed by the Spanish nobility. Consequently, the native nobility was not exempt from paying the fees obligated by its estate or from taking part in the full legal process (it did not have access to the type of expedited justice granted to non-noble Indians). Furthermore, and these distinctions are critical, "the Indian pueblos formed the second exception in this general assimilation to the statutes of miserabilis and of guardianship. As corporate entities, they could take legal action and have legal action taken against them in the common courts, engage legal counsel as they might wish, submit to the ordinary proceedings of Spanish law and pay fees and full costs just as Spaniards did."[108]

The condition in which minors found themselves, however, as people in need of guardianship or as existing in a condition of wretchedness, made it possible to justify the development of a system of justice tailored to indigenous customs—a system in which protection of the Indians was mandated. Yet it is also true that while participating in a justice system that was foreign to them, the Indians, as noted earlier, managed to incorporate many elements from their own culture and to negotiate advantages on behalf of their separate interests. This justice system functioned and cohered to a certain point because the Indians participated in it and also carved out political niches for themselves, a situation that existed not only in New Spain but also in Peru, where the native population—similarly categorized as miserables, as people therefore in need of special protection—manipulated this designation to their advantage.[109]

Given this confluence of factors, it is not surprising that during the viceregal administration of Luis de Velasco, the Crown attempted, through a series of royal decrees, to lower the cost of legal disputes for the Indians, even to the point of totally exempting extremely poor Indians from such costs. From the available evidence, it seems that the audiencia fell in line with these decrees.[110] In general, during this period justice as applied to the Indians functioned no differently than it had during Viceroy Mendoza's time. Numerous disputes were brought before the viceroy. On occasion, he intervened and settled them personally; in other instances, he delegated them to one of the oidores or—depending on the origin of the case—to a lower-level judge outside the capital. Velasco, when he deemed it appropriate, also maintained the practice of using native judges to resolve disputes. In the majority of cases, these disputes were accompanied by codices or pictorial manuscripts, some of which—even at the earliest stage of litigation—were in Nahuatl or included petitions in that language.[111] The disputes the viceroy settled on first hearing (*en primera instancia*) were generally those brought by Indians from Mexico City. Custom held that Indians who lived within the five-league jurisdictional radius of the viceregal capital could, in the first instance, appeal directly to the viceroy to resolve their disputes, a privilege also extended to even the lowliest Indians who lived in this vicinity.[112] During Velasco's fourteen-year viceregal administration, one oidor, Francisco Ceynos, seems to have presided over more trials involving Indians than any other judge. Like the majority of his fellow oidores, Ceynos was largely ignorant of indigenous culture and customs.[113] In contrast, Alonso de Zorita—an oidor with a broad reputation who also heard and settled numerous Indian disputes during these same years—possessed extensive knowledge of the indigenous world, although his opinions occasionally reflected a strong bias toward the native nobility.[114]

From the mid-sixteenth century on, judicial affairs were affected by a new development: namely, a decision by the native population to begin using lawyers when litigating disputes. In this regard, Susan Kellogg notes that at the outset of a case, the Indians generally did not use a lawyer but prepared their own testimony. If this approach proved unsuccessful, however, they turned to a procurador (untitled lawyer), who was usually a creole, to pursue the case in the audiencia. The procuradores were conversant with the law but lacked the legal training lawyers possessed. A further distinction Kellogg draws is that the legal strategies the Indians' lawyers employed were very different from the arguments the Indians themselves presented when a case was initially heard. This difference, reflective of a basic cultural divide, played out markedly over nearly 200 years, from the early sixteenth century through the seventeenth century.[115] Clearly, many of these procuradores, along with the court interpreters, or *nahuatlatos*, played an important role as cultural intermediaries, linking the Indian pueblos with the judicial system. As many members of the religious orders saw it, however, the procuradores frequently deceived their clients and caused their financial ruin. In the experience of the superiors of New Spain's three most important religious orders, the Indians were given to litigate over almost any matter, which meant their already meager resources were expended in paying fees to procuradores and meeting other legal costs.[116]

AUGUSTÍN PINTO: A SIXTEENTH-CENTURY *PROCURADOR*

On these points, it is useful to examine some of the specific strategies procuradores employed in litigation involving the native population. The actions taken by a procurador for the Mexico City Audiencia, Augustín Pinto, during the second half of the sixteenth century serve as an excellent example. On June 22, 1564, the members of the audiencia appointed him to that office following the death of the former procurador, Vicencio de Riberol.[117]

The record of Pinto's performance as procurador begins in 1564. In that year, a group of Indian artisans or skilled manual workers—among them bakers, tailors, and grass gatherers from Mexico City's four Indian quarters (San Juan, San Pablo, Santa María, and San Sebastián)—brought a lawsuit against the Indian governor of Mexico, Don Luis Santamaría Cipac, and the *alcaldes* (judges and *cabildo* members of an Indian town) and *regidores* (councilmen) of the city's Indian cabildo (municipal council). The latter sixteen individuals were Martín Cano, Tomás de Aquino, Tloribio Tlacuchcalcatl, Don Luis Huehuezaca, Diego Tezcacoacatl, Antón Tepan, Don Pedro Tlapaltecatl, Melchior Diez, Martín Yolotécatl, Don Martín, Don Antonio, Juan González, Juan Totococ, Martín Cipac, Pedro Temyluca, and Miguel Sánchez. The artisans accused the governor and the cabildo members of subjecting them to mistreatment, collecting excessive amounts of tribute, and mismanaging government affairs in the city. They also engaged Augustín Pinto as their procurador. For their part, the Indian cabildo members hired a lawyer named Juan Caro, also a good friend of Alonso de Zorita.[118]

An important consideration underlying this case is that it took place at a key time in the evolution of the Indian cabildo in Mexico City. These were the last years in which the council was controlled by members of the old, ancestral native nobility. Following Pinto's legal advice, the artisans accused their noble authorities of having antiquated ways, of retaining idolatrous practices from before the conquest. But an even more serious infraction, they maintained, was that in the actual fulfillment of their duties, cabildo members persisted in letting ancient customs guide them; for example, "that as and when someone dies, they go to the house of the deceased to eat and drink as was the practice and custom in the past century."[119]

Another accusation the artisans made was "that said alcaldes and regidores maintain the custom, in the *mitotes* [dance festivals] which they conduct, of wearing some costumes and decorations which our old ancestors had the custom of donning and wearing when bent upon engaging in worship and upon sacrificing somebody, bringing natural death to him and [that] this should not be allowed simply because of their office." The nobles who formed the membership of the Indian cabildo were also denounced for bathing in sweat houses "stark naked" and for being "drunk." A final accusation the artisans made was that every year the nobles held a secret election to choose who would next be named to the offices of alguacil, constable, and regidor and that those to whom the honor was given were invariably members of their own circle.

Although the document that spells out the artisans' complaints against the cabildo members contains nineteen major charges, what was doubtless really behind their case was a desire to capitalize on the new conditions in post-conquest Mexico so they could wrest local political power from the nobles. With this objective in mind, the artisans provided Pinto with information about the customs the nobles had practiced prior to the conquest. Pinto then used this information to attack the cabildo members during the trial.

In defending themselves against this line of attack, the nobles argued that the artisans did not know how to read or write, "nor do they understand well the customs and experience of the natives of this land, necessary for its judicial administration and proper governance."[120] They pointed out, in addition, that the basis for the attack against them was the artisans' desire to avoid paying the tribute they owed.

Even more interesting is the cabildo's principal figures' attempt to respond to the raft of allegations about their attachment to ancient customs. They explained that on ceremonial occasions, such as funerals and weddings, when they conversed and mingled with people, it was to discharge a social duty undertaken to honor and express feelings for others. Regarding their participation in the mitotes, they replied that the celebrations took place as part of the days of obligatory Christian observance and that they were singing the Lord's praises. With regard to the sweat house baths, they stated that these were evidence of their strict habits of cleanliness and good health.

The artisans' case continued to be heard before the audiencia. The trial record is inconclusive, however. It ends with a court summons issued to the top cabildo authorities, as well as a demand that money be returned to the artisans. Through the entire case, however, Augustín Pinto made clear use of the arguments his

Indian clients provided. Moreover, a second case from 1564 offers another example of Pinto's work as procurador. In this instance, his services were performed
on behalf of the pueblo of San Francisco Iztaquimaxtitlan, located southeast of
the state of Puebla. The Indians of this community were attempting to separate
themselves from the capital to which they had traditionally been attached, the
pueblo of San Juan Iztaquimaxtitlan, arguing that they had not in fact been its
tributaries. This type of case was very frequent beginning in the mid-sixteenth
century. With the weakening of the altepetl and its traditional leadership, numerous subject pueblos successfully engineered their own independence.[121]

Such was the case with San Francisco Iztaquimaxtitlan, whose members
resorted to both the courts and outright rebellion to achieve their independence
from San Juan Iztaquimaxtitlan, whose standing was supported by the missionaries. During the struggle, members of the San Francisco community physically
assaulted those from San Juan, injuring several nobles who served on its cabildo.
This occurrence was depicted in a codex that formed part of the evidence San
Juan introduced in the suit it brought against San Francisco. The latter community, as noted, was defended by Augustín Pinto.[122]

In the top left part of the pictorial manuscript presented by San Juan, the
Indians from San Francisco are seen clubbing several of their opponents with
sticks; blood is running from the faces of the wounded, who are carrying a staff
that identifies them as members of San Juan's Indian cabildo. A similar action is
taking place on the top right side of the manuscript, where two other Indians
from San Juan, both dripping blood, are also being beaten with sticks by Indians
from San Francisco. They are wearing blue crowns (*xihuitzolli*), a symbol of royalty and an indication of their noble lineage. A friar appears between the two
warring parties; a word in the form of a scroll comes out of his mouth, and he
seems to be trying to pacify the Indians from San Francisco, trying to halt them
from abusing the San Juan Indian nobles.

More unruly action is seen taking place in the lower left section of the manuscript, where a monastery appears and some of the San Francisco Indians—
throwing stones—have actually cracked a hole in the wall of the building. Two
bloodied Indian nobles, wearing crowns and carrying their staffs of office, are
seen inside the monastery speaking with a friar, in all likelihood describing the
violent confrontation with the San Francisco Indians. Finally, in the lower right
area of the manuscript, the artist has depicted the denouement of the narrative—punishment is being administered to some of the Indians for their participation in these events, and two are shown hanging by rope in a kind of shack
(place for inflicting impromptu punishment) (Figure 1.6).

Prior to the Spanish conquest, the altepetl of Iztaquimaxtitlan served as an
important Mexica fortress or military garrison for the defense of the Tlaxcalan

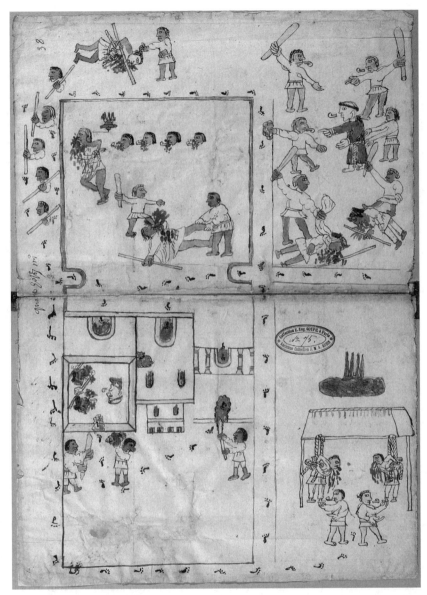

1.6. Reproduction, no. 75 (no. 169 in Glass and Robertson 1975). Date: 1564. Courtesy, National Library of France, Paris.

empire. Because of the sparse documentary record, however, it is not mentioned either as one of the empire's conquests or as one of its tributaries.[123] This altepetl was apparently situated in the upper reaches of a mountain and, from what is known, contained around 5,000 families. Hernán Cortés and his men passed through the site sometime around August 1519 and spent a week there; during his stay, Cortés noted how similar the place seemed to Castilblanco, in Extremadura. The local ruler, who perhaps functioned as a military governor, informed the Spaniards that he was an ally of Moctezuma. Indeed, a short while later, he and his warriors provided military aid to the Mexicas in their confrontation with the Spanish, a gesture that cost Iztaquimaxtitlan dearly a year later when the Spaniards—under the command of Gonzalo de Sandoval—unleashed a violent war of conquest against the settlement.[124]

Yet despite this pre-conquest alliance forged with the dominant Mexica power, the Indians from San Francisco opportunistically asserted, through Augustín Pinto, their lineage as an altepetl and underscored a closeness between themselves and the tlaxcaltecas:

> [F]or twenty, thirty, forty, fifty and four hundred years and more, and sustained by every memory of man, the said pueblo of san Francisco Iztacamatitlan, my clients, called by another name Castilblanco, has been and is a seat of administration and not subject to any other town because, as is shown through its pictographic documents and antiquities, more than 670 years will have passed since the four seats of administration that existed in those parts where the said pueblo is located were under natives of a territory they called Chicomoztoc. They possessed the section and place and lands where the said town is situated and populated and these four persons [the administrators of the four seats] went to live in the city of Tlaxcala where the natives . . . of San Francisco elected and obeyed them, bringing them tribute and other things that were required. And it has always had its church, governors, magistrates, and councilmen.[125]

The origins of the dispute lay in the construction and establishment of a Franciscan monastery and in the decision by the Spanish to elevate the adjacent Indian community to a *cabecera* (head town of a municipality). When the plains of Atzompa—covering an extensive area that had been unpopulated since the pre-Hispanic era—began to be settled, the inflow of people was accompanied by the founding of a pueblo, which was named San Juan Tlaxocoapan. A series of further developments occurred in the mid-sixteenth century, when the Spanish authorities elected to resettle a part of the population of Iztaquimaxtitlan in this new site and move the cabecera, which was renamed San Juan Iztaquimaxtitlan, there. The community of San Francisco, however, refused to be attached to the new cabecera, thus precipitating the confrontation and division.

Ultimately, the Spanish authorities were compelled to recognize both sites—San Juan and San Francisco—as cabeceras. Over time, as the area's flat contours made it a focal point for settlement, San Juan lost its indigenous qualities and became Hispanized—so much so that its original name was changed to San Juan de los Llanos. San Francisco, however, retained its traditional indigenous character.[126]

The Indians from San Francisco who had engaged Augustín Pinto's services tried to exploit whatever loophole might exist in the judicial system. This strategy—to gain advantage by crafting narrow legal arguments based on both indigenous tradition and the new colonial regime and to do so out of context—seems to have proven effective. Furthermore, a skilled lawyer such as Pinto could tie these arguments to Spanish legal doctrine and its sui generis application in the Indies.

Augustín Pinto turns up again on the legal scene in 1565. Earlier in this chapter I referred to a dispute that took place in the pueblo of Tlacotepec, located in the Valle de Toluca. The incident's central figures were two Indians, one Matlazinca and the other Nahua. The procurador for the Nahua Indian was Augustín Pinto. This dispute over houses and land in Tlacotepec is interesting because it points out that the native population frequently managed to influence the legal strategies procuradores employed in carrying out litigation.

Both Indians in this dispute—the Matlazinca, Pablo Ocelotl, and the Nahua, Alonso González—had offered different pictorial representations and other evidence to sustain their respective claims to a house in Tlacotepec and a nearby tract of land with maguey plants. To validate his claim of ownership, Ocelotl had produced titles of inheritance that supposedly guaranteed that these were ancestral lands that had come down to him as his rightful patrimony. As a member of the lower Matlazinca nobility, Ocelotl had also drawn upon a detailed description of his lineage and—going to considerable effort—had called as witnesses several Matlazincas from his pueblo who had known both him and his family for many years.[127]

The pictorial manuscript he presented was impressive. Executed on a sheet of European paper, it depicts Ocelotl's genealogy in the form of a numbered glyph showing 4,000 maguey plants accompanied by a calendar. It also portrays scenes from the Matlazincas' historical past and daily life, surrounding which is found the traditional year count. The latter has thirteen numerals and four year bearers (cargadores): Acatl (Cane, or Reed), Tecpatl (Flint), Calli (House), and tochtli (Rabbit). The calendar begins with the year Reed 1519 and registers forty-seven annual glyphs, bringing it up to the year in which the dispute broke out, House 1565. In form and content it is highly traditional; the bearer tochtli is drawn as a rabbit's head that appears to have been decapitated, with two scrolls rolled out in opposite directions from it, and the bearer Tecpatl is drawn as a "star-like eye" (Figure 1.7). Furthermore, as represented on the sheet, Pablo Ocelotl's genealogy indicates that his lineage is derived from a hill, or tepetl. This imagery symbolizes a family line whose ancestry originates in a cave, which in turn implies a connection to or kinship with the ancient gods.

A specific example of such a connection, or rather of the attempt to establish one, is found in another case involving a cacique of the community of Culhuacán named Don Baltasar. He was accused of having hidden, in 1538, some idols from the principal Mexican temples. During the trial, an Indian artist testified that at the behest of the cacique he had painted a genealogy of the cacique's family, whose history and lineage began with the departure of his ancestors, in the company of some gods, from a cave called Tlaxico.[128]

Unlike the Matlazinca, the Nahua Indian had been unable to demonstrate an ancestral claim to the lands and houses being litigated. Instead, his right of possession was based on the fact that his father, who had arrived in Tlacotepec from the Valley of Mexico, had been given the property and houses by local authorities because Pablo Ocelotl's parents were not actively using them. Although his ownership rested on an illegal foundation, González was able—thanks to the cleverness of his procurador, Augustín Pinto—to keep Ocelotl's houses. Using witnesses who were not from Tlacotepec and who may have been bribed (as Ocelotl charged) and guided by Pinto, the Nahua claimed that he, too, was of noble lineage. His strategy was simply to copy Pablo Ocelotl's line of argument and, through his witnesses, maintain that his was a noble Nahua family from Tlacotepec. This story, however, was completely false; González's witnesses invented a grandfather for him who had supposedly lived in Tlacotepec, with Pinto—mimicking Ocelotl's claim—then asserting that González was a descendant of Tlacotepec nobility. Resorting to this type of legal chicanery, Pinto managed to win the case in 1568, enabling González to come away holding on to Pablo Ocelotl's properties. Further undermining Ocelotl's defense was the fact that his lawyer had built his case purely on the argument—threadbare as it was—that the Matlazinca was a lowly Indian and should not be robbed of what was his. Pinto, as has been seen, took a much more aggressive approach, arguing that his client, Alonso González, was a Nahua of noble lineage whose family had been rooted in Tlacotepec since before the conquest. Clearly, Pinto—who shamelessly appropriated Ocelotl's evidence and case and superimposed them on González—was much more effective than his adversary. The more traditional vantage point of the Indian world to which the Matlazinca clung left him vulnerable to the Nahua, who wisely took advantage of the more flexible, if dishonest, approach the new legal system and environment offered.[129]

Around the same time, in 1566, Augustín Pinto found himself defending the authorities of the pueblo of Temazcaltepec in a criminal claim against the Indian alcalde of Malacatepec. Both communities were located in the present-day state of Mexico. The Malacatepec alcalde, another Pablo Ocelotl, was defended

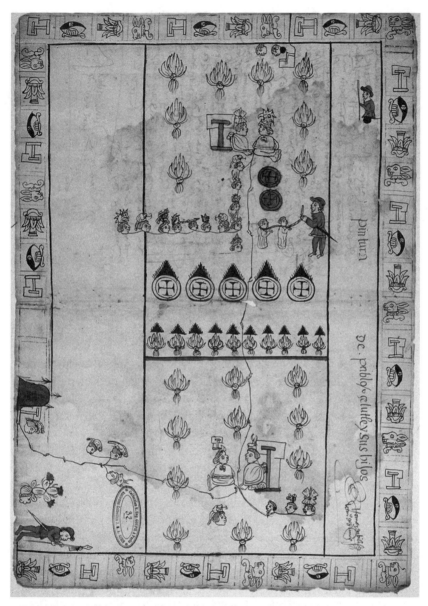

I.7 Reproduction, no. 32 (no. 336 in Glass and Robertson 1975). Date: 1565. Courtesy, National Library of France, Paris.

by Alvaro Ruiz, who—like the lawyer Juan Caro—also maintained a close friendship with the oidor Alonso de Zorita. Zorita had expert knowledge of this region. At the time, Temazcaltepec was an important mining zone and also constituted

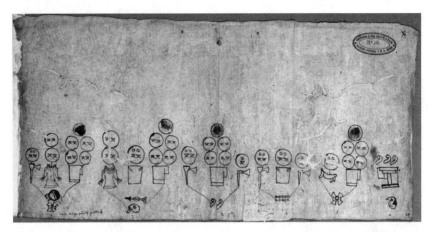

I.8 Reproduction, no. 111 (no. 310 in Glass and Robertson 1975). Date: 1566. Courtesy, National Library of France, Paris.

an *alcaldía mayor* (the jurisdiction of an alcalde mayor), which necessarily made the site a center of Spanish interest.

For reasons never made clear, one evening the Indians from the pueblo of Malacatepec had apparently descended at midnight on two or three outlying settlements of Temazcaltepec, robbing and setting fire to the houses. The Indians from Temazcaltepec introduced a codex on which the stolen objects are represented (Figure 1.8).[130] The Temazcaltepec Indians also depicted on other sheets that the Indians from Malacatepec had placed several Indians from their pueblo under arrest. Through the efforts of Augustín Pinto, they succeeded in getting the audiencia to issue a royal order calling for the arrest of the alcalde of Malacatepec as the result of his pueblo's actions. The alcalde, Pablo Ocelotl, was seized and carried off to the audiencia's jail in Mexico City. This action caused many of the Indians from Malacatepec to flee into the surrounding mountains. Alvaro Ruiz argued in Ocelotl's defense that he had not been at the site of the attacks on the Temazcaltepec settlements or at the arrest of the Indians and thus had not participated in those events. Ocelotl also claimed that the case made by the Temazcaltepec Indians was a series of lies and that, in reality, they had been the instigators and aggressors. Nevertheless, thanks to the work of their procurador, Augustín Pinto, the Indians from Temazcaltepec fought successfully to keep Ocelotl in jail, where several other authorities from this pueblo had also been placed. The dispute persisted and was carried to the next level, where the record of what subsequently happened is unfortunately lost.

Following this case, the trail of Augustín Pinto's legal activities dries up until 1572. In that year the procurador plunged into a case that involved Indian families in the community of Santiago Tlatelolco.[131] Several Indians from that pueblo had filed a suit against Gaspar Carrillo, a Spaniard who was married to a mestiza named Andrea Ramírez, over the disposition of lands and houses located in a quarter of Tlatelolco called San Martín Zacatlán. The lawyer representing the Spaniard and his wife was the ubiquitous Augustín Pinto. Prior to the conquest, in the time of Moctezuma, the properties being litigated had belonged to an Indian called Chimaltzin. This Indian had bequeathed them to his two sons, Mazapuecatl Chimaltzin, the younger, and Atlatzin. Atlatzin, in keeping with his ancestral and noble state, married Ana Papan. They had four daughters who after the conquest were baptized and given the Christian names Marina, Mencia, Marta, and Barbola. During the war of conquest, Atlatzin was killed by the Spanish, causing his wife to flee from Tlatelolco with their daughters and to abandon the family lands and houses. Concerned that the properties not fall into disuse and disrepair, the *xilacale*[132] and headmen of the district asked an Indian named Martín Coata to take care of them. Coata, it seems, had come from Tenochtitlan and was the grandfather of Andrea Ramírez.

The dispute arose when the four Indian sisters, as Chimaltzin's granddaughters, filed suit against Gaspar Carrillo over the houses. In response, the Spaniard argued—through Augustín Pinto—that as the granddaughter of Martín Coata, his wife owned the houses. Chimaltzin's granddaughters countered that Coata had simply been asked to watch over and take care of the houses, which legally still belonged to them. An initial judgment, rendered on June 17, 1572, went in favor of Carrillo and his wife. The granddaughters appealed the verdict, this time calling several witnesses from among the Indian population of Tlatelolco. Perhaps because his clients were a Spaniard and a mestiza, Pinto chose to handle this dispute in a more orthodox way and not construct his defense around arguments drawn from the Indians' experience and view of the world. His approach, instead, was to impute the honesty and integrity of the four Indian sisters, arguing that they had bribed their witnesses to testify, paying each of them four reales. He also tried to undercut the witnesses' testimony by pointing out that they were all Indians, as though that was an unusual development in a dispute that involved the native population. He further argued that they were "friends" of Chimaltzin's granddaughters and—again attempting to impute their character—were just "miserable Indians . . . lowly and of ill fortune and estate."[133]

In this case, however, the procurador's strategy and defense fell short. On May 19, 1573, the audiencia reached a final judgment in favor of two of the granddaughters, Barbola and Mencia, ordering that Carrillo and his wife return the properties to them within nine days.

The last dispute on record in which Augustín Pinto is mentioned occurred some years later, in 1590, when he again became involved in litigation between two Indian pueblos, Santiago Tenexcalco and Tizayuca (located in the present-day states of Hidalgo and México, respectively).[134] The pueblo of Tenexcalco—plaintiff in the case—claimed that although it was a subject community of Tepeapulco, the Indians of Tizayuca, who were subject to the jurisdiction of Otumba, still insisted that Tenexcalco participate in collective labor Tizayuca was obligated to carry out on certain work projects in Mexico City, such as "the repair of water fountains [and] tubes in Chapultepec, drawing from the river of Tenayuca Acalhuacan along with other work they are assigned." In their complaint, the Tenexcalco Indians added that they were not subject to Tizayuca's authority and that if they had assisted the pueblo in doing work in Mexico City that it owed as tribute, it was only because of an arrangement worked out by the Tizayucans.

The procurador for Tizayuca was Juan Palencia and the one for Tenexcalco was the now-famous Augustín Pinto. The problem raised in this case is particularly interesting because it concerns the system by which collective labor was organized prior to the Spanish conquest. As they had noted in their legal submissions, the Indians of Tenexcalco were subject to the political and administrative authority of Tepeapulco, a community whose population had declined. At the same time, while not dependent on Tizayuca, since the time before the conquest Tenexcalco had participated in collective labor activities the former pueblo organized. Thus the Tizayucans stated, in affirming this tradition: "[T]he said settlement of Tenezcalco has always, without expressing any doubt, been accustomed to answering the call of said pueblo of Tizayuca, lending assistance and service on these occasions," declaring further that Tenexcalco's present objection to continuing to participate in the collective labor resulted from its "lack of loyalty."[135]

The tensions and confrontation had in fact been brewing for several years. In 1583, the Tizayucans presented a ruling the viceroy had issued on June 28, 1581, in which he ordered that the residents of Tenexcalco gather to help Tizayuca with the work it needed to perform on projects in Mexico City. Their position strengthened by this precedent, in 1583 the Tizayucans also managed to secure a royal ruling upholding and ratifying the viceroy's earlier order. In this decision, the critical point is that the viceroy, Lorenzo Suárez Mendoza (1580–1583), chose to respect and sanction the tradition in force since before the conquest in which the Indians of Tenexcalco collaborated in helping Tizayuca fulfill its collective labor obligations. The fact that Tenexcalco was under the authority of Tepeapulco, not Tizayuca, was of secondary importance. The viceroy's decision revolved around customs and practices established by the Tizayuca Indians prior to the arrival of the Spanish.

To counter and refute the evidence Tizayuca presented, Augustín Pinto produced a definitive judgment handed down in 1536 by Viceroy Antonio de

Mendoza, under which a division of communities and lands was made between the pueblos of Otumba (to whose authority Tizayuca was subject) and Tepeapulco. This parceling out was done because of the numerous disputes between the two pueblos. As part of the judicial ruling, it was specified that Tenexcalco—along with a group of other Indian settlements—would be subordinated to Tepeapulco's authority. Pinto then argued that the Tepeapulco Indians had hidden from his clients the document that made Viceroy Mendoza's ruling official, with the result that Tenexcalco, out of pure ignorance, had continued its practice of helping the Tizayucans fulfill their collective labor obligations. Nobody had bothered to inform the pueblo that it was not dependent on either Tizayuca or Otumba. To buttress his case, Pinto prepared a questionnaire and called several witnesses to testify.

From the context, it can be inferred that after the conquest, the Indians from Tizayuca had incurred the obligation to provide labor for various work projects in Mexico City and, on the basis of long-standing custom, received assistance from neighboring pueblos—such as Tenexcalco—in fulfilling the obligation. In all likelihood, these pueblos assisted Tizayuca because of a traditional practice of collective labor, not because they were subject to its higher authority. After the division and reordering of pueblos that took place under Spanish colonial rule, Tenexcalco continued to observe this custom. By 1590, however, its attitude had changed. The latest wave of epidemics had reduced Tenexcalco's population, leading the pueblo to want to be relieved of the personal service burden. Yet if this was the motive, why would Tenexcalco clearly emphasize that it was a subject community of Tepeapulco? After all, the latter pueblo was also obliged to perform services in Mexico City. The reason may be that Tepeapulco was virtually depopulated and, lacking manpower, could no longer muster the effort to collect people into a workforce and send them to the city. In 1583, however, Tizayuca was among a group of pueblos that found themselves obligated to share in the physically taxing work of cleaning Mexico City's main irrigation ditch.

In taking the line he did, Augustín Pinto's strategy was to show that with respect to the organization of labor, indigenous customs inherited from pre-conquest times no longer made sense. He argued that the subordinate pueblos should yield to their cabeceras alone, to the political and administrative authority above them, and not to the impositions of an antiquated system. Pinto's strategy proved successful, and on October 26, 1590, the audiencia ruled that Tenexcalco had no further obligation to help Tizacuya fulfill its work quota in Mexico City.

In prosecuting this case successfully, Pinto was not only the architect but also the instrument of his clients' designs. The Tenexcalco Indians furnished Pinto with the substance of his arguments. The procurador then rephrased and recast the arguments in accordance with the terms and principles of Spanish legal doctrine, taking care to place the case within the framework of European practice and tradition. By following this strategy, Pinto backed Tenexcalco's adversaries into a difficult corner.

He had also demonstrated his value as a cultural mediator. The interpreters employed by the courts also played an important role in this respect. A majority of interpreters were Indians, although Spaniards also performed this function. Their work of translating statements and documents first expressed in various indigenous languages made them vitally important during trials but in many instances also led to suspicion that they might be the objects of bribery. Indeed, from the time of Viceroy Mendoza, nahuatlatos had been enjoined from receiving gifts and other favors from both Indian and Spanish litigants.[136]

The practice of bribing court interpreters was widespread. During Antonio de Mendoza's viceregal administration, for example, an Indian interpreter named Hernando de Tapia enjoyed remarkable privileges because of his work. Tapia collaborated closely with the oidor Lorenzo de Tejada, translating for Tejada on numerous occasions when the oidor, resorting to clandestine tactics, stole extensive tracts of land from several pueblos in central Mexico. In return for his help, the nahuatlato received a grant of land bordering some of Tejada's property in the fertile area of Tacuba. Tapia—unconcerned about concealing the quid pro quo—boasted that it was his custom to go strolling through the agricultural fields of the oidor, whom he knew very well.[137] Since the level of interpreters' participation in trials against the native population was very high, it is not surprising that they were subject to bribery by the Spanish.

At the same time, generally speaking, in the sixteenth century the legal and judicial dynamic favored the Indians in many respects—for example, in permitting them to use their own practices and customs, in giving them access to procuradores and interpreters, and in placing them, as vassals of the Crown, under the protective umbrella of the monarch. Not surprisingly, these conditions created an environment in which many disputes that involved the Indian population reached the audiencia. Indicative of this trend is the fact that fully one-third of the cases the audiencia heard over the course of the sixteenth and seventeenth centuries were brought by Indians against Spaniards.[138] Of course, it was one thing for the Indians to engage in legal action against Spaniards and another to emerge victorious. On this point, however, Susan Kellogg has found—significantly—that Indians won the majority of trials in the sixteenth century that involved both them and Spaniards.[139] A similar situation seems to have existed in the viceroyalty of Peru, implying that Spain's New World empire followed a uniform and consistent policy of extending certain protections to its Indian subjects. Thus, to cite Peru as an example, by using the colonial justice system to their advantage, Indians in the Vilcanota region managed to win numerous suits pertaining to arguments over land, and the leaders of their communities developed considerable expertise in legal matters.[140]

THE INDIAN JUSTICE SYSTEM AT THE END OF THE SIXTEENTH CENTURY

After the death of Viceroy Velasco in 1564, however, the justice system that had taken hold in New Spain began to change, as for a time his successors found themselves operating without the tightly centralized jurisdiction Velasco had enjoyed. The Indians responded to this less rigid environment by bringing their legal concerns to the attention of the oidores as frequently as they had to the viceroy. The situation became even more fluid and confusing in 1569, when the government created a new judicial arm, the Sala del Crimen, whose authorities were given jurisdiction to rule in the first instance in disputes between Indians and Spaniards that occurred within a five-league area around Mexico City.[141]

The changes affecting the justice system in the colony became more clearly defined during the administration of Viceroy Martín Enríquez de Almanza (1568–1589). In contrast to his predecessors, this viceroy had a very poor grasp of the reasons underlying the Indians' decisions to initiate legal action, especially when directed against Spaniards. As Martín Enríquez saw it, the Indians had a strong predilection for involving themselves in disputes and—with the justice system constructed as it was—would freely enter into litigation over matters of little consequence. He believed the caciques were particularly disputatious and that the missionaries as well as some mestizos encouraged them in this tendency, for which reason he recommended that, as a broad rule, the native population be given less access to the courts and the justice apparatus.[142]

It was not surprising that Viceroy Martín Enríquez would assume this posture and withdraw support for the Indians' ready access to the judicial system because he was reflecting changes in the political temper and creed that began when Philip II ascended to the Spanish throne in 1556. With respect to colonial policy per se, the interests of Indian communities in general and of the native nobility in particular took a clear turn for the worse beginning in 1564. The king's attempts, in consultation with the members of his Royal Council, to impose overarching control produced one set of changes after another in the formulation of policy regarding the indigenous population. On the spectrum of these changes, the period from 1570 onward assumes fundamental importance for the Spanish empire because of Philip II's declaration of bankruptcy on September 1, 1575.[143]

The fiscal crisis in which the kingdom found itself meant that Philip's government was driven by both a growing need to increase the revenues in the royal treasury and the concomitant need to distance itself from the policies the Royal and Supreme Council of the Indies had followed to that point, policies that had afforded the Crown's Indian subjects limited participation in the colonial enterprise and guaranteed them some rights as well as respect for certain of their customs. By the 1560s, however, especially beginning late in the decade, the stronger pressure exerted by the Crown in collecting tribute from the Indians led to the impoverishment of the indigenous rulers and to the curtailment of both their privileges and their jurisdiction. The native nobility also lost some of the privileges it had enjoyed. As of 1564, for example, the *mayeque*, or Indians attached to specific lands of the indigenous nobility, had to begin paying tribute directly to the king, whereas earlier they had been exempt from this obligation.[144]

This development created a domino effect. It prompted the Indians who worked their noble overlords' lands to abandon them in order to generate the royal tribute they were now obligated to pay the king. In turn, this exodus left the nobles with their lands but with no Indian laborers to cultivate them. A further innovation, implemented by the mid-1560s, was that the tribute pueblos had paid collectively now had to be paid individually. Adult Indians who were married were assessed an annual tribute, or fee, of one peso,[145] as well as half a *fanega* of corn.[146] This change dealt a severe blow to the Indian economy. The pueblos objected in a variety of ways, but to no avail; the new assessment continued to be imposed. The burden was particularly painful and unmanageable for Indians who lived in Mexico City, since—as they argued—they did not have the land from which to extract the new tax. When the governor of México-Tenochtitlan, Don Luis de Santamaría Cipac, failed to persuade the Spanish authorities to abolish the tax, the Indians under his rule rebelled against him.[147] According to the *Anales de Juan Bautista*, the deep unease his people felt and their decision to revolt caused Santamaría Cipac to die prematurely, in 1566. He was the last governor of México-Tenochtitlan to have descended from the traditional Mexica ruling nobility; no member of Tenochtitlan's royal family ever again assumed the governorship of this extended area.[148]

Within the new political scheme, moreover, others besides the Indian nobility experienced a reduction of privileges. The Crown also perceived the religious orders to be a hindrance to its authority because their practice of defending the indigenous population and the degree of political and religious control they exercised over that population set them apart and allowed them to function as an alternative power. For the Crown, it was necessary to mitigate that influence by expanding and strengthening the role of the secular clergy. In addition, the mining sector became an even stronger part of the colonial economy during this period. As an offshoot, legal mechanisms were developed to steer Indian laborers into the mines. This development, together with the outbreaks of disease that periodically swept through the Indian communities, led to a major drop in the native population beginning in 1568. All of these factors, and certain regional occurrences as well, contributed to the consolidation of a colonial economy controlled by the Spanish and left the Indian community on the far margins.[149]

In sum, the changes introduced to the policies that had governed Spanish-Indian relations through roughly the first two-thirds of the sixteenth century had a pronounced effect on the way justice was administered, a central difference being that the colonial authorities no longer sanctioned the same access to, and participation in, the system by the Indian population. Nonetheless, Indians continued—albeit on a reduced scale—to negotiate their disputes in the courts and to present forms of evidence such as codices when doing so. The economic needs of the Spanish and the greater protection accorded their interests—those of the mining and agricultural sectors in particular—by colonial authorities at the highest level also disadvantaged the native population in multiple ways during the last decades of the sixteenth century.

Between 1576 and 1580, a virulent epidemic broke out among the Indians. The ensuing loss of population and demographic crisis greatly affected the Indian pueblos, reducing many to the status of mere phantom communities. As the figures in Table 1.1 indicate, there were 2.65 million Indians in Mesoamerica in 1568; by 1585—less than twenty years later—their estimated number had dropped to 1.9 million. The sharp decline in the indigenous population had immediate economic consequences. The lack of Indian labor was felt in the mines and in the provision of food supplies for the viceroyalty.[150] On top of this demographic collapse, action was taken during Viceroy Martín Enríquez's administration to consolidate the system of *repartimiento* (the compulsory provision of labor by Indians, who were rotated among specific encomenderos and other colonial entrepreneurs). This system traced its beginnings in New Spain to the government of Viceroy Luis de Velasco. Centered initially on agricultural work, it began to be consolidated in 1574. Under the system, Indian labor was drafted for such productive Spanish enterprises as mines, farms, and ranches, in return for which the Indians received a weekly wage of one *cuartillo* (a quarter of a real). To manage this distribution of labor, the viceregal authority relied on Spanish judges—specialists in the matter—who were assisted by Indian interpreters and officials of the Indian cabildos. Each week, the pueblos provided a specified number of Indians to work in the colonial enterprises within a certain jurisdiction, a number represented pictorially on codices or manuscript paintings. The conditions of work imposed on the Indians, especially in the mines, were extremely harsh—so harsh, in fact, that in 1594 the Franciscan missionaries lashed out against them, comparing the labor system to slavery. Among its abuses and consequences, they noted, were the excessively long hours the Indians were forced to work, a violation that resulted in the deaths of many, and the obstacles the Indians faced—because of the time they had to spend elsewhere—in getting their own fields planted.[151]

The repartimiento system was abolished for agricultural work in 1633 but remained in force for the mines.[152] At its high point, the requirement of personal service imposed on Indians was so all-encompassing that even the native artists, or tlacuiloque, of Santiago Tlatelolco were obligated to participate in the system and fulfill a manual labor quota.[153]

As far as commanding indigenous labor is concerned, available documentation seems to indicate that the Spanish had depended on regional variations of pre-Hispanic work patterns until shortly after the middle of the sixteenth century. By the late sixteenth and early seventeenth centuries, however, pressures imposed from without transformed the colonial environment. The immense economic demands now roiling the Spanish monarchy accelerated the process of Hispanicization in the colony and helped fuel the adoption of the more aggressive system of forced Indian labor, whose distribution was overseen by a special group of judges. In this new order, indigenous patterns of work inherited from the pre-conquest period were inevitably displaced. In the long run, moreover, these adjustments marked a transitional phase from the old labor system to that of debt peonage, a new form of servitude that became institutionalized in seventeenth-century New Spain. Debt peonage was a quintessentially colonial and, later, post-colonial phenomenon, unknown in pre-Hispanic Mexico.[154]

An interesting aspect of the repartimiento system is the fact that it was coordinated from within the pueblos themselves, by the Indian cabildos. The cabildos fulfilled the task of selecting community members for specific work assignments: "Ordinarily, those who manage the distribution are the governors, the principal political and judicial authorities, constables, tribute collectors and mayordomos, and a distribution of Indian labor was also made to them."[155] At a later stage, a special judge who was Spanish supervised the distribution of the teams of Indian laborers to the colonists.

The special judge's appearance and intercession helped ensure the delivery of native labor. Within the repartimiento system, however, the role played by the Indian cabildo likely explains Viceroy Martín Enríquez's attempt to reinforce the cabildo's authority, even to the point of allowing it to invoke the use of pre-Hispanic customs. The fact that the viceroy was so motivated is suggested by an interesting case from the time, although the evidence is too limited to permit a definitive conclusion. As has been seen, Martín Enríquez's term as viceroy was hardly characterized by an impulse to protect the native population or to display respect for its customs. Nevertheless, his desire to strengthen the authority of the cabildo so it could more effectively funnel Indian labor to Spanish entrepreneurs may have spurred him to grant it certain symbolic concessions. Thus, on October 15, 1578, the viceroy issued an order designed to enhance the prestige and power of members serving on the cabildo of the pueblo of Calpan (located in the present-day state of Puebla). The order, which was written in Nahuatl and translated into Spanish, stated that "the title and designation of *principal* are hereby given to those named below."[156]

Each of the eighteen members of Calpan's cabildo documented pictorially that he was of noble origin, depicting his lineage and the local quarter of the pueblo to which he belonged by birth. By submitting this material, the Indians on the cabildo sought to make clear that not only did each member have the right, by virtue of ancestral ties, to have a title or designation of authority attached to his name but he also had a right to be granted official confirmation of the same. Each manuscript painting had around it a drawing of a palace, out of which emerged lines that connected the palaces to the heads of noblemen who wore blue crowns, symbolizing royalty. The nobles' heads are united or bound together by thick cords (*mecatl*); grouped together, they represent the lineage of people who hold the right to titles by virtue of inheritance (Figure 1.9). The cords (rather than simple lines) are an unusual graphic detail to express this relationship. It may not be coincidental that they strongly echo the corded heads painted on the upper walls and ceilings of the mid–sixteenth-century *posas* (processional chapels) at each of the four corners of the atrium in Calpan's Franciscan monastery complex. In these images the cords link the heads of angels. In short, it seems possible that, given the colonial belief that their ancestors had become angels, Calpan's nobles sought to express their ancestral lines in the codex in the same manner.[157]

The titles the viceroy granted to the nobles who served on the Indian cabildo of Calpan were tlatquictecuhtli, tlacatecuhtli tlayllotlactecuhtli, tezcachiuh tecuhctli, chichimeca teuhctli, tlacochcalcatl tecuhctli, popocatl tecuhctli, tlauizcal paztecuhtli, tlamacazcatecuhtli, quauitescatl tecuhctli, calmecahuatecuhtli, calnahuacatl tecuhctli, and tlayllotlactecuhtli tezcachiuhca.[158] Observe in the painting in Figure 1.9 that the cabildo members have depicted—with each councilman drawing attention to his own native quarter—the way in which they inherited these time-honored offices or titles from their ancestors.

For the viceroy, it posed no jurisdictional problem or conflict to let these Indian nobles "make use of" their ancient titles and offices, either in connection with discharging their cabildo responsibilities or because doing so bolstered their personal prestige within the pueblo. In the end, what mattered to the viceroy was to recruit the local authorities to his side so they would work to ensure the smooth operation of the repartimiento system—a system the Indians, naturally, did not embrace. Moreover, when a cabildo member attached the ancient title to his name, it reinforced his power only on a symbolic level; he did not accrue additional jurisdictional authority. What is more, granting the nobles the right to this privilege was politically astute on the part of the viceroy. It allowed him to strengthen his authority within the Indian pueblos and gave him a better means

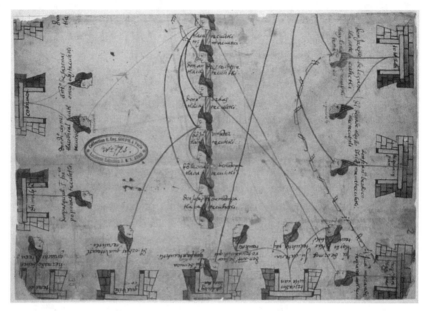

I.9 Reproduction, no. 73 (no. 35 in Glass and Robertson 1975). Date: 1578. Courtesy, National Library of France, Paris.

of seeing that local Indian authorities fulfilled the unpleasant tasks with which they were charged.

Thus, it is not surprising that Viceroy Martín Enríquez would use a policy initially established by Viceroy Antonio de Mendoza in 1536, under which members of the native nobility were granted titles in keeping with their ancient usage to enhance their status in the new colonial order.[159] Mendoza's action, however, had resulted from a different set of political and social imperatives.

In Viceroy Martín Enríquez's case, it could be said that he was engaging in a form of bribery. It is a matter of record that he indeed resorted to this strategy occasionally in his dealings with the Indians. In 1579–1580, for example, the viceroy came to the aid of a Spaniard named Jerónimo López in the latter's efforts to increase the size of his encomienda. López was the encomendero of Ajacuba (Hidalgo). Using his authority and talent of persuasion, he managed to convince the Indians in that pueblo to testify in a trial that the neighboring pueblo of Tetepango, which fell under the administration of a corregidor (that is, it paid tribute directly to the king), was actually a subject community of Ajacuba. Going even further, López bribed the cacique of Tetepango and some of the pueblo's other nobles to swear to the veracity of this declaration. With the knowledge and help of Viceroy Martín Enríquez, the encomendero promised the cacique

Table 1.2. Official Interpreters of Indigenous Languages in the Royal Audiencia, 1591[1]

Name	Language	Salary (in annual pesos)[2]	Indian
1. Juan de Riberol	Nahuatl	200	no
2. Juan Grande	Nahuatl	200	no
3. Pedro López de Barahona	Nahuatl	200	no
4. Juan Mendez de Sotomayor	Nahuatl	200	no
5. Francisco de [Leyva?]	Nahuatl	200	no
6. Bernardino de Leyva	Nahuatl	200	no
7. Nicolás de Castro	Tarasco [p'urhépecha]	200	no
8. [no information]	Otomí [hñahñu]	44[3]	yes
9. [no information]	Mixteco [ñudzahui]	44	yes

Notes:

1. AGI, *México* 22, letter and report to the king concerning persons on the audiencia's royal payroll, May 25, 1591, Mexico City.

2. "These [salaries] are in lieu of collecting fees in the law courts." Ibid.

3. Their annual salary was 20 pesos of ordinary gold, and "they were given eight pesos to help with the costs of celebrating each of the three Easter festivals, which comes to be twenty four pesos and with this each one receives forty four pesos every year." Ibid.

that he would be made governor of Ajacuba. López also granted him a license to carry arms and gave him "clothes such as the Spanish wear and capes made of taffeta."[160] The entire affair came to light when the Indians from Tetepango filed a suit against their cacique for trying to incorporate them into an encomienda.

In the face of such circumstances, and especially following the death of Viceroy Luis de Velasco in 1564, the Indians appealed to various colonial authorities to attend to their complaints. In doing so, however, they caused additional problems for themselves. In 1574, for example, the Indian cabildo of México, headed by Don Antonio Valeriano, attested to the fact that prior to the conquest, disputes among the Indians had been settled quickly and with little or no cost to the parties involved; "now" they were drawn out, costly, and resolved only after much time had elapsed.[161]

Only in the last decade of the sixteenth century did the new viceroy—Luis de Velasco, the younger,[162] the Marqués de Salinas (1590–1595)—begin to devise a new system of justice for the native population. This initiative resulted in the creation of the Juzgado General de Naturales (General Indian Court of Colonial Mexico), an institution that remained intact throughout the entire colonial period (it was not abolished until 1810). By 1591 the audiencia had thirteen procuradores and also employed nine interpreters, each of whom earned a set annual salary (Table 1.2). Two of the nine interpreters were Indians, and the remainder were Spanish. As Table 1.2 indicates, the annual salary of the Spanish translators was 200 pesos and that of the Indians only 44 pesos. The discrepancy in earnings underscores the inferior status of the audiencia's Indian employees and also reflects the scant importance given to their bilingual and even trilingual abilities.

With the creation of the Juzgado in 1591, Viceroy Velasco, the younger, restored the initial consideration and disposition of Indian legal claims and disputes to the viceregal office, a practice, recall, that had been decentralized beginning in 1564. The viceroy also instituted other judicial reforms. The interpreters serving the Juzgado were now prohibited from doing their work and reviewing indigenous cases in their homes, and they were barred from bringing petitions, codices, and pictorial manuscripts on behalf of the Indians. Furthermore, Indians whose claims were being heard in the first instance or by the viceroy were relieved of having to pay any fees or court costs; if their case went to trial, indigenous communities and Indian nobles were required to pay only half of the costs charged to Spaniards. To ensure that he could dispense justice to the Indians in the first instance, the viceroy was assisted and advised by a man of letters. To cover the costs of operating the Juzgado, each Indian family that paid tribute was assessed a special fee of half a real.[163]

The interpreters and lawyers who specialized in dealing with Indian claims objected to the establishment of the Juzgado because of the limits it imposed on the amount of money they could make when involved in such cases. Unmoved and undaunted by their complaints, the viceroy recommended that they be ignored.[164]

A further reform of Viceroy Velasco, the younger, was to appoint two individuals to the newly created post of agent for Indian affairs. The Indians, by paying the half-real assessment, now had access to a special court, and the financial burden the caciques and Indian communities faced in meeting court costs and associated judicial fees had been cut in half. The viceroy held sessions in the Juzgado on Monday and Wednesday mornings and Friday afternoons.[165]

Nevertheless, despite this range of reforms that benefited the native population materially and otherwise, by 1590 the option of preserving indigenous customs as a formal element of the colonial legal system—even to a limited degree— had been forsaken. In his reports to the peninsula, Viceroy Velasco does not even allude to it.[166]

Accordingly, the use of Indian codices as evidence in trials declined notably by the end of the sixteenth century, matched by a corresponding loss of richness in their descriptive power and subject matter. Indeed, for some specialists such as Donald Robertson, the year 1600 marks the end of "manuscript art."[167] As we shall see in Chapter 2, however, this decline was not absolute. Through a process of negotiation in the courts, Indian pueblos still managed to continue to present arguments and evidence that centered on some of their traditional practices and customs. In this context, in the seventeenth and eighteenth centuries the Indians "saw the law as a practical and moral resource that allowed them to gain a measure of control over their lives and to forge a relationship to a distant king."[168]

NOTES

1. Alonso de Zuazo, *Cartas y memoriales (1511–1539)*, ed. Rodrigo Martínez Baracs (Mexico City: CONACULTA, Colección Cien de México, 2000), 245–246.

2. Alonso de Molina, *Vocabulario en lengua castellana y mexicana y mexicana y castellana*, preliminary study by Miguel León Portilla, 3rd ed. (Mexico City: Editorial Porrúa, S.A., 1992), 120r.

3. Fray Bernardino de Sahagún, *Códice Florentino* [facsimile edition of Manuscript 218–220 in the Palatina Collection of the Medicea Laurenziana Library], 3 vols. (Mexico City: Gobierno de la República and Archivo General de la Nación, 1982), 2, book 8, chap. 14, fols. 25v–26r.

4. *Florentine Codex, General History of the Things of New Spain, Fray Bernardino de Sahagún*, ed. and trans. Charles E. Dibble and Arthur J.O. Anderson, 13 vols. (Santa Fe, N.M.: School of American Research and the University of Utah, 1950–1982), book 8, Kings and Lords [1954]: "The name of one Teccalli was Tlacxitlan. There they tried princes and great lords. At once, swiftly, they passed judgment on their complaints or wrong doing," 55.

5. Sahagún, *Códice Florentino*, 2, book 8, chap. 14, fol. 26r; Fray Toribio de Benavente [Motolinía], *Memoriales o libros de las cosas de la Nueva España y de los naturales de ella*, ed. Edmundo O'Gorman (Mexico City: UNAM, 1971), 354; Alonso de Zorita, *Relación de la Nueva España*, ed. with paleography by Ethelia Ruiz Medrano and José Mariano Leyva, 2 vols. (Mexico City: CONACULTA and Colección Cien de México, 1999), 1, 343.

6. Sahagún, *Códice Florentino*, 2, book 8, chap. 14, fols. 26v–27r.

7. *Florentine Codex, General History*, book 8, Kings and Lords: "And the second place where justice was done was named Teccalli. There were the Mexican judges. Sagely they heard the complaint, they recorded it in paintings so that they might take it there to Tlaxcitlan, where they informed the judges who were princes, so that their judgment might be pronounced," 55.

8. Frances F. Berdan and Patricia Rieff Anawalt, *The Essential Codex Mendoza* (Berkeley: University of California Press, 1997), 140–142.

9. Benavente [Motolinía], *Memoriales*, 354; Fray Diego Durán, *Historia de las Indias de Nueva España e Islas de la Tierra Firme*, ed. with paleography and notes by Angel Ma. Garibay K., 2 vols. (Mexico City: Editorial Porrúa, 1984), 1, 184–185; Zorita, *Relación*, 1, 343.

10. *Florentine Codex, General History*, book 8, 54; Alfredo López Austin, *La constitución real de México-Tenochtitlan* (Mexico: UNAM, 1961), 59–61.

11. "And if something was difficult, they took it up to the ruler so that he might judge it [with] those judges whose names were Ciuacoatl, Tlacochcalcatl, Uitznaualailotlac, Ticociauactl, Pochtecatlailotlac, Ezuauacatl, Mexicatl tezcacoactl, Acatliacapanecatl, Milnauatl, Atlauhcatl, Ticociauacatl, Ciuatecpanecatl, and Tequixquinaoacatl." *Florentine Codex, General History*, book 8, 55.

12. The term, signifying *atl-tepetl altepetl* (water and mountain) in Nahuatl, generally refers to a territory ruled over by a lord. On this point, see James Lockhart, *The Nahuas after the Conquest: A Social and Cultural History of the Indians of Central Mexico, Sixteenth through Eighteenth Centuries* (Palo Alto: Stanford University Press, 1992), 14–58.

13. Jerome Offner, *Law and Politics in Aztec Texcoco* (Cambridge: Cambridge University Press, 1983), 147.

14. Ibid., 55–56.

15. Benavente [Motolinía], *Memoriales*, 354.

16. Ibid., 355–357; Offner, *Law and Politics*, 283–287.

17. Benavente [Motolinía], *Memoriales*, 353; Zorita, *Relación*, 1, 339 (quote).

18. Benavente [Motolinía], *Memoriales*, 354; Zorita, *Relación*, 1, 347.

19. Natan Wachtel, *La vision des vaincus: Les Indiens du Pérou devant la conquête espagnole* (Paris: Éditions Gallimard, 1971), 238. My thanks to Professor Guilhem Olivier for this information.

20. Benavente [Motolinía], *Memoriales*, 353–354.

21. Zorita, *Relación*, 1, 339.

22. Benavente [Motolinía], *Memoriales*, 354.

23. Ibid., 355.

24. Susan Kellogg, *Law and the Transformation of Aztec Culture, 1500–1700* (Norman: University of Oklahoma Press, 1995), xxvi–xxvii.

25. Molina, *Vocabulario*, fol. 1v.

26. Ibid., fol. 73v.

27. Fray Francisco de Alvarado, *Vocabulario en lengua mixteca* (Mexico City: Instituto Nacional Indigenista and INAH, 1962), fol. 3v.

28. Ibid., fol. 118v.

29. Fray Juan de Cordova, *Vocabulario en lengua zapoteca* (Oaxaca: Ediciones Toledo, 1987), fol. 3r.

30. Ibid., fol. 117r.

31. "Arte de la lengua matlatzinca compuesto por nuestro padre maestro Fray Diego de Basalenque, padre de esta provincia de San Nicolás Tobutino de Michoacan de la orden de nuestro padre San Augustin," Año de 1640, Manuscript in European paper, Biblioteca Nacional of the Museo Nacional de Antropología, Mexico City, fols. 195v, 199v.

32. James Krippner-Martínez, "The Vision of the Victors: Power and Colonial Justice," *Colonial Latin American Review* 4, 1 (1995): 3–28.

33. Ibid.; Archivo General de Indias (hereafter cited as AGI), Justicia 108, 1530: "[T]rial conducted of the herein named Cazonzi, by the President and Captain General Nuño de Guzmán, the army finding itself in those provinces, and in which, his treasonous and idolatrous activities being proven, resulted in his being sentenced to death."

34. *Códice de Templo Mayor o Códice Moctezuma*, Biblioteca del Museo Nacional de Antropología e Historia, Mexico City, no. 35-26. I am grateful to Ignacio Silva for the translation of the text from Nahuatl.

35. Stephanie Wood, *Transcending Conquest: Nahua Views of Spanish Colonial Mexico* (Norman: University of Oklahoma Press, 2003). Wood addresses this point at length in chapter 2.

36. Benavente [Motolinía], *Memoriales*, 469.

37. Charles Gibson, "Llamamiento general, Repartimiento, and the Empire of Acolhuacán," *Hispanic American Historical Review* (hereafter cited as HAHR) 36 (1956): 1–27.

38. National Library of France (hereafter cited as BNF), no. 374. I thank Ignacio Silva for the translation of the Nahuatl gloss into Spanish.

39. Among the numerous monographs that deal with the twin subjects of encomienda and tribute in these years, the most important continue to be Silvio Zavala, *La encomienda indiana* (Mexico City: Editorial Porrúa, 1973); Lesley Byrd Simpson, *The Encomienda in New Spain: The Beginning of Spanish Mexico* (Berkeley: University of California Press, 1982); and José Miranda, *El tributo indígena in la Nueva España* (Mexico City: El Colegio de México, 1980). Regarding the encomienda system and the Indians in this period, see Charles Gibson, *The Aztec under Spanish Rule: A History of the Indians of the Valley of Mexico* (Palo Alto: Stanford University Press, 1964). On Cortés and his world, see José Luis Martínez, *Documentos Cortesianos*, 4 vols. (Mexico City: UNAM and Fondo de Cultura Económica, 1990); and Martínez, *Hernán Cortés* (Mexico City: UNAM and Fondo de Cultura Económica, 1990).

40. Zavala, *La encomienda*; Simpson, *The Encomienda*.

41. Ethelia Ruiz Medrano, "Las primeras instituciones del poder colonial," in Bernardo García Martínez, ed., *Gran historia de México ilustrada*, 4 vols. (Mexico City: Planeta DeAgostini and CONACULTA-INAH, 2002), 2, 41–60.

42. Ibid.

43. Zavala, *La encomienda*; Simpson, *The Encomienda*. The members of the First Audiencia were President Nuño de Guzmán and judges Licenciado Matienzo and Licenciado Delgadillo. The audiencia was dismissed in 1530 following numerous complaints leveled by Bishop Zumárraga, who was reacting to the failures of the government headed by these officials.

44. Zavala, *La encomienda*; Simpson, *The Encomienda*.

45. Ethelia Ruiz Medrano, *Shaping New Spain: Government and Private Interests in the Colonial Bureaucracy, 1535–1550* (Boulder: University Press of Colorado, 2006).

46. Ibid.

47. Ibid.

48. Ibid., 19–32; AGI, Justicia 232.

49. Madrid, July 28, 1533, El Consejo al Rey, AGI, Indiferente General 737, no. 29.

50. Lewis Hanke, *The Spanish Struggle for Justice in the Conquest of America* (Philadelphia: University of Pennsylvania Press, 1949); Anthony Padgen, *Spanish Imperialism and the Political Imagination* (New Haven: Yale University Press, 1990).

51. Mario Góngora, *Studies in the Colonial History of Spanish America* (Cambridge: Cambridge University Press, 1975), 33–40.

52. The *Siete Partidas* (or simply *Partidas*) was a body of legal codes, drawn up during the reign of Alfonso X (1252–1284) to standardize juridical practice in his kingdom. Originally called the *Libro de las leyes*, it received the name by which it is currently known near the outset of the fourteenth century because of its division into seven sections.

53. Beginning in 1516, the list of royal titles was expanded to include (together with the names of other peninsular places) "King of the Indies, islands and terra firma of the Ocean Sea." Moreover, as a result of the election that took place in Frankfurt at the end of June 1519, the sovereign who ruled over Castile and other areas of the Iberian Peninsula also became "Emperor of the Romans," although he was not crowned as such by the pope until 1530, in Bologna. The Spanish Crown now inherited the universalist ethos symbolized in the designation "Roman," which had been passed down through the Hapsburg royal line since the Middle Ages. Góngora, *Studies in the Colonial History*, 44.

54. Ibid., 43; Anthony Pagden, *Spanish Imperialism*, 5–6.

55. Hanke, *Spanish Struggle*.

56. Henry Raup Wagner, *The Life and Writings of Bartolomé de las Casas* (Albuquerque: University of New Mexico Press, 1967), 209–240.

57. Ibid., 209–220.

58. Ross Roland Dealy, "Vasco de Quiroga's Thought on War: Its Erasmian and Utopian Roots" (PhD diss., Indiana University, Bloomington, 1975), 35–36.

59. Ibid., 150.

60. Padgen, *Spanish Imperialism*, 5–6.

61. Antonio Muro Orejón, Studies and Notes, *Las Leyes Nuevas de 1542–1543. Ordenanzas para la gobernación de las Indias y buen tratamiento y conservación de los Indios* (Seville: Escuela de Estudios Hispano-Americanos, 1961, facsimile edition), fols. 4v–5r.

62. Francisco Miranda, *Don Vasco de Quiroga y su Colegio de San Nicolás* (Morelia, Mexico: Fimax Publicitas, 1972), 19.

63. Ibid., 19–21.

64. Roland, "Vasco de Quiroga's Thought," 33, 35–36, 42, 45.

65. Marcel Bataillon, *Erasmo y España: Estudios sobre la historia spiritual del siglo xvi* (Mexico City: Fondo de Cultura Económica, 1996), 831.

66. Robert Ricard, *La conquista espiritual de México* (Mexico City: Fondo de Cultura Económica, 1986); George Baudot, *Utopia and History in Mexico: The First Chroniclers of Mexican Civilization (1520–1569)* (Boulder: University Press of Colorado, 1995).

67. Donald Robertson, *Mexican Manuscript Painting of the Early Colonial Period: The Metropolitan Schools*, 2nd ed. (Norman: University of Oklahoma Press, 1994), 62n67.

68. Woodrow Borah, *Justice by Insurance: The General Indian Court of Colonial Mexico and the Legal Aides of the Half-Real* (Berkeley: University of California Press, 1983), 6–13.

69. It can be said that spaces in which to attain justice, peasant associations, and spaces for negotiation in general are all places, or contexts, in which the "weak" find the possibility of deploying in a routine fashion their best defensive "weapons" without having to resort to open rebellion. On this theme, see James Scott, *Weapons of the Weak: Everyday Forms of Peasant Resistance* (New Haven: Yale University Press, 1985).

70. Kellogg, *Law and the Transformation*.

71. Ethelia Ruiz Medrano and Perla Valle, "Los colores de la justicia. Códices jurídicos del siglo XVI en la Biblioteca Nacional de Francia," *Journal de la Société des Américanistes de Paris* 84, 2 (1998): 227–241.

72. The study of religious and historical codices has a long tradition and has produced an enormous number of works dealing with issues of style, content, and special character- istics. Among the themes emphasized by specialists in this field are the great complexity of these manuscripts, the particularities of different schools and regions, details of style and color, and the presence of multiple religious meanings. A handful of classic works includes *Códice Borgia*, ed. with commentaries by Eduard Seler (Mexico City: Fondo de Cultura Económica, 1963); Karl Antón Nowotny, *Tlacuilolli: Style and Contents of the Mexican Pictorial Manuscripts with a Catalog of the Borgia Group*, trans. and ed. George A. Everett Jr. and Edward B. Sisson (Norman: University of Oklahoma Press, 2005); Elizabeth Hill Boone, *Cycles of Time and Meaning in the Mexican Books of Fate* (Austin: University of Texas Press, 2007); and, with specific reference to historical codices, Robertson, *Mexican Manuscript Painting*; Elizabeth Hill Boone, *Stories in Red and Black: Pictorial Histories of the Aztecs and Mixtecs* (Austin: University of Texas Press, 2000).

73. *Historia tolteca-chichimeca*, ed. Paul Kirchoff, Lina Odena Güemes, and Luis Reyes García, 2nd ed. (Mexico City: CIESAS and Fondo de Cultura Económica, 1989).

74. Robert Barlow, "Las joyas de Martín Ocelotl," *Revista Yan* 3 (1954): 56–59.

75. This hypothesis is developed in detailed form in Ethelia Ruiz Medrano, "The Lords of the Earth: Historical Context of the Mapa de Cuauhtinchan no. 2," in David Carrasco and Scott Sessions, eds., *Cave, City, and Eagle's Nest: An Interpretive Journey through the Mapa de Cuauhtinchan no. 2*, foreword by John H. Coatsworth (Albuquerque: University of New Mexico Press, 2007).

76. AGI, *Justicia* 227, número 7, ramo 3; John R. Hébert et al., *Códice de Huexotzinco* (Mexico City: Ediciones Multiarte and Coca Cola de México, 1995).

77. Arthur Scott Aiton, *Antonio de Mendoza: First Viceroy of New Spain* (Durham, N.C.: Duke University Press, 1927); Ruiz Medrano, *Shaping New Spain*.

78. Aiton, *Antonio de Mendoza*, 8–9.

79. On the administrative level, New Spain was a viceroyalty of the Spanish Crown, but in reality, given the prevailing economic and political conditions, it operated as a col- ony of the kingdom of Castile. Castile's colonies in the Americas were never referred to as colonies; technically, they were viceroyalties or governing audiencias, but in actuality they functioned and served as overseas colonies.

80. Lewis Hanke and Celso Rodríguez, *Los virreyes españoles en América durante el gobierno de la Casa de Austria, México I*, Biblioteca de Autores Españoles desde la Formación del Lenguaje hasta nuestro Días, continuación de la Colección Rivadeneira, Tomo CCLXXIII (Madrid: Real Academia Española, 1976), 36.

81. Borah, *Justice by Insurance*, 65–66.

82. Ibid., 66.

83. Hanke and Rodríguez, *Los virreyes*, 41.

84. Ibid., 41–43.

85. Robertson, *Mexican Manuscript Painting*, 56–57.

86. Carmen Herrera and Ethelia Ruiz Medrano, *El entintado mundo de la fijeza imaginaria, el Códice de Tepeucila* (Mexico City: INAH, 1997); Ethelia Ruiz Medrano, "En el cerro y la iglesia: La figura cosmológica *atl-tépetl-oztotl*," *Relaciones*, El Colegio de

Michoacán 22, 86 (Spring 2001): 143–183. This article includes a large number of examples of water glyphs found in both pre-Hispanic and colonial codices.

87. Herrera and Ruiz Medrano, *El entintado mundo.*

88. Ibid.

89. Ibid.

90. Ibid.

91. Barry D. Snell and Susan Kellogg, "We Want to Give Them Laws: Royal Ordinances in a Mid-Sixteenth Century Nahuatl Text," *Estudios de Cultural Nahuatl* 27 (1997): 325–367.

92. Hanke and Rodríguez, *Los virreyes,* 51.

93. *Códices indígenas de algunos pueblos del Marquesado del Valle de Oaxaca publicados por el Archivo General de la Nación para el Primer Congreso Mexicano de Historia celebrado en la Ciudad de Oaxaca* (Mexico City: Talleres Gráficos de la Nación, 1933), Códice no. 30, Códice no. 19.

94. The codices the Indians presented are found in the map section of the Archivo General de la Nación (hereafter cited as AGN); the related records are in the AGN, Hospital de Jesús, leg. 276, exp. 79.

95. Ruiz Medrano, *Shaping New Spain.*

96. Some examples are found in the BNF.

97. The word sometimes used to denote "wonder" or "marvel" is *mahuiztlamatini.* Some of the trials recorded in Nahuatl are AGN, Tierras, 20, 1ª Parte, exp. 3; 22, 1ª Parte; 30, exp. 4; 39, 2ª Parte, exp. 3; 51, exp. 2; 55, exp. 2 and exp. 3. Many other cases in Nahuatl, accompanied by codices, that were heard in Mexico City are in *Documentos nahuas de la Ciudad de México del siglo XVI,* ed. Luis Reyes Garcia et al. (Mexico City: CIESAS and AGN, 1996).

98. "[P]robá deste poco vino que lo traigo de unas tierras [de Tolpetlac] que he comprado y porque tengáis dello memoria os lo manifiesto y hago saber porque si por ventura en algún tiempo se arrepintiere el que me las vendió que se llama Acxotecatl natural [del barrio] de Tolpetlac." *Documentos nahuas,* 76.

99. AGN, Tierras, 22, 1ª Parte, exp. 4. My thanks to Ignacio Silva for the translation from Nahuatl to Spanish.

100. Spaniards called the puma "lion" and the jaguar "tiger." Ibid., 2719, exp. 8; *Códices indígenas de algunos pueblos.*

101. AGI, Justicia 1013, no. 1.

102. Some scholars consider that the ahuizotl is an otter. BNF, no. 115, Collection Ex-Aubin, unedited, booklet with twelve leaves.

103. "3 Yten, si saben que cada una de las tres cabeceras eran de por sí, y tenían justicia apartada, dividida, sin que en una cabecera tuviese sujeción a la otra, ni la otra a la otra, ni se entremetiesen en la administración de justicia, más de juntarse los señores naturales de las dichas tres cabeceras para los negocios de guerra, e cuando algún pueblo e provincia se rebelaba y alzaba contra alguno de ellos. La cual junta hacían de ochenta en ochenta días, una vez en la una, una vez en la una, otra vez en la otra y otra vez en la otra por su rueda [y termino], para dar orden e concierto según les pareciera, e [proveer] los cargos de justicia y gobernación, y hacer las mercedes que [querían], e cada uno en su gobernación

y señorío e cabecera por su tercia parte de gobernación de esta Nueva España, según esta dicho, digan [esto]. 4 Yten, si saben que cada una de las dichas tres cabeceras tenía e tuvo siempre sus provincias sujetas de por sí cada una por su tercia parte, y acudía cada provincia a su cabecera con sus tributos, servicios y llamamientos, e poniendo cada cabecera las personas que le parecía [proveerlos] y lo [demás] que le convenía, digan [esto]." AGI, Justicia 1029.

104. Ibid.

105. "En el pueblo de Xiquipilco del Valle de Matalçingo de esta Nueva España a tres días del mes de abril de mil quinientos y sesenta y cinco años yo Gomez Davila escribano de su Majestad di a sacar esta pintura de otra original que esta en el proceso que presentó Pablo Oçelutle y sus hijos y la sacó Francisco Yquixitotl indio otomite del dicho pueblo de Xiquipilco y otro indio de Metepeque y mediante Gaspar Borjes intérprete de esta Audiencia en la lengua mexicana y el español y Francisco intérprete en la lengua mexicana y otomite se tomó y recibió de ellos juramento por Dios y por Santa Maria y por una señal de la cruz en forma de derecho y los que la tradujeron so cargo de que declararon que la dicha pintura va cierta y verdadera y fielmente sacada del original que esta en el dicho proceso presentada e que en ella no hay yerro ninguno en sustancia según Dios y sus conciencias en lo que ellos alcanzan y esto es la verdad e lo que pasaba estando a lo que dicho es presentes por testigos Luis de Leon y Diego Lopez estantes al presente en el dicho pueblo de Xiquipilco." Pasó ante mi Gomez Davila escribano de su Majestad, BNF 32, in Ethelia Ruiz Medrano and Xavier Noguez, *Dos pictografías del Estado de México: El Códice de Tlacotepec* (Zinacantepec, Mexico: El Colegio Mexiquense, 2004), 38.

106. "[E]n la primera casa [casilla, section, division] de hacia la mano izquierda dice que significaba la estancia de Atenco. Preguntado que sigue para la segunda casa donde esta una cabeza dijo que sigue para los macehuales de la dicha estancia que son en número de ciento y cuarenta y uno. Preguntado que significaba la tercera casa dijo que el maíz que tributaban los dichos macehuales a los dichos principales que lo habían . . . que eran ciento cuarenta medidas cada uno de los cuales dichos macehuales conforme a la dicha cuenta daba una medida de aquel tiempo que sería como tres medias . . . de las de ahora poco más o menos porque la vio este testigo y la cotejó con los de ahora. . . . Fue preguntado que significa la primera cuenta en la cuarta casa y dijo que dice diez y seis mantas y media y dos huipiles. Fue preguntado que significa la quinta casa y última dijo que una carga y [460] cacaos." My thanks to Professor Patrick Lesbre for sharing this interesting extract with me. From AGN, *Vínculos* 234, 258r–268r, Tezcoco, June 14, 1575.

107. Paulino Castañeda, "La condición miserable del indio y sus privilegios," *Anuario de Estudios Americanos* 23 (1971): 319–321 (quote); Juan de Solórzano y Pereyra, *Política Indiana. Edición facsimilar tomada de la de 1776 (Madrid)*, 2 vols. (Mexico City: Secretaría de Programación y Presupuesto, 1979), vol. 1, chap. 28, 206–213.

108. Woodrow Borah, "El status jurídico de los indios en Nueva España," *América Indígena* 45, 2 (April–June 1985): 263–264 (quote); Borah, *Justice by Insurance*, 57–58.

109. Ward Stavig, "Ambiguous Visions: Nature, Law and Culture in Indigenous-Spanish Land Relations in Colonial Peru," *Hispanic American Historical Review* 80, 1 (2000): 88.

110. María Justina Sarabia Viejo, *Don Luis de Velasco virrey de Nueva España, 1550–1564* (Seville: Consejo Superior de Investigaciones Científicas and Escuela de Estudios Hispano-Americanos, 1978), 27.

111. *Documentos nahuas,* ed. Reyes García.

112. Gretchen Koch Markov, "The Legal Status of Indians under Spanish Rule" (PhD diss., University of Rochester, Rochester, N.Y., 1983), 14.

113. Kellogg, *Law and the Transformation,* 12.

114. Zorita, *Relación.*

115. Kellogg, *Law and the Transformation,* 13–14.

116. AGI, Audiencia de México 280, "Carta de religiosos en material de justicia," July 26, 1561.

117. AGN, Civil 2224, exp. 1.

118. *Códice Osuna. Reproducción facsimilar de la obra del mismo título editada en Madrid, 1878. Acompañada de 158 páginas inéditas encontradas en el Archivo General de la Nación (México) por el profesor Luis Chávez Orozco* (Mexico City: Ediciones del Instituto Indigenista Interamericano, 1947); AGN, Ramo Civil, no. 644. Concerning this matter, see also the testimony reproduced in Juan Bautista, *¿Cómo te confundes? ¿Acaso no somos conquistados? Anales de Juan Bautista,* introduction, study, trans., and ed. from Nahuatl by Luis Reyes García (Mexico City: Centro de Investigaciones y Estudios Superiores en Antropología Social and Biblioteca Lorenzo Boturini y Nacional Basílica de Guadalupe, 2001).

119. *Códice Osuna. Reproducción facsimilar;* AGN, Ramo Civil, no. 644.

120. Gibson, *The Aztec,* 50–54.

121. Ibid.

122. BNF, no. 75.

123. Pedro Carrasco, *The Tenocha Empire of Ancient Mexico: The Triple Alliance of Tenochtitlan, Tetzcoco and Tlacopan* (Norman: University of Oklahoma Press, 1999), 292, 397.

124. Peter Gerhard, *A Guide to the Historical Geography of New Spain* (Cambridge: Cambridge University Press, 1972), 228.

125. "[D]e veinte, treinta, cuarenta, cincuenta e cuatrocientos años y más tiempo y tanto que memoria de hombres no es en contrario el dicho pueblo de san Francisco Iztacamatitlan mi parte, que por otro nombre se llama Castilblanco, ha sido y es cabecera y no sujeto a otro pueblo alguno porque como parece por sus pinturas y antigüedades habrá más de 670 años que las cuatro cabeceras que hubo en aquellas partes del dicho pueblo está situado que fueron naturales de una tierra que llamaron Chicomoztoc. Poseyeron la parte y lugar y tierras do está el dicho pueblo situado y poblado y estas cuatro personas se fueron a vivir a la ciudad de Tlaxcala a donde los naturales . . . de San Francisco los eligieron y obedecieron, acudiéndoles con tributos y lo demás que eran obligados. Y siempre . . . ha tenido su iglesia, gobernadores alcaldes y regidores." BNF, no. 75.

126. Bernardo García Martínez, *Los pueblos de la Sierra. El poder y el espacio entre los indios del norte de Puebla hasta 1700* (Mexico City: El Colegio de México, 1987), 160–161.

127. Ruiz Medrano and Noguez, *Dos pictografías del estado de México.*

128. Robertson, *Mexican Manuscript*, 35.

129. Ruiz Medrano and Noguez, *Dos pictografías del estado de México*.

130. BNF, no. 111.

131. AGN, Tierras 20, exp. 2.

132. I have searched unsuccessfully for the meaning of this term, but from the context it seems to refer to some type of responsibility held by the district's indigenous authorities.

133. AGN, Tierras 20, exp. 2.

134. AGN, Civil 2224, exp. 1.

135. Ibid.

136. Kellogg, *Law and the Transformation*, 23–24.

137. Ruiz Medrano, *Shaping New Spain*, 163, 167, 181, 232, 238n34, 243n111.

138. Kellogg, *Law and the Transformation*, 29.

139. Ibid.

140. Stavig, "Ambiguous Visions," 87.

141. Borah, *Justice by Insurance*, 77.

142. Hanke and Rodríguez, *Los virreyes*, 205.

143. Charles Jago, "Philip II and the Cortes of Castile: The Case of the Cortes of 1578," *Past and Present* 109 (November 1985): 25.

144. On these matters it is useful to read the letters of the *visitador* (royal inspector) Valderrama, who was in charge of carrying out reforms concerning the payment and collection of tribute in New Spain. See France V. Scholes and Eleanor B. Adams, eds., *Documentos para la historia del México colonial [Cartas del licenciado Jerónimo de Valderrama y otros documentos sobre su visita al gobierno de Nueva España, 1563–1565]*, vol. 7 (Mexico City: José Porrúa e Hijos, 1961); AGI, México 92: "Cartas para su majestad del licenciado Valderrama, visitador de la Audiencia de México y de los comisarios que fueron al negocio de la rebelión desde el año de 1563 hasta el de 1568"; Miranda, *El tributo indígena*.

145. One peso was the equivalent of eight reales or silver coins.

146. One fanega equaled a dry weight of about 1.5 bushels. Regarding the administrative directives of this period and contemporary discussion of these fiscal policies, see Miranda, *El tributo indígena*; Scholes and Adams, *Documentos*.

147. Ethelia Ruiz Medrano, "Fighting Destiny: Nahua Nobles and the Friars in the Sixteenth-Century Revolt of the Encomenderos against the King," in Ethelia Ruiz Medrano and Susan Kellogg, eds., *Negotiation with Domination: Colonial New Spain's Indian Pueblos Confront the Spanish State* (Boulder: University Press of Colorado, 2010), 45–78.

148. Bautista, *¿Cómo te confundes?*

149. Zorita, *Relación*, 59–92; Carlos Sempat Assadourian, "La despoblación indígena en Perú y Nueva España durante el siglo XVI y la formación de la economía colonial," *Historia Mexicana* 38, 3 (1989): 425–426, 440; Assadourian, "Memoriales de fray Gerónimo de Mendieta," *Historia Mexicana* 37, 3 (1988): 357–422.

150. Antonio F. García-Abásolo, *Martín Enríquez y la reforma de 1568 en Nueva España* (Seville: Excelentísima Diputación Provincial de Sevilla, 1983), 67–86.

151. AGI, México 289: "Parecer del padre provincial y otros religiosos teólogos de la orden de San Francisco dado en México a ocho de Marzo de 1594. Acerca de los indios que dan en repartimiento a los españoles."

152. Gibson, *The Aztec*, 226–227, 248; García-Abásolo, *Martín Enríquez*, 111–124.

153. AGN, Padrones, 9, exp. 293, leaf 144, dated January 14, 1621.

154. Gibson, "Llamamiento general," 26.

155. AGI, México 289.

156. BNF, no. 73.

157. Sixteenth-century native texts attest to this belief, to include the *Cantares mexicanos* collection of devotional songs when, together with the colonial ecclesiastical elite, at death native nobility were said to take wing to a watery paradise. In addition, the strong presence of sculpted angels with strongly indigenous facial features (and sometimes indigenous haircuts and dress) in the native-executed religious iconography of the same period again suggests that rather than join the angels in (the Christian) heaven, the native elite were converted into such celestial beings. Eleanor Wake, personal communication 2008. See also chapter 6 of Wake's *Framing the Sacred: The Indian Churches of Early Colonial Mexico* (Norman: University of Oklahoma Press, 2010).

158. BNF, no. 73.

159. Pedro Carrasco, "Rango de Tecuhtli entre los Nahuas trasmontaños," *Tlalocan* 5, 2 (1966): 133–160.

160. AGI, México 70, ramo 2.

161. Ernest J. Burrus, S.J., ed., *The Writings of Alonso de la Veracruz: V. The Original Texts with English Translation. Spanish Writings: II Letters and Reports* (Rome: Jesuit Historical Institute, 1972): "Memoria de las cosas en que los indios principales y naturals de la Ciudad de México pedimos y suplicamos a su Magestad del rey don Felipe, nuestro señor, sea servido de mandarnos desagraviar," March 13, 1574, 291–296.

162. The son of the first viceroy with the same name, he was known as "the younger" viceroy during his two terms of service in New Spain. He was also named president of the Royal and Supreme Council of the Indies in 1611.

163. Borah, "El status jurídico," 261.

164. AGI, México 22, letters of Don Luis de Velasco to the king: October 28, 1591, February 20 and March 6, 1592.

165. Borah, *Justice by Insurance*, 100.

166. Ibid., 88–91.

167. Robertson, *Mexican Manuscript*, 55.

168. I thank Professor William Taylor for this reference: Brian Owensby, *Empire of Law and Indian Justice in Colonial Mexico* (Stanford: Stanford University Press, 2008), front cover.

Indigenous Negotiation to Preserve Land, History, Titles, and Maps

SEVENTEENTH AND EIGHTEENTH CENTURIES

HISTORICAL SETTING

Throughout the seventeenth and eighteenth centuries, the colonial justice system witnessed the Europeanization of such basic institutions of Mesoamerican indigenous society as the family, marriage, and access to property. This transformation took place with greatest effect within the Indian population of Mexico City and nearby areas.[1] While European influence predominated in the colony, many cases were still argued during this period in which the Indian pueblos' use of traditional customs and practices in the defense of their lands continued to play an important role.

Although the General Indian Court continued to function during this period, many Indian claims were heard in the first instance in regional tribunals and only received consideration by the Audiencia of Mexico City if they were not resolved at the lower level. This situation was especially true with regard to litigation over land involving Indian pueblos. In 1722 the Spanish Crown issued a decree formalizing the establishment of a new judicial institution, the Tribunal de la Acordada. This was the colony's sole tribunal with unlimited territorial jurisdiction, and it answered only to the viceroy. Although the tribunal's jurisdiction was originally confined to rural areas, Mexico City and other urban centers were brought under it in 1756, thus empowering its judges and agents to operate anywhere in New Spain. The court heard cases involving criminal prosecutions.[2]

On the juridical level, the Indians' status continued to be that of miserables. To the original meaning of this designation—people uninstructed in the faith—the notion was gradually expanded to include a population characterized by "its stupidity, backwardness, poverty, and cowardice." While it might be said that these associations differed little from those regarding the peasantry and other poor residents in the kingdom of Castile, there was a growing tendency in the seventeenth and eighteenth centuries to equate poverty with idleness and vagrancy and to see them as morally hazardous for society. In this sense, the quality of miserable associated with the Indians and with the poor in general possessed a negative social connotation as early as the seventeenth century. It also implied that only through work (whether voluntary or obligatory) could the Indians and the poor redeem themselves.[3]

As a result of this adverse condition, the king was obliged to grant the Indians his highest level of favor. Consequently, when the Indians succeeded in undertaking legal challenges, the colonial courts were required to hear them and (theoretically at least) to execute the royal will in summary fashion. Moreover, the laws at the time recommended serious punishment for Spaniards who abused Indians, especially "if said injuries are inflicted on Indian caciques or nobles."[4]

The circumstances that prevailed in the seventeenth and eighteenth centuries lent credence to the idea that the Indians should enjoy protection. The violent backdrop of conquest, epidemics, forced labor, and the beginning of the program of *congregación* (moving dispersed groups of Indians into nuclear settlements for religious and administrative purposes) had wreaked havoc on Indian communities. By the middle of the seventeenth century, the indigenous population had reached its demographic nadir. Conversely, the colony's other ethnic groups experienced a significant rise in numbers. At the time, New Spain had approximately 150,000 whites, 130,000 blacks and mulattos, at least 150,000 mestizos, and between 300,000 and 400,000 Indians.[5] It was not until 1671 that colonial authorities noted, via the tributary rolls, a slow recuperation among the indigenous population.[6]

Despite the drop in the Indian population during the seventeenth century, productive work in the colony still depended almost exclusively on the Indian labor force. In 1610 the majority of mine workers were Indians. Similarly, the areas of high agricultural production—including Tlaxcala, Tecamachalco, Atlixco, Toluca, and the Bajío—depended on indigenous labor. Public works in urban centers such as Mexico City were also supported by Indian labor. During the seventeenth century, the colony's white settlers complained repeatedly about a lack of Indians to do work, as well as an increased number of vagrants as the result of the growth of the mestizo and mulatto populations.[7]

The Indians' traditional way of life came under assault by Spanish and creole entrepreneurs eager to exert greater control over indigenous lands and labor. In Tlaxcala, for example, hacienda owners fought to abolish the corregimiento system and replace it with municipal councils, which would have allowed the European settlers to assume control over the administration of local government in Indian pueblos.[8] These pressures and assaults tore apart the Indians' social fabric and caused high rates of alcoholism among them. Also during the seventeenth century the Spanish witnessed growing delinquency among the Indian population, especially in urban centers.[9] This development was also linked to the Indians' increasing tendency during this period to migrate to and resettle on the periphery of Spanish cities, drawn by the possibility of earning greater incomes and also of escaping the control of the *mandones* (native bosses in charge of organizing work details) and the political leaders of their pueblos.[10]

In many cases the Indians' flight resulted from the excessive amounts of tribute their communities were obliged to pay to the colonial authorities or to an encomendero. During the first years of the conquest, the tribute requirements the Spanish imposed on the Indians were managed from within the surviving pre-Hispanic social structure, but that situation soon changed.[11]

The Spanish authorities wasted little time in altering the concept of tribute the Indians had held prior to the conquest. By the end of the sixteenth century, tribute had been redefined as an individual rather than a collective responsibility, and its payment was increasingly required to be made in money, not in-kind. The epidemics that swept through the native population also affected the tributary policies adopted by the Spanish. When the loss of Indian population was particularly acute—as, for example, in 1577—the colonial authorities sought to prevent Indians from abandoning the fields and lessened the tributary burden by allowing it to be paid in-kind, especially in corn and wheat. Each Indian who owed tribute was required to farm a parcel of land 8.5 square meters in size (equivalent to 10 varas, in the measurement of that day).[12] The only members of the native population exempt from this requirement were the governors and local magistrates. Income earned from the sale of crops had to be used to pay community expenses.[13] Many of the pueblo's outlays were handled through a community treasury, or strongbox (*caja de comunidad*). By 1554, these funds had been established by order of the Crown so Indian pueblos could guard their money safely. To that end, the strongbox was equipped with three locks.[14] The amount of money many pueblos kept under lock was relatively modest, since the tributary burdens they faced were weighty and numerous: "[I]n the early seventeenth century an average Indian tributary in the Valley of Mexico was required to pay

8 reales (one peso) and one-half fanega of maize to the encomendero or crown, one real for the *Fábrica* and *Ministros* and four reales for *Servicio Real* [Royal Service]. He also contributed to the treasury of his community on the basis of ten varas of agricultural land."[15]

During the eighteenth century, a series of additional expenses was imposed on Indian communities. The first of these occurred in 1770, when the colony ordered that a teacher be placed in each pueblo and that the teacher's salary be paid out of community funds. The second new expense followed sixteen years later, when the Indian pueblos were ordered to use 2 percent of the annual income from their common fund to pay part of the salaries of colonial intendants.[16] In addition to these taxes, the pueblos bore the financial burden of supporting their parish priests.[17] This chain of unjust obligations caused many Indian pueblos to fall behind in their payments and accumulate large debts. In the eighteenth century, the colony's cumulative total of unpaid tribute equaled 1.5 million pesos.[18] Near the end of the century, in 1790, ideas about political freedom and emancipation permitted the development of a campaign to abolish Indian tribute, although as late as 1809, Indian political leaders were still incarcerated for delays in paying tribute. In 1810, as a consequence of the independence movement, the regency council formally decreed the abolition of tribute payments.[19]

Apart from the exaction of tribute, recall that the members of Indian pueblos were obligated to render personal service to Spanish enterprises through the system of repartimiento. With the exception of the mining sector, a prohibition against repartimiento was adopted in 1632 and went into effect on February 1, 1633.[20] From that point on, Indian labor was salaried, and the wages Indians were paid for their work were stabilized to a considerable degree during the remainder of the colonial period.[21]

Against this general backdrop, which was hardly beneficial to the indigenous population, the Indians were further disadvantaged in the seventeenth century when the Crown became much less discriminating about whom it selected to govern New Spain. The new colonial officials, who were responsible for maintaining institutional order and protecting the Indians, were much less prepared than their counterparts the previous century. Furthermore, the king began to sell the most important offices to the highest bidder, without regard to the individual's capacity to assume the responsibilities of a political post. Thus it was that massive corruption began to pervade the colonial administration, beginning in the seventeenth century in particular.[22]

The corregidores were a prime example of such corruption. Established in 1531 with the purpose of limiting the power of the encomenderos over Indian pueblos, the *corregimiento* was eventually transformed into an institution that operated against the interests of Indian communities.[23] In the seventeenth century, the viceroys started noting that the corregidores were embezzling tribute from the pueblos under their administration. They exploited in particular the so-called tributary *derramas*. In the colonial context, these referred to unauthorized tribute or tribute that exceeded the amount required. For the corregidores, the derramas represented the possibility of additional economic gain.[24]

Moreover, the corregidores used their office to engage in commerce. They were in charge of receiving tribute the Indians paid to the king, whether in-kind or in money. Starting at the end of the sixteenth century and continuing through the seventeenth century, the corregidores sold tributary wheat and corn as well as other products the Indians gave as tribute, such as poultry. In the seventeenth century, furthermore, they broadened their activities, speculating in goods and merchandise and attempting to gain control over local markets. The corregidores further enriched themselves by buying goods from the Indians for petty amounts and then forcing other Indians to buy the same goods at prices that greatly exceeded their market value. Beginning in this period, too, the Indians found themselves obligated to purchase cows, mules, alcohol, and silk stockings from their corregidores at exorbitant prices.[25]

It is not surprising, then, that eighteenth-century colonial society freely acknowledged that a corregidor's total income was not limited to his salary but included everything he could amass from the purchases and other transactions the Indians within his jurisdiction were obligated to make. Thus, an appointment as corregidor of a prosperous pueblo, such as one near Mexico City, was a prize these royal functionaries greatly coveted. The corregidores who served in this area lived in the capital and openly transacted business. Charles Gibson came across a 1777 guide that ranked the corregimientos according to the economic benefits they offered their corregidores. The top spot was occupied by the corregimiento of Chalco, which was surrounded by rich, productive land and numerous haciendas. The author of the guide observed that if the corregidor made good use of its commercial prospects, his corregimiento would yield 16,000 pesos annually—an amount thirty times a corregidor's official salary at the time.[26]

During the seventeenth century and part of the eighteenth century, then, the majority of these officials devoted themselves primarily to transacting business with the pueblos, exploiting the power they possessed over the Indians and acting like any other Spanish entrepreneur. Unlike the latter, however, the corregidor was responsible for administering government in his jurisdiction, a situation that gave him a virtually unlimited opportunity to abuse and exploit the Indians. In general, this characterization was also true of the alcaldes mayores. Nevertheless, despite their disadvantaged position, the Indian pueblos tried to use the legal norms and institutions of colonial society to block and counter these abuses. In 1604, for example, the Indians of Chinacamitlan (in the present-day state of

México) produced a document for the government in Nahuatl denouncing the alcalde mayor for compelling them to render him personal service and provide him with food. In addition, they asserted that he subjected them to physical mistreatment and abuse.[27]

Exceptions to the general pattern of corregidor wealth did exist, however, especially in the poorer, more remote pueblos where the corregidores and alcaldes mayores enjoyed few privileges. For example, Don Juan de Berver Machuca y Miranda, the alcalde mayor of Iguala (located in the present-day state of Guerrero), began his tenure in 1681 under conditions that could hardly have been worse. In January of that year, the royal offices of Iguala had burned. During the commotion, his predecessor took off with the administrative records. In addition, within the entire jurisdiction of the alcalde there was no scribe to assist him. As a result, he was forced to handle all the paperwork himself. In addition, a month into his assignment the alcalde incarcerated an Indian official. The Indian, who knew how to write and understood his rights, was accused of being a dangerous shaman.[28]

The case against the shaman began to unfold on August 23, 1681, when Berver Machuca received an official letter, composed in Nahuatl and delivered on behalf of the municipal council of Santa Ana Tasmalaca, an Indian pueblo in his jurisdiction. After several days, the alcalde found someone who could translate the letter and explain its contents. The Indians of Santa Ana Tasmalaca explained that inasmuch as the alcalde had been sent by the king to administer justice, they were denouncing an elderly member of their pueblo named Pedro Juárez, who kept books and "the bones of deceased persons" in his house. The cabildo emphasized that Juárez did not "have a good heart" and was a well-known shaman who caused the deaths of everyone who crossed his path. His unfortunate victims died very painful deaths, vomiting up blood as well as "white pulque, hair, and charcoal." Through the spells he cast, this shaman also caused ulcerous sores to sprout on his enemies' necks before they died.[29]

The cabildo explained that as a result of this situation, the pueblo had made four unsuccessful attempts to kill the shaman. On one occasion, everyone in the pueblo had whipped him as though he were a wild "horse"; although tied up, he still managed to escape. Powerless to inflict punishment on such a dangerous master of witchcraft, the cabildo members explained that they had decided "to place him in your hands so that you can render justice.... [W]e kiss the hands and feet of our alcalde mayor, may God watch over you always." Tasmalaca's Indian leaders had artfully rid themselves of a problem by officially handing it over to the representative of Spanish authority. They likely surmised that if the shaman, out of vengeance for all that had happened, caused someone to die, it would not be one of them but the alcalde who would be his victim.[30]

Yet this type of case, which occurred in a relatively poor pueblo a considerable distance from New Spain's capital, was not common. A recently completed study has demonstrated that the corruption permeating different spheres of the colonial administration played a major role in the revolt that broke out in various Indian quarters of Mexico City in 1692. In that year, an important segment of the capital's indigenous population, with assistance from other groups, rose up against the viceregal authorities. To some extent, the causes of this uprising were rooted in the bad harvest the previous year and the resultant lack of food for the general population, as well as in the poor handling of the pulque business and the distribution of corn. Nevertheless, the uprising was also caused by the Indians' realization—among their leaders in particular—that negotiation with the Spanish authorities had failed and the viceroy would not meet their demands for food. The Indians believed that New Spain's administrators had acted in a patently dishonest manner and that they governed incompetently. The next step was the revolt, which resulted in the viceroy fleeing and subsequently being removed from office.[31]

Predictably, the authorities' corruption accrued to the social and economic benefit not only of the governing class but of other locally powerful groups as well, such as the creoles—all to the detriment of indigenous interests. The ownership of land, a driving issue in the sixteenth century, assumed even greater importance in the early 1700s, when the Spanish exhibited a growing interest in possessing the most desirable Indian lands. This development spurred an ever greater number of Spanish colonists to turn their attention to agriculture. The seventeenth century was thus increasingly marked by the commercialization of land.

Spaniards' access to land was facilitated by Crown policies as well as by the active intervention of the colonial officials who assumed office starting in the last quarter of the sixteenth century. As noted, these policies weakened the Indian nobility's jurisdictional authority over their communities, a development that gained greater momentum after the Crown reformed the tributary system in 1564. Furthermore, these policies were instituted not only to circumscribe certain traditional rights of the Indian nobility but to curtail the power of encomenderos and missionaries as well. The implementation of these reforms by the colonial authorities thus accomplished a key objective of the Crown: to prevent Spanish settler families from holding an encomienda for more than three generations. Thus, with few exceptions, a large majority of New Spain's encomenderos had diversified their economic interests by the end of the sixteenth century—moving into land, mining, and textile factories. Encomenderos who had not made the transition ended up as simple pensioners of the Crown.[32]

With regard to the church and its evangelization effort, the power of the religious orders was lessened by the secularization of the majority of Indian pueblos. This change meant that the indigenous population would be under the spiritual (or not so spiritual, as the case may be) control of the secular clergy and its hierarchy—the archbishop, bishops, and parish priests. Indian pueblos and their leaders in particular were directly affected by the change. Traditionally, they had been allies of the missionary friars. In 1583, swayed by the arguments of Archbishop Pedro Moya de Contreras, the Crown (under its exercise of the *patronato* [royal authority over the church in the American colonies]) officially granted the bishops the right to secularize Indian parishes, subject to certain conditions.[33] This policy was strengthened and consolidated in the seventeenth century, although not without fierce opposition from the most important religious orders: Franciscans, Dominicans, and Augustinians. Indeed, the transfer of responsibility for parish work from one branch of the church to another led to the formation of two opposed camps. Seventeenth-century New Spain was thus characterized by an alliance of corregidores, missionaries, Indian nobles, and other indigenous leaders on one side against creoles, parish priests, and bishops on the other.[34]

The Crown had actively begun to assert the political power of the secular clergy against the missionary friars beginning in the 1560s, and it endeavored to have the tithe collected from the Indians as a way of aiding the secular clergy economically. Although the members of the religious orders argued strenuously against this policy, they suffered several reversals starting at the end of the sixteenth century and continuing into the next that greatly limited their once commanding influence over the Indians. Indicative of their loss is that by the seventeenth century the Indians (apart from the Indian republic's officialdom) no longer cared whether their parishes were in the hands of the secular or the regular clergy. The indifferent reaction that greeted Bishop Juan de Palafox y Mendoza's secularization of thirty-six Indian parishes in 1641 is evidence of the changed environment.[35]

While the decline in the indigenous population as a result of the colony's periodic epidemics had deprived the religious orders of a large number of supporters, their loss of influence during these years was also caused by internal decay and a weakening of spiritual fervor. The new contingents of missionaries who arrived in the seventeenth century were spiritually removed from the problems and hardships their Indian parishioners faced. At least in part, this difference was a function of changes in their training. In the militant environment of counterreformation Spain, the impulse that had once driven the religious orders to recruit as novices those molded in the tradition of Christian humanism slowly flickered out. During the seventeenth and eighteenth centuries, the missionaries appointed to serve in New Spain largely had the same negative views of the native population as did creoles and ordinary Spaniards.

At the beginning of the seventeenth century, then, two institutionalized groups—the traditional indigenous nobility and the missionaries—that in the preceding century had provided strong social support to the Indian pueblos now found themselves in a much weakened political condition. In addition, the colonial authorities under whose care the vassals of the king had been placed were immersed in promoting their own economic interests. In addition to these factors, Spanish colonists in this era received strong support for their agricultural, mining, and cattle ranching pursuits—all of which made deep inroads into indigenous lands and water supplies and required constant infusions of Indian labor.

For example, both creoles and Spaniards who farmed agricultural land acquired extensive irrigation rights, enabling them to privatize and monopolize for their own benefit water equally needed by Indian pueblos in the same vicinity. Hacendados in the region around Puebla exercised full control over water by the end of the eighteenth century.[36] These landowners went so far as to depute their servants to guard the water, referring to them as "water sentinels," and they restricted the pueblos' access to water. Although they lacked official legal status, the guards were a de facto constabulary of the hacendados, especially in the area around Puebla in the eighteenth century.[37]

Ever since the sixteenth century, the Spanish Crown had tried to act in a guardianship role with respect to the Indians' access to land. Their acquisition of recognized communal lands came about through specific viceregal grants, made only after the Indians submitted a formal request. Lands assigned to indigenous communities on this basis fell within the pueblos' already existing boundaries. Pueblos with rich lands that could be readily cultivated had been quickly despoiled of them. The Spanish employed a variety of techniques to grab the land, including exploiting the Indian communities' frequent failure to confirm their previous possession of extensive areas of land through later, formal grants.[38] Starting in the sixteenth century, some Indian pueblos also managed to obtain grants of land from the authorities for the communal rearing of cattle, sheep, and goats.[39]

In the seventeenth and eighteenth centuries, furthermore, many Indian pueblos found it necessary to lease their lands to individuals—Spaniards in particular—to secure the funds with which to satisfy ever-pressing daily needs. Various cases existed in which Spaniards rented lands that belonged to an Indian pueblo in exchange for paying part of its tributary obligations.[40]

The lease agreements were sometimes simply letters the Indians composed in their own language, generally Nahuatl, in which they agreed to turn over the use of their land in exchange for rent. The parties who rented these lands, including clerics, came to feel that they owned them and protested angrily to the authorities if the Indians tried to rescind the lease agreement.[41]

Generally speaking, as of 1567 the Indian cabildos were strongly convinced that indigenous communities held their lands on a communal basis.[42] In that year New Spain's viceroy (1566–1568), Gastón de Peralta, the Marqués de Falces, created the legal entity for an inherited corporate patrimony, stipulating that each Indian pueblo was granted 500 varas of land "extending in all four directions," to be measured beginning with the last house in the pueblo.

Later, in 1687, the amount of land granted was increased to 600 varas (approximately 101.12 hectares, or 1 square kilometer). By 1695, however, the Crown had modified its stance, indicating that the 600 varas were to be measured beginning at each pueblo's church, ordinarily located in the center of the pueblo. This alteration, which effectively reduced the size of Indian pueblos, resulted from successful opposition by Spanish entrepreneurs to the earlier ruling placing the initial point of measurement at the pueblos' outer edges.[43] It can thus be said that the legal entity—the entity in which the land reposed—was the Indian pueblo, to which other lands held cooperatively could also be ascribed. For example, in 1573 the Crown ordered that the Indian pueblos be endowed with a parcel of common land amounting to one square league (4.18 square kilometers) for pasturing their cattle. In the eighteenth century, Spanish entrepreneurs complained because only indigenous communities that had a church, a native governor, and a corregidor were given standing as pueblos, thereby excluding pueblos of recent creation—many of them subject communities broken off from the seats of administration—that failed to meet these conditions.[44] Also in the eighteenth century, some small groups of Indians—beginning with the working populations of haciendas—came together as settlements and, on occasion, even tried to obtain the status of Indian pueblos.

In 1802 the Indians of Santa Bárbara, situated near the town of Dolores (in the present-day state of Guanajuato), claimed that a hacendado, Pedro Juan Gutiérrez, had denied them access to their chapel. The priest refuted the claim, insisting that the chapel did not belong to the Indians who, he maintained, were merely laborers on Gutiérrez's hacienda. In addition, the Indians were also accused of seeking access to the chapel so they could hold dances and other nonreligious activities there. To sustain their claim, the Indians introduced as evidence the painted image of a cross (Figure 2.1). The most interesting elements of the cross are its painted markings of a jaguar's coat. This imagery denotes the connection the Indians forged between a symbol of power—such as the jaguar—which they held before the conquest, and the power of the Catholic faith, as represented for them by Christ and the cross. The "painted manuscript" of the Santa Bárbara cross is noteworthy in two other respects. First, it dates from a very late period; second, it was done by Indians from the Chichimeca region of the Bajío. The gloss on it alludes to Indian leaders as founders, either real or imaginary: "Praise

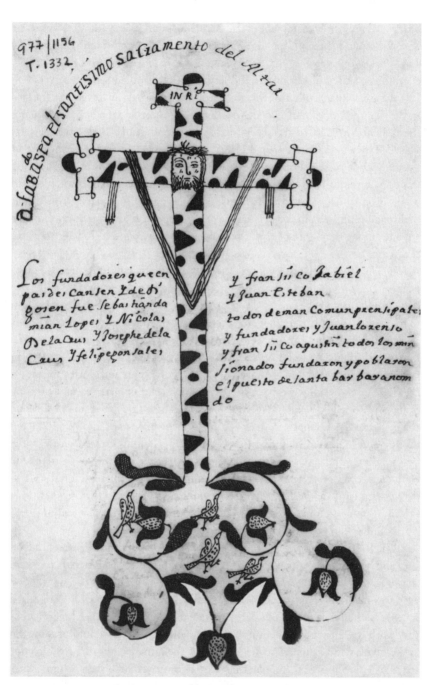

2.1 Reproduction, no. 998. Date: late eighteenth century. Courtesy, Archivo General de la Nación, Mexico City.

be [to] the most holy sacrament of the altar. The founders, may they rest in peace, were Sebastián Damián López and Nicolás of the Cross and Joseph of the Cross and Felipe González and Francisco Gabriel and Juan Esteban. They and others, commoners and nobles, founded and settled the place called Santa Bárbara."[45]

A case similar to that of the chapel of Santa Bárbara involved the Indians in the community of San Diego Xocollocan in Tlaxcala, who appeared before the audiencia in 1796 to argue persistently for certain lands. Their adversary was Felipe Núñez de Villavicencio, a priest and the owner of the hacienda of San Diego Socoyuca. The priest claimed that San Diego Xocollocan was nothing more than an outlying settlement, or ward, and that the Indians therefore had no basis on which to sue for the lands. For their part, the Indians claimed that their community was in fact a pueblo, with a proper cabildo, but as no scribe or anyone among them knew how to read or write, they found it difficult to prove their case.[46]

During the legal proceedings, the San Diego Indians exhibited a "map" (Figure 2.2) on which the date "1540" could be discerned. This date may have represented the year the viceregal authority had granted them official recognition of their lands. The pictographic document was divided into three planes. Various Indian authorities appear on the top plane, with what resembles a river shown underneath them. A church is seen in the middle plane, with a hill—drawn in typical indigenous fashion—positioned at its right. Other authorities appear on the bottom plane, all wearing eighteenth-century clothing and several carrying staffs of justice, likely intended to represent their municipal council. Despite the map and the emphasis in their complaint of the fact that they maintained a cabildo and a church, the Indians' case was found wanting and the verdict went against them. The case demonstrates, however, that in the waning years of the eighteenth century, New Spain's Indians still used a traditional pictorial style to depict their land and its geographic location. It also illustrates that, by that time, few indigenous communities that were not long-established seats of administration could hold on to adjacent lands.

The Indian pueblos or administrative seats that existed in the sixteenth century and had served as the legal entity or vehicle for viceregal grants of land were not prevented from acquiring additional territory. An important adjunct, however, was that lands controlled by Indian nobles were not part of the communal scheme; rather, they were considered private. By the end of the eighteenth century, with the increase in the number of Indian pueblos, few could prevent the estate owners and ranchers who surrounded them or neighboring pueblos, for that matter, from encroaching on their legal allotment of 600 varas. This conflict was especially evident in the Valley of Mexico, where 160 haciendas had sprung up by the end of the colonial period.[47]

2.2 Reproduction, no. 1855 (no. LVIV in Luis Reyes García, *La escritura pictográfica en Tlaxcala. Dos mil años de experiencia mesoamericana* [Tlaxcala: Universidad Autónoma de Tlaxcala/Centro de Investigación y Estudios Superiores en Antropología Social, 1993]). Date: late eighteenth century. Courtesy, Archivo General de la Nación, Mexico City.

THE POLICY OF *CONGREGACIÓN*

The farthest-reaching physical and social reorganization of New Spain's Indian pueblos took place between the end of the sixteenth century and the beginning of the seventeenth century, through the process known as congregación. Colonial authorities had originally intended to implement this program prior to 1570, but for various reasons they did not do so until the end of the sixteenth century.[48] The policy was motivated by several concerns and served a variety of interests, both civil and ecclesiastical. First, Indian pueblos tended to be widely dispersed, which made it difficult for the Spanish to control their lands and populations. Under the program of congregación, numerous Indians from different settlements were collected and resettled—generally by force and against their will—in newly founded communities. These communities were designed and laid out in a uniform way, with a church, municipal council building, and jail arranged around a central plaza—all visible symbols of the colonial order and the place the Indian pueblos occupied within that order. The congregating of pueblos as an instrument of control and domination remains one of the most underresearched topics in colonial Mexican history.

The church had an equally strong interest in the outcome of this program. In 1591 Viceroy Luis de Velasco, the younger, noted that while serving in the same capacity decades earlier, his father had wanted to congregate the Indians to facilitate their conversion to the Christian faith and secure for them a better system of justice. He also argued that the pueblos' dispersed settlement pattern hampered their social and political organization. Finally, the viceroy informed the king that he had accepted the advice of the oidores, bishops, and religious orders regarding the problem and taken measures to begin to congregate the pueblos of Apasco, Atitalaquia, and Mizquihuala, located in the present-day states of México and Hidalgo. The Crown responded favorably to the viceroy's initiative, although various organizational details still needed to be worked out, including—prominently—the costs of the operation.[49] Velasco's solution to this problem, as he noted in a 1592 letter to the king, was that the Indians themselves should subsidize the program. He proposed to justify this expense to the Indians by explaining to them that it would be made for their "well-being and protection" and that, in return, the Crown would exempt them from paying "the fees incurred by their legal claims and business transactions." The viceroy was concerned, as he explained to the Crown, about one thing—he was uncertain how the Indians of Tlaxcala would react to this plan, since in return for allying themselves with the conquistadors, they had negotiated a unique exemption from paying tribute to the Spanish. As the viceroy noted, it "would be necessary to manage them artfully," that is, to deceive them.[50]

Even though the Indians were to be made to bear the initial expenses of their forced relocation, they were soon targeted in another way. In 1601 the Crown ordered that the viceroy exercise care to see that newly founded Indian pueblos were established near mines,[51] so this sector of the colonial economy—which directly benefited the royal coffers—would be guaranteed an ample supply of labor.

The program of Indian resettlement was fully consolidated under the administration of Viceroy Gaspar de Zúñiga y Acevedo, the Count of Monterrey (1595–1603). To accomplish that objective, the viceroy named district judges recruited from among the creole population. The judges, who earned an annual salary of 1,000 pesos, were required to hold consultations as part of the process of moving Indians to new communities administered by secular clerics and members of the religious orders.[52] Not surprisingly, however, many of these judges soon evidenced a loyalty to the interests of hacendados, cattle ranchers, and wealthy farmers—who identified for the judges land of poor quality on which to establish new pueblos and then took over the productive land the Indians had been forced to abandon.[53] The district judges were given a year to select and mark off the sites of new Indian communities, after which the viceroy appointed a second group of officials, the *jueces congregadores*, to oversee the actual relocation of Indians to the designated sites. These latter judges, generally provincial-level chief magistrates, were accompanied by a notary, interpreter, and constable. They were also equipped with a police force, since many Indians did not submit voluntarily to being moved, especially when they saw the inferior quality of the land on which they were being forcibly resettled. The process of moving the Indian population was supposed to be completed within a year but ultimately took twenty years or more.[54]

For the Spanish, the congregación program clearly opened up the possibility of acquiring new land. In this respect the Mexico City cabildo, as the embodiment of colonial power, was particularly opportunistic. Under the cabildo's plan, every inch of land that belonged to Indian pueblos around the city would be expropriated in favor of the white population, with its former owners and residents pushed to new territory in outlying districts.[55] The viceroy abetted the Spanish land grab by making formal grants of land to colonists, who quickly fanned out and settled on all the land the Indians had been forced to vacate.[56] Systematic annexation of indigenous land by the Spanish thus became an accomplished fact.

Although the implementation of the Indian resettlement program was rife with corruption, the Crown—on a higher level—was emphasizing that Indian pueblo lands should be protected. The official royal directive was that the lands the Indians had been made to abandon were still theirs, as designated reservation land, and remained under protection.[57] The reality, of course, was different. The celebrated Spanish cleric Fray Juan de Torquemada denounced the fact that, as carried out, congregación simply gave the best land to the Spanish and the worst to the Indians.[58] Its practical effect was to create concentrated pockets of Indian populations, thus enabling hacendados to have more direct access to an indigenous labor force. In addition, then, to transferring Indian lands to Spanish hands, resettlement of the native population contributed to the formation of the classic seventeenth-century hacienda, especially in the Valley of Mexico.[59]

In its manner of implementation, the program also failed to uphold chapter 12 of the law of congregation, stipulating that, if necessary to achieve a fair exchange, some lands belonging to Spaniards should be expropriated and awarded to newly established Indian pueblos. In addition, the law specified that the amount of land granted for new pueblos should take into account expected future increases in the native population and that Indian nobles and officials of Indian cabildos should receive more land than the *macehuales* (Indian commoners).[60]

Events surrounding the resettlement of the pueblo of Xalpantepec (present-day Jalpan, in the state of Puebla) illustrate many of these points. On July 8, 1599, Rodrigo de Zarate, one of the judges appointed by the king, arrived in Xalpan-tepec and immediately called on its authorities to meet with him in the church. As soon as the judge determined that four languages—Nahuatl, Tepehua, Otomi, and Totonaca—were spoken in the pueblo, he appointed two interpreters, from whom he learned that the pueblo's lands contained abundant water and were very productive, yielding three harvests of corn every year. In spite of this information (or perhaps because of it), the judge informed the Indians that he was going to move them to a better place where they would enjoy "spiritual and temporal comfort." The judge then toured the pueblo, accompanied by its governor and other authorities. He noted that it had been founded on the slope of a hill, creating a pattern of irregular settlement, and that it lacked a "good" church and had no jail or hospital. The authorities told him that the pueblo had 100 tributaries, at which point the judge suspended his activities.[61]

The following day, Zarate visited all of the Indian communities subject to Xalpantepec and informed them about his resettlement plan. He also summoned their authorities to appear at the church the following Sunday. At this point, the judge had verified that there were 360 tributaries within the pueblo's jurisdiction. On July 10 he sought the opinion of a group of people regarding possible sites on which to relocate the pueblo. The group included a mulatto, a Spaniard, and two ladino Indians (in this context, Spanish-speaking Indians), who had been familiar with Xalpantepec for several years. They all agreed that the pueblo should be moved to Jalpan. Zarate followed their advice, announcing that same day that he would be relocating the Indians to Jalpan. His decision was made official on July 11, when Xalpantepec's authorities—who had been given advance word through the interpreters—received it at the church. At the conclusion of the ceremony, the judge asked the authorities if they agreed with the decision, to which the general answer was that the pueblo's Indians were "pleased" with it. Zarate reimbursed the Indians for the food and assistance he and his entourage had received, and he withdrew.[62] The resettlement experience was set down and recorded in

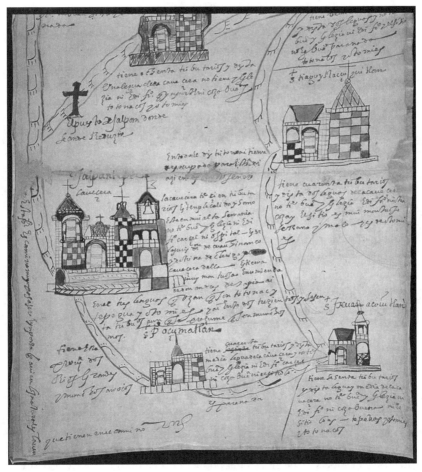

2.3 Reproduction, no. 2064. Date: 1599. Courtesy, Archivo General de la Nación, Mexico City.

a pictorial manuscript. The document depicts, in the form of churches, both Xalpantepec and its subject communities, with different roads leading to these places (Figure 2.3).

The case of Xalpantepec raises three central questions: Why did the Indians accept the exchange of their own fertile lands for other lands? Why were the Indians not asked where they would prefer to be resettled? What happened to the rich lands of Xalpantepec, which produced three harvests of corn per year?

Besides the loss of land, the Indians suffered other setbacks as a consequence of their resettlement. As a rule, to discourage the Indians from returning to their original pueblos, the churches in those pueblos were destroyed and the houses burned. In many cases, in addition, the uprooted Indians arrived in their new pueblos only to discover that they lacked shelter or housing. The colonial authorities had decided that the Indians should be responsible for constructing their own thatched mud-and-wattle houses. Thus, on top of the injury of being forced out of their traditional pueblos, the Indians had to live—for some time—without any dwelling places, exposed to the cold and rain. This abrupt and violent transition exacted a very high toll. Not surprisingly, the colonial authorities received reports that many Indians died in transit, while others fled before being moved or, in some cases, took their own lives. At one point, the Spanish expressed the fear that the resettlement operation would provoke a wider contagion of the epidemics that ravaged the native population.[63]

In sum, the Indians' forced separation from their places of origin traumatized them. Their pattern of life and cultural inheritance had engendered a powerful attachment to their native territory. It held great symbolic and spiritual importance for them, as the place where their ancestors had arrived in the distant past after long journeys of migration and were now buried, where they themselves would be laid to rest, and where the hills, caves, and rivers that surrounded them served as sacred sites for worshipping the gods.

THE POLICY OF *COMPOSICIÓN*

Given the fragmentation and disruptions the Indians experienced, it is difficult to construe that some pueblos would manage to carve out an area of negotiation with the colonial powers. Nonetheless, various representatives of Indian communities, as well as individual Indians, mounted efforts to ameliorate the harsh effects of the colonial system and defend their rights in Spanish courts. More interesting still, some members of the indigenous population demonstrated a strong desire to recount for colonial authorities the history of their pueblos during pre-Hispanic and colonial times—the latter in particular—motivated by the impulse to preserve their land. This phenomenon first occurred in the seventeenth century and continued through the 1700s. Documents of the period—such as land titles (called primordial titles at the beginning of the nineteenth century), pictorial maps, codices of the Techialoyan variety, and records of colonial legal cases—bear eloquent testimony to this negotiation process.

The documents referred to as the Techialoyan codices were produced in the seventeenth and eighteenth centuries on amatl paper and consisted of several sheets. The sheets contain Nahuatl glosses accompanied by large-format images, generally depicting local rulers. Since all these codices are executed in a similar style, they are viewed as forming a distinct type or genre. The majority come from pueblos in Central Mexico and the area around Puebla. Thematically, the

Techialoyan codices are characterized by the retelling of the local history of the altepetl and the recording of its boundaries.[64]

Some of the primordial titles, on the other hand, focus on depicting sources of water that assumed importance for the Indians at that juncture in the history of their pueblos when they were resettled.[65] Other themes in this category of documents are the introduction of the Catholic faith and the arrival of the Spanish. Along with pictorial maps, the Indians showed these materials to the Spanish authorities with the purpose of safeguarding their lands. In the seventeenth and eighteenth centuries the courts grew accustomed to having Indians introduce these documents as evidence to validate their claim of long-held ownership of particular lands.[66] This fact is noteworthy, since it contradicts the colonial authorities' disinclination, emergent at the end of the sixteenth century, to allow the Indians to incorporate traditional customs and practices within the colonial justice system. An even more glaring contradiction is that starting at the end of the sixteenth century, the Crown had promoted the adoption of laws that prohibited the Indians from recounting their pre-Hispanic past.

In furtherance of this objective, on April 22, 1577, Philip II ordered Viceroy Martín Enríquez to impound all works and writings that made reference to the Indians' pre-Hispanic past and their ancient customs and religion. The order stipulated that any such work be sent to the Royal and Supreme Council of the Indies in Valladolid. The official prohibition against the publication of works about the civilization of pre-Columbian Mexico lasted until 1820. It also mandated that any publication or piece of writing that referred, even obliquely, to Mexico's ancient history be confiscated and sent to Spain. As a consequence of this prohibition, numerous tomes written by missionaries that dealt with the history of the ancient Mesoamerican kingdoms—works similar to those produced by Sahagún, Motolinía, las Navas, Olmos, and others—perished.[67] This occurrence resulted from the Crown's desire to erase the history of New Spain's indigenous population. Eliminating the historical memory of the subject population was a way to reinforce and consolidate the power of the king. Moreover, in pursuing this course, the Crown had a related goal in mind: to stop the descendants of the traditional Mexica tlatoque from making any attempt to recover their pre-Hispanic dominions and to suppress any revanchist tendencies of Indian rulers in other parts of the colony.

Despite the prohibition's sweeping nature, it did not succeed in stamping out the Indians' collective memory of their past. The recollection of an earlier civilization came to life in accounts they wrote to present before the audiencia to demonstrate that they had long possessed certain lands. Further, the prohibition did not eradicate the accounts of ancient journeys of migration or the ancestral worship accorded to founders of the pueblos.[68] These stories continued to be handed down through the pueblos' oral traditions and in certain instances can be detected in the narratives of the primordial titles and the iconographic representations of maps and pictorial manuscripts.

For example, some of the maps the Indians produced during the colonial period reveal the figures of large heads, which seem to represent the Indians' ancestors. This figuration occurs on the lienzo of San Juan Cuauhtla, from the Sierra Negra (Puebla), on which the oversized heads of both women wearing indigenous headdress and anthropomorphic beings with headdress are depicted (Figure 2.4). The lienzo's description of the migration journey to and founding of the pueblo suggests that the heads symbolize its original founders. The document's Nahuatl text refers to different places in which various persons with supernatural characteristics founded settlements, erected churches, and carried out penances. The place names evoke ancient religious beliefs and practice. One fragment, for example, reads "the god of women"; another reads "here, San Juan Guautla, is where we do penance, my name is Xihuitototli, hill of the owls and hill of the deer. Here is where we make things . . . and we say, here we have our houses and we nobles have always wanted it to be thus."[69]

Although the Crown had rejected the Indians' heritage—going so far as to proscribe any reference to it in printed works—and tried to reshape the colonial legal landscape to reflect that policy, many Indian pueblos nevertheless found ways of negotiating with the colonial authorities and overcoming this rejectionism. Their success, apparent especially in the central part of the colony and in the region of the present-day states of Puebla and Oaxaca, enabled them to continue to present pictorial documents—maps in particular—in numerous judicial proceedings. In the mid-seventeenth century, furthermore, they introduced a new line of argument in the courts as a means of defending their corporate interests. Especially in litigation over land issues, they addressed their history, providing oral testimony and submitting written briefs—usually in Nahuatl—that described their ancestors' migration journey, ceremonies of arrival in the new pueblo, and the rites by which they took "possession" of their lands. They accompanied these narratives and texts with pictorial manuscripts, in many instances passing them off as having great antiquity in an effort to lend more force to their historical argument.[70] The primordial titles and the Techialoyan codices form a large part of this type of documentation.

The Indians' effort to preserve their lands was at the core of their production of titles composed in the native languages, as well as of maps, codices, and pictorial representations. Responding to this effort, Spanish colonial authorities generated their own body of historical-administrative records and documents. Land was not the Indian pueblos' sole preoccupation, however. The materials they elaborated depicted other matters of symbolic importance to them. Their concerns and way

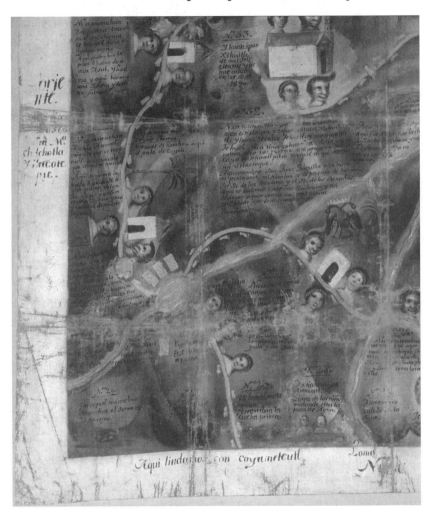

2.4 Reproduction, detail from pictorial representation of San Juan Cuauhtla, no. 35-134. Date: 1740. Courtesy, Instituto Nacional de Antropología e Historia, Mexico City.

of operating during the colonial period were therefore multidimensional: to produce documentation that would address and satisfy their needs of the moment through the use of historical records that confirmed the legitimacy of their rights over lands they claimed as their own. This dynamic could occur within a single document or within a series of interrelated documents, such as grants of land, normally made in the sixteenth century for cattle ranches or farms; it could also occur in a resolution over water rights. Further, the dynamic could apply to documents grounded in a pueblo's oral history, produced to demonstrate its original or long-held possession of lands under litigation. At times, the records of a particular case were composed of several types of documents. When they lacked official documents, some Indian pueblos resorted to forging them, although the authorities were generally able to detect such counterfeits without difficulty. One such case involved the Indian residents of Xuchitepec, Chalco (in the present-day state of México), in 1748.

In that year the pueblo filed a suit through its governor against Francisco de la Cotera, a Mexico City judge and cabildo member who owned land in Tlalmanalco, Chalco, and maintained that certain tracts of land in Xuchitepec belonged to him as well. Unable to produce documents that would prove its ownership of the disputed land, the pueblo—led by its governor—decided to elaborate a set of counterfeit sixteenth-century royal grants and a map. The Indians' attempt was easily foiled, however. In demonstrating to the audiencia that the documents were false, the expert who detected the fraud pointed out: "Taking some woodworm . . . from the supporting beams and cooking it with *tequesquite* [a type of limestone mixed with corn to make dough], white paper of any kind, sprinkled with water and humidified[,] takes on a color that makes it look very old. And then these same sheets of paper are placed in an oven to dry until they get crisp, when examined, though, the paper markings are from modern-day[,] not old[,] paper."[71]

Some titles the Indians produced, however, were not confined simply to information extracted from official colonial documents but instead included specialized information reflecting local conditions. These were rendered in native languages, generally Nahuatl, and were accompanied by a recently completed Spanish translation. The translation was clearly vital if tribunals were to allow them to be introduced as evidentiary documents. This class of titles has drawn the greatest attention of specialists. The information they contain was apparently set down within the framework of an oral history, narrating details about the local experiences of either the *altepeme* (capitals) or their subject pueblos. They usually pertain to the founding of pueblos and the circumstances surrounding their origin. In some instances they refer to the support the colonial authorities gave to the pueblo's founding, in which case—as Stephanie Wood has noted—three figures almost always play a central role: the colony's first two viceroys, Don Antonio de Mendoza (1535–1550) and Don Luis de Velasco "the elder" (1550–1564), as well as Hernán Cortés.[72] The local history of indigenous communities was obviously affected by these three individuals for a long period.

From the perspective of law and legislation, the origin of this type of historical evidence, submitted by the Indians to preserve or augment their lands, is not entirely clear. A precipitating factor, however, may have been an effort the Crown began in 1581 to consider the possibility of selling off pasturelands (*dehesas*) supposedly reserved for communal use by the Indians. The project, conceived of by a monarchy in urgent need of revenue, was nevertheless discouraged by the second Viceroy Velasco. In 1591, though, a new land policy known as *composición*, involving the legalization of titles to land through the payment of fees, did go into effect under Velasco's stewardship. On the basis of two royal decrees, the monarchy announced that as the owner and master of all New World lands, it wished to make "a grant" of the same to both the Spanish and the Indians. Having learned that some people possessed land without holding title to it or, in other cases, by holding defective or invalid titles, the Crown ordered a "general restitution of lands already appropriated, leaving to the Indians what was necessary for their subsistence."[73] To avoid sanctions and hardships stemming from such irregularities, individuals would be allowed to legalize their titles through payment; in addition, land that was vacant would be available for legal purchase. Funds that accrued to the royal coffers through this source of revenue, the Crown explained, would be used to help pay for a fleet of ships to protect the colony's maritime commerce from being intercepted by pirates and enemy countries.[74] Initially, composición progressed slowly, but the process moved ahead rapidly at the beginning of the seventeenth century when monastic establishments managed (despite legal impediments) to gain official title to different land grants and Spanish colonists began to directly purchase lands from the Indians.[75]

The commercialization of land as an integral part of royal policy was underscored by an order issued by the Crown in 1615, enabling royal land grants to be bought at auction. This action was taken despite the opposition of colonial authorities, who looked askance at putting up for sale something that until then had been the centerpiece of a compensatory system, through which in return for services that benefited both Spaniards and Indians the viceroys could reward colonists with land.[76]

The composición program had gathered significant momentum as of 1629 and reached new plateaus in 1631, 1635–1636, 1643, 1645, 1675, and 1697–1698, by which time a large majority of New Spain's haciendas had secured definitive title to their land.[77] The program was expensive for the Crown because its operation required the appointment of a special group of judges. Nevertheless, it was kept alive, although the revenue it produced did little or nothing to alleviate the economic exigencies of the Spanish monarchy. The high price of running the program was justified on the grounds that it helped finance the fleet of ships, in particular the armada of Barlovento, that defended the Indies.[78]

The first step in the full process of composición began with an order the *juez privativo de composiciones* (land composition judge) issued to the Spanish official in charge of a district in which land titles were going to be legalized. The judge's order, ordinarily issued in fulfillment of a royal decree requesting the same, called on the official to produce a list of names of Indian pueblos, the owners of water rights and lands, and the amount of royal or vacant land in the district's jurisdiction. Once he had this information, the judge named a panel of *jueces comisarios* (land title legalization commissioners), who were almost always the province's alcaldes mayores.

Those who owned water rights and land and wanted to regularize their titles, as well as Indian pueblos that wanted to do the same as of 1707, came before these authorities and declared the name of their property, the land and water it contained, and its boundaries or limits. They showed the authorities the titles they held to the property (or properties) and offered a sum of money to "resolve matters" with the Crown. In addition to the parties themselves, the judge requested the appearance of three or more witnesses to attest to the validity of the declaration made by those seeking to have titles legalized. If any irregularity was encountered, the judge organized an eyewitness inspection by the juez comisario, who recorded the land and its limits and took testimony from all householders and property owners to prevent the usurpation or wrongful assignment of land. If the comisario found that all was in order and that the declaration did not contain any excess of water or land, he so informed the juez privativo, who then accepted the sum of money offered for the legalization of titles as "a gracious donation to the Crown" and issued an official statement that covered either land or water, declaring that its owner had fulfilled the royal order.

If, however, excessive claims of land turned up during the on-site inspection, the property owner had to appear at the Royal Treasury and pay the amount of money he had offered or more, depending on the decision of the judge privativo. After he had done so, "he was furnished with a receipt as proof of payment. Next, the judge privativo granted him a statement of legalization compensating him for and relieving him of any error, or defect, or omission in the title(s)." The most interesting aspect of this little-known mechanism for legalizing titles is that it was applied "in the same way when dealing with Indian common lands, lands belonging to religious orders and the jurisdictions of caciques, and properties situated in towns or cities."[79]

These protocols are very important, since some scholars have seen in them and in the larger corpus of law underlying composición the origin of the Techialoyan codices and the primordial titles of Indian pueblos. While the two developments do coincide, from the inception of the land legalization program in 1591 through all its seventeenth-century iterations, both Indian pueblos and Indians as individuals remained—without exception—officially outside the program.[80] The Indians were not brought into the process until the issuance of the royal decree of August 15, 1707. A large number of Indian pueblos figured in one of the last general spurts of land title legalization in New Spain, which occurred between 1709 and 1717. During this period, more than 600 legalizations were approved in the Puebla area alone.[81] The program continued to operate sporadically and to include Indian pueblos and individual Indians until the end of the eighteenth century. The number of cases continued to drop steadily, however, since most individuals and pueblos had already regularized their titles, whether voluntarily or under coercion.[82]

RECOUNTING HISTORY AS A MEANS OF DEFENDING LAND

Recall that the pueblos produced primordial titles and the Techialoyan codices during the seventeenth and part of the eighteenth centuries of their own volition, unencumbered by any legal obligation to come forward with such records. Their reason for doing so was probably to prevent the Spanish, who were compelled to fulfill the Crown's dictates regarding composición, from appropriating land that belonged to them or to Indian caciques. The Spanish had various channels at their disposal; they could lodge false claims, augment their holdings by taking extra land, or exploit the ineptitude or corruption of the jueces privativos and alcaldes mayores—who in return for bribes could secure for Spaniards titles to land that belonged to the pueblos. The mark of how valuable the primordial titles and related records were to the Indians is that even in the Puebla region, Spanish ranchers involved in litigation against Indian pueblos over land and water would resort to stealing the titles from the pueblos to deprive them of their legal-historical evidence.[83]

During the seventeenth and eighteenth centuries, therefore, the Indian pueblos tended to produce maps and pictorial documents to assert and defend their rights to water and land. Occasionally, however, a pueblo found it impossible to produce a map or painted manuscript because it lacked either a resident with even a rudimentary understanding of how to execute the work or the money to pay someone to do it. Pueblos regularly found themselves in this situation. Confronted with this problem, some seized upon ancient pictographic documents that had been produced for different reasons and—under the pressures of the moment—tried to deceive the tribunals into thinking they were primordial titles. Other pueblos used a variation on this theme by taking ancient pictorial maps and manuscripts, which were sometimes simple genealogical accounts of their lines of nobles, and retouching them so the courts would mistake them for the appropriate documents—a tactic I refer to as the "readjustment" of a pictorial document. Various examples exist of both types of attempted deception.

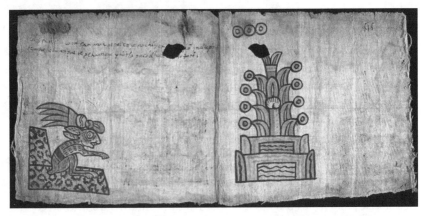

2.5 Reproduction, detail, no. 824 (no. 69 in Glass and Robertson 1975). Date: sixteenth century. Courtesy, Archivo General de la Nación, Mexico City.

In 1733, for example, the Indians living in the district of Concepción launched a determined and protracted struggle against the Indians of the neighboring district of Santa Mónica. Both communities were located in Cuetzalan (Chiutla de la Sal, Puebla). The conflict was triggered by an argument over land, which seemed at the point of resolution in 1749. At the last moment, however, the Concepción Indians mentioned through their lawyer that they had some "instruments," which were "primordial," that "justified their right to the land."[84] One of the "instruments" consisted of two fragments of codices on amatl—likely from the sixteenth century—which appear to be part of an ancient calendar, since they include symbolic representations of the Mesoamerican year. According to the records of the case, the Indians—probably because of their concern over land—had made annotations on both fragments during the eighteenth century. The annotations referred to different boundaries of their territory. It is clear from examining one of these fragments that the image on it (Figure 2.5) does not relate to land or suggest any type of title. It is simply a small piece of a perhaps much larger codex the Concepción Indians rescued—probably from among other documents—and presented to the authorities because its antiquity would be seen to validate their claim to historical possession of the disputed land.[85] The fragment's vivid traditional symbolism made it a good candidate to serve as the community's primordial title. The Rabbit sign, or *tochtli*, is represented by an elaborate headdress of quetzal feathers and is shown planted on a seat covered with the coat of a jaguar, a very important symbol of power among the native population of Mesoamerica. The gloss, which lies above, seems much more recent than the drawing beneath it. The figurative symbol of the Rabbit year is fronted by that of Reed, or Acatl (3 Reed), depicted in a very elaborate manner.

The codex was apparently admitted as evidence, and there is an interesting aside from the person interpreting for the audiencia—an observation befitting a man of some enlightenment. He commented with respect to the two fragments—which he called a "map"—that they were undoubtedly the pictorial representation of pre-Hispanic monuments that served to delimit the Indians' lands:

> [T]he two Cues [pre-Hispanic temples] seen opposite to each other in the form of a pyramid are nothing more than burial mounds which, in the time when they were gentiles, the Indians placed over the tombs of their princes, or they are altar stones [for sacrifices] highly venerated among them, which in Peru are called huacas, and all those entombed in them are numbered with the little circles edging the altars; nowadays known as teteles [pyramids], they are used in the fields to denote the limits or boundaries of the lands possessed by the pueblos or [to] mutely testify that the sites where they are now seen were those inhabited by their ancestors.[86]

Similarly, some pueblos presented ancient pictorial documents that had been embellished with landscape scenes, writing, or images of people during the eighteenth century. Examples include the *Codex Colombino* (of pre-Hispanic origin and from Tututepec, on the Oaxaca coast), the codex *Veinte Mazorcas* (from the Tlapa region, Guerrero), and one of the Cuauhquechollan (Huaquechula, Puebla) codices. Also worth mentioning is the *Codex Tulane*, which was painted on animal hide in the mid-sixteenth century and is a genealogical manuscript from the nobility of Acatlan in the Mixteca Baja. The codex was readjusted as a map in the nineteenth century by the Indians of San Juan Ñumi (Mixteca Alta) in a land litigation.[87]

Thus, the reworked documents, primordial titles, and Techialoyan codices all form part of a nexus of indigenous negotiation that stemmed from Crown initiatives to curtail the loss of land; they were not required under the law. Even more telling, nobody during the seventeenth century ever asked the Indians to confirm their landholdings by producing a set of legal-historical documents or to present arguments to justify their long-held possession of particular lands. Instead, the Indians took these actions and submitted these materials to the colonial tribunals as a precautionary measure, or at least this was the rationale until the early eighteenth century. As noted, the primordial titles and the Techialoyan codices were presented by Indian pueblos whose lands fell within territory coveted by the Spanish, a situation that occurred in the central part of the colony and in the region around Puebla in particular. The geographic origin of the Techialoyan codices is very clear; it includes the Valley of Toluca, the basin of Central Mexico, and parts of the present-day state of Morelos. These regions contained zones of rich, fertile land with a growing Indian population; Spanish-owned haciendas undergoing major expansion; and, therefore, strong competition to secure the rights to exploit water, forestland, and other natural resources.

Beginning in the seventeenth century, however, Indian pueblos in various parts of Mesoamerica sought to contain this threat and to protect their land by creating written and pictorial narratives of their history. Thus, for example, a title in Nahuatl that originated in the region of Colima, toward the northern part of New Spain, ostensibly describes events that occurred in 1523, when Hernán Cortés made grants of land to various pueblos. The title itself dates to a much later time, probably 1650, and portrays the conquistador as the protector of indigenous lands against the rest of his countrymen:

> Here, in the pueblo named Santiago Tecoman and in the ward called San
> Pedro Petlatzonican and also in all of the remaining pueblos: San José
> Tecolapan Xictlan; San Sebastian Tecpan Mixpanic where the water is yellow;
> Petlatlan; Ayutlan de Castilla; Tlillan; San Andrés Coatlan; Coyotlan, which
> were esteemed by the great tlahtoani the Marqués del Valle, who lived here,
> and then stated "that my fathers should dwell here may they not take fright."
> And so we accomplish it; much honor is bestowed upon us and with it they
> respect, for always and in due manner[,] my beloved land and you will be my
> children always, placed next to me, and you and your children will live and
> nobody will cause you to be poor; the people of Castile will be at our backs
> but nobody will die, nobody will suffer, nobody will be made to cry.[88]

Another example of titles in this vein exists for the region of the Bajío (the present-day states of Querétaro and Guanajuato). In this case, an eighteenth-century Indian nobleman narrates in his language, Otomi, all of the vicissitudes his forbears experienced, as well as the aid they gave to the Spanish during their conquest of the Chichimeca region. The narration repeatedly makes clear that without the assistance of the Otomi, the Spanish would have found it impossible to assert control over an area rich in agricultural and mineral resources.[89]

Finally, consider a much more remote example, one that deals with a title originating in Guatemala, from the pueblo of Santa María Ixhuatán. It probably dates to the eighteenth century and still reposes in that community. This large manuscript describes a series of events that both precede and follow the conquest. The narrative centers on the migration journey to, and subsequent founding of, the pueblo, events in which members of the local nobility are the central figures—in particular a nobleman called Don Pedro de "Albarato Xilomiqui de Guazacapan," who probably served as the pueblo's first native governor in the wake of the European conquest. The Indian nobleman's lineage is traced back to the Toltecs, and the command to elaborate the primordial titles is said to have come from the Toltecs of "Señor Quetzalcoatl." According to the narrative, the founder nobles emerged from a mythical cave bearing the name Chicnauztepetl (Nine Hill) and then crossed the water. After founding the pueblo, they declared that the "grandfathers and grandmothers" are in the *mictlan* (the underworld, the place of the dead) inside the cave, where the gentiles also go because they do not believe in "our great tlahtoani God," who—as the titles relate—died on the cross "so that men should not journey to the mictlan." Apparently, the Indians who set down these titles had before them a pictorial document or codex, since the manuscript frequently uses such expressions as "here one sees," "here there appears," and "here is."[90]

In this way, then, Indians from different regions of Mesoamerica presented colonial tribunals with titles and maps before the Crown had imposed the obligation on them to negotiate their land titles (*componerse*). They took this action primarily out of the need to preserve their land. It was usually indigenous leaders, both nobles and Indian cabildo members, who presented these documents to the Spanish authorities. Even though—with few exceptions—their power had been substantially eroded during the seventeenth and eighteenth centuries, they nevertheless managed to win some of these cases, despite the advantageous position the Spanish colonists enjoyed.

The titles, Techialoyan codices, and some pictographic maps the Indians employed in legal wrangles over land depict and describe local indigenous elites as wielding important influence.[91] The events narrated in these documents about the local histories of Indian pueblos are clearly difficult to confirm, yet this obstacle should not deter us from studying them. Rather, we need to look more deeply into them in the attempt to unravel and understand their meaning. The documents constitute a unique source that opens a window onto indigenous culture and society.[92]

During the colonial period, as mentioned, some Indian pueblos prepared forged documents. Not surprisingly, this development occurred more often in areas with large numbers of Spanish haciendas, where Indian lands faced greater threats.[93] In some cases the Indians recopied original colonial documents pertaining to visits by officials collecting tribute, royal grants, and permissions given to Indian rulers to use daggers or to travel on horseback. The primordial title of the pueblo of San Miguel Chignautla, located in the Puebla area, is an example of such a practice. Its opening lines state that "in the year of [1552] I, juez visitador general Don Diego Ramírez y Mendoza, for Don Fernando Cortés conquistador of this New Spain of the Indies, do make this grant." In 1552 Diego Ramírez was empowered to revise the tribute exacted from Indian pueblos in the central part of the colony. As an honest official who reduced the pueblos' tribute burden, he earned the gratitude of the Indians and the enmity of the encomenderos.[94] My supposition is that in producing this title, the Indians had recourse to official documents in front of them, such as a tributary roll composed by Ramírez. They proceeded to add the surname of the colony's first viceroy, Mendoza, whom they recast as an envoy of Hernán Cortés. The title also states:

> [A]nd the foot of the hill of Chachelotepeque Ymiquexco Chiyucan and Tecolotepeque is meant for your cattle, goats, sheep, mules, [and] horses.... And when it is thus[,] notice will first be given to the high government of his excellency señor viceroy don Luis de Belasco count of Corona . . . and to ensure the defense of the recorded lands under his care and control the alcalde don Juan López Chicnamiqui was granted the right to bear arms, harquebus, dagger, sword, arrow, garments, doublet, silk stockings, [and] wig for the adornment of his person.[95]

From the title, it is evident that the Indians of this pueblo probably adapted part of its content from earlier documents, including a grant of cattle and a viceregal concession made to one of the community's nobles allowing him to carry a dagger. The title thus combines elements foreign to indigenous culture with the pueblo's own oral tradition.[96]

Given the complexity of these sources, the Indians' ways of conceptualizing their past need to be taken into account. From the indigenous perspective, different ideas of reality imply different ideas of history,[97] which, in turn, are woven into the strands of the Indians' traditional oral histories. This oral narrative is dynamic, constantly refashioned. For example, when the Bribri of Costa Rica rework their myths, they evoke the conquistadors and European colonizers as a way of absorbing and integrating that which is culturally alien and threatening.[98]

Similarly, when the Indians of New Spain set down part of their oral history in written and pictorial documents, they blended in Spanish colonial figures as mediators or included the founding of churches to represent one dimension of their acceptance of Christianity. These, as well as fragments of their pre-Hispanic past, were used in the Indians' effort to obtain titles to their lands, which they then used to defend their ownership and possession of the lands and the community life they supported against the dominant power.[99]

This predilection among the Indians to record the traditional narrative of their history was eminently pragmatic. For the native population of Mesoamerica, truth did not reside in what was written but rather in the tradition passed down from one's ancestors: "[I]ndigenous tradition was not indestructible; its continuity did not reside in the preservation of 'authentic' objects such as books, but in the survival of the social group that transmitted it and gave it life."[100]

Consider, for example, the Indian cabildo of the district of Santa María Magdalena Mixuca, which was subject to the authority of the Mexico City Indian community of San Juan. The Magadalena cabildo first asserted in 1639 that for an untold number of years, its district had possessed two areas of swampland that were rented to a Spaniard, Manuel Copado. The cabildo members were taking legal action against Copado on the grounds that he would not let them onto the property to cut grass and that he also mistreated them. Over time, the situation surrounding Magdalena's swamps intensified, and in 1702 a contingent of the district's Indians appeared in court with a pictographic map that seemed of considerable antiquity. They proceeded to describe, through oral testimony, the many glyphs that appeared on the map. As they did so, an interpreter translated the Indians' explanations, and a scribe wrote down what they said regarding the map:

> I see and recognize some figures on the first sheet that seem to be the caciques who ruled in that time, the first is the one who ruled for four years = and the years are on the margin, where I recognize that it is the first year of their rule and it is called Tecpatha [Tecpatl] which means flint = and the second year that follows is Acatle [Acatl] which means caña = and the third year is tuchil [*tochtli*] which means rabbit = and the fourth is cali [Calli] which means house, where the months of the year are shown.[101]

The map's glyphs are extensive, taking up several sheets. This case indicates that during the eighteenth century the Indians were still capable of "reading" the traditional glyphs. Many of the glyphs were intricate and involved, as will be noted in the next passage, which describes a punishment inflicted on an Indian by a group of judges in the presence of a tlatoani wearing a headdress that has a ribbon with his name emblazoned on it. This example illustrates graphically that for the Indian pueblos, oral tradition as conveyed in pictorial and written documents still held uppermost importance in this era:

> On the second sheet there is a seated cacique who has four heads, and another cacique in front pointing to said heads. And to the side there is another seated cacique at whose foot there is a head with its *copil* [a conical headdress, xiuhuitzolli?, or turquoise crown worn by the rulers] and a black line that is going to meet where it says Rabbit [*tochtli*] and in the middle there is a gallows and a boy hung from it and a brazier with heated coals, the devil is there blowing on it, these were the judges who render justice; because according to what I see on said map, the great lord is seated in his place of honor, the garment is that of the cacique and king who rules them and who is set apart and has his copil and from his head another black line comes out that is going to run into a head which seems to be that of a *sierpe* [serpent] or some other animal.[102]

RETELLING THE PAST AMONG INDIAN PUEBLOS

For the Chamula Indians of Chiapas, history—the past—is forever intertwined with the present and "is reaffirmed in the face of the needs, hopes, and threats that infuse their present-day life."[103] Like their Mayan forbears, the Chamula think and organize experience in terms of temporal cycles. In their view, all events occur according to established patterns that inevitably recur. The historical cycle is therefore a key element in their way of looking at the past. Yet, somewhat paradoxically, the needs they face today have become a force that constantly conditions and reshapes the content of their history. For example, the Chamula believe ladinos are the survivors of their "Third Creation," an epoch during which people spoke Spanish and fought constantly among themselves. Later, to prevent wars, the pueblos were separated by the "Sun Father." The Chamula, who speak Tzotzil, believe they have evolved beyond that stage but that the ladinos have not, by virtue of the fact that they still speak Spanish. In addition, as descendants of the people of the Third Creation, ladinos have a quarrelsome, bellicose nature.[104] With respect to the two (or more) social groups, this outlook reveals a logical relationship between past and present for the Chamula, in which they occupy a preponderant and more evolved position. Thus, for the Indians, mythical thinking and historical consciousness can develop simultaneously within a single society and even within individual discourse.[105]

Another group, the Ch'oles of Chiapas, also views the transmission of knowledge from the past as serving a pragmatic function. The activity, however, is centered in the present.[106] This situation is not unique to Mexico's Indians; the Andean pueblos share a similar dynamic link between past and present. In the Andean Indians' way of thinking, the past is ever latent in the present; it "endures and is reformulated in terms of present experience."[107]

Indeed, the formulations of the past that indigenous groups elaborate serve as a resource for undertaking social action in the present.[108] Thus, for Colombia's Nasa people, historical events did not occur as they actually did but rather as the Nasa would have had them occur. Past events are used to explain and render intelligible the concerns of the present, even if in the retelling those events are changed, details are omitted, or the wider narrative itself is restructured.[109] The events have no importance in themselves. In this sense, Nasa historical narrative is fundamentally different from what we consider historical "truth." In the retelling of their history, what truly matters for the Nasa is that it benefits their present interests.

In this way, when an Indian pueblo conveys information in its primordial titles that does not correspond to rigid historical "truth"—for example, in trying to link itself with other pueblos of greater past importance, such as Tlaxcala or México-Tenochtitlan (or even to pueblos that may not have possessed such importance)—it is demonstrating how historical knowledge is used to create a moral continuity between the past and the present.[110] This tendency describes what some Indian pueblos, such as Tzinacapan, located in the sierra of Puebla, are doing at present in Mexico. Through the elaboration of a historical narrative, the Indians of this community have forged a direct link with the prestigious pre-Hispanic past of the Mexica.[111]

In observing the Nasa, Joanne Rappaport offers an insight that could be applied to the Indians of Mexico and even to indigenous peoples across Latin America more broadly: "[T]o be a good Nasa historian, one must have more than a grasp of the past: one must also be capable of articulating past and present in order to change the future."[112] Consequently, all the information about their past, about the image they held of their own history, that Mexico's Indians set down in the Techialoyan codices, primordial titles, painted maps, and other pictographic and written documents constitutes a process of negotiation. It is not something fixed and frozen in texts but something fluid, something that must be studied in its social, political, and historical specificity.[113] In the act of recovering their history, certain members of the Indian pueblos play a predominant role. Their leaders, for example, serve as the principal repository of the pueblo's collective memory, its history and folklore. The memories or stories they transmit are shaped by present-day concerns. In their practices, the K'ulta of Bolivia exemplify this overlapping and intertwining of past and present.[114]

To succeed in preserving their past and transmitting it into the present, Indian communities have had to resist the colonial and national states alike, both of which consciously attempted (and, in the case of some national states, may still attempt) to redesign and mold the indigenous past as part of their strategies of colonization and domination.[115] Clearly, "colonialism produces not only a contention of societies and cultures but also a conflict of history."[116] Although the Indians have highly valued (and continue to value) books and the culture of written law, they have deeply respected and continue to respect oral tradition as well.[117] Oral tradition enables the Indians to recount their past in a dynamic and fluid way; it entails a continuous process of creative and collective transformation.

The art of memory requires not only remembering but also what has been called "structured forgetting."[118] Thus, both Frank Salomon and Thomas Abercrombie have argued that the contradiction, in seeking to reduce oral narrative to writing, lies in the reality of two irreconcilable notions of time and history. The Spaniards' perception of historical time as linear and unitary and as a sequence that lacks any repetition of events makes it impossible for them to absorb and comprehend the distinctly different perception of historical time found in the Andes, where the validity of a sequence of episodes in a narrative does not require that it fit neatly into a single master narrative.[119]

This argument is equally valid for the Indians of Mexico. In Mexico as in the Andes, the primordial titles are held on to and transmitted among indigenous authorities and families from generation to generation because they serve to protect the land, which, in turn, harbors the memory of the pueblo founded by their ancestors and, as such, must be safeguarded for future generations. Each boundary marker of the Indians' lands likewise helps protect them and helps preserve historical memory. In keeping with this tradition, marking off the boundaries of a pueblo's lands has been and remains today a ritualized act in which the pueblo as a whole was and is fully engaged. When Indian pueblos take up arms to defend their lands, it is a sign not of their descent into irrational violence but instead of their determination to protect a history and identity that must be passed on to future generations.[120] For the indigenous peoples of Mexico and the Andes, their history has been recorded three-dimensionally—in codices and pictorial maps, in textile designs and *khipus* (Andean data-recording device made of cord that can be knotted), in songs and dances, and in rituals and sacrifice.[121]

The primordial titles in particular have a series of elements that reveal what the Indians had to say, in the stories they first told and later set down in writing (principally in Nahuatl but in other native languages as well) about the origin of their pueblos. The titles describe ritual journeys of migration, struggles and conflict, and the founding of the Indians' pueblos. They interweave mythical tales and history. As a general rule, they explicitly mention several Spanish personages: Emperor Charles V, his son, King Philip II, and high-level local functionaries. As noted previously, they also repeatedly mention Viceroys Antonio de Mendoza and Luis de Velasco, as well as missionaries and conquistadors—above all Hernán Cortés—who played a mediating role in enabling the Indians to receive grants of land. Characteristically, the dates, names, and offices assigned to these individuals are often unreliable. Names are confused one with another or even mixed up, and events are given impossible dates (that, for example, Cortés had granted a certain pueblo its lands in 1510).

Yet, if one takes into account the salient facts about the malleable nature of indigenous historical narrative and adds what is learned from the work of Yukitaka Inoue regarding Nahuatl titles, the apparent "confusion" of dates, personages, and historical events that characterizes many of the titles can be better understood. In pre-Hispanic Mexico, the founding of the various altepetl took place under the will and protection of the gods. For the Indians who elaborated primordial titles during the colonial period, the equivalent of their ancient gods was the Christian God. Land, as the titles indicate, was received from God. This notion—that land was received by men from the deities—was undoubtedly part of pre-Hispanic thinking. In this way of thinking, the Spanish monarchs, conquistadors, and royal officials were ultimately agents of God. Thus, when making grants of land to the Indians, they were not acting autonomously but as instruments of God's will and higher power. It was therefore unimportant, for those producing the primordial titles, whether the names of these Spanish agents were expressed correctly.[122]

For example, in the Tlaxcalan Indian community of San Bartolomé, tradition has it that when a conflict over land broke out between that community and the nearby pueblo of Contla, a multitude of people came to its rescue and were led by Saint Bartholomew himself, thanks to which Contla ended its claim over the land.[123] In this case, the protector of the pueblo's land is the saint, acting in a God-like capacity. Another example that illustrates even more clearly the link between God and the land is found in the invocatory words of the primordial titles of Tepehuexoyucan (Asunción Tepezoyuca, in the state of México):

> And now our great lord and god looked upon us compassionately . . . spiritually we newly believe in the Christian faith, the beloved priest whom we follow looks upon us compassionately. . . . [W]e are all believers and spiritually love the moral virtue that he with the greatest grace has given us. And now in this time the one who measures land has come here by order of our great lord Don Antonio de Mendoza who arrived in [the] last year, epochal count [1534] years.[124]

In addition, the primordial titles contain detailed descriptions of a pueblo's boundaries while in some cases also referring to rituals and community feast days and their musical accompaniments. They also include the narration of seemingly disconnected events and facts. This last element occurs in a title, bearing the unlikely date of 1529, that belongs to the Indian community of Tlalpan, in Mexico City. Part of the title states:

> The boundary of San Agustín is where the *ajuejotes* [a variety of tree] stand. Diego Xochimantzin. Stone and sand wall, where [the flute] is played. In the sandy area. It stopped there; the narrow boundary was drawn here. Miguel Tecpatl. The limits of the ajuejotes. The road for Mexico passes [through here]. Juan Aguacatzin. The place where the sun comes out. The San Lorenzo quarter. Sebastián Chichitomitl, died from an arrow. There is where a snake crossed their path. The boundary of Ahuehuetitlan.[125]

Some titles also mention the ritual that was followed when pueblos received a grant of land, during which—in certain cases—they also burned copal (a type of incense). The use of copal figured prominently in both pre-Hispanic and colonial-era indigenous rituals, as it does to this day: "[W]e the natives of this pueblo of San Miguel Nepantla [state of México] proceeded right away to take possession of all these lands in the name of the king, our lord, people in all four directions cut grass, tossed stones, walked about burning copal as a sign of taking possession."[126]

Titles also exist that, in addition to all the elements already mentioned, include fragments of dialogue among the founders of the pueblo:

They went to the spot called Tetexalpa Sansacatlalpa. Afterwards they went to the place called Quauhxayacatitlan. And there they went to meet all of the elders by the boundary of Atlacotecatli. They played flute music there and put down some benches and ate fish and ducks and birds and hares from the marshes and everything that's from and goes about in the water and when they finished eating there an old man got up and said[,] come here all of you children of the pueblo, young boys, lads, and the littlest ones and those who are yet unborn[;] you don't know how the elders with hard work won possession of the pueblos, the lands, and all of the water and the marshes lowlands.[127]

It seems clear from the details in these passages that the information set down in the titles formed part of an oral discourse and tradition the community knew and perhaps continued to enact. The written version of the titles generated on the basis of this oral tradition, however, was assuredly directed at the Spanish authorities.[128] In part, the confusion or disconnectedness of people and events narrated in these texts derived from their origin; they were part of a cultural tradition the Indian pueblos transmitted orally, only to express later in written form because of the urgent need to protect their lands.

Even today, Indian communities that have been subject to relocation are prone to reinvent their memory of the past to accord with their new circumstances. The ideas of the biblical exodus or the promised land, for example, are incorporated into their historical narrative in light of their move to a new region.[129]

RECALLING THE PAST AND LOCAL INDIGENOUS POWER

Among the numerous examples of titles, pictorial maps, and the Techialoyan codices, the figures of the Indian nobility—those known as native lords, caciques, and tlatoani or tlatoque (the plural form in Nahuatl)—stand out in particular. Local indigenous rulers are generally pictured historically as "those who governed"; almost invariably they are the central figures in the stories that relate the founding of pueblos. The Indian nobility sanctioned the history of pueblos and confirmed a community's legitimacy with respect to the lands it held.

Representatives of the indigenous nobility began to appear in the primordial titles in the first years of the seventeenth century. In 1635 the pueblo of Ayotzingo, Chalco (present-day state of México), probably produced a loosely bound book on paper that contained descriptions in Spanish of important events in the community since the year 1519. These jottings are accompanied by a map of the pueblo's lands on which a cacique is depicted. The cacique is portrayed in the style typical of the Techialoyan codices. This fact is interesting, since it demonstrates that these codices' particular style was developed before the mid-seventeenth century (Figure 2.6). The map marks a beginning, after which—year

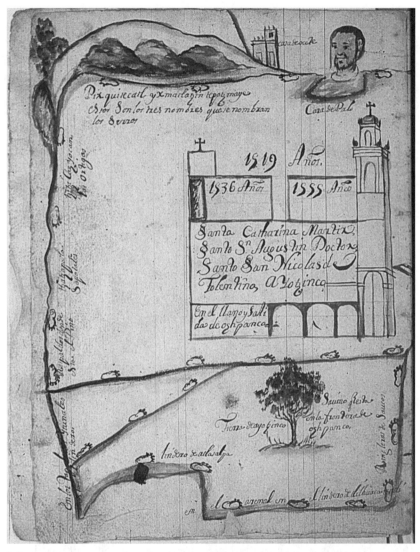

2.6 Reproduction, detail, no. 84 (no. 18 in Glass and Robertson 1975). Date: 1607–1635. Courtesy, National Library of France, Paris.

after year—the pueblo's artists painted images of its different ruling nobles. What is most interesting is to view both the stylistic variation in the depiction of the nobles and the combining of different styles in some of the documents (Figure 2.7). The fusing of styles indicates that different artists were involved in the production of the maps. Stylistically, the drawing technique in the last group is

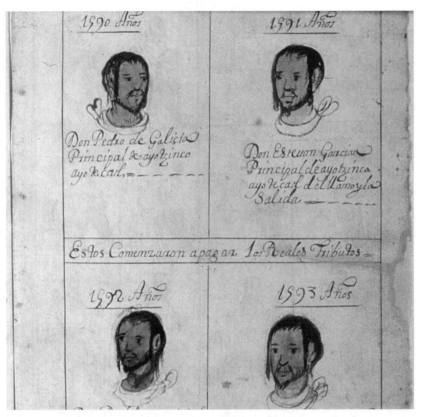

2.7 Reproduction, detail, no. 84 (no. 18 in Glass and Robertson 1975). Date: 1607–1635. Courtesy, National Library of France, Paris.

almost juvenile (Figure 2.8). The pueblo has left, as it were, a pictorial gallery of its local governors.

These images recall an oil painting produced in 1801 that forms an attachment to a group of titles belonging to the community of San Sebastian Tepatlachico, or Tepatlasco, Tepeaca, Puebla: a series of native nobles dressed in the eighteenth-century European style can be seen in the upper part of the image (Figure 2.9). From left to right, they bear the names Don Pablo Moctezuma, "legitimate cacique"; "I, don Felipe Chichimeca Tequeytli witness" (Chichimeca teuhctli is a title found in sixteenth-century documents that probably pertained to native nobility of the pre-Hispanic era); "I, don Bartolomé Zitlalpopoca legitimate cacique and witness"; and finally, "I, don Alonzo de Juan Bautista witness." Interestingly, the event to which they are witnesses is found in the document to which the "painting" is attached, indicating that it is the pictorial representation

2.8 Reproduction, detail, no. 84 (no. 18 in Glass and Robertson 1975). Date: 1607–1635. Courtesy, National Library of France, Paris.

of what is written in the document. Some of the nobles were witnesses to the preparation of this title, which—among other things—describes:

> Translation from the Mexican to the Spanish language of the title belonging to the pueblo of San Sebastián Tepatlasco and of don Francisco Quapinto granted to me by my god and later by my king don Luiz [Luis] de Velasco Charles the Fifth king of Spain and I was given three plots of land on which I serve my father San Sebastián and the boundaries of my land begin where the sun comes out, running alongside Santa María Magdalena and adjoining San Antonio and adjoining Santa Isabel on the north and marking a border in front of Matlacuey and adjoining the lands of Tlaxcala where the wolf gets warm and where you make a turn where the cypress is and where a corner stone is buried and then you go down through Ocosingo where the sun appears and adjoins San Agustín and you come to a stop in Agucatitlan.[130]

2.9 Reproduction, no. 2403. Date: 1801 (black-and-white photograph of the original, found in the Tepeaca[?] pueblo). Courtesy, Archivo General de la Nación, Mexico City.

In the execution of traditional maps, as the titles for the Indian communities of San Salvador Chachapan, Puebla, and San Juan Quetzalcuapan, Tlaxcala, indicate, local caciques were still depicted as guarantors of land at the very end of the colonial period.[131] In this respect, a map produced in 1817 by Indians from Santiago Tlaxoyaltepec, located in Etla, Oaxaca, depicted the caciques in western dress but also showed Indian fighters clothed in the manner of pre-Hispanic eagle warriors.[132] This latter element recalls the cloth map and titles that belonged to Santa Cruz Xoxocotlan, Oaxaca, on which the figure of an Indian governor is painted, perched on a type of throne or seat of authority (*icpalli* in Nahuatl) and dressed as an eagle warrior. The document states that the map was presented in 1660, when the boundary lines of Xoxocotlan's lands were demarcated.[133]

On this point, codices that employed a sophisticated style developed prior to the conquest were being produced in the Mixteca (upper, lower, and coastal) during the sixteenth century. On some of these codices, which the pueblos introduced in tribunals as part of their efforts to defend their land, members of the indigenous nobility were depicted as pairs of governors, generally shown perched on seats of power (*tayu* in Mixteco). One of many examples of the continuing use of this style in the early colonial period is the 1585 *Codex of Yucumana*.[134]

A seventeenth-century pictorial manuscript, found in the French National Library, depicts four tlatoque from México-Tenochtitlan mounted on jaguars. The image represents the genealogy of the Cano Moctezuma family; the names of the tlatoque are Quauhnochtli, Moteuhcoma, Acamapiltzin, and Don Francisco Sano (Cano?). This painted manuscript convincingly demonstrates that for the seventeenth-century descendants of the ancient native nobility, a clear association existed between indigenous royalty and vital symbols of pre-Hispanic power such as the jaguar.

A date, composed in indigenous numerals, appears on the right-hand side of the manuscript with a gloss that reads "date of the original map." Beneath this is the inscription "One hundred and forty-five years marked off since the founding of Mexico," thus placing the date of the manuscript at 1666 (Figure 2.10).[135]

The Indians of pre-Hispanic Mexico undoubtedly believed their leaders were endowed with special powers that distinguished them from the rest of the community. In addition to presiding over ritual events and celebrations, they served as intermediaries between men and the gods.

One can posit, therefore, that an association also existed between the image of power attached to the native nobility and the historical legitimacy the Indian pueblos asserted in the colonial period with respect to their lands. It would otherwise be impossible to explain why in so many maps, codices, and pictographs, as well as various written documents, the Indians took such pains to "show" their land as linked to and united with the power of their native lords, since in many regions the native nobility had long since lost its high social and political status. That effort was accompanied by a parallel effort to assert the legitimacy of noble lineages.

Yet in some pueblos in the regions of Puebla and Oaxaca, Indian noble families were still accorded exceptional recognition as figures of power. Indeed, in the

2.10 Reproduction, no. 388 (no. 37 in Glass and Robertson 1975). Date: seventeenth century. Courtesy, National Library of France, Paris.

pueblo of Cuauhtinchan, which has produced splendid pictorial documents[136] such as the *Mapa de Cuauhtinchan no. 2,* with its powerful images of ritual sacrifice and sacred statuary, the descendants of the pre-Hispanic ruling lineages have maintained power and lands to the present day.[137]

The fact that the native nobility, the legitimate indigenous governing authorities, continued to possess great symbolic power throughout the colonial period was in part a result of the important role oral tradition played within Indian pueblos. The symbols of power surrounding ancient members of the native nobility were tied to and transmitted by this tradition. Similarly, a long-held tradition underlay the symbolic power of the indigenous "native lords," or local governors, and their forbears—who occasionally merge into a single entity and are imaginatively represented as the mediators of divine forces. In 1795, for example, the Indians of Huizquilucan (state of México) were denounced by the *provisor* (an ecclesiastical judge who oversaw the Indians' religious affairs) for having constructed, with great enthusiasm, a "chapel or place of worship" devoted exclusively to venerating the ancient Mexica emperor Moctezuma. The offending edifice was located on a hill near the pueblo, which also bore the emperor's name. On top of this outrage, according to the provisor, some caves in the surrounding area contained the images of several idols (representations of the Indians' ancient gods).[138] This episode demonstrates that at the end of the colonial period, the Indians still beheld their ancient rulers in a sacred light.

Based on his recent analysis of the first folio of the *Historia tolteca-chichimeca* (superbly edited by Kirchhoff and Luis Reyes), Michael Swanton has shown that an ancient text existed in the Popoloca language that was apparently related to a rite by which rulers were enthroned. The text was probably invoked in a carefully guarded way by those entrusted with watching over it and also, perhaps, by those responsible for administering the ritual.[139]

This interesting hypothesis helps reinforce the idea that the *Historia tolteca-chichimeca* is intended to exalt the lineage of a ruling family of Cuauhtinchan. In my opinion, it also reveals something else about the *Historia*—that it helps substantiate the theory that the history of Indian pueblos, the history of the land on which they sit and that surrounds and encloses them, is indissolubly tied to local government and the exercise of local power.

Up to a certain point, this type of association between governing authority and land is more readily made when a relatively early and vivid example—such as that embodied in the *Historia tolteca-chichimeca*—is at hand. But has a similar source for this association been left to us from the later colonial period, when the power and authority of many Indian noble lineages suffered a slow and inexorable dissolution? I believe the association lasted longer than might be thought.

One indication that it did endure is found in primordial titles from colonial Cuernavaca. Several of those titles focus particular attention on a sixteenth-century Indian noble named Don Toribio Sandoval de San Martín Cortés. In the documents, Don Toribio is portrayed as a local hero linked in a timeless way to the *tlatocayotl* (domain) of Cuernavaca.[140]

Similarly, in 1698 the residents of a district called Texinca, which belonged to the pueblo of San Miguel Atlatlauca—which, in turn, was subject to the jurisdiction of Tlalmanalco (located at the southern tip of the Valley of Mexico)— submitted in court that their pueblo had possessed its own lands prior to being absorbed into San Miguel in the seventeenth century under the program of congregación. In particular, they called attention to certain lands, now threatened, that had belonged to them from time "immemorial."[141]

The circumstances of the case followed a familiar pattern. In 1606, as happened to many other indigenous communities at different times, the Indians of Texinca were resettled into a larger pueblo, one whose location better suited the Spanish colonists and administrators—in this case, San Miguel Atlatlauca. Prior to leaving their lands, the Texincans received a kind of security bond, signed by the juez congregador, that guaranteed their lands.[142] This document, given its official nature, would supposedly impede Spanish ranchers from opportunistically taking over land that had been "abandoned" as a result of the forced relocation of Indian pueblos.[143] The documents given to the Indians certified that the lands they left behind belonged to them, regardless of the distance that separated those lands and the Indians' new place of settlement. In practice, because of the distances involved, Indian pueblos often rented their old lands either to Spaniards or to other Indian communities in order to gain revenue and to maintain ownership over them.

The community of Texinca had decided to give the governor of the pueblo to which they became subordinate, San Miguel, the legal authority to rent their lands. In 1698, however, the parties who had succeeded that authority tried to sell the lands to a rancher named Baltasar de Mellado, who lived in the vicinity. Although they had not administered their lands for more than ninety years and operated at a disadvantage given their subordinate status as a district of the pueblo of San Miguel, the Texincans decided to lodge a formal protest.[144]

In doing so, they displayed a series of documents that clearly demonstrated the association that existed among the history of specific governing lineages, the governed, and their land. More particularly, they produced a royal grant from the sixteenth century that established that the lands under dispute were theirs. They also presented the official document issued by the juez congregador in 1606, certifying their possession of the lands, as well as a letter sent to them by a cattle rancher in the mid-seventeenth century expressing his appreciation to them for having rented the lands to him.[145] Finally, the Texincans decided to draw up a map that would convincingly validate their ancient possession of the lands, a map depicting the arrival in the territory of the pueblo's first noble governors, the *teochichimecas*, after their migration. The map is accompanied by an explanatory gloss that highlights the noble lords' different ranks, or categories of status: "*do[n] Martín Tlitecatzinchichimeca Teuctli*," "*Juan Toyaotzin chichimeca teuctli*"[146] (Figure 2.11).

This last rank, or station, within indigenous society also appears in a document pertaining to nobility of the Puebla region in the mid-sixteenth century,[147] as well as in the gloss on the manuscript entitled *Mexicain no. 73*, housed in the French National Library, which comes from the pueblo of Calpan (see Chapter 1).

These documents and their depictions underscore that the titles of the ancient indigenous nobility continued to be passed down through the pueblos' oral history, even in pueblos as fragmented and small as Texinca, reduced to simply a district of San Miguel. Perhaps even more interesting, however, is the way the Texincans represented members of the nobility, portraying them as historical chichimecas. The figure and gestural characteristics of one of these nobles can be compared with his equivalent in the *Mapa Tlotzin*, elaborated more than 140 years earlier in the Tezcoco region. In the Texinca map, two other essential features can also be observed: the traditional use of a toponym (*tecuancalc, tequan-*

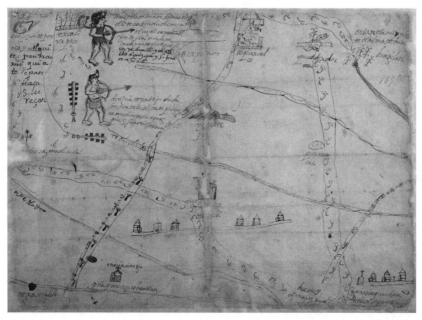

2.11 Reproduction, no. 1175. Date: seventeenth century. Courtesy, Archivo General de la Nación, Mexico City.

calco) and the recourse to ancestors as rulers who legitimized the historical possession of certain lands.

This association of pueblo, land, and noble authorities was so widespread during the colonial period that the Spanish themselves used it, in an apocryphal way, to gain legal sanction of their purchases or improper usurpations of land from the Indian pueblos. Indeed, ranchers and hacendados sometimes ordered the forging of documents and maps that purported to show the purchase and sale of lands by a region's ancient Indian caciques as a way of proving legitimate ownership of their cattle ranches and farms.

One such case, from the mid-eighteenth century, involved a Spanish constable, Juan de Palafox y Rivera. The constable sold a group of Nahuatl documents, as well as a codex executed on cloth (Figure 2.12), to a hacendado who lived in the Tlaxcala region. Once in possession of these "indigenous documents," the hacendado tried to maintain that they were the authentic property titles that had originally belonged to an Indian—a descendant of caciques—from whom he had purchased the land.[148]

The hacendado apparently engaged in these machinations because he lacked any legal proof of ownership and had been accused of illegally appropriating land

2.12 Reproduction, no. 890. Date: eighteenth century. Courtesy, Archivo General de la Nación, Mexico City.

belonging to the Indian cabildo of Tlaxcala. The *"pintura"* depicts the supposed cacique, Don Diego Naxaxa, and his spouse in the manner of Spaniards, attired in Spanish dress. "His people" are sporting feathers, blankets, and loincloths (*maxt-latl*) and are also wearing xihuitzolli. The host of conquering Spaniards looms at the left. It is noteworthy that two opposite associations are made in this work: the Indian nobility is represented entirely in the image of Europeans, whereas the Indian commoners are represented as barbarians.

The important lesson to be drawn from this document is that the Spanish themselves occasionally set out to justify their possession of land by resorting to the claim that it had been ceded or sold to them by one or more Indian nobles, native lords, or caciques. In this particular case, the scheme was exposed. Events and Indians from the sixteenth century had been re-created and, in an attempt to make them look old and authentic, the writings and painted manuscript were roughed up and wrinkled. In addition, a royal decree bearing the signature of Emperor Charles V, ordering that the lands belonged to the Indian noble "Don Diego Naxaxa y Becerra," had been forged. As the final piece of his evidence, the hacendado presented a Nahuatl document and map, dated 1559, describing and illustrating boundary markers and land that conveniently coincided with or formed part of his hacienda.

Criminal charges of producing forged documents were brought against the constable Palafox and the hacendado, and both confessed that an Indian woman from the outskirts of Tlaxcala had done the work for them. The audiencia's judges made a point of emphasizing that the false titles should be destroyed, but for some reason the map eluded this fate.

As noted previously, actions taken by the Crown beginning in the final years of the sixteenth century led to a steady loss of power among the native nobility. To a great extent, these measures by the Crown deprived the nobles of the Indian labor they had traditionally commanded. As a consequence, the tlatoque and pipiltin took to selling or renting their lands, especially those near Mexico City and Puebla, where the loss of the Indian workforce was felt most acutely. In many cases, moreover, the tlatoque were losing not only economic but jurisdictional power as well. Indicative of this trend is the fact that in various pueblos during the seventeenth and eighteenth centuries, the membership of Indian cabildos began to be filled by commoners and mestizos, whereas previously cabildo members had been Indian nobles. In addition, on the basis of forged documents, some Indians in the eighteenth century managed to have their cacicazgos—whether real or fictitious—legally recognized by the Spanish authorities.[149] A portion of them even claimed in these documents that Hernán Cortés had accorded them recognition as caciques in 1521. Other Indians, such as those from Calpulalpan in the Sierra Juárez of Oaxaca, incorporated symbols of power that were important for Spaniards as well as for native Americans, such as the two-headed eagle.[150]

In this period, furthermore, some communities that had never had a tlatoque were accorded the status of those that did by successfully inventing a descendant of a nonexistent noble lineage as a resident of the community. At the end of the colonial period, the established nobility who belonged to pueblos near Mexico City continued to enjoy a privileged status of sorts, but its members no longer functioned as authorities, and many now lacked any power to command. In some areas, however, the native nobility did maintain its traditional power through the eighteenth century. Such was the case, for example, in the areas of Tecali and Cuauhtinchan, near Puebla.[151] There, the native Mixtecan lords (*iya* in Mixteco) retained substantial power well into the nineteenth century.[152] In general, native rulers across Mesoamerica incurred the loss of jurisdictional power; within this broad pattern, though, some Indians of noble lineage continued to enjoy a preeminent position in their communities, as well as a degree of economic and political power, throughout the colonial period.

In many instances, however, another colonial-era indigenous institution that often drew up titles or mandated that action and that sometimes served as a political refuge for noble leaders did not retain its power and prestige. That institution was the Indian cabildo, or municipal council, which the colonial authorities established in New Spain in the mid-sixteenth century. The Indian cabildo became the mechanism through which the traditional tlatoque were drained of their power to rule over the native population.[153] While at the outset cabildo service may have been the purview only of Indian nobles, over time the fact that the council members were made salaried officials and that their period of service was limited led to the bureaucratization of this sector of indigenous society. These functionaries' salaries came from the community's treasury. Initially, the Indian cabildo—supported by the missionaries and the colony's first viceroys—carried out ceremonies and celebrations that gave its work a special aura. During the sixteenth century, for example, the cabildo of Tlaxcala produced a series of magnificent mural paintings featuring Emperor Charles V and King Philip II. Tlaxcala may have been a special case, since its cabildo was the most important indigenous municipal council during the colonial period, but it was not unique.[154]

By the end of the eighteenth century, this sense of ceremony had gradually dissipated, especially in the pueblos of the Valley of Mexico. Indian cabildo members now devoted themselves mainly to collecting the despised tribute and to jailing the chronically inebriated among the native population. As a further sign of the decline, the word *tecpan*, which referred to the ruler's palace or to the seat of government during the colonial period, had become synonymous with a jail; in addition, many Indian municipal buildings had fallen into a noticeably disreputable state.[155] Although by the eighteenth century most Indian cabildo members in the Valley of Mexico could sign their names,[156] that ability did not extend to their counterparts in areas away from urban centers. With the exception of some sectors of its leadership, the majority of New Spain's native population was alphabetically illiterate.

The members of Indian cabildos were chosen through elections held in one of several places—the tecpan, the local church, or the cabildo offices—and their service generally rotated. The viceroys had the prerogative of ratifying these elections, and they exercised control over them through the corregidores. Another person who intervened in the elections held by cabildos during the eighteenth century was the parish priest who served the Indian pueblos. The members of Indian cabildos had to adhere to a number of conditions: they could not be found drunk, they could not arrange for their immediate reelection, they had to cooperate with the Spanish authorities, and they had to be of pure Indian blood, although in many cases mestizos managed to hold the office. During the seventeenth century, the colonial authorities made an unsuccessful attempt to require that cabildo members understand Spanish.[157] Throughout the colonial period, Indians elected to serve on their municipal councils maintained the custom of traveling to Mexico City to have their post confirmed by the viceroy. Once confirmed, they were authorized to use their staffs of office.[158]

The functions Indian cabildo members—governors and magistrates in particular—carried out included administering justice in lower-level cases. Each pueblo had a jail in which Indians convicted of disturbing the peace could be locked up by order of the authorities. In Charles Gibson's opinion, the records of judicial proceedings conducted by the Indian cabildos demonstrate a highly cultivated legal consciousness among the Indian authorities.[159] Along with the cabildos, the pueblos also maintained councils or bodies of elders, which, according to Gibson, implied the existence of a community power that had survived the imposition of Spanish colonial authority.[160] These councils served a symbolic function; they were probably responsible for preserving the pueblo's history as well as its long-held documents.

Both the cabildo's authorities and the Indian nobles who drew up or presented titles and documents to defend their lands in the courts occasionally used arguments that were not only based on the pueblo's actual history but that were also in line with the traditional Mesoamerican view of the world. The actions of two Oaxacan pueblos provide a case in point. In the last decade of the seventeenth century, embroiled in litigation over land, the pueblos presented Spanish authorities with primordial titles in both Nahuatl and Mixtec and a map. All three documents supposedly dated back to the 1520s. The Nahuatl title, which belonged to the pueblo of San Martín Mexicapan, stated that in 1520, four warriors from Central Mexico responded to a request for help made by a great "noblewoman of the Zapotecs." The noblewoman complained that the Mixtecs had threatened her people and had committed acts of cannibalism on a rescue party she had dispatched (interestingly, an alliance existed in the fifteenth century between Nahuas and Zapotecs against the Mixtecs). The woman had warned the Nahuas that they should document these events in writing, to leave a record of them for posterity.[161]

The warriors, according to the Nahuatl title, approached Hernán Cortés, "the lord of the children of the sun," and feigned a battle in an attempt to convince him that they could achieve success where others had failed. Impressed by the warriors' strength, Cortés sent them into battle. They fought as they journeyed through the mountainous Mixtec region and descended into the Valley of Oaxaca, where they confronted and defeated the Mixtec in the midst of a violent storm and an earthquake. As a reward for this victory, they and their descendants were given land. When Cortés arrived in Oaxaca, however, the alliance collapsed, and the Spaniards and Nahuas prepared to battle each other. The Nahuas confused and frightened the Spaniards by causing a flood, which induced the Spaniards to sue for peace. The Nahuas proudly proclaimed that they had defeated everyone and had even captured some African slaves. These "renowned Mexicans" referred to their victory as "the original conquest."[162]

The Mixtec titles from the second pueblo, San Juan Chapultepec, a subject community of Cuilapan, narrated the actions in a less grandiloquent way and rejected the Nahua version of events in favor of their own. These Mixtec claimed that they welcomed Hernán Cortés when he reached Oaxaca and gave land to him and to the men in his party. All went well until Cortés returned with a group of Nahuas from Central Mexico, at which point the Mixtec began to fight them. The Spanish intervened only when the Mixtec forced the Nahuas to surrender. The Mixtec ruler cooperated with Cortés and accommodated the interests of each party, finding a site where the Nahuas could settle down. Henceforth, according to the Mixtec titles, the Mixtec, Nahuas, Zapotecs, and Spanish had coexisted peacefully in the Valley of Oaxaca.[163] The Nahua version of the story is especially interesting because it introduces magical forces into their confrontations with the Mixtec and the Spanish—for example, when the Nahuas call down floods and earthquakes to help them during battle.

These examples, which manifest themselves in primordial titles submitted by the pueblos, illustrate the survival of old, pre-Hispanic modes of thought among the Indians. Few traces of this predilection, however, are found in other documents emanating from the Indian cabildos, which overall are rather scarce. In addition, no other information exists that might reveal precisely how the indigenous authorities went about negotiating matters of vital importance to their pueblos with high-level colonial administrators. The *Actas de cabildo* (official records of the municipal council), such as those from Tlaxcala and Tula, Hidalgo, shed interesting light on the councils' daily activities but rarely disclose anything relevant to understanding the persistence of traditional thinking in their work or anything that might yield insight into the pueblos' reaction to the policies civil and ecclesiastical authorities followed regarding them.[164]

The annals of indigenous tradition compiled by the cabildos do offer, in a smattering of cases, a small amount of information about matters that, because of their secret nature, are rarely detected in public records. One such example is *El Libro de los guardianes y gobernadores de Cuauhtinchan*, which covers the sixteenth century. This record provides details concerning the political and theological discussions that took place between the missionaries assigned to the pueblo and the nobles who served on its cabildo.

The tome records a variety of happenings, year by year and in both Nahuatl and Spanish. The Nahuatl section, for example, mentions the appointment of local officials and the outbreak of epidemics, while the Spanish part records events that occurred in the Iberian Peninsula, which were undoubtedly the subject of frequent conversation among missionaries in the Cuauhtinchan convent.[165]

In the latter category, for example, the Cuauhtinchan annals record that in 1559, the remains of Dr. Constantino were committed to the flames and that

Dr. Agustín Cazalla was tossed into a fire and burned alive, along with many others.[166] These events were inspired by Philip II's organized persecution of the Erasmists. In another epoch, Dr. Constantino—who, because of the accusation that he was a follower of Erasmus, had languished and died in the dungeons during the Inquisition—would have served as confessor to Emperor Charles V. He was also a disciple of Bartolomé Carranza de Miranda, a close friend and associate of Fray Bartolomé de Las Casas. The condemnation of Constantino and other Erasmists undoubtedly disturbed Cuauhtinchan's Franciscan missionaries, since in the late 1550s some members of the order still operated under the influence of Erasmus's ideas. Indeed, a catechism that Fray Juan de Zumárraga wrote in 1546 drew its inspiration from his reading of Constantino's work.[167] There is a hint, an echo in the Cuauhtinchan annals, of the discussions over political, religious, and philosophical issues that the missionaries may have held with the pueblo's Indians. Such discussion was at the root of the persecution of the Erasmists.

Since allusions to this type of information or discussion were rare in the Indians' writings, we can only draw veiled inferences from the documentation that does survive. Of interest in this context is that some Indian cabildos retained codices and pictorial manuscripts that open a window to their ancient world and way of life. This understanding can be glimpsed in two lienzos still kept under lock and key in the town hall of San Miguel Tequistepec, a pueblo located in Oaxaca's Valle de Coixtlahuaca. Its original inhabitants were cholotecas (*ngigua*), but they stopped speaking the local language long ago. In an earlier era, the lienzos had been under the care of the pueblo's Indian cabildo. One of them (Figure 2.13), dating from the sixteenth century and executed on cloth, contains a complex genealogy grounded in myth as well as historical-cartographic imagery. Two pairs of kings or native lords, the sovereigns of Tequistepec and Coixtlahuaca, respectively, appear conspicuously in the center. Both pairs are mounted on jaguars, the symbol of power par excellence. The toponym (place name) of the pueblo, represented as a hill with a seashell inside it, appears under them and to their side.

Little is known about this lienzo.[168] The present-day inhabitants of Tequistepec generally believe it narrates the history of a king.[169] In this sense, the lienzo would seem to be metaphorical, since in effect it depicts the genealogy of the ancient governors of Tequistepec, whose origins lie in the birth of its royal ancestors at the point of the "Great River." The lienzo, interestingly, was not seen by outsiders until 1970.[170] Because of a legal matter that affected the pueblo, however, the representation of a corral—enclosed with animals—was added to the lienzo sometime during the colonial period (Figure 2.14). When the various images are compared, the style in which the corral was drawn appears fairly simple in contrast to the rest of the lienzo. This sharp difference clearly emerges, for

2.13 Reproduction, digital photograph of details from the *Lienzo of Tequixtepec*. Original found in the pueblo of San Miguel Tequixtepec. Date: sixteenth century. Courtesy, Instituto Nacional de Antropología e Historia, Mexico City.

example, in the image of the native rulers mounted on jaguars, which is striking in its execution.

It is evident from this lienzo and from its handling that the pueblo of Tequistepec has placed considerable value on preserving its traditions. The secrecy with which the lienzo was guarded until the twentieth century underscores the great symbolic power Tequistepec's caciques exercised over the pueblo. This power came to light in 1586, when Tequistepec's cacique was jailed after facing charges of idolatry. The cacique, Don Diego de San Miguel, was accused of having the pueblo's elders and members of its cabildo accompany him to the local church, where he warned the Indians not to forget their ancient gods. He also visited the Indians who lived around the pueblo at night to issue the same warning. The cacique was accused of possessing ritual codices, which he brandished threateningly before the Indians, and of sacrificing birds in his house. There seems little doubt that in his manner of living, he was guided by ancestral customs. Furthermore, although the cacique's father, Don Miguel, had been buried in the pueblo's church around 1565, funeral ceremonies that followed pre-Hispanic religious ritual were still being conducted for him. For example, gold objects and silver coins were spread out for the cacique to accompany him on his journey to the great beyond.[171] According to present-day residents of Tequistepec, the pueblo's titles were taken to the Archivo General de la Nación, and they had been "lined with human skin"[172]—a practice that recalled ancient rituals of human sacrifice that preceded the ceremonial founding of a pueblo.

2.14 Reproduction, digital photograph of details from the *Lienzo of Tequixtepec*. Original found in the pueblo of San Miguel Tequixtepec. Date: sixteenth century. Courtesy, Instituto Nacional de Antropología e Historia, Mexico City.

This disposition to link on a metaphorical level particular places and the founding of pueblos with human sacrifice occurs throughout Mesoamerica. In the Nahua community of Atliaca (in the present state of Guerrero), for example, people say that the pueblo's "ancient" bridge (a small bridge of colonial vintage) has human blood in its mortar and that the blood is also present in the church tower.[173]

The fact that during the colonial period the pueblos' traditional authority figures and members of Indian cabildos still kept alive a complex cosmology inherited from the past is brought into even sharper relief by contemporary data about gatherings and assemblies that have taken place in various Indian pueblos. Between 1950 and 1960, for example, several families in Atliaca managed to take over the majority of the pueblo's wells. The pueblo evidently had five wells; three were being used by these families, which left the remaining two for the pueblo's other residents. Weary of this injustice, the campesinos held a meeting to discuss the matter. The *topile* (constable) of Atliaca recalls that as the discussion progressed about whether a suit should be filed against the families, a man named Don Diego—who was accustomed to looking for water in different parts of the locale—told the people assembled that they need not file a suit, since he was able to tell them where there was water; in fact, he explained, it was only necessary "to pick up or remove the stone and the water would gush forth." Nevertheless, after much debate, the pueblo decided not to follow Don Diego's advice because "the gentlemen" (*caballeros*) would be upset and perhaps, therefore, disinclined to help them. They therefore decided to carry their complaint to the courts.[174] By "gentlemen" the Atliacans mean the beings, or superior powers, who cause rain to fall and fight against "evil" forces so that water might exist. These caballeros fly through the heavens and at night "are the meteorites and when they are seen it is because they are fighting and give off sparks."[175]

Following the same logic, the Ch'oles, an indigenous Mexican people who live in Chiapas, maintain a body called the community committee (*junta comunitaria*). This committee, an institution of fundamental importance in Ch'ole social organization, meets when important issues need to be reviewed. The committee is a pivotal concept in Ch'ole social thought, the underlying principles of which are rooted in ancient Mayan mythology. The junta's meetings sometimes take place in caves, a classic setting for religious worship.[176]

These chronicles and stories indicate that in the realm of local discussion and decision, as embodied in the workings of the colonial Indian cabildo, problems both mundane and supernatural were discussed with equal interest and vigor. To the European way of thought, this proposition seems unreal, but to the indigenous folk, both were aspects of a single timeless reality.

TRADITIONAL INDIGENOUS TITLES AND MAPS IN THE CONTEXT OF THE SACRED

The Indians' sacred bundles or vessels were made up of objects associated with the gods. These objects were generally wrapped in cloth and, in Nahuatl, were called *tlaquimilolli*. The tradition of assembling bundles of sacred objects extended across a wide geographic zone and did not stop at the borders of Mesoamerica. In pre-Hispanic times, these objects were worn by priests and kept in the temples.[177] Among other functions, they enabled men to communicate with the gods.[178] Moreover, society in ancient Mexico was punctuated by a clear association between the sacred bundles and rituals of power.[179]

Under the Spanish a new regimen was installed, and these sacred objects that connected men to the gods were banned, along with their worship. There are indications, however, that on occasion during the colonial period some of the objects continued to be used and to serve their intended function. One such example occurred in 1745, when Indians from the pueblo of Tenango del Valle (present-day state of México) surreptitiously made their way to a nearby cave in which they had hidden idols they continued to worship. The cave also contained a flint mask, guarded zealously by the Indians, "which, when worn over your face enabled you to look upon everyone and to see these parts of the world which so many people wanted to see."[180] Thus, in the second half of the eighteenth century the Indians continued to display reverence for sacred objects that possessed magical powers, such as the flint mask. Although such cases were infrequent, they nonetheless occurred throughout the colonial period. Occurring much more frequently among the Indians was the practice of associating items they perceived as holding symbolic power for the Europeans with their own traditional sacred objects.

Papal bulls emanated from the pontifical chancellery and were used to put a seal of authenticity on church documents. In 1594 Pope Sixtus V broadened the Bull of the Holy Crusade, extending its reach to the dominions of the Spanish empire and thus to the New World. The bull was a form of papal concession, granting indulgences to the faithful. The church issued the indulgences on paper, to be purchased—at various prices—by those who wanted them. The Indians of New Spain became enamored of this practice and soon acquired a considerable number of indulgences. Reflecting their newfound passion, in 1599 a compendium was published in Nahuatl describing "the virtues of the Bulls of the Holy Crusade."[181]

In the early seventeenth century, however, the Crown reversed its policy with respect to the Indians' access to papal bulls. King Philip III ordered the heads of religious orders in the Indies to gather up all the papal Bulls of the Holy Crusade the native population possessed. In 1621 the Crown specifically ruled that Spaniards alone were allowed to acquire, handle, and collect these bulls. Furthermore, all of the bulls in circulation had to be tallied and inventoried to ensure that the Indians no longer possessed any. The order was universal—not a single copy of the Bull of the Holy Crusade could remain under the control of Indian pueblo authorities or commoners. Following the 1621 edict, royal instructions relative to papal bulls specified that they had to be printed in Spanish and not in Latin.[182]

The steps taken to deny the indigenous population access to papal bulls probably stemmed from the magical use some Indians made of them. Although the bulls formed part of the official rites of Catholic faith and observance in the Indies,[183] the Indians occasionally interpreted and treated the documents in a very heterodox way. The bulls, as we shall see, were sometimes added to the sacred bundles the Indians used in their rituals; they were used to help give the traditional codices or some other type of non-Christian practice more power. The bulls' strength and power resulted from their sacred character, which the Indians believed could be released and transferred to elements of pre-conquest indigenous religion. For the native population, the use of the bulls accomplished a double objective: it invoked and increased the power of the ancient gods while

133

adding to that power the strength of the Christian God. The fact that the bull was a physical object that could be readily incorporated into indigenous ceremonies and rites made it, by its very nature, a symbol of power. For example, in mentioning the tribute collected from the Indians, the sacred book of *Chilam Balam de Chumayel* states that the burden was lifted through a bull. The passage refers to a decree passed by the Cortes of Cádiz in 1806:[184] "And that is the coming of the bull with six parts to it. Three times the bull will be brought. Then will arrive the judge's bull. Either the collector of the money will be judge."[185]

On these points, John Chuchiak has noted the importance the papal bulls had for the colonial-era Maya as sacred objects and has shown how they were incorporated into traditional Mayan beliefs. Underlying these observations was his desire to understand why a well-known pre-Hispanic Mayan codex, the *Códice Madrid*, should have had a papal bull attached to it. The bull, a Bull of the Holy Crusade, was made from paper that dated to the late sixteenth or early seventeenth century and was probably attached to the codex during that time span. The person who had placed the bull on the codex was possibly a native Mayan.[186] The Maya, even those who taught the catechism, failed to understand the true nature of the bulls; sermons delivered in the Mayan tongue generally stressed that they were "sacred" and miraculous.[187] Beginning at the end of the sixteenth century, some Maya accepted the bulls as sacred reliquaries and began to treat them as they treated any other sacred object—for example, by offering sacrifices to them and using them in dances and celebrations. Chuchiak refers to an Englishman, Jon Chiltern, who traveled through Mexico in 1579 and remarked, with respect to the papal bulls: "[T]he spiritual value of the 'Bulas de la Cruzada' was not fully understood by the Indians, as they would tear them up into little pieces, sticking them onto the walls of their houses, with the hope of gaining pardons for thousands of years."[188]

Thus, a Mayan scribe or Indian nobleman may have placed the copy of the bull onto the codex as a way of blessing it.[189] Or he may have used the bull as a means of drawing in the power of the Christian religion,[190] so that it adhered to an object—the codex—the Maya considered sacred. In these years, priests with Indian flocks informed the ecclesiastical authorities that the population of literate Indians included some who wrote codices and hid them, later reading them in secret nocturnal gatherings.[191]

In 1684 a group of Zapotec Indians from the pueblo of San Francisco Caxonos was put on trial on charges of committing idolatry. During the trial, the Spanish authorities were told about an Indian woman who—with great secrecy—had wrapped up sheets of *yaguichi* paper (made of cloth from maguey bark), together with some feathers, and stored them in a house. The yaguichi, according to the report, was "an instrument of idolatry proving their [the Indians'] gentile state."[192] Another Indian had apparently removed the bundled papers from the house and carried them off. Upon being discovered, he abandoned them. The Spanish authorities described the contents of the wrappings: "a small pouch of palm leaves, a sheet of *Yaguichi* bark paper hammered into a piece about two yards long, and eight small wrappings tied up with little cords made of the same *Yaguichi* and inside them some green and red feathers and some small branches of leaves from the pine tree, and all of the wrappings seem to have been freshly made and were very bloody."[193]

The Indians on trial also had another small palm leaf pouch with two old bundles. The pouch contained several items: the leaf of a cornstalk enclosing strands of hair, a bird's head, feathers, a squash with powdery substances, a piece of yaguichi, and "a holy bull of the fourth sermon of the ninth conception of Paul V," along with a piece of coarse muslin-like cloth.[194] The sacred bundles the Indians of Caxonos used in their rituals were composed of these sorts of objects.

It is also clear that New Spain's native population incorporated the papal bulls into the rituals it devoted to the ancient gods. Like the Maya who attached a bull to the *Codex Madrid*, Indians elsewhere in the colony did the same with other codices. A Bull of the Holy Crusade, for example, appears in the earlier-cited record of the pueblo of Magdalena Mixuca, located on the outskirts of Mexico City.[195] Similarly, an eighteenth-century (although bearing the date 1672) codex from San Luis Huexotlan (state of México) that depicts the local nobility and their lands has a copy, apparently granted in 1700, of the Bull of the Holy Crusade attached to its reverse side.[196] In a 1764 legal proceeding, the Indians of Amecameca (state of México) produced an extensive record of titles containing documents pertaining to their jurisdictional rights and boundaries, pictorial maps, pictures of their early rulers, and a papal bull.[197] A further example is found in the pueblo of Tepezintla, located in the northern sierra of Puebla, where the Indian residents have kept and preserved a strip of paper from the eighteenth century on which the caciques of the pueblo are represented. This fragmentary document, with a Nahuatl gloss, is again bound up with a Bull of the Holy Crusade dating to 1596.[198]

A clear association exists in each of these cases between the primordial titles, pictorial documents, maps, and the traditional native nobility on the one hand and the use of papal bulls on the other. A Testerian codex, produced in 1719, provides a vivid example of this linking of Christian and traditional indigenous power. The Testerian painted manuscripts were used by the church in Mexico from the sixteenth to the nineteenth centuries to teach Christian doctrine to Indians unfamiliar with an alphabetic writing system. In Elizabeth Hill Boone's opinion, for the colonial indigenous nobility, some of the Testerian codices were the equivalent of what the Book of Hours represented for the European nobility.[199]

Tellingly, inserted into the 1719 Testerian codex was a 1700 Bull of the Holy Crusade.[200]

In addition to its sacred character, the power of the papal bull lay in the fact that it was written alphabetically. As the case of the Indians from Caxonos indicates, both literate and illiterate Indians could use the bulls when conjuring magic. In colonial Mexico, as recent research has shown, ritual texts—containing calendar dates, magic spells, and other devotional jottings that mixed the two religions, old and new—circulated among the Indian pueblos. Some of these written texts had been passed down through generations, and the pueblo's spiritual authorities took great care with them, given their secretive nature.[201] In their zeal to possess them, the Indians sometimes stole books from the Spanish; because of their perceived magical powers, liturgical books may have been especially coveted. Prior to 1669, some Indians were hanged publicly in a convent in San Sebastián (location unknown) for the crime of having stolen "many books" from its premises.[202]

The attraction these artifacts held for the Indians is not surprising. Even today, books and other written texts of ritual character continue to play a role in the activities of some indigenous spiritual leaders. For example, in 1951 Pedro Carrasco discovered that the curanderos in the Oaxacan Chontal pueblo of Tequixtlatec used ritual texts—which they composed in their own language—dealing with such varied subjects as hunting, the agricultural seasons, and life cycles. The ritual writings were interspersed with drawings.[203]

Similarly, one of the Nahua curanderos of Atliaca—an unschooled Indian named Julio, nicknamed "the tipsy one"—had the habit some years ago of asking his fellow Atliaca, the lawyer and schoolmaster Modesto Vázquez Salgado, to purchase for him in the Merced Market in Mexico City—"where they sell books on witchcraft"—a book by Saint Cyprian.[204] This book, popularly known as "Ciprianillo," is a compendium of magic formulas, in particular those reputed to lift spells that have been cast over hidden treasures. In Vázquez Salgado's opinion, this book was "very large" in the past but is "much smaller" today. When he had the book, the curandero would head for the pueblo's church to have it blessed. Inside its pages, Don Julio "searched for what he needed to treat the sick." Armed with the book, he would carry out rituals in a cave in an area near Atliaca called Huezquizostoc. Apparently, the power that resided in the book gradually dissipated over time until it magically disappeared from the curandero's hands. Vázquez Salgado thus noted that the book "gives you courage to face evil forces, then at any moment it is lost, goes missing, the evil forces are purged because that book serves to cure what produces them."[205] Accordingly, Vázquez Salgado was prevailed upon to bring the curandero the same book on two occasions, which prompted him to ask the curandero—rather testily—if he had perhaps lost it while in a drunken state. The curandero replied that he had not lost the book;

instead, the book had "disappeared." This "disappearance" of the book could be associated with the loss of power contained in certain magical objects. For example, in the pueblo of Santiago Tlacotenco, located in the Valley of Mexico, the curanderos use stones called *chalchiuhteme*, or "jade stones," to heal people. These stones come from caves. When they "work" they give off a brilliance, but when their power diminishes they turn opaque and mysteriously disappear.[206]

The Indians' ritual use of books as magical objects is seen even more clearly in the case of an elderly Mixtec from the pueblo of Santa María Cuquila, in Oaxaca's Mixteca Alta. To divine the future and cure the misfortunes that befall those who come to him, this Indian uses a European book of magic published in the second half of the nineteenth century. The old man places a needle, hung from a thread, on top of the book. He then reads the passage in the book at the point where the needle has slid and come to rest, concentrating on interpreting its meaning for the person he is attending. Numerous people from surrounding pueblos consult the old man about various matters; on one occasion—as I witnessed firsthand— some people from the Mixteca Alta pueblo of Santiago Nuyoo sought him out because they had failed to receive news of relatives who had immigrated illegally to the United States. They hoped, or expected, that through his power the old man could reveal how their relatives were doing. The talk in Cuquila was that the Indian, Don Domingo Melchor, had learned his vocation in the mid-twentieth century from a trusted friend.[207] With respect to the old man's method of operation, John Monaghan has observed that for some Mesoamerican pueblos the act of reading is an extension of looking into the heart of things. In turn, the ability to see or visualize things is considered an expression or instance of wisdom. Shamans, in fact, possess the gift of being able to see the gods; a ritual connection exists between seeing a deeper reality and reading.[208]

Nonetheless, the dynamic can also work inversely. Just as the Indians see the papal bulls as an important symbol of power and therefore worthy of being linked to their titles and pictorial manuscripts, so, too, in some cases they demonstrate an interest in tying their own pictographic tradition to Christian symbols. The Zapotec pueblo of San Bartolo Yautepec provides an example of the latter. The pueblo's authorities had delivered choral books from 1600, containing Gregorian chants, to conservators for restoration. The conservators discovered—undoubtedly to their great surprise—that one of the books had a deerskin cover with religious glyphs on it, painted in a style dating prior to the Spanish conquest.[209] The book was originally owned by a literate Zapotec Indian. Another example is in the Schoyen Collection in the National Museum of Norway in Oslo, where there is a sixteenth-century book in Nahuatl that has an inserted Mexican codex that apparently deals with Indian tribute. The Nahuatl text that has been translated to English by Mark Z. Christensen, and refers to a heterodox version of San

Paul's conversion and about San Sebastian's ministry. It is reasonable to think that indigenous fiscals added the codex to the book.[210] This association can clearly be likened to the *cristos de caña*, the hollow papier-mâché–like images, made of cornstalks or other plants, of Christ on the Cross. The Christ figure of Mexicaltzingo is a prominent example.[211]

The church of Santo Domingo Tlaquiltenango, in Morelos, offers a similar example. In 1909 one of its walls was found to be covered with more than 100 fragments of codices. They were all the work of Indians.[212] In both cases—that of the cornstalk Christ figure and the one of the church—the codices were from the sixteenth century and dealt with the tribute and taxation exacted from the pueblos during that period. These cases are not incidental; several others exist, and I believe they express the Indians' intermixing of Christian and indigenous symbols of power. Yet the resulting synthesis demonstrates more than an overarching cultural dynamism; it also reveals the importance of the primordial titles and codices in the pueblos' affirmation of their identity.

The important legal uses to which the Indians put their maps, titles, and other pictorial documents, as well as books and papal bulls, clearly unfolded within the wider colonial context. Yet that context also enables us to see into the world of the Indian pueblo and to grasp something of the traditional thinking underlying it. The question is whether the legal, historical, and personal use of the codices, maps, and titles continued after the eighteenth century or whether it was confined to the colonial period. The record of independent Mexico provides an answer.

NOTES

1. Kellogg, *Law and the Transformation.*

2. Colin M. MacLachlan, *Criminal Justice in Eighteenth Century Mexico: A Study of the Tribunal of the Acordada* (Berkeley: University of California Press, 1974).

3. Amos Megged, "Poverty and Welfare in Mesoamérica during the Sixteenth and Seventeenth Centuries: European Archetypes and Colonial Translations," *Colonial Latin American Historical Review* 6, 1 (1997): 1–29.

4. Solórzano y Pereyra, *Política Indiana*, 1:206–210.

5. Jonathan I. Israel, *Race, Class and Politics in Colonial Mexico* (London: Oxford University Press, 1975), 21–22, 27.

6. Ibid., 27–28.

7. Ibid., 25–26, 28.

8. Ibid., 33–34.

9. Ibid., 51, 57.

10. Ibid., 39–41.

11. Gibson, *The Aztec*, 194.

12. A vara was a unit of measure, usually about 33 inches or 0.836 meter.

13. Gibson, *The Aztec*, 203.

14. Ibid., 213.

15. Ibid., 205.

16. Ibid., 215.

17. Ibid., 214; William Taylor, *Magistrates of the Sacred: Priests and Parishioners in Eighteenth-Century Mexico* (Stanford: Stanford University Press, 1996), 125–150.

18. Gibson, *The Aztec*, 218.

19. Ibid., 219.

20. Silvio Zavala, *El servicio personal de los indios en la Nueva España 1600–1635*, vol. 5, part 1 (Mexico City: El Colegio de México and El Colegio Nacional, 1990), 92–93.

21. Gibson, *The Aztec*, 251.

22. Israel, *Race, Class, and Politics*, 35.

23. Regarding the beginnings of this institution, see Ruiz Medrano, *Shaping New Spain*, esp. chapter 1.

24. Gibson, *The Aztec*, 93–94.

25. Ibid., 94.

26. Ibid., 95–96.

27. AGN, Tierras, 2811, exp. 5.

28. AGN, Bienes Nacionales, 596, exp. 12.

29. Ibid.

30. Ibid.

31. Natalia Silva Prada, *La política de una rebelión: Los indígenas frente al tumulto de 1692 en la Ciudad de México* (Mexico City: El Colegio de México and Centro de Estudios Históricos, 2007).

32. Zavala, *La encomienda*.

33. Israel, *Race, Class, and Politics*, 47.

34. Ibid., 50–51.

35. Ibid., 55.

36. Sonia Lipsett-Rivera, *To Defend Our Water with the Blood of Our Veins: The Struggle for Resources in Colonial Puebla* (Albuquerque: University of New Mexico Press, 1999), 151.

37. Ibid., 32–33, 37.

38. Gibson, *The Aztec*, 261–262.

39. Ibid., 211–212.

40. Ibid., 212.

41. Among numerous such cases, see AGN, Tierras, 1622, exp. 5 (1652); 2918, exp. 3 (1813).

42. Borah, "El status jurídico," 263–264.

43. Eusebio Buenaventura Beleña, *Recopilación sumaria de todos los autos acordados de la Real Audiencia y Sala del Crimen de esta Nueva España,* introduction by María del Refugio González (Mexico City: UNAM and Instituto de Investigaciones Jurídicas, 1991, facsimile ed.), 1:67–68, no. 122. On the change from 500 to 600 varas, see María Teresa Sepúlveda y Herrera, *Los lienzos de San Juan Cuauhtla, Puebla* (Mexico City: INAH and Miguel Angel Porrúa, 2005), 88; Gibson, *The Aztec*, 292–293.

44. Gibson, *The Aztec*, 293.

45. "Alabado sea el santísimo sacramento del altar. Los fundadores que en paz descansen y de [ileg.] gocen Fue Sebastián Damián López y Nicolás de la Cruz y Joseph de la Cruz y Felipe González y Francisco Gabriel Y Juan Esteban. Todos [demás] común y principales fundadores todos los mencionados fundaron y poblaron el puesto de Santa Bárbara nombrado." AGN, Tierras 1332, exp. 3. The original copy lacks color.

46. Ibid. 2722, exp. 3.

47. Gibson, *The Aztec*, 285–289.

48. Peter Gerhard, "Congregaciones de indios en la Nueva España antes de 1570," *Historia Mexicana* 26, 3 (1977): 347–395.

49. AGI, México 22, letter from Viceroy Luis de Velasco to the king, Mexico City, May 24, 1591.

50. Ibid., March 25, 1592.

51. *Recopilación de leyes, de los reinos de las Indias*, prologue by Ramón Menéndez y Pidal, preliminary study by Juan Manzano Manzano (Madrid: Cultura Hispánica, 1973), 4 vols. Law 10: That efforts be made to found pueblos de indios near the location of mines. Philip II, Valladolid, November 24, 1601.

52. Ernesto de la Torre Villar, *Las congregaciones de los pueblos de indios* (Mexico City: UNAM, 1995), 24–26.

53. Ibid., 26.

54. Ibid., 27, 54.

55. Gibson, *The Aztec*, 283.

56. Ibid., 283–285.

57. AGN, Tierras, 1663, exp. 1.

58. Torre Villar, *Las congregaciones*, 34.

59. Gibson, *The Aztec*, 285.

60. Ibid., 283–284; Torre Villar, *Las congregaciones*, 29.

61. AGN, Tierras 2764, exp. 1.

62. Ibid.

63. Torre Villar, *Las congregaciones*, 283n150.

64. Donald Robertson, "Techialoyan Manuscripts and Paintings, with a Catalog," in Howard F. Cline, ed., *Handbook of Middle American Indians*, vol. 14: *Guide to Ethnohistorical Sources*, part 3, 253–280 (Austin: University of Texas Press, 1975); Wood, "El problema de la historicidad."

65. López Caballero, *Los títulos primordiales*. See, for example, the titles belonging to Metepec, 132–143; San Antonio Zoyatzinco, 251–271; and San Matías Cuixinco, 272–302.

66. Ibid. See the titles belonging to San Bartolomé Capulhuac, 93–103; San Martín Ocoyoacac, 104–115; Metepec, 132–143; San Lorenzo Chiamilpa, 144–147; San Pablo Chapultepec, 152–155; Cuernavaca, 156–172; "Códice municipal de Cuernavaca," 178–191; San Gregorio Atlapulco, 196–203; Santa María Nativitas, 204–209; San Francisco Cuacuauzentlalpan, 210–218; Asunción Milpa Alta, 219–229; San Andrés Mixquic, 231–233; San Nicolás Tetelco, 234–237; Santa Marta Xocotepetllpan, 238–250; San Antonio Zoyatzinco, 251–271; San Matías Cuixinco, 272–302; de los Reyes, 309–320; San Juan Tenango, 321–329; Santiago Sula, 330–339; and San Miguel Atlauhtla, 340–349.

67. Baudot, *Utopia and History*, 491–524.

68. López Caballero, *Los títulos primordiales*; see, for example, the titles belonging to San Bartolomé Capulhuac, 93–103; and Coatepec de las Bateas, 116–130.

69. "Aquí se nombra San Juan Guautla aquí hicimos penitencia, mi nombre es Xihuitototli y cerro de los tecolotes y el cerro de los venados. Aquí es donde hacemos . . . y decimos aquí tenemos nuestras casas y que desde lejos lo deseamos los principales." Map of San Juan Huautla, Biblioteca del Museo Nacional de Antropología, Colección Códices. I am grateful for the assistance of Ignacio Silva in interpreting the Nahuatl text. María Teresa Sepúlveda y Herrera's *Los lienzos de San Juan Cuauhtla* contains a general study of this pictorial document. At least one copy of the map exists in a private collection, its source unknown, and I thank Sr. José Muñoz Medina for having allowed me to view it.

70. Roskamp, *La historiografía indígena*; Wood, *Transcending Conquest*; Stephanie Wood, "The Social vs. Legal Context of Nahuatl *Titulos*," in Elizabeth Hill Boone and Tom Cummins, eds., *Native Traditions in the Postconquest World,* 201–231 (Washington, D.C.: Dumbarton Oaks Research Library and Collection, 1998); Wood, "El problema de la historicidad"; Wood, "Don Diego García de Mendoza Moctezuma"; Oudijk, *Historiography*; López Caballero, *Los títulos primordiales*; Terraciano and Sousa, "Original Conquest."

71. "[T]omando un poco de polilla de madera . . . de las soleras y cociendo esto con agua de tequesquite [un tipo de piedra caliza que se mezcla con el maíz para hacer la masa] cualquier papel blanco, nuevo rociado y puesto en humedad toma el color que parece muy antiguo. Y a más de esto estar estos mismos papeles puesto a secar en horno hasta que se tostaron, fuera de esto las marcas de dichos papeles son de las modernas y no de las antiguas." AGN, Tierras 1907, exp. 1, map no. 1305. Because the documents were false, the audiencia ordered that they be housed secretly.

72. Wood, *Transcending Conquest*, 119.

73. François Chevalier, *La formación de los latifundios en México* (Mexico City: Fondo de Cultura Económica, 1976), 326.

74. Ibid., 226–227.

75. Ibid., 228.

76. Ibid., 229.

77. Ibid., 329–335; María Cristina Torales Pacheco, "A Note on the Composiciones de Tierras in the Jurisdiction of Cholula, Puebla [1591–1757]," in Simon Miller and Arij Ouweneel, eds., *The Indian Community of Colonial Mexico. Fifteen Essays on Land Tenure, Corporate Organizations, Ideology and Village Politics,* 87–102 (Amsterdam: Centro de Estudios y Documentación Latinoamericanos, 1990).

78. Alejandra Vigil Batista, *Catálogo del Archivo de Tenencia de la Tierra en la provincia de Puebla. Sección de manuscritos Fondo Reservado, Biblioteca Nacional* (Puebla: Gobierno del Estado de Puebla and Comisión Puebla V Centenario, 1992), 23.

79. Ibid., 28–29.

80. Ibid., 25.

81. Ibid., 26–27.

82. Ibid., 28.

83. Lipsett-Rivera, *To Defend Our Water*, 25–26.

84. They were referring to primordial documents or titles. AGN, Tierras, 689, exp. 1.

85. Ibid. Reproductions of the fragments were published in *Códices indígenas de algunos pueblos*, Códice no. 32. Robert Barlow has also provided a learned commentary on these fragments in "[N47:III:1] El Códice de Coetzalan, Puebla," *Tlalocan: A Journal of Source Materials on the Native Cultures of Mexico* 3, 1 (1949): 91–92.

86. "[L]os dos Cues [templos prehispánicos] que en forma de pirámide se ven en dos reversos que no son más que unos túmulos que sobre los sepulcros de sus príncipes levantaban en el tiempo de su gentilismo, o aras [altares para el sacrificio] muy veneradas entre ellos que en el Perú llaman huacas, y cuantos en ellos tenían sepultados los numeraban con los círculos pequeños con que dichas aras se ven orladas; conocerse hoy por teteles [pirámides] sirven en los campos de limites o mojones a las tierras que los pueblos poseen o de una muda insinuación de que fueron habitables de sus mayores aquellos parajes donde hoy se ven." AGN, Tierras, 689, exp. 1.

87. I thank Professor William Taylor for directing me to this magnificent Mixtec codex: Mary Elizabeth Smith and Ross Parmenter, *The Codex Tulane* (New Orleans: Tulane University, Middle American Research Institute, 1991).

88. "Aquí, en el pueblo llamado Santiago Tecoman y en el barrio llamado San Pedro Petlatzonican y también en todos los demás pueblos: San José Tecolapan Xicotlan; San Sebastian Tecpan Mixpanic donde el agua es amarilla; Petlatlan; Ayutlan de Castilla; Tlillan, San Andrés Coatlan; Coyotlan, los cuales fueron atesorados por el gran *tlahtoani* el Marqués del Valle que vivió aquí, dijo mencionó el *tlahtoani* Marqués del Valle luego dijo: 'que aquí vivan mis padres que no se espanten.' Y así lo haremos; recibimos mucha honra y con ello respetaran mi amada tierra en buena forma y para siempre y ustedes siempre serán mis hijos junto a mi estarán colocados serán todos y estarán y vivirán ustedes y sus hijos y a ustedes nadie los hará pobres; las personas de Castilla vendrán por nuestras espaldas pero nadie morirá, nadie sufrirá, nadie los hará llorar." AGN, Tierras, 113, exp. 1. The documents come from pueblos in Colima, named Coyotlan and Santiago Ticoman, that still exist today. The title is in Nahuatl, dated 1650. I am grateful to Ignacio Silva for his assistance in translating the text from Nahuatl to Spanish.

89. David Wright, *Conquistadores otomíes en la Guerra Chichimeca* (Querétaro, Mexico: Secretaría de Cultura Bienestar Social and Gobierno del Estado de Querétaro, 1988), 43–51.

90. The titles of Santa María Ixhuatán, composed in Pipil Nahuatl, are found in their original form in the pueblo. They were discovered in the early 1990s by Professor Alain Ichon. Karen Dakin and Berenice Alcántara are currently translating them into Spanish. I am grateful to Alcántara for furnishing a summary version, in Spanish, of this remarkable document.

91. Wood, "Social vs. Legal Context," 203.

92. Ibid., 203–204n4, 5.

93. Ursula Dyckerhoff, "Forged Village Documents from Huejotzingo and Calpan," in *Actes du XLII e. Congrès International des Américanistes. Congrès du Centenaire, Paris, 2–9 Septembre 1976,* 52–63 (Paris: Société des Américanistes, Musée de l'Homme, 1979), vol. 7.

94. Walter V. Scholes, *The Diego Ramirez Visita*. University of Missouri Studies 4 (n.p.: University of Missouri, 1946).

95. "[Y] al pie del cerro de Chachelotepeque Ymiquexo Chiyucan y Tecolotepeque es para que tengan sus ganados vacunos cabríos ovejas mulas caballos ... y cuando esto sea así primero se dará cuenta al superior gobierno del excelentísimo señor virrey don Lois de Belasco conde de Corona ... y para guarda de su defensa por el registro de la tierra que quedan a su cargo se le concedió el alcalde don Juan López Chicnamiqui de cargar armas arcabuz daga espada flecha vestido chupa medias de seda peluca para el aderezo de su persona." Primordial titles of San Miguel Chignautla, found in the Tribunal Unitario Agrario, no. 37, Puebla. I am grateful to Lic. René Marneu Villavicencio for facilitating my access to this source.

96. Another example of seventeenth-century titles in which the Indians used a document with pictorial content that formed part of Diego Ramírez's mid–sixteenth-century visit is the one found in AGN, 1871, exp. 1, involving the pueblo of Huautla in the province of Pánuco.

97. Pedro Carrasco, "Sobre mito e Historia en las tradiciones nahuas," *Historia Mexicana* 39, 3 (1990): 677–686; Alfredo López Austin, "Del origen de los mexicas: ¿Nomadismo o migración?" *Historia Mexicana* 39, 3 (1990): 663–675; Federico Navarrete, "Medio siglo de explorar el universo de las fuentes nahuas: Entre la historia, la literatura y el nacionalismo," *Estudios de Cultural Náhuatl* 27 (1997): 156–179.

98. Anja Nygren, "Struggle over Meanings: Reconstruction of Indigenous Mythology, Cultural Identity, and Social Representation," *Ethnohistory* 45, 1 (1998): 31–61.

99. Wood, *Transcending Conquest.*

100. Federico Navarrete, "Los libros quemados y los nuevos libros. Paradojas de la autenticidad en la tradición mesoamericana," in Alberto Dallad, ed., *La abolición del arte. El Coloquio Internacional de Historia del Arte* (Mexico City: Instituto de Investigaciones Estéticas and UNAM, 1998), 53.

101. "En la primera foja veo y reconozco en el unas figuras que según parecen son los caciques que gobernaban en aquel tiempo que es el primero el que gobernó cuatro años = y al margen están los años, por donde reconozco que es el primer año que antiguamente se gobernaban que es y se llama *Tecpatha* [*tecpatl*] que interpreta pedernal = y el segundo año que sigue *Acatle* [*Acatl*] que se interpreta caña = y el tercer año es *tuchil* [*tochtli*]que se interpreta conejo = y el cuarto es *cali* [*calli*]que se interpreta casa, donde se señalan los meses que son." Biblioteca del Museo Nacional de Antropología, Mexico (BMNA), A II 8-2, Documento de la Magdalena Mixuhca, fols. 8r–16v.

102. "En la segunda foja esta un cacique sentado con cuatro cabezas, y otro cacique delante señalando las dichas cabezas. Y a un lado esta otro cacique sentado al pie de éste está una cabeza con su copil [tocado cónico, ¿*xiuhuitzolli*? o diadema de turquesa utilizada por los gobernantes] y una lista negra que va a dar do dice *tochi* [*tochtli*] y en el medio está una horca y un muchacho colgado en ella y un brasero de lumbre, soplando el brasero donde está el diablo soplándola, estos eran los jueces que hacían justicia; porque según veo en dicho mapa esta el gran señor en su sitial sentado, el traje es de tal cacique y rey que los gobernaba, el cual esta separado y tiene su copil y le sale a la cabeza otra línea negra que va a dar a una cabeza que al parecer es de sierpe [serpiente] u otro animal." Ibid, fol. 9r.

103. Gary H. Gossen, "Cuatro mundos del hombre: Tiempo e historia entre los Chamulas," *Estudios de Cultura Maya* 12 (1979): 180.

104. Ibid., 187–188.

105. Jonathan D. Hill, *Rethinking History and Myth: Indigenous South American Perspectives on the Past* (Urbana: University of Illinois Press, 1988), 7–9.

106. José Alejos García, *Mosojäntel etnografía del discurso agrarista entre kis ch'oles de Chiapas* (Mexico City: Instituto de Investigaciones Filológicas and UNAM, 1994), 166.

107. Rosaleen Howard-Malverde, "Talking about the Past: Tense and Testimonials in Quechua Narrative Discourse," *Amerindia* 13 (1988): 125–155.

108. Hill, *Rethinking History and Myth*, 9.

109. Joanne Rappaport, *The Politics of Memory: Native Historical Interpretation in the Colombian Andes* (New York: Cambridge University Press, 1990), 66.

110. Ibid., 66, 76.

111. Alessandro Lupo, "Los cuentos de los abuelos: Un ejemplo de construcción de la memoria entre los nahuas de la Sierra Norte de Puebla, México," *Anales de la Fundación Joaquín Costa* 15 (1997): 263–284.

112. Rappaport, *Politics of Memory*, 195.

113. Ibid., 200–201.

114. Thomas A. Abercrombie, *Pathways of Memory and Power: Ethnography and History among an Andean People* (Madison: University of Wisconsin Press, 1998), 85.

115. Ibid., xxiv, 85.

116. Ibid., 16.

117. Ibid., 18.

118. Ibid., 117.

119. Ibid., 195; Frank Salomon, "Chronicles of the Impossible: Notes on Three Peruvian Indigenous Historians," in Rolena Adorno, ed., *From Oral to Written Expressions: Native Andean Chronicles of the Early Colonial Period*, 9–39. Latin American Series, Foreign and Comparative Studies Program 4 (Syracuse, N.Y.: Maxwell School of Citizenship and Public Affairs, Syracuse University, 1982).

120. Abercrombie, *Pathways of Memory and Power*, 287–288, 290.

121. Ibid., 411.

122. Yukitaka Inoue, "Fundación de pueblos indígenas novohispanos según algunos *Títulos primordiales* del Valle de México," *Institute of International Relations and Area Studies* (Ritsumeikan University) 5 (2007): 107–131.

123. Luis Reyes García, *Documentos históricos Cuahixmatlac Atetecochco* (Tlaxcala: Departamento de Filosofía y Letras de la Universidad Autónoma de Tlaxcala, Instituto Tlaxcaltera de la Cultura, Comisión para escribir la historia de Cuahuixmatlac, 2001), 17.

124. "Y ahora nuestro gran dios y señor nos vio compasivo . . . espiritualmente acabamos de creer en la fe cristiana nos vio compasivo el amado sacerdote fuimos con él . . . creímos todos y adoramos espiritualmente la virtud moral que graciosamente nos dejó. Y ahora en este tiempo ha llegado acá el medidor de tierras de orden de nuestro gran señor Don Antonio de Mendoza que arribó el año que acaba de pasar época que cuenta [1534] años." AGN, Sección de *Títulos primordiales*, caja 17, exp. 5. I do not know the location of the original; this is a photocopy the AGN keeps in this section. The original

is in Nahuatl; the photocopy is a transcription and translation into Spanish done in the nineteenth century.

125. "El lindero de San Agustín es donde están formados los ahuejotes [un tipo de árbol] Diego Xochimantzin. Barda de piedra y arena, en donde se tocó [la flauta]. En el arenal. Allí terminó, ahí se trazó el lindero angosto. Miguel Tecpatl. Límite de ahuejotes. [Aquí es donde] pasa el camino de México. Juan Aguacatzin. Lugar por donde sale el sol. Barrio de San Lorenzo. Sebastián Chichitomitl, murió por una flecha. Allá es donde se les atravesó una serpiente." Lindero de Ahuehuetitlan. Santos Herrera de la Rosa and Ignacio Silva Cruz, *Transcripción y traducción del plano de San Agustín de las Cuevas, hoy Tlalpan* (Mexico City: AGN, 2002), 18.

126. "[E]n seguida procedimos a dar posesión a los naturales de este pueblo de San Miguel Nepantla [Estado de México] de todas estas tierras en nombre del rey nuestro señor, las gentes a los cuatro vientos cortaron yerbas, tiraron piedras se anduvieron paseando quemando copales en señal de tomar posesión." AGN, Tierras, 3706, years 1639 and 1769. This is a transcription and photocopy of the original document whose location, if it still exists, is unknown.

127. "Fueron a donde se llama Tetexalpa Sansacatlalpa Después fueron por donde se llama Quauhxayacatitlan Y allí fueron a encontrar todos los viejos por el lindero de Atlacotecatli. Allí tocaron chirimías de flautas y pusieron unas bancas allá comieron pescados y patos y pájaros y liebres de ciénega y todo lo que hay y lo que anda en el agua y cuando acabaron de comer allí salió un viejo dijo venid acá todos los hijos del pueblo mozos y muchachos y los más chiquitos y a los que no han nacidos ahora no sabe como ganaron los viejos los pueblos y las tierras y todo el agua y los ciénegas con mucho trabajo." Ibid. 3032, exp. 3, titles for Milpa Alta and the Federal District, whose dates are supposedly the end of the sixteenth century.

128. Inoue, "Fundación de pueblos," 130.

129. Oscar García González, "Memoria colectiva de un éxodo. Los nuevos poblados zapatistas en la selva," *Anales de Antropología* 39, 2 (2005): 51–87.

130. "[T]raslado del idioma mexicano al castellano del título perteneciente al pueblo de San Sebastián Tepatlasco y de don Francisco Quapinto que me concedió mi dios y después mi rey don Luiz [Luis] de Velasco Carlos Quinto rey de España y me dio tres sitios de tierra en que le sirvo a mi padre San Sebastián y empiezan mis linderos por [d]onde sale el sol linda con Santa María Magdalena y linda en San Antonio y linda en Santa Isabel por el norte que le llaman y linda adelante de Matlacuey linda con tierras de Tlaxcala por [d]onde se calienta el lobo y da la vuelta por [d]onde esta un ciprés y [d]onde esta enterrada una piedra esquinada y luego baja por Ocosingo por [d]onde entra el sol y linda en San Agustín y va parar en Agucatitlan." AGN, Tierras, 3362, exp. 3: "traducción del idioma mexicano al castellano y traslado de los documentos pertenecientes al pueblo de San Sebastián Tapatlasco."

131. Archivo General del Registro Agrario Nacional, pueblos of San Salvador Chachapan and San Juan Quetzalcuapan.

132. AGN, 2603, map with traditional elements, 1817, Santiago Tlaxoyaltepec, Etla, Oaxaca.

133. AGN, 18-1, primordial titles of Santa Cruz Xoxocotlan, n.d.

134. Housed and cared for today in the pueblo's community museum in the Mixteca Alta.

135. In the church of San Francisco Tepeapulco, an arch reveals personages mounted on lions. I thank Professor Eleanor Wake for letting me know about this interesting motif.

136. They include the well-known *Historia tolteca-chichimeca* and four other pictorial maps.

137. Ruiz Medrano, "Lords of the Earth."

138. AGN, Bienes Nacionales, vol. 638, exp. 84.

139. Michael W. Swanton, "El texto popoloca de la *Historia Tolteca-Chichimeca*," *Revista Relaciones* (El Colegio de Michoacán) 22, 86 (Spring 2001): 115–140.

140. Robert Haskett, "Visions of Municipal Glory Undimmed: The Nahuatl Town Histories of Colonial Cuernavaca," *Colonial Latin American Historical Review* 1, 1 (1992): 1–36.

141. AGN, Tierras, México, 1663, exp. 1.

142. Ibid.

143. One example of this situation, which affected all of central New Spain during this period, is the one found in AGN, *Títulos primordiales*, caja 12, exp. 1, Malinalco: "Legal brief of the Indians of the district of San Martín in Malinalco regarding lands in Xocotla against the Spaniard Juan de Prave. These lands were left when the Indians of this district were resettled; the Spaniard wanted them evicted, 19 August 1613."

144. AGN, Tierras, México, 1663, exp. 1.

145. Ibid.

146. Ibid.

147. The document was discovered by Pedro Carrasco. See his "Rango de Tecuhtli."

148. This case is explained in greater detail in Ruiz Medrano, "El espejo y su reflejo."

149. Gibson, *The Aztec*, 162–163.

150. Archivo General del Estado de Oaxaca, Oaxaca, Legajo 59, exp. 1.

151. John K. Chance, "Indian Elites in Late Colonial Mesoamerica," in Joyce Marcus and Judith Francis Zeitlin, eds., *Caciques and Their People: A Volume in Honor of Ronald Spores,* 45–65 (Ann Arbor: Museum of Anthropology, University of Michigan, 1994); Chance, "Mesoamerican Ethnographic Past," *Ethnohistory* 43, 3 (Summer 1996): 379–403; Ruiz Medrano, "Lords of the Earth."

152. Monaghan, "Mixtec Caciques."

153. Lockhart, *Nahuas after the Conquest*, 30.

154. Pablo Escalante Gonzalbo, "Pintar la historia tras la crisis de la conquista," in *Los pinceles de la historia. El origen del reino de la Nueva España* (Mexico City: Museo Nacional de Arte and UNAM, 1999), 38.

155. Gibson, *The Aztec*, 191–192.

156. Ibid., 149.

157. Ibid., 177–178.

158. Ibid., 179.

159. Ibid., 180.

160. Ibid., 193.

161. Terraciano and Sousa, "Original Conquest," 359.

162. Ibid., 349.

163. Ibid., 350.

164. Eustaquio Celestino Solís, Valencia R. Armando, and Constantino Medina Lima, *Actas del Cabildo de Tlaxcala, 1547–1567* (Mexico City: AGN and CIESAS, 1985); James Lockhart, Frances Berdan, and Arthur J.O. Anderson, *The Tlaxcalan Actas: A Compendium of Records of the Cabildo of Tlaxcala (1545–1627)* (Salt Lake City: University of Utah Press, 1986); Lockhart, *Nahuas and Spaniards: Postconquest Central Mexican History and Philology* (Stanford: Stanford University Press, 1991).

165. Constantino Medina Lima, paleography, introduction, and notes, *Libro de los guardianes y gobernadores de Cuauhtinchan [1519–1640]* (Mexico City: CIESAS, 1995).

166. Ibid., 50.

167. Bataillon, *Erasmo*, 825.

168. Ross Parmenter, *Four Lienzos of the Coixtlahuaca Valley* (Washington, D.C.: Dumbarton Oaks, Trustees for Harvard University, 1982); Sebastián van Doesburg and Olivier van Buren, "The Prehispanic History of the Valley of Coixtlahuaca, Oaxaca," in Maarten Luis Reyes García, ed., *Códices, Caciques y Comunidades,* 103–160 (Ridderkerk, Holland: Asociación de Historiadores Latinoamericanist, 1997).

169. From a January 2007 interview in San Miguel Tequistepec with Don Juan Cruz Reyes, founder of the pueblo's community museum.

170. Parmenter, *Four Lienzos.*

171. Sebastián van Doesburg, *Documentos antiguos de San Miguel Tequixtepec, Oaxaca. Los primeros cien años de la colonia [1533–1617]* (Leiden: Research School of Asian, African and Amerindian Studies, University of Leiden, 2002), 241–291.

172. Information supplied by Tequistepec resident Don Juan Cruz Reyes, in my 2007 interview with him in San Miguel Tequistepec.

173. From a November 30, 2003, interview in Atliaca with Nahua lawyer and teacher Modesto Vázquez Salgado.

174. Ibid.

175. Ibid.

176. Alejos García, *Mosojäntel etnografía,* 67. "The cave is considered an abode of the gods, a center of power and for that reason 'to reach agreement in the cave' confers on the junta a formal, solemn, sacred character. Caves are, moreover, a place of worship, a refuge in the wake of such disasters as war, the eruptions of volcanoes, epidemics, and plagues," 67n16.

177. Guilhem Olivier, "The Sacred Bundles and the Coronation of the Aztec King in Mexico-Tenochtitlan," in Julia Guernsey and F. Kent Reilly, eds., *Sacred Bundles: Ritual Acts of Wrapping and Binding in Mesoamérica,* 199–225 (Barnardsville, N.C.: Boundary and Archeology Research Center, 2006).

178. Ibid., 206.

179. Ibid., 208.

180. Archivo del Arzobispado, caja 62, exp. 7.

181. Jaime Morera, *Pinturas coloniales de animas del purgatorio* (Mexico City: Instituto de Investigaciones Estéticas and UNAM, 2001), 101–104.

182. F. John Chuchiak, "Papal Bulls, Extirpators, and the *Madrid Codex*: The Content and Probable Provenience of the M.56 Patch," in Gabrielle Vail and Anthony Aveni, eds., *The Madrid Codex: New Approaches to Understanding an Ancient Maya Manuscript* (Boulder: University Press of Colorado, 2004), 80.

183. Mónica Patricia Martín, *El indio y los sacramentos en Hispanamerica colonial. Circunstancias adversas y malas interpretaciones* (Buenos Aires: PRHISCO-CONICET, 1993), 251.

184. S. Munro Edmonson, trans., *Heaven Born Merida and Its Destiny: The Book of Chilam Balam of Chumayel* (Austin: University of Texas Press, 1986), 47. My thanks to Professor Guilhem Olivier for bringing this text to my attention.

185. Ibid., 259, paragraph 6295.

186. Chuchiak, "Papal Bulls, Extirpators," 76.

187. Ibid., 76–77.

188. Ibid., 77.

189. Ibid.

190. Ibid., 78.

191. Ibid., 74–75.

192. Archivo Histórico Judicial, Oaxaca, Villa Alta Criminal, Legajo 3, exp. 11. The citation is to a transcription of the document found in *Apuntes históricos por el ilustrísimo y reverendísimo Sr. Dr. Dn. Eulogio G. Gillow Obispo de Antequera, Diócesis de Oaxaca. Facsimilar de la edición de 1889 realizada por la Imprenta del Sagrado Corazón de Jesús, Mexico* (Oaxaca: Ediciones Toledo, 1990, first facsimile ed.), 123.

193. "[U]na petaquilla de palma, una corteza de papel de *Yaguichi* batido de dos varas de largo, poco más o menos, en una pieza, y ocho envoltorios pequeños anudados con unos cordelillos hechos del mismo *Yaguichi* y dentro de ellos unas plumas verdes y coloradas y unas ramillas de hojas de árbol de ocote, y todos los dichos envoltorios al parecer muy ensangrentados y nuevamente hechos." *Apuntes históricos por el ilustrísimo*, 123–130, quotation in this note on 124.

194. Ibid.

195. See note 101 in this chapter.

196. Biblioteca del Museo Nacional de Antropología, no. 35–64, *Codex of the Nobles of San Luis Huexotlan and San Lorenzo Axotlan*.

197. AGN, *Títulos primordial*, caja 20, exp. 5.

198. Rodolfo Becerra Mora, "La tira de Tepetzintla (Un estudio regional)" (master's thesis, Estudios Mesoamericanos, UNAM, Mexico City, 2002).

199. Personal communication from Elizabeth Hill Boone, 2007.

200. Anne Whited Norman, "*Testerian* Codices: Hieroglyphic Catechisms for Native Conversion in New Spain" (PhD diss., Tulane University, New Orleans, 1985). This Testerian codex is housed in the National Library of France, *Fond Mexicain*, no. 77.

201. Eduardo David Tavárez, "La idolatría letrada: Un análisis comparativo de textos clandestinos rituales y devocionales en comunidades nahuas y zapotecas, 1613–1654," *Historia Mexicana* 49, 2 (October–December 1999): 197–251.

202. From a slender leather-bound book of twenty-three sheets, entitled "Baptismal Registry of San Sebastián. In leather, from 27 May 1669 until 3 March 1681." The sheets

have tears on the margins; the writing style is that of the seventeenth century. The manuscript is in private hands. My thanks to Sr. Filiberto Flores for having informed me about this book.

203. Pedro Carrasco Pizano, *Pagan Rituals and Beliefs among the Chontal Indians of Oaxaca, Mexico* (Berkeley: University of California Press, 1960), 87–117.

204. Interview with Modesto Vázquez Salgado in Atliaca, May 2005.

205. Ibid.

206. Guilhem Olivier, *Mockeries and Metamorphoses of an Aztec God: Tezcatlipoca, "Lord of the Smoking Mirror"* (Boulder: University Press of Colorado, 2003), 354n91.

207. Fieldwork in Santa María Cuquila, carried out in October 2005.

208. John Monaghan and Byron Harmann, "La construcción cultural de la lectura en Mesoamérica," in Constanza Vega Sosa, ed., *Códices y documentos sobre Mexico. Tercer Simposio Internacional* (Mexico City: INAH, 2000), 486–487.

209. I had the opportunity to observe this codex personally in the Biblioteca Francisco Burgoa in Oaxaca. I thank María del Refugio Gutiérrez, restorer, for letting me see her work with this interesting codex. Personal communication from Aurelio Tello, Mexico City, 2010.

210. Mark Z. Christensen, "The Tales of Two Cultures: Ecclesiastical Texts and Nahua and Maya Catholicisms" (*The Americas*, Volume 66, Number 3, January 2010, pp. 353–377) 361–364, Appendix.

211. Abelardo Carrillo y Gariel, *El Cristo de Mexicaltzingo: Técnicas de las esculturas en caña* (Mexico City: Dirección de Monumentos Coloniales, 1949). This codex, known as the *Códice del Cristo de Mexicaltzingo*, is located today in the National Museum of Anthropology and History, Mexico City.

212. These fragments belonged to what became known as the *Codex Mauricio de la Arena*. Six of the fragments are housed at present in Mexico City's National Museum of Anthropology and History. The remainder, nearly 100, are in the American Museum of Natural History in New York City. See Glass and Robertson, "A Census," 212.

3	Indigenous Negotiation to Preserve Land, History, Titles, and Maps

NINETEENTH AND TWENTIETH CENTURIES

INDIAN PUEBLOS AND INDEPENDENCE: GENERAL CONSIDERATIONS

As the eighteenth century drew to a close, New Spain's Indian communities faced continuing challenges and threats. A new set of issues made their relationship with the colonial authority even more complex. Two factors in particular—an increase in the native population and a pronounced effort among Spaniards and creoles to develop commercial agriculture—intensified the pressure on Indian lands.[1] Furthermore, as a consequence of the Bourbon reforms introduced in the 1760s, the Indian pueblos were compelled to rationalize their financial affairs. Although they tried to do so by renting their unoccupied or "surplus" lands, the new policy ultimately benefited rural estate owners, miners, and merchants rather than the indigenous communities.[2]

The native population was also affected by the creation in 1786 of a new political-administrative unit, the intendancy, under whose authority the indigenous communities were placed. Intendancy officials became personally involved in regulating the pueblos' financial business, which in turn led to greater involvement by Spanish authorities in the affairs of indigenous government[3] and Indian authorities' loss of some of their local political strength.[4]

Not surprisingly, the changes that took place as a result of the Bourbon reforms created a growing unease among the colony's Indian pueblos, which erupted in a series of revolts and disturbances at the end of the colonial period.[5] Eric Van Young contends that the Indians' discontent, which flared between the end of the eighteenth century and the first decade of the nineteenth century across 150 pueblos, had three principal causes: increased tributary requirements, land problems, and problems internal to local indigenous government.[6] Furthermore, the majority of these uprisings were led by the communities' authorities, generally the governors of the pueblos, who were accustomed to confronting Spanish officials over matters relating to their power and authority.[7] The colony's first steps toward political independence from Spain, and the armed rebellions that accompanied those steps between 1810 and 1820, were taken against this general backdrop.

Van Young points out that, contrary to what is often asserted, the principal participants in the war of independence were not drawn from Mexico's mestizo population. In reality, the independence movement was composed of hundreds of thousands of the colony's Indians, an understandable development given that they constituted a large majority of the population. In 1810, New Spain's population was approximately 60 percent Indian, 20 percent Spanish, and 20 percent black and mixed race.[8] Moreover, Indians continued to form a majority of the population throughout the nineteenth century: they represented 50 percent of the total population in 1857 and approximately 43 percent in 1876.[9]

Some scholars have noted that the independence movement in Mexico, which broke out in 1810, had its origins in the various Indian pueblo uprisings of the late eighteenth century. In this outlook, the rural population's great discontent, which flowered into the independence movement, resulted in part from an increase in the Indian population that created a burgeoning demand for land. Two other precipitating factors were the implementation of "modernizing" policies, which threatened the survival of Indian communities, and changes affecting access to land, which favored large-scale ownership of land. Another factor was the growth of commercial agriculture, which benefited large producers. To one degree or another, the impetus for many of these developments started with the Bourbon reforms. The outbreak of the independence movement was also fueled by a crisis within New Spain's agriculture, which produced famine conditions in the colony during the years 1808–1811. For Van Young, however, these and other problems of a political and economic nature are only part of the reason a substantial element of the Indian population chose to participate in the 1810–1820 independence movement. Their participation was also motivated by a long process of cultural resistance to the various internal and external forces that helped bring about the changes noted.[10] The central elements of this cultural resistance included a sense of separate ethnic identity, a feeling of belonging to a different community, a distinct indigenous religious sensibility, and "a certain style of political thinking that was all their own."[11]

During the war of independence, various Indian pueblos displayed both a messianic-like fervor toward, and a loyalty to, the Spanish monarch. Indeed, Indian insurgents often expressed their desire for change through the cry "long live the king and death to bad government." They clearly harbored feelings against the Spanish, as represented by the colonial authorities and the local oligarchy, while maintaining an attachment to the king and to the Virgin of Guadalupe—although the latter's influence on the Indians' religious life had diminished during most of the colonial period. An interesting counterpoint to this fact lies in William Taylor's revelation that the Indian pueblos' tripartite linking of the virgin, justice, and a sense of nationalism originated during the war of independence, after which it continued to be strengthened in their perception.[12]

At the same time, the enactment of liberal legislation, which took place in the context of a weakened Spanish monarchy, offered the Indian pueblos hope of attaining greater benefits for themselves and their wider communities. In 1812 the liberal-inspired Constitution of Cadiz was formally adopted, providing the basis for the organization of Mexico's future national state. Under this instrument, the state's provincial-level administrative division was established. The organization of municipal power also flowed out of the Constitution of Cadiz, as did the principle of equal rights among Americans, Spaniards, and Indians—resulting in the abolition of tribute, the encomienda, and the institution of personal service. The constitution was likewise the mechanism through which communities with at least 1,000 inhabitants were made to establish *ayuntamientos*, or town councils, whose members—as with the colonial cabildo—were to be elected by vote. This turn of affairs was advantageous to the Indian pueblos, since—in contrast to other societal groups—they were familiar with elections. Between 1820 and 1830, Indians participated in municipal elections on a wide scale. During the colonial period, the rules governing the election of officials to fill positions on the Indian cabildos varied according to local custom, but that variability soon ended. In the post-independence period, only males above age twenty-five were eligible to participate in the election of persons to municipal offices, and the chosen method of voting was indirect.[13]

The Indian communities associated the idea of citizenship with the payment of taxes and the right to vote for municipal officials, who in turn gained the ability to control resources. The ceremonies governing the election of town officials in the early national period were in fact very similar to those followed by New Spain's Indian cabildos. As Peter Guardino has observed, the commonality was logical, since both sets of ceremonies were derived from the same Spanish municipal traditions.[14]

Above the town councils in the hierarchy of political authority were the provincial councils, or *diputaciones provinciales*. In theory, when the previous intendancy system was eliminated, its local representatives (*subdelegados*) were stripped of their duties as well. In practice, however, the subdelegados remained a potent force, "functioning as justices in the first instance, and as officials responsible for matters of war." Broadly speaking, revolutionary Mexico's new legal and legislative landscape met with enthusiastic approval among many Indian pueblos, since the citizenship conferred on their members made them newly free and autonomous while also enabling them to opt out of further participation in the political arena. Their enthusiasm, however, was not shared by the colonial authorities and local-level white oligarchs. The subdelegados in particular viewed the Indian town councils as potentially circumscribing their own political and judicial authority.[15]

As a consequence of Ferdinand VII's failed attempt to reinstitute absolute monarchy in Spain, the Constitution of Cadiz was suspended in 1814. Six years later, however, it was readopted in New Spain. The backwash of these political upheavals was felt in the Indian pueblos. For example, the officers of Tlaxcala's venerable cabildo—its caciques, governor, and councilors—who under the indigenous system ruled in perpetuity, were relieved of their duties and offices in 1812. In 1814, with the suspension of the constitution, they reassumed them, only to be superannuated again—this time permanently—in 1820. The caciques addressed their uncertain and confusing political situation in an 1822 letter to Mexican emperor Agustín de Iturbide (1822–1823). By creating the town councils, they explained, the Constitution of Cadiz had eliminated the traditional indigenous offices of governor and municipal councilor, held by their incumbents in perpetuity. They further argued that as a result of their loss of power, they had been held up to public ridicule by those who succeeded them as officials on Tlaxcala's newly formed town council. Their situation, the native rulers emphasized, recalled the experiences of forbears who had been dispossessed of "that cushion"—an allusion to the ancient indigenous seat of royal status and authority. They stressed again, however, that when "the Constitution was abolished down by the Royal Decree of [May 4, 1814], we were restored to our earlier posts and offices, and in the midst of a climate that gave free expression to all manner of disgraceful passions, we turned away from a constant stream of offensive acts and confined ourselves strictly to fulfilling the duties and responsibilities of our offices."[16]

Their period of recovered service was brief, however. With the readoption of the Constitution of Cadiz in 1820, the Tlaxcala caciques were again compelled to relinquish their posts. In their letter they recounted all these occurrences, explaining that the new town councilors of Tlaxcala, "without showing us any consideration . . . called for the documents, records, and other official papers in the municipal archive, all of which we handed over forthwith, without so much as obtaining an acknowledgment of receipt for our own safekeeping." This abrupt turn of political fortune provoked a "new despondency" among the caciques; they repeated that they found themselves in "low spirits and a state of confusion . . . without the law, justice and reasoned reflection being able to alter their fortune." Given these developments, they beseeched the emperor that the March 24, 1813, decree of the Regular and Extraordinary Cortes of Cadiz be fully respected. Under that decree, deposed authorities—such as themselves—were to maintain the "distinctions, special treatment, honors, and use of the uniform which they had possessed at the time the new [town councils] were created."

Having been deprived of real political power, the indigenous rulers argued that they should be allowed to command their time-honored symbolic power by continuing to receive special honors and distinctions. The issue resonated with particular force in the Indian community of Tlaxcala because after strenuous effort in the wake of the Spanish conquest, its cabildo had managed to extract special privileges and concessions from Emperor Charles V and King Ferdinand II. Three centuries later, Tlaxcala's surviving line of caciques continued the struggle to maintain a residue of these privileges in an independent Mexico.

The caciques closed their petition to Iturbide by pledging their loyalty and respect, just as their colonial ancestors had done in the numerous letters they had sent to the Spanish monarchs beginning in the sixteenth century. Thus, in their 1822 letter the caciques stated that "now that we have the privilege of kissing for the first time your sacred staffs of office, we submit this humble and respectful representation, which promises us the greatest consolation and the most favorable relief from misfortune."[17]

It is instructive that, from the vantage point of their traditional political culture, the caciques endeavored to accommodate the new circumstances of independent Mexico. The Indian nobility faced a difficult situation, lacking as it did the resources to anchor itself politically and economically during the unsettled times. Even Moctezuma's descendants complained bitterly in 1814 that they had not been paid their stipend for a considerable time.[18] It was not only Indian rulers who confronted this situation; the Indian pueblos in general were swept by instability. Despite this fact, as observed in the Tlaxcala caciques' letter to Iturbide, they carried on, displaying a "notable ideological flexibility, aimed at reclaiming a place in the national society and before the state, a task which they managed to accomplish by adopting new political systems while simultaneously keeping alive practices stemming from colonial times."[19]

INDIAN PUEBLOS DURING THE FIRST HALF OF THE NINETEENTH CENTURY

During the first half of the nineteenth century, the Indian population continued to manifest great ideological flexibility; within this orbit, their traditional cultural practices played an important role. For the Indians, the environment posed major challenges, since through the legislation passed first by Cortes of Cadiz and then by successive liberal and conservative national governments, the pueblos lost the unique juridical protection and separate court system the monarchy had afforded them. Henceforth, they had to coexist with other groups unshielded by the legal-legislative barriers—fragile as they might have been—erected by a "paternalistic" monarchy. Supposedly, in terms of legal and civil rights, the Indians were now on an equal footing with other social and ethnic groups. The reality, however, was different. The Indian pueblos scrambled to master the new rules of successive governments, which, although their political ideologies differed, were nonetheless alike in considering the Indians a hindrance to the formation and consolidation of a modern state.

At the same time, the glorification of the country's indigenous past played an important role in the development of a distinct sense of national patriotism as early as the eighteenth century. After 1810 some Mexican liberals, including Carlos María Bustamante, continued to harbor and express this sentiment. In their eyes, they and the sector of white society they represented were the true descendants of ancient Mexicans. Accordingly, for some years the legitimacy of the country's nation-building enterprise rested in part on the legitimacy and perceived eminence of its pre-Hispanic civilizations, that of the Mexica in particular. The creole patriots did not hold their Indian contemporaries in such high esteem, however. On the contrary, they saw them as a people who had been socially and politically degraded as a consequence of three centuries of colonization. After independence, both liberal and conservative political groups in Mexico gradually stopped exalting the country's pre-Hispanic civilization. Instead, that heritage was viewed with indifference or simply neglected. By the mid-nineteenth century the transformation was complete. Mexico's governing authorities reached the point of believing that the Spanish conquest and colonization had actually been of great service to the Indians, who were merely "savage animals," incapable of aspiring to the state of civilized beings.[20]

Thus, in 1821 some Mexican legislators debated the Indians' physical and moral capacities. The discussion found advocates both pro and con, although in general, members of the political elite throughout the nineteenth century considered the Indians a backward people, totally lacking in education and refinement.[21] Such thinking notwithstanding, legislation emanating originally from the Constitution of Cadiz and later from Republican Mexico enabled the Indians to enjoy specific benefits. In 1822 the government did away with the *medio real de ministros*, or tax that had been levied on each tributary since the early seventeenth century to help defray the costs of Indian litigation and, after its creation in the later part of that century, the expenses of the General Indian Court of Colonial Mexico—now abolished. Other financial burdens eliminated in post-independence Mexico were the half-real tax each Indian tributary paid for the *hospital de naturales* and the one-and-a-half-real tribute they had been obliged to pay into their community treasury.[22]

Of course, while they were relieved of a significant part of their previous tributary burden, the Indians also faced a world without a special Indian-centered system of justice or hospitals designed exclusively for their care. The laws passed in this period emphasized that the Indians had the right to be admitted to any hospital, on the same basis as any other citizen of the state. On a practical level, however, the new nation—politically unstable and economically impoverished—lacked the infrastructure to address the legal difficulties and serious health deficiencies of its large indigenous population.[23] To make matters worse, in 1841 the government decreed that each person sixteen years of age and older would be required to make a personal contribution to the state. Thus, after independence the Indians' economic situation was only a little less bleak than it had been under Spanish imperial rule.[24]

At the same time, the privileges they were accorded as citizens allowed the Indians to negotiate certain benefits, notably, preserving elements of their "traditional rights and practices."[25] In this connection, it is critical to note that in the Indians' view, citizenship was at bottom another form of belonging to their own communities; it embodied a vision of the national community as an extension of the local community. For the Indians, what was entailed in being a citizen was centered not on the individual but rather on the possibility of belonging to a wider community—still conceived of as the pueblo—that encompassed the nation, in which everyone had rights and obligations without distinctions of race or class.[26] As acknowledged "Mexicans," the Indians evolved strategies to preserve the colonial order in various aspects of their lives, in particular as it concerned the governing of their pueblos.[27] In this way, the response of Indian pueblos to the changes and assaults that impinged on them from without during the first half of the nineteenth century contained important traditional cultural elements.

I would like to consider this point in depth by examining several cases. The first set brings us back to the Indians' traditional beliefs as they played out on a local level during the first half of the nineteenth century. I subsequently describe an occurrence that illustrates how, following independence, many Indians longed for a special political autonomy, as represented in the election of a native king. Finally, I deal with a case that involves the attempt by some pueblos to advance their interests by arguing their position and engaging in politics on the national level. Through these cases, I hope to demonstrate that the Indians combined great ideological flexibility with a deep attachment to their own traditions.

In February 1815 the Indian governor of the pueblo of Zacualpan, which fell within the jurisdiction of Cuautla Amilpas (in the present-day state of Morelos), had ordered the arrest and imprisonment in the town hall of several Indians from the pueblo. By taking extreme measures, such as hanging them from the ceiling by their hands, the indigenous authorities tried to get the Indians to confess to acts of witchcraft of which they stood accused by neighboring residents in the pueblo. The affair came to the attention of the district judicial officer, who decided to intervene and set the imprisoned Indians free.[28]

The Indians had been accused of making a woman in the pueblo fall ill. Carrying her to the town hall, the woman's husband accused several of the pueblo's inhabitants of being witches and demanded that its governor, Don Martín Santiago, take steps to enforce justice. Santiago summoned the accused and then, in front of the entire pueblo, ordered each "witch" to cure the stricken woman. Complying with the order, the Indians tried to apply remedies to her as she lay on the ground in front of them. One after another, "they began . . . to press down on her stomach and others gave her herbal drinks." They also suffused her with aromatic herbs and sucked on her body, head to foot, with mouthfuls of water—all to no avail. At that point, Santiago ordered that the alleged witches be imprisoned and, in an effort to make them confess to their evil doings, had them tortured. Learning of this outcome, the Spanish official demanded that the pueblo's governor explain why he had invoked such extreme punishments instead of approaching the Spanish authorities. Santiago replied that he done so because "a considerable number of his people asked him to, pained that these men were killing and sickening whom[ever] they will." Moreover, he had not brought these matters to the magistrate's attention, "since he hoped that the sick woman would be cured, as they had promised and furthermore because the justice system would not credit that these things happened, and, set free after two or three days in jail, they would come out and cause harm to those who [had] complained against them."[29]

The magistrate set out to question the Indians, who explained that "their elders believed in witchcraft, although the priests instructed them not to believe in it." It seems that sorcery had been performed on the sick woman as part of an act of vengeance, with the perpetrator of the evil receiving as payment two reales and a jug of pulque. The magistrate ruled that the accused men should be set free, should take communion during Holy Week, and should continue to work on the nearby sugarcane plantations.[30]

This case illustrates that the inhabitants of Zacualpan believed that the existence of witch doctors in the pueblo, and the problems that resulted from their presence, required the intervention of their own authorities. To this end, they had tried, through their governor, to exact justice against the dangerous parties. In the interests of the common good, Santiago had rendered justice against the witch doctors in a traditional manner. He avoided the Spanish authorities, who lacked the ability to understand the delicate nature of the matter and would simply have set the guilty parties free, enabling them to inflict more harm through their special powers. Furthermore, the armed conflicts during the independence war had inflicted considerable hardship on the region's native population; as one example, the church of an Indian community near Zacualpan had been burned to the ground.[31] In the Spanish system of justice, on the other hand, it was not sufficient to simply liberate the mistreated Indians; they were needed to work on the sugarcane plantations. For the Spanish authorities, the output of the plantations was paramount.

During the nineteenth century, then, some indigenous communities tried to administer justice and resolve conflicts internally, without recourse to external law and authority. At times, as a case involving the Indians of Pueblito (in Querétaro) illustrates, they linked old and new traditions within the small world of their local community. In 1817 their priest accused the Indians of Pueblito (likely Otomís) of being "superstitious." The community maintained the tradition of solemnly guarding a cross, which its members called the "Cross of Justice." The Indians performed nighttime ceremonies around the cross, joined regularly by many Indians from neighboring pueblos. The Pueblito Indians had also constructed a chapel in the home of a local curandero, Patricio García.[32] Evidently, as a result of the general political instability, the authorities had turned a blind eye to this case, and the Indians managed to continue their rituals in an atmosphere of relative calm.

Nevertheless, the wider distractions of the time did not mean that the government and its agents would not eventually reinvoke the colonial policy of censuring the Indians' traditional ways, especially in matters involving religious belief and practice. In 1819, for example, several Otomí Indians from the pueblo of Lerma (present-day state of México) were tried on charges of carrying out religious practices foreign to Catholicism. Thus, two years before Mexico became an independent nation and the Spanish royal army was defeated, Spanish ecclesiastical authorities were still devoting time and energy to trying a group of Indians for committing "idolatry."

This particular case revolved around the fact that a large number of Lerma's Indians had gathered at night in the home of a blind neighbor, Francisco Domingo, to perform a ritual. They placed in front of them an altar, divided into two tables, on which were images of the Virgin and of Christ on top of crosses, as well as tamales, stewed duck, eggs, fruit, and pulque. In the middle of the altar

3.1 Reproduction, no. 4719. Date: nineteenth century. Courtesy, Archivo General de la Nación, Mexico City.

was a *chiquihuite* (basket) that contained dolls representing people and animals (dogs and roosters), surrounded by multicolored pieces of wool. The Indians danced around the altar, holding cigars in their hands and singing praises to one of their ancient gods, Llemixintte (Yemixintt), whom they declared to be the god of the mountains. In their songs, the Indians asked Llemixintte to protect them, in return for which they would honor him in ceremonies. As part of the ritual, the Indians also used a "painted manuscript"[33] (Figure 3.1) on which they depicted a flying pole with people descending from it, encircled by men and women (one of the women appears to be grinding corn). There are also people dressed as coyotes or dogs and a bundle with flags stuck to it. Some crosses and a church are in the upper part of the painting, and above them is what seems to be the image of a sun and stars. The drawing on the manuscript has deteriorated substantially; the dye has faded, and the brushstrokes are not well executed. Yet despite these limitations, the different elements noted here can be identified with some clarity. The artifact seems to be describing some type of festive ceremony, perhaps a carnival, and its imagery reveals why the Indians kept it with them during their nocturnal celebrations.[34]

More than likely, through its performance this ritual enabled Lerma's inhabitants to maintain a sense of communal cohesion; the blind Indian may have been a curandero, and the ceremony appears to have originated from the Indians' desire to ask their pantheon of supernatural beings to protect them and their families. When caught by the local priest, they fell back on the excuse that while the ceremony had indeed been conducted in the manner of their "ancestors," the idea behind it was not actually theirs but had been given to them by a resident of Puebla, whom they had met in Mexico City. More particularly, Francisco Domingo stated that he was in Mexico City selling charcoal when one of his customers, a man from Puebla, assured him that he could be cured of his blindness if he carried out a ritual in the same way his "ancestors" had. The stranger described everything he needed to do. Domingo further explained that he had purchased the "painting" in a Mexico City market, telling the woman who sold it to him that he wanted it for "a game." The blind Indian insisted that he never knew the name of the mysterious *poblano* (person from Puebla) who gave him this advice, nor had he learned exactly where the man lived.

In short, Domingo claimed that neither he nor any of the other Lerma Indians would have been capable of carrying out the ceremony without the advice proffered by the poblano. Given the depth of knowledge of traditional practices the ritual entailed, however—practices embedded in the cosmology of the Indian pueblos—the blind man's story is hardly credible. Nevertheless, the ecclesiastical judges declared that they were satisfied with the Indians' response, asserting in the sentence they handed down that the incident was the result of ignorance, incapacity before the law, and the Indians' "lack of instruction" in matters of faith. They terminated the case by releasing the guilty parties from jail and ordering that they take communion and listen to Mass for two weeks.

The pueblos, though, were enmeshed in more than religious issues during these years of political uncertainty and turmoil. Some of them tried to capitalize on New Spain's independence to gain separate independence for the Indian pueblos. In the first years of the nineteenth century, some native groups conveyed this ambition by their expressed desire to have their own king. For example, in 1801 the Indians of Tepic (located in the present-day state of Nayarit) rose up in a messianic movement that encapsulated their expectations of social and political change. Under the banner of this movement, the Indians announced the arrival of a king of Tlaxcaltecan origin whose coronation would take place in Tepic.[35] Such an occurrence was not confined to Tepic; after independence, the call to have their own king, as embodied in the person of Tlaxcala's ruler, was heard in other native communities.

On October 4, 1824, the United Mexican States formally came into existence as a federal republic, with Guadalupe Victoria (1824–1828) elected president. By virtue of this election, the rumor began to circulate among some Indian pueblos that "the *gente de razón* [Spaniards, creoles, and, broadly, Hispanicized elements of the population] proclaim as emperor Guadalupe Victoria and the Indians proclaim [as their ruler] the governor of Tlaxcala."[36] In that same year, President Victoria received a report informing him that an Indian, said to be the "Tlaxcala messenger," had arrived in the small pueblo of San Francisco Galilelo (Querétaro). In his traveling case, the Indian carried "a half sack of wool" along with numerous letters, originating in Tlaxcala, to be sent to the person governing the Indians in the northern reaches of the country, the area known as Tierra Adentro. The report explained:

> The new was that the gente de razón[37] proclaimed Señor Don Guadalupe Victoria as emperor, and the Indians proclaimed [as their ruler] the governor of Tlaxcala. The notion that the gente de razón proclaimed your excellency as emperor could have originated in the fact that the Indians will have learned of your excellency's election to the presidency of the United Mexican States but do not have any real idea of the nature of this office, new to our country, yet the business they are said to have of proclaiming [as their emperor] a governor of Tlaxcala and the letters meant to be sent off to Tierra Adentro . . . have caught the attention of this government.[38]

Indeed, the government was sufficiently preoccupied with this turn of events that the onetime governor of Tlaxcala, Juan Ignacio Lira, took refuge in a hacienda while the city's chief political official kept a careful watch over the movements of a group of Chichimec Indians who had arrived in Tlaxcala from Guanajuato—supposedly on a pilgrimage to the sanctuary of the Virgin of Ocotlán. The authorities, however, suspected that their true motives lay elsewhere, namely in the rumor that the Indians planned to crown the indigenous governor of Tlaxcala as their king. Not long before this development, government forces in Guanajuato had suppressed a revolt by Indians from the pueblo of San Pedro Piedra Gorda. The authorities had imprisoned a number of Indians, stripping them of their bows and arrows. The Indians confessed that the governor of Tlaxcala had called them to participate "in a mass that would be solemnly celebrated in Tlaxcala, our brother Indians from all of the pueblos received the [governor's] call to come to the said event."[39]

Although the plan of some Indian pueblos to crown Tlaxcala's governor as king ended badly for them, it nonetheless possessed a certain inner logic. During the colonial period, Tlaxcala's municipal council had enjoyed the highest degree of favor and privilege to which any Indian cabildo could aspire. Its prestige among the native population gave Tlaxcala's governor the standing to call the Indians together to invest him with the leadership of a new government, separate from that of New Spain's white, black, and mestizo populations. To the Indians, the conditions for such a movement seemed especially ripe after the conclusion of the war of independence and the ensuing collapse of the colonial order.

This clear desire to achieve autonomy was not evident in other indigenous movements of the period. After 1810, Indian revolts focused on either local grievances or on issues of wider import, but the greater significance of Indian participation in public life after independence was that it helped mold the nascent Mexican state. Indians' political involvement in the creation of what today is the state of Guerrero is an excellent example of this fact.

Under the 1824 constitution, Mexico became a federal republic, with a representative form of government. From 1829 to 1831, Vicente Guerrero—a popular leader of the revolutionary forces—served as the country's president. Guerrero (assassinated in 1831) enjoyed strong support from the Indian pueblos. His brief presidency and the federal system in general opened a wider field of political participation for Mexico's Indians. First, the number of municipalities across the country's federated regions was approximately equal to the number of Indian republics existing during the colonial period; second, the practice of extending universal suffrage to all males was guaranteed by the constitution. Further, although the Indians faced the burden of paying taxes to their municipality, all money collected was administered locally. For many Indians, the term "federalism" equated to the "diffusion of power at the local level."[40] While some municipalities were controlled by whites and mestizos who maintained strong regional interests and wielded power over the indigenous communities that belonged to their municipalities, many municipalities were under full Indian control.

The federal system lasted only until 1834, however, at which time the centralists took power. Their ascendancy (1835–1841) affected the Indian communities dramatically. Under the centralist government, municipalities were reduced in number, and many came under the control of both the creole elite and mestizos, who lorded that fact over the Indian pueblos within their respective jurisdictions. During these years, moreover, the government raised taxes. This move greatly upset the Indians, who reacted against the measure by rebelling openly—especially in the region of present-day Guerrero. The final blow the centralist government dealt to the Indians was the restriction it placed on universal suffrage. Starting in 1836, only males with an annual income of between 100 and 200 pesos were eligible to vote, a requirement that completely disqualified the Indian peasant population from participating in elections.[41]

These changes provoked several Indian pueblos in both the coastal and mountainous parts of Guerrero to take up arms against the central government. The initial uprising broke out in Chilapa, after the municipality's white and mestizo elite tried to exercise control over dependent neighboring Indian pueblos by manipulating their internal political affairs. The local grievance rapidly escalated into a wider campesino revolt, which erupted in 1840.[42]

The rebel Indians in the Chilapa area were joined by many other pueblos similarly opposed to the laws the centralist government had adopted. The tax issue in particular sparked a major movement against the central government that spread over extensive parts of present-day Guerrero. In addition, the government was weakened by serious internal divisions, which leading members of its non-Indian political opposition—among them the federalist Juan Álvarez—exploited. Álvarez, who supported the Indians' demands, was a key figure in the creation of the state of Guerrero in 1849. In return for his promise to make good on their grievances, Álvarez received critical support from the Indians in his effort to secure statehood for Guerrero. Of course, the impending fall of the centralist government was caused not only by internal factors but also by the U.S. invasion and subsequent loss of national territory resulting from the U.S.-Mexican War (1846–1848). During the war, Álvarez fought against the U.S. Army, employing guerrilla tactics and supported by a large contingent of Indians from Guerrero.[43]

With the Indian uprising concluded and the centralists deposed, the country returned briefly, from 1850 to 1852, to a federalist form of government. In 1852 the government, headed by Mariano Arista, fell as a result of strong pressure exerted against it by both conservatives and the allies of former president López de Santa Anna. The political climate having shifted, Santa Anna returned from exile and was again named president. In the state of Guerrero, however, Álvarez and other important federalist politicians refused to accept the new order and rebelled against it. In 1854 they drafted and proclaimed the so-called Plan de Ayutla, designed to provide the basis for a renewed popular federalism. As they had on previous occasions, the Indian communities of Guerrero's mountainous region joined forces with the federalists, this time to help wage a guerrilla war against Santa Anna's government. Although Santa Anna hoped to put down the rebellion swiftly and mercilessly, he was unsuccessful in doing so. The movement against him soon grew, bolstered by pueblos and groups in Michoacán, the state of México, present-day Morelos, Tamaulipas, Oaxaca, Nuevo León, Jalisco, San Luis Potosí, Zacatecas, and Mexico City—all of which subscribed to the Plan de Ayutla. Powerless against the mounting offensive, Santa Anna was deposed and sent into exile in August 1855. Juan Álvarez was elected president that same year and made his entrance into the capital accompanied by the rebel Indian forces. Several months later Álvarez resigned and was replaced as president by Ignacio Comonfort.[44] A notable aspect of this political movement is that the Indians formed alliances with groups of fellow Indians who spoke different languages (Mixtecs, Tlapanecos, Amuzgos, Nahuas). They communicated through written Spanish, and they shared a broad political agenda with those among the non-Indian population who wanted to see federalism triumph.

In elucidating these cases, I have tried to show how the expression and use of certain traditional elements of indigenous culture helped preserve a sense of cohesion within Indian communities during the first half of the nineteenth century. At the same time, however, the actions the Indian population took in the face of external changes and pressures were clearly varied and reflected the notable ideological flexibility its members displayed. The country's Indian communities possessed a long tradition of political organization. This experience enabled them on occasion to voice their political wishes and demands on a national level, to engage effectively in collective action with non-Indian sectors of society, and to play a part in the formation of the Mexican national state.

During the nineteenth century, furthermore, the Indian pueblos generally opted to interact and negotiate with government authorities by following the same approach and strategy they had used during the three centuries of colonial rule. More often than not, their understanding of how a specific piece of legislation would affect them precipitated and guided such negotiation. Under the new institution of the town council, the Indians managed to hold on to old political practices dating from the colony. In this transition, "the designation of governor of the [Indian] republic was replaced by that of chief political officer."[45]

In this regard, the case of Oaxaca is instructive. Oaxaca's 1825 constitution set down two conditions for the creation of a town council. The first specified that communities with more than 3,000 inhabitants would have the right to form such a council, while the second stated that communities with at least 500 inhabitants would be recognized as republics. This legislation was advantageous to the Indian pueblos, since the republics enjoyed the same administrative attributes and functions as the town councils. The arrangement enabled many small Indian pueblos, in Oaxaca at least, to enjoy a degree of autonomy and to govern their own internal affairs. Also, as with the colonial Indian cabildo, the republic's officials were appointed on the basis of popular representation.[46] At the local level, significantly, government authority and decisions remained in the hands of the Indian pueblos throughout the nineteenth century, whatever the country's wider domestic problems. The 1857 Mexican constitution reformed the administration of local government by making municipal presidents the leaders of town councils. Moreover, communities (or Indian republics) with at least 500 inhabitants were now allowed to become municipalities. Thus, through the skillful political participation of indigenous leaders, as well as the precedent of the 1825 law, many Indian pueblos in Oaxaca attained the status of municipalities and, in doing so, managed to retain the land they had secured legally during the colonial program of composición.[47]

Although they did not benefit from legislation similar to Oaxaca's, Indian pueblos in other Mexican states also managed to hold on to their lands. The hurdles were greater in Puebla, where the law stipulated that only settlements with more than 3,000 inhabitants were eligible to become municipalities. In the state of México, the bar was set even higher, at 4,000.[48] A greater threat to the interests of indigenous communities loomed there, however. According to an 1825 law, the communal lands belonging to Indian pueblos within a particular district of the state could be assigned to the capital town (*cabecera municipal*) of that district. Through this device, the cabecera could augment its revenues by collecting rent on the land—which it held in usufruct—from the Indians. Although the law was in place, it was poorly understood. In addition, the cabeceras lacked an effective cadre of agents to enforce it. For their part, the pueblos actively defended their possession of the land, hiring lawyers and exposing holes in the law in an effort to prevail in the courts.[49]

The pueblos' assertiveness reinforced a long tradition of legal and political resistance by the Indians, for whom land was not only an economic resource but also a fount of political rights and communal freedoms against the countervailing power of the state.[50] Mounting legal defenses served as an important tool for the Indians; yet for government authorities and for much of Mexican society in general, this resistance by the pueblos was artificial, deliberately stirred up by the Indians' lawyers, whom their critics referred to contemptuously as "shysters."[51] The Indians' tenacity in pursuing redress through the courts was so pervasive that in 1853 the states of México, Veracruz, and Guerrero, as well as the Federal District, prohibited Indian pueblos from litigating issues involving land.[52]

During the nineteenth century, as these developments indicate, Mexico's Indian population could on occasion take measures to assert its political rights and protect the integrity of pueblo lands. Devising legislation and taking cases to court were important options in this effort. On the other hand, during the national period successive Mexican governments were generally not inclined to guarantee the survival of indigenous communities. They preferred, in fact, to have communal lands pass into private hands. Not surprisingly, some Indian communities came to regret the disappearance of the colonial regime, pointing out that the Indian pueblos had enjoyed greater protection under the Spanish monarchy.[53]

INDIAN PUEBLOS, LAND, AND TITLES FROM THE REFORM LAWS ONWARD

Although a succession of national and state governments in Mexico attempted to de-communalize various types of Indian pueblo lands between 1821 and 1850,[54] it was in 1856, under a liberal government, that the Indians' collective rights to land suffered a major blow. In that year the government passed the law of desamortización, or disentailment, aimed at forcing the sale of urban and rural corporate properties previously held in mortmain.[55] The enabling legislation allowed the pueblos' communal lands to be divided, distributed, and particularized, but its effects were not felt for some time. Eventually, the law led a great many pueblos to lose the right of usufruct over their common lands. Although the law was sponsored by liberals, it was also supported by political conservatives and owners of rural estates.[56]

Recent studies have shown, however, that many Indian pueblos managed to preserve their lands by finding loopholes in the legislation while appealing their cases. For example, lands devoted to public use were exempt from the law. As the law read, the Indians' community lands (ejidos) and village sites could fall into this category.[57] The pueblos could also evade the law by converting themselves into agrarian societies and adopting the policy of joint ownership.[58] Thus, some pueblos with land generally not coveted by whites or mestizos managed to gain title to it in the name of their settlers—effectively maintaining the collective control they would otherwise have lost.[59] As a final tactic, the Indians resorted to extreme measures—such as organizing violent rebellions—to avoid losing their lands. The law of disentailment could also be deflected through more exotic loopholes or exceptions, as occurred with some descendants of the Mixtec caciques. Although the system of *mayorazgo* (inheritance of titles and property by the eldest son) had been abolished shortly after independence, some Indian caciques in Oaxaca—especially in the region of the Mixtec—succeeded in keeping their cacicazgos intact despite the passage of the 1856 law. For example, one of the largest cacicazgos in the Mixteca, Chazumba, remained in the hands of José María Bautista y Guzmán until he died, sometime between 1870 and 1880. He had inherited the cacicazgo from his father, Joaquín Antonio Bautista y Guzmán, whose family line went back at least to the sixteenth century.[60]

This gamut of responses by the pueblos demonstrates their marked capacity to negotiate and defend community lands. One of the Indians' more interesting strategies in seeking the latter objective, a strategy their authorities began to pursue starting in the mid-nineteenth century—spurred on by the disentailment law—was to search for their primordial titles, either by themselves or through their representatives.[61]

Some pueblos, however, had begun to search for their titles prior to passage of the legislation, and they continue in this endeavor to the present day. As early as 1830, the pueblos requested through their authorities that searches be made for their titles in the Archivo General de la Nación for the purpose of protecting pueblo land. By 1869, Mexico's national archive had created a special section, the Archivo de Buscas y Traslado de Tierras, to house all the data pertaining to the pueblos' attempts to locate their primordial titles.[62] In general, the formalities of the process were straightforward: the pueblo sent a letter of request to the director of the national archive, stating that, as a requirement of some legal transaction or lawsuit, it needed to secure a certified copy of its primordial titles. In turn, the archive appointed someone to search for the titles and have copies made for the pueblo.[63] In addition, some pueblos that had retained and safeguarded their titles began to take them to the national archive to have them transcribed and certified. A considerable number of pueblos undertook research on the history of their community. The record of requests and responses documenting title searches made between 1869 and 1991 takes up 175 thick volumes, imparting some idea of the sheer number of Indian pueblos that have attempted (and go on attempting) to locate and obtain their primordial titles from the national archive.[64]

Article 97 of the 1846 regulations governing the archive stipulated that the institution "will furnish copies to those individuals who need certain documents to consolidate their rights or to fulfill some other purpose."[65] Even more interesting is Article 102, which stated that "the copies issued as prepared are to be fully accepted in all of the tribunals, courts, and offices of the Republic," signifying that on the basis of the regulation, copies furnished by the national archive were deemed legally valid. By 1920 the service had an expanded definition, to include "the issuance of certified copies of primordial titles, grants, maps, and other original materials existing in it [the national archive] which might in some way be used by the public."[66] Between 1830 and 1904, copies of primordial titles, which in many instances included maps and Techialoyan codices, were produced in manuscript form by exceptionally talented paleographers and illustrators, who hand-colored their illustrations (Figure 3.2). In 1904 the archive began to produce copies on a typewriter.[67]

One of the archive's most distinguished nineteenth-century paleographers was Don Francisco Rosales, who over a number of years transcribed numerous primordial titles for Indian pueblos, in many cases translating them from the original Nahuatl into Spanish. In 1854 Rosales was named "by the supreme government, [as] interpreter and translator of the Mexican language in the Archivo General de la Nación"—an office he fulfilled without an official salary, his sole means of support consisting of what the pueblos paid him for his translations.[68] Rosales customarily took the records to his house and did the work there. For many years he was the archive's only paleographer and translator; he was still working at this task in the early 1870s.[69]

In 1830 the pueblo of Santiago Competepec (known today as Celaya, in the state of Guanajuato) requested a copy of its primordial titles through its auxiliary political chief. This request, which the pueblo needed because it had filed a lawsuit against hacendados who had usurped its lands, is the earliest of its type recorded in the national archive.[70] Two years later the Indians of San Cristóbal

Niz omoniquili yn huey cuauhtlecoatzin niz tococ huey tlalochpanco
tlalticpac tlaxilacali. OO.

Aquí murió el cuauhtlecoatzin, fui aquí enterrado en el lugar de
la gran carrera, arriba de las tierras del Barrio.

3.2 Reproduction, no. 2582 bis. Date: nineteenth century. Courtesy, Archivo General de la Nación, Mexico City.

Pajacuaran (Zamora, Michoacán) submitted a similar request. Both pueblos are located in the Bajío region, an area of rich agricultural land, suggesting that the first pueblos to request their primordial titles in the nineteenth century were those encountering strong pressure from hacendados and independent agriculturalists eager to absorb the pueblos' lands.

These two requests were the tip of the iceberg. Soon thereafter, numerous pueblos across the country took similar action. In general, during the nineteenth century the copies furnished to Indian pueblos were made from records located in the section of the archive known as the Tierras and consisted of such varied colonial documents as grants, fragments of legal claims, and maps—some of which were extremely old. In 1854, for example, the pueblos of San Mateo and Santiago Tepopula (Chalco, state of México) asked the archive to search for their titles—which, it turned out, consisted of the decision rendered in a lawsuit dating to 1536. In that year the Indians living in Chalco and Tlalmanalco were sued by the "Indian caciques and governors" of Mexico City and Tlatelolco, who claimed that some lands reaching from "the sierra of Coatl to the summit of the sierra of Ocotepec" were rightfully theirs, having belonged to their families since pre-Hispanic times. As a result of the Spanish conquest, they alleged, the lands had been illegally seized by the Chalco and Tlalmanalco Indians. The authorities who heard the case in the sixteenth century, however, rejected the testimony of Mexico City's and Tlatelolco's leaders and sided with the defendants. Their finding in this case served as the legal basis on which the pueblos of San Mateo and Santiago Tepolula successfully defended their lands in 1854.[71]

On the whole, the title requests submitted by pueblos were uncomplicated. Normally, pueblos simply cited the 1846 regulation granting them the right to receive copies of their titles from the archive.[72] In some cases the request incorporated information the pueblo's leaders learned about their community's origins and early history from stories told by pueblo elders. This type of information was included as an aid to the paleographer and translator in their search for primordial titles. For example, the Indian community of Santa María Sauceda (in the state of Guanajuato) explained in its 1869 title request that its name in the sixteenth century had been Chichimequillas, which it knew through stories told in the community for hundreds of years. Moreover, it had been called Chichimequillas because

> in its surrounding hills and mountains dwelled the Chichimecan tribes, a
> thoroughly ignorant, barbarian people; and the caciques of the pueblo of
> Xilotepec came there [to Chichimequillas] in order to escape the ravages and
> robberies committed by the Chichimeca people, the settlement was founded
> by travelers making their way from Zacatecas to Mexico City, with the license
> and approval of the Spanish government, and the Spanish monarch granted

them the right to not pay any tribute for many years along with many other privileges and considerations.[73]

Santa María Sauceda's authorities stressed that they lacked any documentation to substantiate this history; their only source was the community's oral tradition. It was thus imperative that the archive search for their titles. Similarly, some pueblos included a description of their ancient boundary markers as a way of documenting their land, while noting that they lacked any written records and relied on information passed down orally from one generation to the next for this knowledge. The 1870 request by the pueblo of Santiago Yauhnahuac (state of Puebla) for copies of its primordial titles is an example of this type of case.[74]

Primordial titles copied and translated into Spanish from the original Nahuatl frequently narrate events connected to the pueblo's founding and very early history. In 1869, for example, Francisco Rosales copied and translated the titles belonging to the pueblos of San Jerónimo Acapulco and Santa María de la Asunción Tepehuexoyuca, Tenango del Valle (in the state of México). Rosales produced his work from a colonial Techialoyan codex the Indians had guarded with care; the codex was constructed and formatted like a book and consisted of twenty sheets of amatl paper on which the names of the pueblos' founders, "Don Salvador Moctezuma and don Miguel de San Martín," were written.[75]

The request for its primordial titles submitted to the archive in 1861 by the pueblo of San Miguel Atlatlauca (Chalco, Mexico) offers a similar case. San Miguel's titles, again translated by Rosales from Nahuatl into Spanish, supposedly date to the year 1521. The document contains a description of eleven mythical founders of the site. Three names stand out among the eleven: "the elders Miguel Axaxayacatzin . . . atlauhteco, Pedro Maexochocotzin, [and] Bartolomé Cuauhxochitzin." These founders likely embody the oral survival of traditions that antedate the Spanish conquest. On this point, the title also mentions that the Indians' efforts to mark off their land provoked serious confrontations: when "the boundaries of the settlement were set . . . the elders clashed violently, the pueblos fought each other, for which our fathers, grandfathers, and grandmothers admired them when the matter of the land was finally regulated."[76]

San Miguel Atlatlauca's title also contains unambiguous allusions to pre-Hispanic Mesoamerican cultural traditions. In mentioning, for example, that authorities in Mexico City sent instructions concerning the sacrament of baptism, the title associates the capital with a particular set of symbols: "the essence inside the water, the wolf's water, site of the rattlesnake's water where the eagle flaps its wings, place of respect, Mexico City." In this connection, the document also warns that the pueblo's inhabitants should hand down to their descendants information about the pueblo's origin and physical boundaries:

> You will say to your children that you are their father, and to those who will come later, to those of Anahuac you will say it, to those who are beginning to stand, to those who are toddlers, and to those still crawling and dragging themselves about, to those who turn themselves head first, to those in the womb as yet unborn, to those of our line who will come in the future, to those who from behind come crawling on all fours, so that they understand what they must keep hold of.[77]

Another primordial title laden with traditional indigenous elements was presented to a court in the present-day state of Jalisco by the Indians of Tonalá in 1848. Containing fifty-eight sheets, the document freely mixes different types of information, including an account of the Spanish conquest, a religious chronicle, and material recording the qualifications and service records of individuals in the pueblo. In addition, those who crafted the title tried to tie their governor's ancestral line to the royal house of the Mexica; thus, "Don Salvador Alvarado Cortes, who bore the name Mascaron Chiptalpopoca," was proclaimed a brother of Moctezuma. Similarly, they tried to liken Tonalá with Tlaxcala, describing the pueblo as a place of great wealth: "this great Province of the great Pueblo of the Cuchilmingalad, the Suchiilmingalas, chucalco, chitalpopocas, who bear these names because they were born in the great Pueblo of Tonalá, founded on the richest land that our Lord the King has in all his crown, lo, all of the land is silver."[78]

From the content of titles such as Tonalá's, it is apparent that the local histories and oral traditions included in some colonial titles continued to have legal relevance for Indian pueblos in the second half of the nineteenth century. Moreover, the archive copied and sometimes translated the material so the Indians could use it as part of the legal defense of their lands.

Also in this period, pueblos that still possessed old maps and documents inscribed more information on them to bring them up to date so they could be introduced as evidence in the courts, with the intent of serving the Indians' efforts to protect communal lands. This strategy was followed, for example, by the pueblo of Chiconquiaco (state of Veracruz), with an old map and colonial grants of land it had safeguarded. In 1877 the pueblo had the map copied from its original amatl paper onto ordinary paper.[79] The map records and illustrates the pueblo's mythical origins and also contains noteworthy dates from the pre-Hispanic Mesoamerican calendar. When copying the map, Chiconquiaco's Indians added the names—in Totonaco, Nahuatl, and Spanish—of places that held importance for them. Five years later, in 1882, the pueblo's leaders had the royal colonial land grants copied as well.[80]

Pueblos that possessed any form of documentation had a natural legal platform from which to argue their case, but what happened to pueblos whose searches for primordial titles in the Archivo General de la Nación came up empty or who lacked any internal documents from the colonial period to present in the courts as a way of authenticating their community's history and antiquity? Under these circumstances, some pueblos decided to produce counterfeit documents and pass them off as original and timeworn—similar to what was done in the seventeenth century with both primordial titles and the Techialoyan-style codex.

In 1887, for example, the pueblo of San Lucas Xochimanca, located in the jurisdiction of Xochimilco, asked the archive to certify a map and some documents it had safeguarded. The map and accompanying documents showed 1552 as the year when the pueblo's boundaries were marked off. The Indians also indicated that once they had certified copies of their documents, whose cover sheet read "Titles of the pueblo of San Lucas Xochimanca, the year 1552," they would donate the latter to the archive. When the documents were examined in the archive, however, they were seen to be false. The report the archive issued specifically noted that the documents contained two counterfeit seals and that the map had a fake drawing of the Spanish coat of arms on it.[81]

This was not an isolated case. In 1871 several pueblos in the state of Tlaxcala furnished the government with a group of titles and maps as part of an effort to protect their lands. State officials apparently realized that the maps and titles were counterfeit and subsequently arrested people they believed had likely perpetrated the crime. They decided to send all the falsified documents as well as the suspects to the city of Puebla, where the head of the counterfeiting ring lived. In court, various campesinos from different pueblos in Tlaxcala testified before the judge, Antonio Rivera, that they had bought the titles and maps. Evidently, the counterfeiting operation was headed up by two non-Indians—Melesio Yañez, a resident of Puebla, whom the Indians described as dressing in a "suit," and his friend Vicente Poblano, who lived in the Tlaxcalan community of San Jerónimo Las Caleras. The two accomplices employed a third man, José Manuel Tello, who forged the titles and painted the maps. Tello revealed that he received instructions from some of the pueblos' authorities about what he should write and paint.[82]

In addition to Yañez, Caleras, and Tello, fifteen others were involved in the scheme. The two lead suspects were incarcerated. The first, Antonio Guerrero, was a campesino and rural schoolteacher from San Bartolo, a settlement belonging to the pueblo of Santa Ana Chautempan (state of Tlaxcala); the second was his father-in-law, Francisco Coca, an illiterate campesino from the same community. Both of the accused testified that they were farmhands who worked for Vicente Poblano and that Poblano had drafted them into the scheme.

Both Guerrero and his father-in-law further declared that their boss, Poblano, sent them to pueblos in Tlaxcala to speak with the Indian authorities, informing them that they knew the identity of a private party who had the colonial-period documents germane to their pueblos' lands. The majority of the Indian authorities fell for the story and accepted Guerrero and Coca's proposal, explaining that they "needed" those documents. In essence, the proposal entailed buying the material for a price that varied from 100 to 150 pesos. In some cases the two also asked for an animal, such as a lamb, to seal the agreement. Once the discussions had concluded, the Indian authorities immediately called the pueblo together and, cooperating among themselves, pledged the money to pay for the titles. The pueblo generally made the payment in two or three installments, since it took time to collect the full amount.[83] Some pueblos further declared that they felt pressured to buy the titles to prevent them from being sold to nearby hacendados.

As a rule, the titles and maps were not delivered for several months. The pueblo authorities who bought the counterfeit documents explained that they tried to learn the identity of the person who possessed their titles but that Guerrero and Coca stopped them from doing so. The two insisted that they could not reveal the person's name because he was very sensitive about this matter, but they assured the Indian authorities that they need not worry since they—Guerrero and Coca—were his "agents."

Before it was broken up, the gang of counterfeiters had sold documents and maps to more than twenty-five pueblos, the majority located in the state of Tlaxcala. They included:

Santa María de Jesús Acapetlahuayan, Acapetlahuacan, Atlixco

Santa Margarita Mazapyltepehco, Tlaxcala?

San Bartolomé Cuayxmantla, doctrine of Santa Ana Chautempan, Tlaxcala

San Martín Tepetomatitla, doctrine of San Pablo Apetlatitla, Tlaxcala

Santa Inés Zacatelco, Tlaxcala

San Antonio Acuamanala, Tlaxcala

San Lorenzo Teposantitlan, Tlaxcala

San Matías Tepetomatitlan, Tlaxcala

San Pablo Apetatitla, cabecera of Santa Ana Chautempan, Tlaxcala

San Diego Acapulco, jurisdiction of San Francisco Acapatlahuacan, Tlaxcala?

San Rafael Tlanamilolpan, doctrine of San Martín Texmelucan

San Pedro Tlalauapan, Santa Ana Chautempan, Tlaxcala

San Jerónimo Tenextlatlatylolla, Tlaxcala?

San Mateo Ocotlán, Tlaxcala

Bartolomé Cuahuaxmatl, Tlaxcala

San Antonio Acuamanala, Tlaxcala

Santa María de Jesús Acapetlahuacan, Tlaxcala?

Santa Margarita Maapiltepexco, Tlaxcala?

Santísima Trinidad Tetatsi Tenellecac de Techalollan, Tlaxcala?

San Hipólito Tepetzoltic, Tlaxcala?

Santo Toribio Xicotzinco, Tlaxcala

When Tello was apprehended in his workshop, the authorities were able to observe his technique firsthand because they discovered a map he was still painting. Similarly, the primordial titles were touched up in a particular way to make them appear as though they were old and worn. Many of the confiscated titles bore dates from the sixteenth century. They were preceded by a cover with a title on it, such as "Possession of lands occupied by the pueblo of San Lorenzo Teposantitlan, as found in the registry of the archive of the natives of the Noble (City?) of [the region of] Tlaxcala, in the year of 1546."[84] On the hundreds of sheets on which he counterfeited titles, Tello consistently used a large, very ornate style of manuscript lettering. He also tried, rather unconvincingly, to imitate colonial orthography by frequently using the letter "k," a practice he also followed—likewise excessively—in the glosses accompanying the maps. The style of the lettering varies. At times it is in the form of block printing; in other instances it is elongated and "chained," with the letters attached to each other in long sentences in an obvious effort to imitate the official style of legal script used at the end of the sixteenth century and the beginning of the seventeenth century, known as *procesal encadenada* (run-together script).

The information contained in the titles varies but is consistent in simulating, in a very confusing and unrealistic way, official documents produced during the colonial period, complete with seals and descriptions of the boundary markers of the pueblos affected. Regrettably, the purchased titles contain few references to the pueblos' local history. San Lorenzo Teposantitlan's titles, for example, begin with this description: "By virtue of the carefully considered measures subsequently brought before the honorable senate of this titleholder's hall, in order that the list of titles contained in the registry be found to cite and include the present primordial document, with the full legal and worthy approval of this preliminary authority in the name of our lord king Karlos V, be it faithfully and respectfully recorded in this main archive."[85]

The peculiar, stilted style of this text was repeated in the maps, both on the maps themselves and in the glosses that accompanied them. The maps are richly colored and at first glance appear to have been done in a nontraditional style. Nonetheless, their illustration of boundary markers and some brief historical data they contain leave the impression that they were produced with information furnished by persons living in the places they represent. Some of the maps depict the founders of the pueblo, along with their written names. The map of Santa

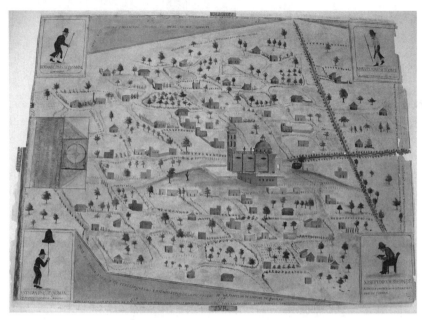

3.3 Reproduction, government records of Puebla, Mexico, 1871. Date: nineteenth century. Courtesy, Library of Congress, Washington, D.C.

Inés Zacatelco, Tlaxcala (Santa Ines Sakatelko), for example, contains an image of one of the pueblo's founders, represented as an elder ringing a bell (lower left-hand side). The local authorities, all dressed in the nineteenth-century manner, are depicted in the other corners of the map (Figure 3.3).

Similarly, the map of San Antonio Acuamanala, Tlaxcala (San Antonio Akuamanala), contains both the image of the oversized head of a man, who is identified as an authority figure, and a drawing of Saint Anthony. Below the map is a serpent confronting a tiger, with the term "coatl" (snake in Nahuatl) inscribed above the serpent. Recall in connection with these maps that their colonial counterparts also depicted the founders of indigenous pueblos. In addition, colonial titles and pictorial manuscripts frequently contained images of local authorities as well as saints, and the Indians' tradition of depicting animals on codices and maps predates the Spanish conquest.

This nineteenth-century attempt to replicate a distinct type and style of traditional indigenous map may have resulted from the fact that the illustrator who drew the copies knew the style and defining characteristics well and, in addition, received information from the Indians who lived in the pueblo whose territorial holdings he was depicting. For example, the gloss accompanying the image of a great serpent on the map of San Pablo Apetatitla, Tlaxcala, indicates that the

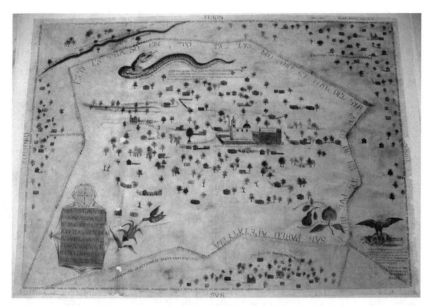

3.4 Reproduction, government records of Puebla, Mexico, 1871. Date: nineteenth century. Courtesy, Library of Congress, Washington, D.C.

mammoth creature attacked various people in 1711, wreaking havoc in the region (Figure 3.4). Another instance of these associations is the map of Santa María de Jesús Acapetlahuacan, Atlixco (Puebla) (Akapetlahuakan), on which the illustrator painted traditional scenes of local life—some of which depict birds with distinct coloration and contain references to human remains encountered in the seventeenth century. The map also depicts a woman lying on the ground, struck by a bolt of lightning as punishment for having committed horrendous crimes. As a final example, the map of San Matías Tepetomatitlan, Tlaxcala (San Matyas Tepotomatytlan), contains an image of pre-Hispanic statuary, accompanied by a gloss that reads "ancient statue" (Figure 3.5). Coincidentally, the Techialoyan-style colonial codex from the pueblo of Santa María de la Asunción Tepehuexoyuta in the Valley of Tenango (state of México) also uses a pre-Hispanic image to represent a place called "the site of infidelity [where] the pueblo's lands lie."[86] All of this information seems to have been derived from local stories the Indian residents told to the person who produced the maps in the nineteenth century.

These maps and titles were not only used by some of the pueblos in Tlaxcala but have also been diligently preserved by them. A map Tello produced for Santa Inés Zacatelco, for example, reposes to this day in the sacristy of the pueblo's church, as do various documents and maps from the colonial period. Tello's counterfeit map, as we shall see, was put to legal use by Zacatelco's inhabitants in the

3.5 Reproduction, government records of Puebla, Mexico, 1871. Date: nineteenth century. Courtesy, Library of Congress, Washington, D.C.

twentieth century. Similarly, the pueblo of Tepeticpac has preserved four lienzos in the sacristy of its church. One of the lienzos, dating from the sixteenth century, records important information about the pueblo prior to the Spanish conquest. Another, entitled *Lienzo de Tepeticpac 2*, supposedly produced in 1535, in reality came out of Tello's workshop and can be identified as such by its stylistic properties and the use of the letter "k" in the accompanying gloss. Given its provenance, it is believed to be a copy of a colonial-era map of Tepeticpac.[87]

The decision by residents of both Zacatelco and Tepeticpac to preserve Tello's counterfeit maps is a strong indication that the maps might have been legally useful at some point. Moreover, the fact that they were preserved along with colonial-era maps or codices already in the residents' possession underscores the intense, centuries-old desire by Indian pueblos to accumulate a corpus of documents—including some shown to be false—that would uphold their claims to communal lands. The impulse was eminently pragmatic.

At the same time, it is difficult to establish with complete certainty whether the pueblos that acquired these documents realized that they were counterfeits. In their testimony against the counterfeiting gang, the residents and authorities of the pueblos caught up in the scheme consistently maintained that they believed they were purchasing legitimate documents. On the other hand, Tello's confession states that he produced the material in accordance with the guidance and instructions he received from the pueblos' authorities. What is undeniably true is that Indian communities needed, searched for, and found maps and related colonial-period documents describing their history as a means of preserving their lands and that the laws of the Reform, which broke up and particularized communal lands, helped drive this movement. The pressure to locate ancient maps and titles created a market for apocryphal documents, a market toward which the Indian pueblos were naturally drawn. As we have seen, this same dynamic existed in the seventeenth and eighteenth centuries, making it likely, despite the absence of clear corroborating evidence, that operations such as Tello's also existed in those days. The fact that so many Indian communities were involved in Tello's scheme reinforces this possibility.

In this context, it is instructive to consider an example that takes us past the nineteenth century. During the twentieth century, Indians from the community of San Salvador Chachapan, Puebla, presented their primordial titles and a colonial-era map dating to 1722 to authorities of the National Agrarian Agency.[88] The map (Figure 3.6) is plain, done on paper, with its traditional indigenous elements consisting of a near-glyphic depiction of water as well as a path marked with footprints and, on the lower part, a representation of the sierra of Amozoc. Curiously, another map almost identical to this one has been preserved by the Indians of San Bartolomé Coatepec, in the state of México. The only element of the San Bartolomé map (described by H. R. Harvey in a 1966 issue of the *Boletín del Instituto Nacional de Antropología e Historia*) that distinguishes it from its Chachapan counterpart is that the water (identical in form to the water in the Chachapan map) appears at its center.[89]

Just as in the foreground of the Chachapan map, a person dressed in the style of the colonial period is standing next to a church, his left arm raised and a hat in his right hand. Below these images appears a mountain range, similar to the depiction of the sierra of Amozoc in the Chachapan map. On the upper left-hand part is a shield bearing the title of the map, the only difference being that the date on the Coatepec map is 1639. In addition, the Coatepec map uses the word "croquis" to refer to the map proper, a term—as Harvey notes—that came into use beginning in 1832.[90] Both maps are late creations from the early–twentieth-century copyist Manuel Ramírez de Arellano. No other circumstance would so readily account for the remarkable similarity between the two maps, supposedly dating from the colonial period and hailing from two very different regions of Mexico—the states of Puebla and México, which are separated from each other by a considerable distance.[91]

In sum, between the promulgation of the laws of the Reform in 1856 and the Mexican Revolution more than half a century later, Indian communities were

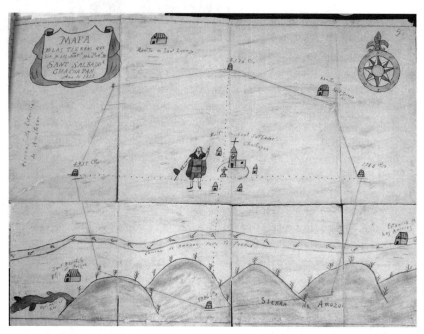

3.6 Reproduction. Date: twentieth century? Courtesy, Archivo General Agrario, Mexico City.

embroiled in a constant battle to ward off the division and loss of their communal lands. Interestingly, their only reprieve from this effort came during the imperial interlude of Maximilian of Austria.

Before he met his death by firing squad in 1867, Maximilian briefly ruled as emperor of a restored monarchy in Mexico, installed following the 1863 invasion of Mexico by French forces and the subsequent fall of the government headed by President Benito Juárez. Although Mexican conservatives had helped engineer Maximilian's designation as emperor, the youthful Hapsburg prince harbored distinctly liberal tendencies. Some Indian pueblos fought alongside the deposed liberals against Maximilian's government and the French military units that propped it up. The Indians of the Puebla sierra were particularly distinguished in combating the expeditionary army of Napoleon III.[92] Many Indian communities, however, supported the new monarchy, motivated especially by the favorable stance Maximilian had taken toward them during his abbreviated period as emperor. As a harbinger of that support, in 1864, when the imperial couple traveled from Veracruz to Puebla, they attended numerous receptions to accept greetings of welcome in Nahuatl from indigenous authorities, with translations provided by a member of their entourage, Galicia Chimalpopoca. In many pueblos the Indians presented the emperor with bouquets of flowers, and native leaders were invited to converse with Maximilian and his wife, Carlota.[93]

Maximilian decided to restore communal landholdings suppressed by the 1856 legislation; in addition, the notice of the restitution—published in both Spanish and Nahuatl—stipulated that pueblos with more than 400 inhabitants but that lacked ejidos and the community sites on which to situate them would henceforth have the right to obtain both. Besides their municipal sites, pueblos with more than 2,000 inhabitants would have the right to gain additional land to be used for ejidos and the cultivation of crops. The lands so granted to the pueblos would be obtained by the government from vacant land or through expropriation.[94] This redirection of policy provided great relief to the Indian communities. Furthermore, in 1865 Maximilian established a new government office, the Junta Protectora de Clases Menesterosas (Committee to Protect the Needy Classes), as a forum in which matters that affected the indigenous population—matters involving land in particular—could be legally aired. In addition, the emperor had granted public audiences on Sundays starting in 1864.[95] These initiatives, warmly received by many Indian pueblos, resembled those followed during the colonial period, when a special tribunal existed to consider indigenous affairs. As a final, critical step, Maximilian restored a distinct legal identity and standing to Mexico's Indians: "[P]etitions from the Indians that reached the emperor allowed him to tamp down conflicts and grasp the reality of his subjects, a function that such petitions had for the European monarchs."[96]

The committee was presided over by Faustino Galicia Chimalpopoca, who held the post of "imperial tutor" in the Nahuatl language at the Colegio de San Gregorio and also served as the administrator of two large Mexico City Indian wards, Santiago and San Juan.[97] This formally educated Nahua was in charge of vetting the problems the Indians brought before the junta. Those problems generally concerned water and land issues that pitted the Indians against hacendados.[98] To help ensure a successful outcome for their claims, Indian pueblos frequently retained lawyers, and they kept abreast of the latest laws and legislation.[99] They also acted in concert, presenting claims collectively. Equally compelling is the fact that in seeking legal redress, the Indians used the same language in their petitions that they had used when writing to the king and viceregal authorities during the colonial period: "[T]he rhetoric used with the emperors—which resurrects the style and forms of address used in colonial times—beseeching protection as helpless and ignorant subjects, contrasts strongly with the language which they had employed in earlier decades and would again employ after the restoration of the Republic, when they claimed their rights as citizens who formed part of the Mexican nation."[100]

Maximilian's policy favoring the Indians was not a momentary whim. On the contrary, he was genuinely interested in the history and archaeology of pre-Columbian Mexico. On his orders, the imperial coat of arms bore the sacred Mexica symbol of the eagle, perched on a cactus and devouring a serpent. Similarly, frescoes painted on the walls of Maximilian's castle in Chapultepec featured pre-Hispanic subjects and landscapes. Both the emperor and his consort were favorably predisposed toward their Indian subjects. The imperial court, for example, issued a decree requiring that all government regulations involving the indigenous population appear in Nahuatl as well as Spanish, and the emperor sympathetically received delegations of Indians. In this vein, Maximilian's policy toward the Indians definitely defused conflicts brewing within the pueblos as a consequence of the 1856 Reform laws.[101] In the opinion of historian Niceto de Zamacois, the enthusiasm Maximilian generated among the Indian pueblos resulted largely from the fact that "it was a novelty for them [the Indians] to witness themselves invited to take part in public affairs."[102]

When the liberal opposition toppled the empire in 1867, however, the pendulum swung back. Not only were the laws adopted by Maximilian's government abrogated, but the 1856 legislation affecting communal lands was fully restored.[103] This legislation was an important springboard for the agrarian policy Porfirio Díaz implemented during his thirty-five years as president of Mexico (1876–1911). For Díaz, Indian communities and the various forms of collective ownership of land constituted a serious obstacle to his plan to mold Mexico into a liberal, modern nation.

In 1883 Díaz's government launched a major legal offensive against the tradition of indigenous landholding through its Decree on Colonization. The decree mandated the demarcation of all the country's vacant or undeveloped land. The idea behind this initiative was to cede such land to foreign immigrants and Mexican settlers. The decree also authorized private companies to carry out the work and awarded them a third of the total land they surveyed and demarcated.[104] Virtually all of these companies were U.S. businesses. One of the aims of the 1883 decree was to create a true national map that charted all of the nation's territory and revealed the actual dimensions and boundaries of its different states. However, since Mexico's government lacked the resources to carry out a complete topographic survey of the country, it opened the field for private companies to do so, "so by this means they undertook the survey work, took ownership of the land, and turned around and sold it."[105]

In 1894 President Díaz issued a sister law dealing with "the occupation and alienation of the vacant lands of the United Mexican States." Under the terms of this law, vacant and virgin lands—or lands not already granted for the benefit of public use—as well as extensions of land and land that belonged to the federal government, could be awarded to any person who "claimed" them, with no upper limit placed on the acreage claimed.[106] This law "continued the program under which small landholdings, as well as agricultural and pasturing lands held communally, were killed off and disappeared." Powerless to stop the process, during this period many Indians lost their land and were forced—as the price of survival—to become laborers on farms and estates. The legislation was intentionally skewed in favor of medium- and large-scale landownership. It benefited foreign interests, surveying companies, landed estates, and President Díaz's cronies and associates. It likewise helped relax restrictions on the exploitation of labor.[107] As a consequence of the legislation, by 1889, companies had surveyed and demarcated 38 million hectares—one-third of Mexico's national territory—and received as compensation 12.7 million hectares. On top of this transfer of land, the Porfirian regime sold an additional 14 million hectares to the survey companies at absurdly low prices. The legislation of 1883 and 1894 thus accomplished two things: it provided ammunition and opportunity to the critics of communal landholding, and it facilitated the legal acquisition of extensive tracts of property by the richest sector of the population.[108]

Although these developments undermined the interests of Mexico's Indian pueblos, the notion that Indians and peasants universally lost their land during Díaz's time as president does not stand up to scrutiny. While many pueblos indeed suffered this fate, others—reflecting specific regional dynamics—managed to uphold and preserve the community-based administration of their lands. Their success in doing so resulted in part from their capacity for negotiation, long a vital element of indigenous culture, and in part from the fact that their lands were neither particularly fertile nor located in a place of strategic importance to enterprises such as the railroad. The municipality of Tepenene, in the Mixteca Alta of Oaxaca, provides one such example. From the end of the nineteenth century into the early 1900s, Tepenene continued to administer its communal lands; some were reserved for ejidos, some supported the running of its municipal government, and some were rented out to individuals. The pueblo's authorities used the rental income to help pay part of the fee for a lawyer they had hired to represent them in litigation over land.[109]

Clearly, with respect to the defense of land mounted by Indian pueblos during the Porfiriato, the more one explores and studies regional cases, the more insight one gains into the strategies the Indians pursued. For now, however, we can confidently assert that the search for primordial titles in the Archivo General de la Nación and the presentation of "ancient" documents were among the key strategies employed. Instances abound in which Indian pueblos sought to defend their land in these ways. In 1887, as we have seen, the community of San Lucas Xochimanca, located in the jurisdiction of Xochimilco, asked the archive to certify the authenticity of several documents as well as a map that showed the pueblo's boundaries as they had been marked off in 1552. Similarly, in 1891 the authorities of Santa María Cuetzalan, in the district of Chiautla (Puebla), submitted an "urgent" request to the Archivo General de la Nación that it search for the pueblo's primordial titles because a surveying company was demarcating land in the area.[110] In 1892, in a third case, officials of San Bernabé Amajac, in the state of Tlaxcala, not only asked the archive to search for the pueblo's titles; they also donated to the archive some ancient documents the pueblo had preserved, requesting in return a transcription of the material.[111]

Even more dramatic, in 1910, Indians from the pueblo of Xixingo (Puebla) participated successfully in a topographic exercise directed by an engineer assigned to identify the boundaries of the pueblo's lands that fell on the line separating the states of Puebla and Oaxaca. The Indians assisted by translating place names from Nahuatl to Spanish and explaining stories carried down through the community's oral traditions; they related, for example, that the remnants of pre-Hispanic sculptures—"idols"—had existed in certain sites, noting that "long ago the pueblo's inhabitants came across many idols believed by the Mexicans to be the gods of their [the Indians'] primitive pagan religion."[112] We can well visualize, at this critical moment on the eve of the Mexican Revolution, the Indians of Xixingo recounting for the engineer from Puebla stories of their ancient past and recalling the Nahuatl names and special sites that marked their lands.

In short, the Indians' talent for negotiation and their flexible ideological posture enabled some pueblos to retain their lands. Moreover, they did so against a political backdrop, engineered by state power, that placed severe constraints on their negotiating strategies up to the beginning of the military phase of the revolution in 1910.

LAND, INDIANS, AND TITLES AFTER THE REVOLUTION

In spite of all the efforts described previously, by 1910 a large proportion of Mexico's indigenous and peasant population was landless. This situation unsettled the countryside and, starting at the end of the nineteenth century, caused many pueblos to rebel against the government, despite its actions to repress dissent.[113] In 1911 Emiliano Zapata and his followers published the Plan of Ayala, which not only repudiated the government of President Francisco I. Madero (1911–1913) but also enunciated the principle that Mexico's land should be distributed to its communities. From 1910 to 1919, Zapata championed and led a sweeping movement for agrarian reform. Recent studies also demonstrate that Zapata's movement produced a far-reaching, coherent plan for the global transformation of a complex society ("Zapatismo generated a radical, class-based, and coherent political plan for the global transformation of a complex society"). The movement's proposals were not static either. As the struggle over the distribution of land advanced, they, too, evolved, although the political program sketched out in the Plan of Ayala—which served as their foundation—was unchanging.[114]

For the Zapatistas, the agrarian community constituted the nation's basic social unit. The agrarian problem thus became the central theme in the plan to reorder Mexican society. The latter goal depended on two requirements: first, that lands be returned to the communities that had historically possessed them; and second, that these communities have the autonomy to determine how they would organize the productive use of their land, in keeping with their resources and traditions. The movement's leaders envisioned that their plan could succeed by transforming free and newly autonomous municipalities into the nation's core political unit. In addition to restoring communal lands to the pueblos, the Zapatista program proposed making nontransferable grants of land, in which the land would be owned and managed by cooperatives. To accomplish these goals, all of the land not in the hands of small landowners would be expropriated and brought immediately under government control by force of arms. The owners of expropriated land would have to present their land titles before revolutionary courts. This all-embracing proposal was designed to transform the nation's agrarian structure. In addition, both the state and federal governments were viewed above all in functional terms; they existed to provide services and coordination. As such, the governors of the different states and the president of the republic would be appointed by councils composed of revolutionary leaders.[115]

The partisans of agrarianism had woven their demands into the rhetoric of the revolution through the Plan of Ayala. The institutional answer to those demands was the ejido. For the peasant insurgents, the pueblo's ejidos were the lands they had always controlled and cultivated; they were a pueblo's entire complex of lands, known during the colonial period and the nineteenth century by various names—*terrenos de común repartimiento* (common croplands), *propios* (lands that supported village governments), *fundo legal* (lands that comprised the site of a pueblo), and ejido (a pueblo's agricultural and pasturelands). After 1856, however, this mix of lands was referred to simply by one name: ejidos. In Dana Markiewicz's opinion, the change and simplification in terminology may have resulted from the language in Article 8 of the Ley Lerdo (the disentailment law) of June 28, 1856. That article exempted the ejidos from disentailment, prompting some pueblos to argue that all of the land still under their control fell into the category of ejidos.[116]

To recover these ejido lands, Indians pueblos took up arms and fought during the revolution. Francisco Madero's government and later the government of Venustiano Carranza (1917–1920) rejected the peasantry's claims, however, since to do otherwise would have undermined the validity of the land titles held by many large-scale landowners and, ultimately, the validity of private property itself. Accordingly, the institution of the ejido that emerged from the revolution was far more the creation of Mexico's peasants than of the new post-revolutionary regime.[117]

In 1915 the faction known as *constitucionalistas*, which included Carranza, promulgated a less radical agrarian law than the one set down in the Plan of Ayala. On January 6, 1915, the constitutionalists' law took concrete form through the creation of a National Agrarian Commission. Established to allocate and restitute land as well as to enlarge existing ejidos, the commission also helped regularize the classification and definitions of small landholdings, land held communally, and land managed cooperatively in the form of ejidos. Local commissions were established in the states to assist the national commission in fulfilling its charge. The National Agrarian Commission set the stage for the adoption of Article 27 of Mexico's 1917 constitution. In January 1934 the commission was replaced and its functions were taken over by a new federal agency, the Departamento Agrario.

Through these initiatives and by restoring the pueblos' juridical standing and identity, the government tried to take control of, and find a solution for, the agrarian problem. In 1915 one of its first actions was to "restitute" to the Indian pueblos the lands they had lost as a consequence of the 1856 Reform laws. The restitution policy fueled a headlong rush by the pueblos to reconstruct their history by producing their primordial titles or by having the titles searched at the Archivo General de la Nación. The pueblos also submitted evidence regarding specific lands they had possessed prior to the 1856 legislation in the form of oral testimonies by elderly community members. The search for primordial titles was likewise intensified by the terms of Article 27 of the 1917 constitution. To advance this work, the National Agrarian Commission engaged paleographers to transcribe the colonial documents the pueblos used as evidence to substantiate the antiquity of their landholdings.[118]

Good intentions notwithstanding, the restitution program fell well short of resolving the agrarian problem because many pueblos could not locate the historical documents that would have proven their loss of land. The government's response was to allocate other land and permit the formation of new agrarian concentrations. The Indians were caught in a vicious cycle, however, because this initiative also had preconditions. The pueblos had to either furnish their primordial titles or provide documentary evidence of "the date on which the pueblo was founded and a copy of its articles of association."[119] Although Indian pueblos had endeavored since before the mid-nineteenth century to locate their primordial titles in the Archivo General de la Nación and continued to do so both prior to the creation of the National Agrarian Commission and after the revolution, the legislation that emanated from the revolution caused them to accelerate their efforts.

In 1912 and 1915, for example, authorities of the pueblo of Coatlán del Río, in the state of Morelos, informed the archive's administrators that the contents of their municipal archive had been destroyed during the revolution. Among the lost documents were their primordial titles. They were therefore asking the archive to search for its copies of the same. The archive was able to fulfill their request by providing a copy of a 1773 document from its Tierras section.[120] Similarly, in 1912 Don Francisco Cuautli (a Nahuatl surname derived from the word for eagle, *cuauhtli*), the auxiliary president of the pueblo of San Antonio Cacalotepec, part of the municipality of San Andrés Cholula (Puebla), submitted a search request to the archive for the pueblo's primordial titles.[121]

Documents that recorded their history thus continued to have profound importance for indigenous communities, even more following passage of the 1915 agrarian legislation. Furthermore, many of the pueblos that had success-fully preserved centuries-old documents preferred to turn them over to the archive for safekeeping after they had used them to defend their lands. The case of Cuajimalpa, a pueblo located in the Federal District, provides such an example. In 1913 the pueblo's authorities decided to donate their primordial titles, contained in a Techialoyan-type codex produced on amatl paper, to the Archivo General de la Nación.[122] Their titles, as transcribed, copied, and translated from Nahuatl to Spanish by Francisco Rosales in the nineteenth century, contain information about the region's pre-Hispanic governing lineages: "The domain of the great and worthy ones of the land of Xihuitltemoctzin began here, possessors of the white vestments at the time the Spaniards arrived."[123]

The use of counterfeit primordial titles also continued. For example, in 1913 the pueblo of San Nicolás Tetitzintla, located in the district of Tehuacan (Puebla), asked the Archivo General de la Nación to certify the authenticity of its primordial titles. It needed the documents to secure newly received ejido lands. The archive, however, determined that the titles were counterfeit; its authorities, in fact, found the wording and style of the titles "nonsensical."[124] Cases such as Tetitzintla's occurred during this period because government agrarian authorities lacked the rudimentary historical knowledge to evaluate the colonial-period and nineteenth-century documents the Indian communities presented to them.

The case of another pueblo, Santa Inés Zacatelco (Tlaxcala), exemplifies this situation. In 1933, Santa Inés's inhabitants produced a copy of a map of their pueblo that supposedly dated to the colonial period. The map, however, was actu-ally one of the counterfeit maps from José Manuel Tello's workshop that had been made in 1871 for the pueblos in the state of Tlaxcala (Figure 3.7). The copy of the counterfeit map contains interesting alterations. Its coloring is much more vivid than the "original," and—as one measure of its supposed antiquity—its bor-ders have motifs styled in typical pre-Hispanic fashion (Figure 3.8). Pueblos that

187

3.7 Reproduction. Date: nineteenth century. Courtesy, officials of the steward's office, Church of Santa Inés Zacatelco.

had managed to preserve maps from an earlier time thus had them copied by a member of the community after the revolution to substantiate the pueblo's long history and, on this basis, to obtain the allocation of land.[125] Some of these maps were counterfeit, however, and in the case of Santa Inés Zacatelco the convolutions were even greater, since the pueblo's inhabitants copied a supposed colonial-era map—actually produced in 1871—to secure a 1933 distribution of land. More interesting still is that to this day the pueblo possesses genuine colonial maps and genealogies.[126] In 1933, as we see in Figure 3.9, the pueblo's inhabitants copied a complete genealogy that seems to be from the colonial period. In addition, the pueblo copied a genealogical tree of its caciques that was probably sixteenth-century in origin (Figure 3.10). Clearly, for pragmatic reasons, the residents of Santa Inés Zacatelco simply tried to amass as large a body of evidence as was available.

A case similar to Santa Inés's involved the pueblo of Santa María Acuitlapilco (Tlaxcala), where in response to the post-revolutionary environment the Indians also copied a lienzo preserved by the community since colonial times. In addition, the sacristy of Santa María Acuitlapilco's church has an oil painting dating to the same period that contains extremely interesting motifs.[127] Possibly done in the eighteenth century and still in good condition, the picture, or map—clearly

3.8 Reproduction. Date: nineteenth century. Courtesy, officials of the steward's office, Church of Santa Inés Zacatelco.

of indigenous origin—is painted on both sides on cloth, accompanied by a gloss in Nahuatl. A series of caves with lagoons inside them is depicted on the front, and in the top center of the map is the image of a white, fair-haired woman with the green-colored double tail of a serpent, bearing the gloss *cihua xochla cuitlapilco* (lady of this place who bears a tail?). The woman is surrounded by Indians with white blankets and by smaller serpents. A childlike figure with western features appears in the center of the painted map. He seems to be a little white-skinned nahual, who carries a lance while in the act of hunting. On his head he wears a helmet, which takes the form of an eagle's head and bears the gloss *quauhpiltzinti-ipe nahual tlachixqui* (the royal nahaul eagle child who looks at or takes care of something?). There is also a path with footprints on it and figures of Indians, either seated or kneeling, painted around the path. The reverse side of the map seems to be sixteenth-century in origin. A friar, shown atop a hill with a serpent at his shoulders, appears in its upper part. The friar seems to be preaching to a group of Indians who are dressed in white blankets and are listening to him with heads lowered. Buildings, such as chapels, are depicted at the bottom of the map.

The two sides of the map appear to depict contrasting or opposite states: on the reverse, a scene showing a missionary's work of evangelization and on the

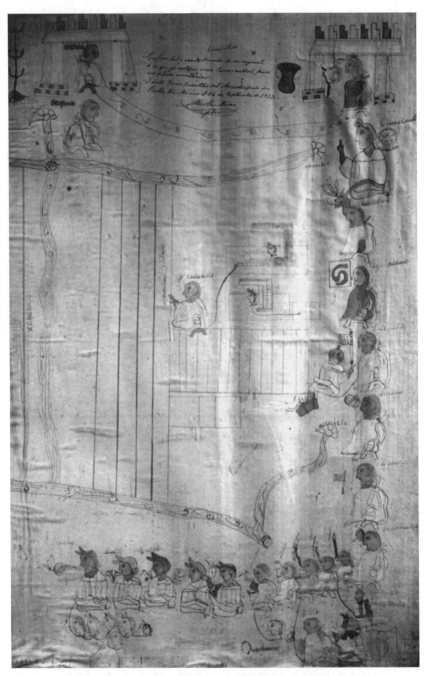

3.9 Reproduction. Date: 1933. Courtesy, officials of the steward's office, Church of Santa Inés Zacatelco.

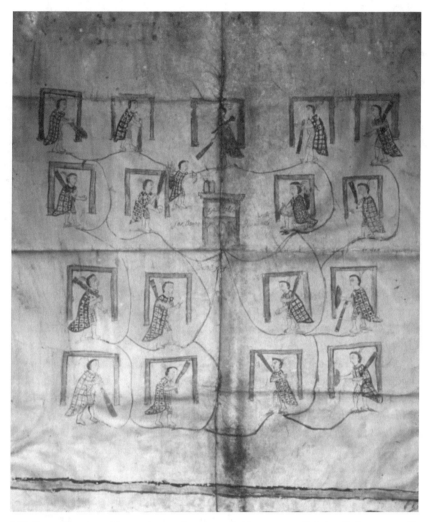

3.10 Reproduction. Date: sixteenth century? Courtesy, officials of the steward's office, Church of Santa Inés Zacatelco.

front, a representation of the Indians' "idolatrous" beliefs held before the arrival of the Spaniards. A recent study of the pueblo, which at one time stood by a lagoon (now dried up), mentions that between 1930 and 1970, people in the locale believed in the existence of a siren, a woman with the tail of a fish, who watched over the lagoon of Acuitlapilco. In recent years, as the water gradually dried up and disappeared, the siren's place was taken by another woman who terrified those who at night came near the spot where the lagoon had been located.[128] Evidently, during these same decades the Indians of Acuitlapilco also thought (returning to the image of the serpent) that green- or blue-colored serpents lived in the clouds and brought rain during the sowing season.[129] In addition, they believed in the existence of *nauales*, "persons of male sex who turned into predatory animals like the wolves or coyotes that lived in the hills."[130] The front of the Acuitlapilco map appears to make reference to these beings. Next to the original map sits a twentieth-century copy, which seems to be painted only on one side. It is not clear whether the evangelization scene was copied. In the copied version, most of the colors have a blue tinge, and, although it also seems to have been changed in some ways, the Nahuatl gloss is much clearer than in the original. An inscription, read only with difficulty, appears at the bottom: "copied M. Ll Riera or Rieza."

The care Indian pueblos took after the revolution to re-elaborate and present historical evidence was not accidental. By this time, they had a total of almost 400 years of experience in mounting legal defenses to protect their lands from outsiders' greed. The revolution and its rhetoric notwithstanding, the Indians understood that their hold on the land was not guaranteed, that the hacendado class would fight to take it away from them, and that government authorities' commitment to restitute and allocate land was relative. A pueblo like Santa Inés Zacatelco easily grasped this reality; it had been surrounded by hacendados since the colonial period.[131]

In 1921, Zacatelco's inhabitants had managed to obtain a provisional allocation of ejido land, a development that affected the interests of the owners of nearby haciendas who enjoyed the protection of the governor of the state of Tlaxcala. In light of this fact, the foremen on two of the haciendas, Santa Águeda Cuacualoya and San Isidro Pinillo, armed themselves with carbines and threatened the Indians of Zacatelco unremittingly. Their terror tactics included shooting at the peasants as they tried to sow the land the government had allocated to the pueblo. Zacatelco's authorities claimed that the hacendados had accused their fellow villagers, in front of the governor, "of having blown up a bridge and also of ripping up a long stretch of road that connected the hacienda of Santa Águeda to the Panzacola station, all of which is nothing but slanderous lies on the part of these estate owners." Such dealings by hacendados were common. As a rule, they called in the police force, known as the white guards, to prevent the campesinos from taking possession of the ejido lands granted to them. Some hacendados even had detachments of the federal army on their payroll.[132] Large landowners and their foremen typically viewed the leaders of the agrarian movement as "despotic types" who stirred up destitute and backward communities with their promises of land. For some, these agrarian activists were akin to "witch doctors."[133]

At last, in 1923, Zacatelco obtained its allocation of land in definitive form.[134] The struggle was long and hard. From 1914 to 1918 the claimants were led by a peasant revolutionary named Domingo Arenas, who succeeded in rousing to arms a large number of Tlaxcala's campesinos.[135] A statue of Arenas still stands in Zacatelco, and every year, on August 30, the pueblo—convinced of the importance of preserving his memory—stages a parade to honor him:

> The legacy of Domingo Arenas, we celebrate the festivity recognizing that he fought for land when campesinos had almost no land, the hacendados monopolized all the land, harvesting all of it, giving what they wanted to the campesinos, so then Domingo Arenas rose up in arms and made it known to them that they had to fight for these lands which would be shared out among all those who had no land yet worked it, all those who were made to work the entire day and got what little handouts of corn the hacendados wanted to give them, to sustain their households, for this reason, then, this man rose up in arms and fought a revolution here in Zacatelco and indeed, yes, he succeeded, they recovered their lands.[136]

The hacendados' resistance to the land distribution program deepened the unity among the Indian pueblos and enabled them to craft a stronger legal position in their negotiations with the state to recover or obtain land. These negotiations advanced on several fronts and involved a series of actions: searching for documents recording the history of pueblos and their lands, approaching the government's agrarian authorities, obtaining assistance from other official agencies, and drafting extensive correspondence to send to various functionaries—correspondence whose terminology demonstrated the pueblos' adherence to the ideals and aims of the revolution. Between 1917 and 1940 alone, more than 400 pueblos sought to regain lost land through restitution.[137]

In Dana Markiewicz's opinion, the agrarian reform program was distinguished more by its limitations than by its accomplishments. It served as a brake on campesino unrest and rebellion, created some adjustments in patterns of landownership, and—critically important—helped to institutionalize the new political order that emerged from the revolution. Its limitations resulted from a lack of political will among post-revolutionary governments to realize the promise of comprehensive land redistribution. Stated bluntly, government leaders never had much interest in either bettering the campesinos' lot or addressing the nation's agrarian problem, and their indifference colored the essential design of agrarian reform policy. The agrarian law permitted small landholdings. That provision, coupled with the constitutional guarantee of the right to possess land, enabled large landowners to mask themselves as small landholders in the eyes of the courts. The only exception to this situation occurred during Lázaro Cárdenas's presidency (1934–1940), when a record amount of land was distributed to campesinos—an amount that had not been reached previously and has yet to be exceeded.[138]

Thus, very little land was distributed during Venustiano Carranza's administration, and the percentage of decisions made in favor of campesinos was similarly low. From 1917 to 1920 they received slightly less than 400,000 hectares of land, a mere 0.3 percent of all the country's agricultural land. Although Article 27 of Mexico's constitution stipulated that the division of land belonging to haciendas was to be completed through the passage of federal and state legislation, both Carranza and his successor, Alvaro Obregón (1920–1923), deferred resolution of this troublesome matter to the states. Federal law permitted the expropriation of land on behalf of the pueblos yet, at the same time, placed no limits on the amount of land that could be owned either individually or by a company. Laws passed between 1918 and 1923 brought some measure of control over this muddled situation, but they were rarely enforced.[139]

Moreover, state laws permitted landowners to maintain large extensions of land and generally granted them extended periods of time in which to sell acreage that exceeded state-imposed limits. On occasion, state laws also granted exceptions to such regulations in the interest of the efficient operation of large estates. Furthermore, when an expropriation occurred, its beneficiaries were not only required to pay the state government for the land they received, but the owners of the land had the right to compensation as well. In this way, agricultural laborers and poor campesinos were obstructed from benefiting from agrarian reform laws, since they lacked the funds with which to buy land.[140] In addition, as we saw in the case of Santa Inés Zacatelco, many large landowners were supported by the state governors and used arms to enforce their will. Given these conditions, the agrarian reform envisioned in the constitution was destined to fail.

Under the administration of Plutarco Elías Calles (1924–1928), only a small fraction of the campesino population received agricultural credits, in part because of pervasive corruption within the government. As of 1928, only 4 percent of the nation's agricultural land had been distributed, and only 10 percent of existing haciendas had been affected by the allocation or enlargement of ejidos. These statistics underline the power of large landowners to block agrarian reform, reinforced by state support during this period. In 1930 President Calles voiced the opinion that the agrarian reform program should end. In doing so, he was echoing the wider political reality. The distribution of land had come to a halt across the country, and the number of presidential resolutions was likewise in decline. Approximately 2.5 million people were landless in Mexico. At the beginning of the 1930s, the country had 4,189 ejidos and 898,413 recipients of ejido land, each of whom, on average, had around 2.2 hectares of land to cultivate. At the same time, only 5,565 haciendas had been affected by the agrarian reform program; of the 41.3 million hectares of land controlled by large landowners, only 6.9 million hectares (17 percent) had been expropriated.[141]

The country embarked on a new course during Cárdenas's government. Both Cárdenas and the people around him understood the importance of the campesino population to the nation's life and well-being. Under his administration a high priority was placed on consolidating the revolutionary regime and implementing its social aims. From 1935 to 1940 Cárdenas signed 11,000 presidential resolutions, through which 774,000 campesinos received 19 million hectares of land. By 1940, ejidos accounted for 57.4 percent of the country's irrigable land—a sharp contrast to the situation a decade earlier, when the percentage of such land under ejido control was only 13.1 percent. Although the distribution of land increased significantly during Cárdenas's time in office, progress in achieving underlying agrarian reform moved more slowly—affected by international events, disagreements inside the government, and class-based domestic struggles. Nonetheless, the majority of changes in the nation's agrarian structure took place from 1936 to 1938.[142]

The strong push for land distribution came to an end in 1940 with Ávila Camacho's ascendancy to the presidency (1940–1946). At the outset of his term, the country still had 308 large estates, with an average size of 100,000 hectares. Haciendas larger than 1,000 hectares, which represented only 0.8 percent of national landholdings, controlled 79.5 percent of the total land. Furthermore, the distribution of land among the country's ejidos was highly uneven. While 9.1 percent of the recipients of ejidos controlled just 1 percent of the ejido lands under cultivation—working plots that on average covered less than 1 hectare—2.5 percent of all ejido recipients controlled 13.8 percent of cultivated ejido land, with plots of 20 hectares on average. The government made no effort to mitigate this development. Moreover, the sale of ejido lands, which impoverished some ejido recipients while enriching others, was a common practice in these years.[143]

Under the Cárdenas administration, many hacendados had lost land, but starting in 1940 they returned with greater force, bolstered by support from the state. In addition, the ejidos lost the resources and assistance they had previously received. The agrarian policy of Ávila Camacho's government targeted agricultural development and production, not social reform. These trends were reinforced during the first year of Miguel Alemán's presidency (1946–1952), when, in legal proceedings involving agrarian issues, the practice of *amparo* (granting an injunction suspending the effects of legal dispositions seen to violate constitutional guarantees of individual rights) came back into force. This decision effectively spelled the end of the agrarian reform begun in 1915. Alemán, declaring that agrarian reform and economic development were mutually exclusive, modified Article 27 of the constitution to permit landowners to bring challenges in court against expropriations, an action that deprived the ejidos of their main legal bulwark against hacendados. The years 1940 to 1965 were a golden age in Mexico for large-scale commercial agriculture. Financial and political resources were put at the disposal of this capitalist sector. For ejidos, however, the future was bleak. Having lost the support of the government and stripped of their ability to contest the interests of private agriculture, they entered a period of decline.[144]

Given the implacable obstacles they faced, the only recourse for the country's Indians and campesinos, the only way out of the straitjacket, was to sell pueblo lands. In November 1991 Article 27 was modified yet again—this time by Carlos Salinas de Gortari's government (1988–1994)—to permit lands held in the form of ejidos to be rented or sold, with an eye toward stimulating private investment and promoting the injection of foreign capital into Mexico's agricultural sector. In tandem with this development, Salinas announced that the agrarian reform program initiated in 1915 had ended. Government representatives tried to argue that these new measures would modernize, not destroy, the ejido. Their adoption, though, was an implicit acknowledgment that the political sands had shifted and that the support of the ejido campesinos—once so critical to the coalitions sustaining successive Mexican governments—was no longer needed. The country's peasant organizations viewed these changes as a collective disaster for *ejidatarios*, agricultural laborers, and Indian pueblos.[145]

This landmark reform led to the creation of a new government initiative, the Program for Certification of Ejido Rights (PROCEDE), through which lands could be registered on an individual basis—thereby facilitating the sale of what had once been communal land to privately incorporated entities. This process, in turn, fueled rampant greed and the illegal sale of communal and ejido lands. The field was tilted sharply in favor of the privatization of Indian pueblo lands and their natural resources.[146]

An equally or even more serious consequence of these reforms has been the disappearance of a large number of state offices and agencies (responsible for extending loans, regulating prices, dispersing agricultural inputs such as seeds and fertilizers, and similar tasks) that promoted rural social welfare by ensuring that state resources reached the countryside.[147] For example, when the Mexican Coffee Institute ceased to exist, a guaranteed price for the commodity disappeared along with it. The reform package thus freed the state from its historical obligation to promote production and guarantee minimum prices. The support the state had long given the country's agricultural population vanished, bringing parts of the Mexican countryside to a virtual standstill.[148]

Despite these adverse conditions, Indian pueblos continued to defend their lands by arguing their position both in the courts and through direct contact with state- and national-level authorities. As we have seen, after passage of the 1915 and 1917 agrarian legislation, they maintained the practice of searching for their primordial titles or of using the titles and other documents they and their forbears had safeguarded for generations. On this matter, Indian pueblos across the country continue to consult with the national archive's Department of Paleography, Diplomatics, and Document Certification. Every day the departmental staff consults reams of colonial documents and furnishes transcribed, certified copies of primordial titles to the communities requesting them, "since, for the pueblos, these documents attest to their possession of land":

> When the pueblo representatives arrive [in the national archive], they are taken to the main reference area, where they first sign in and then submit their title search request. If it happens that no such documents are located, the cause is not lost, because if the resolution of some dispute over their land is found, that resolution becomes the title. If old maps turn up, they serve to identify the boundaries of pueblos. At times, documents—sometimes with seals on them—are found and turn out to be apocryphal, and others, produced with dye and from the late nineteenth century, are also located.[149]

For all this work, which may take months, pueblos pay only the cost of the certified copies. The time and labor expended are provided gratis. From time to time, the staff must deal with difficult situations. For example, representatives from pueblos contesting the same lands may find themselves in the archive at the same time, in which case departmental personal need to mediate between them so disputes do not break out while title searches are under way. Pueblos customarily ask the archive to certify every document that makes reference to their communities, not simply the primordial titles. As a rule, the pueblo's authorities travel to the archive to present a search request. They often spend two or three days in uncomfortable circumstances—sleeping, for example, in bus stations—in the hope that their primordial titles will be found quickly. Archival staff members frequently plead with them to return to their communities, explaining that document searches can take a considerable amount of time.[150] An Indian peasant with whom I conversed explained that the Indians make their way to the archive like children following at their father's heels, to receive the documents that define their heritage.[151]

Indian pueblos, then, continue—as they have done for centuries—to use and copy primordial titles, as well as maps, codices, and a host of related documents, to validate their landholdings and protect them in the judicial arena. For example, the pueblo of San Miguel Ecatepec, Tequicistlán, located in the Oaxacan district of Tehuantepec, presented a "faithful copy" of a colonial codex to the agrarian authorities (Figure 3.11). The copy, done in black and white on paper and certified by the municipality's agent, was produced in "San Miguel Yautepec, Oaxaca, on 5 November 1941." It contains large-size Spanish-language glosses and depicts a man and a woman paired as caciques, with the expression

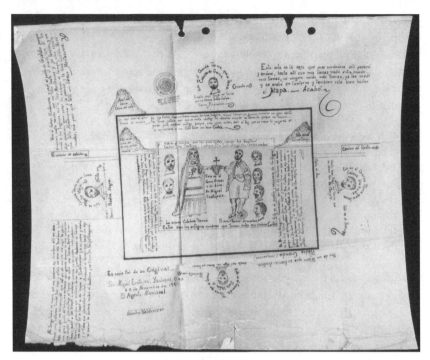

3.11 Reproduction. Date: 1941. Courtesy, Archivo General Agrario, Mexico City.

"the tender snake lady" appearing beneath the woman, matched by the words "lord, trunk of many" under the man. Below their names is written "These were their names of old before [Hernán] Cortés arrived." The glosses indicate that the codex deals with caciques, and one of the glosses describes what sounds like a history of mythical origin:

> The lady tender snake, the lord Log of many, these are the ancient names they had before the arrival of Cortés. I am absent both father and mother who brought me into this world; I am an orphan, there in [crossed out], where they found me the earth shook for thirteen days and three days after they found me, a rainbow also appeared, I saw the people gather me up, with great delight, from the foot of the rainbow, and they reared me, attending to me in high spirits; then, having grown up, the time arrived for me to measure off my lands, I battled with many and slaughtered the valiant Zapotecos when I wanted to do so, a clap of thunder was heard and all of the people died. After a time, I escaped and went off to bring my woman to Xuchitepeque, and also her father and mother and all the servants. After more time, my child was born, the lady took great cheer, and it was baptized, and is named D[o]n Felipe Gregorio.[152]

This document clearly incorporates aspects of an important local oral tradition, as well as information gleaned from what seems to be a colonial codex. The pueblo's authorities presented it to an agrarian tribunal to verify their community's long history. The fact that Indian pueblos would still copy codices in the mid-twentieth century is interesting enough, but lending greater interest to these exercises—undertaken over matters of land—were their recovery and recounting of ancestral myths and stories.

As we have seen, indigenous communities attached great importance to these documents. When they lacked their primordial titles, they invoked other strategies for negotiating the preservation of their lands with the state. The latter option was used, for example, by the pueblo of Iztapan, in the state of México. Since its inhabitants were apparently bereft of old documents, they decided at the beginning of the twentieth century to take a leather-bound book with religious illustrations and inscribe on its front—in white letters over a black background—"Títulos de Iztapan. 1639" (Figure 3.12).

The instances in which Indian community members have made and continue to make use of historical documents to defend their lands are too numerous to describe here. The essential point is that even today they feel strongly connected to these documents. Employing the documents as a legal tool, they have carried on the fight for their lands for centuries, lands on which they continue to perform ceremonies and rituals as part of marking off boundary lines and confirming their possession of territory—as is done, for example, by the Ayuk (Mixe). In the Oaxacan community of Alotepec, when the line, or boundary stone (*mojonera*), that marks the intersection of the territorial limits of three pueblos (*punto trino*) is going to be laid down, the members of its council of elders "go [to the site] and perform a ceremony with prayers and ask nature's permission, they pray that all go well and they make offerings of roosters and chickens, of mescal and tobacco. They sever the heads of the animals, their wings and tiny legs, and bury them above the other items, and they place the boundary marker on top."[153]

This value that the land holds for the Indians and the land's interconnection with ancient documents, primordial titles, and local tradition are difficult to grasp from a purely historical vantage point. In my judgment, the pueblos' historical process and their contemporary reality must be examined together. Thus, in Chapter 4, I analyze the importance the recovery of their documents and their past holds for Indian pueblos today, as well as the link to their lands these documents carry, as elements in the way they view and make sense of their world. In turn, I hope to lend support to the idea that history and anthropology are disciplines that, pursued jointly, bring us closer to understanding the past, present, and possible future of the Indian pueblos.

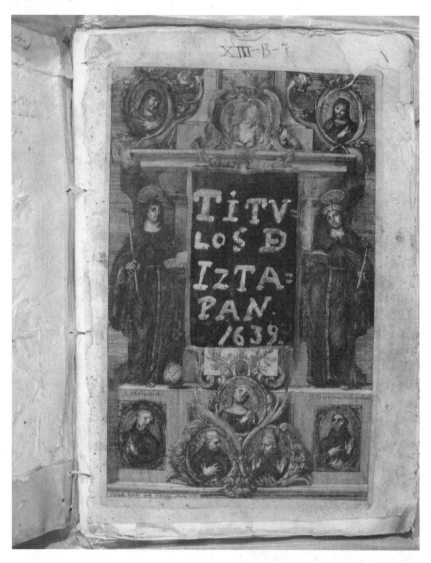

3.12 Reproduction. Date: twentieth century. Courtesy, Archivo General Agrario, Mexico City.

NOTES

1. John Tutino, "Globalizaciones, autonomías y revoluciones: Poder y participación popular en la historia de México," in Leticia Reina and Elisa Servin, eds., *Crisis, reforma y Revolución México: Historias de fin de siglo*, 25–85 (Mexico City: Taurus, Consejo Nacional para la Cultura y las Artes, and INAH, 2002), 29; Felipe Castro, *La rebelión*

de los indios y la paz de los españoles (Mexico City: CIESAS and Instituto Nacional Indigenista, 1996), 40.

2. Margarita Menegus Bornemann, "Los bienes de comunidad y las Reformas Borbónicas (1786–1814)," in Antonio Miguel Bernard Rodríguez, ed., *Estructuras agrarias y reformismo ilustrado en la España del siglo XVIII* (Madrid: Ministerio de Agricultura Pesca y Alimentación, 1989), 383–389.

3. Wayne Smyth Osborn, "A Community Study of Meztitlán, New Spain, 1520–1810" (PhD diss., University of Iowa, Iowa City, 1970), 197–198.

4. William Taylor, "Conflict and Balance in District Politics: Tecali and the *Sierra Norte de Puebla* in the Eighteenth Century," in Arij Oweneel and Simon Miller, eds., *The Indian Community of Colonial Mexico: Fifteen Essays on Land Tenure, Corporate Organizations, Ideology and Village Politics* (Amsterdam: CEDLA, 1990), 270–294.

5. John Tutino, *From Insurrection to Revolution in Mexico: Social Bases of Agrarian Violence, 1750–1940* (Princeton: Princeton University Press, 1986), 140–141.

6. Eric Van Young, *The Other Rebellion: Popular Violence, Ideology, and the Mexican Struggle for Independence 1810–1821* (Stanford: Stanford University Press, 2001), 408–415.

7. Ibid., 423.

8. Ibid., 46, 498.

9. Dolores Pla Brugat, "Indios, mestizos, y blancos, según algunas estadísticas elaboradas en México en el siglo XIX," in *Diario de Campo* (Mexico City: Nacional de Antropología and INAH, 2007), 43, 106–111. The accuracy of population censuses in nineteenth-century Mexico is problematic. These statistics from Pla Brugat are therefore approximations: in 1810, Mexico was 18 percent white, 60 percent Indian, and 22 percent mestizo; in 1857 the country was 17 percent white, 50 percent Indian, and 33 percent mestizo; in 1876 it was 20 percent white, 43 percent Indian, and 37 percent mestizo; in 1885 the percentages were 19 white, 38 Indian, and 43 mestizo (the latter-most either self-declared or so considered, although we do not know what the defining attributes of mestizo were); and finally, in 1921 the national population consisted of 10 percent whites, 29 percent Indians, and 59 percent mestizos. These figures are curious, indicating a flat or minimal level of growth within the white population, followed—as reflected in the 1921 percentages—by a sudden drop in its numbers. In contrast, the censuses show a distinct rise in the mestizo population beginning in 1885. These figures may be deceptive, however, since they pertain to social and cultural, rather than biological, race mix. Taking this factor into account, new studies demonstrate that the indigenous population remained in the majority throughout the nineteenth and twentieth centuries. See Federico Navarrete, *Las relaciones interétnicas en México* (Mexico City: UNAM, 2004).

10. Young, *The Other Rebellion*, 496.

11. Ibid., 503.

12. Taylor, *Magistrates of the Sacred*, 296–297.

13. F. Peter Guardino, *Peasants, Politics, and the Formation of Mexico's National State Guerrero, 1800–1857* (Stanford: Stanford University Press, 1996), 92–93.

14. Ibid., 92.

15. Alicia Tecuanhuey Sandoval, "La resistencia del subdelegado de Atlixco a los ayuntamientos en los pueblos del partido, 1812–1814," in *Memorias de la Academia Mexicana de la Historia correspondiente de la Real de Madrid,* 15–36 (Mexico City: n.p., 2002), quote on 35–36.

16. "[A]bolida la Constitución por el Real Decreto de [4 de mayo de 1814] se nos repuso en los destinos antes dichos (volvieron a ocupar sus puestos de gobierno) y pudiendo haber desahogado entonces vergonzosas pasiones huimos constantes de bajezas y nos limitamos únicamente a el lleno puntal de nuestras atribuciones e incumbencies." AGN, Gobernación 34, "Quejas y reclamaciones. Los caciques, gobernador y regidores perpetuos de la N.C. [Noble Ciudad] de Tlaxcala se les expida el rescrito correspondientes para el goce de los honores de que se hallaron despojados por el Nuevo Ayuntamiento," December 4, 1822. Signed by "Don Francisco Vásquez, Don José de Molina, Don José Ignacio de Lira y Don Juan Tomás de Altamirano y Don Rafael Morales Caciques todos de la N[oble] C[iudad] de Tlaxcala."

17. Ibid.

18. AGI, Indiferente General 1612.

19. T. Michael Ducey, "Hijos del pueblo y ciudadanos: Identidades políticas entre los rebeldes indios del siglo XIX," in Brian Connaughton, Carlos Illanes, and Sonia Pérez Toledo, eds., *Construcción de la legitimidad política en México* (Mexico City: El Colegio de Michoacán, Universidad Autónoma Metropolitana, UNAM, and El Colegio de México, 1999), 127.

20. Rebecca Earle, "Creole Patriotism and the Myth of the 'Loyal Indian,'" *Past and Present* (Oxford) 172 (2001): 125–145.

21. Lucina Moreno Valle, *Catálogo de la Colección Lafragua, 1821–1853* (Mexico City: Instituto de Investigaciones Bibliográficas and UNAM, 2001), document no. 129, 13. This attitude and state of affairs applied not only to Mexico but to Peru as well. See Mallon, *Peasant and Nation,* 16.

22. AGN, Gobernación 40, 7, exp. 6, 1822: "Decree of the Provisional Governing Junta regarding the suppression of the half real of ministros, half real for the Hospital, and the one and a half real contributions heretofore paid by the Indians. Hospitals are also obliged to admit Indians as patients, no differently than any other citizen."

23. Moreno Valle, *Catálogo,* document 741, decree of February 21, 1822.

24. Antonio Escobar Ohmstede, "Introduction: La 'modernización' de México a través del liberalismo. Los pueblos indios durante el juarismo," in Antonio Escobar Ohmstede, ed., *Los pueblos indios en los tiempos de Benito Juárez (1847–1872)* (Mexico City: Universidad Autónoma Metropolitana, 2007), 19.

25. Ducey, "Hijos del pueblo," 130 (quote); T. Michael Ducey, "Viven sin ley ni rey: Rebeliones coloniales en Papantla, 1760–1790," in Victoria Chenaut, ed., *Procesos rurales e historia regional (sierra y costa totonacas de Veracruz)* (Mexico City: CIESAS, 1996), 24.

26. Guardino, *Peasants,* 91–92.

27. AGN, Gobernación 40, 4, exp. 67, 1822, Guadalajara: "request to do away with the words mulatto, negro, Indians and in their place to use the word Mexicans."

28. AGN, Criminal 175, exp. 5, Zacualpan, 1815.

29. "[P]or esperar a que curasen a la enferma como lo tenían prometido y a mayor abundamiento porque luego no nos creen las justicias esas cosas, y con tenerlos dos o tres días presos los ponen libres y salen a hacer daño a los que contra ellos se quejan." Ibid.

30. Ibid.

31. AGN, Justicia, vol. 14, exp. 8, 1821: "Melchor de los Reyes, governor of the pueblo of Ixcatepec, jurisdiction of Zacualpan, on behalf of the Indians of the pueblo, [urges] that its sole church, which was burned down during the revolution, be rebuilt."

32. AGN, Inquisición 1465, sheet 87.

33. AGN, Mapa, no. 4719.

34. AGN, Bienes Nacionales 663, exp. 19.

35. Carlos Ruiz Medrano, "Los rebeldes de Colotlán en 1780 y la llegada del rey Mariano a Tepic en 1801: Episodios de la resistencia indígena en las postrimerías del período colonial mexicano." Unpublished manuscript, 2008.

36. AGN, Gobernación 75, exp. 19, 1824.

37. In this period the term generally referred to the white population and implied that the Indians lacked the qualities of rationale people.

38. "[L]a novedad que había era que la gente de razón proclamaba por emperador al Señor Don Guadalupe Victoria, y los indios proclamaban a su gobernador de Tlaxcala. La especie de que la gente de razón proclamaba por emperador a vuestra excelencia podrá haber tenido origen de que los indios por precisión habrán sabido las elección de vuestra excelencia para la presidencia de los Estados Unidos Mexicanos y no tendrán un concepto verdadero del carácter de este supremo empleo, nuevo en nuestra patria, pero la empresa que dice tienen ellos de proclamar a un gobernador de Tlaxcala y las cartas que se asienta se llevaban para Tierra adentro . . . han llamado la atención de este gobierno." AGN, Gobernación 75, exp. 19, 1824.

39. Ibid., 68, exp. 16, 1824.

40. Guardino, *Peasants*, 95.

41. Ibid., 96, 107, 174.

42. Kyle, "Land, Labor, and the Chilapa Market."

43. Guardino, *Peasants*, 147–177.

44. Ibid., 178–210.

45. Edgar Mendoza García, *Los bienes de comunidad y la defensa de las tierras en la Mixteca oaxaqueña. Cohesión y autonomía del municipio de Santo Domingo Tepenene, 1856–1912* (Mexico City: Senado de la República, 2004), 90.

46. Ibid., 90–93.

47. This development accounts for the great number of municipalities that still exist in the state of Oaxaca, which has more municipalities than any other Mexican state. Ibid., 93.

48. Guardino, *Peasants*, 94.

49. Ibid., 104–107.

50. Escobar Ohmstede, "Introduction," 17.

51. Antonio Escobar Ohmstede and Teresa Rojas Rabiela, *La presencia indígena en la prensa capitalina del siglo XIX. Catálogo de noticias I* (Mexico City: Instituto Nacional

Indigenista, Centro de Investigaciones, and Estudios Superiores en Antropología Social, 1992), 292.

52. AGN, Gobernación 422, exp. 1, 1853.

53. Osborn Smyth, "A Community Study," 206–208.

54. J. Robert Knowlton, "El ejido mexicano en el siglo XIX," *Historia Mexicana* 48, 1 (1998): 76.

55. Fabila, *Cinco siglos de legislación* 1, book 5, 109–115.

56. J. Donald Fraser, "La política de desamortización en las comunidades indigenas, 1856–1872," *Historia Mexicana* 21, 4 (1972): 627.

57. The last part of Article 8 states: "With respect to properties belonging to municipal governments, the buildings, lands, and ejidos given over exclusively to the public service of the communities which own them will also be exempted." Law of Disentailment of Properties Held in Mortmain, Mexico, June 28, 1856.

58. "Joint ownership entailed a property that belonged to various owners, who did not enclose their individual plots of land but maintained them as a part of the unified whole, each was aware of his own land and shared in the payment of taxes and in the costs associated with litigation over other properties." Antonio Escobar Ohmstede and Ana María Gutiérrez Rivas, "El liberalismo y los pueblos indígenas en las Hustecas, 1856–1885," in Antonio Escobar Ohmstede, ed., *Los pueblos indios en los tiempos de Benito Juárez (1847–1872)* (Mexico City: Universidad Autónoma Metropolitana, 2007), 256.

59. Escobar Ohmstede, "Introduction."

60. Monaghan, Joyce, and Spores, "Transformation," 132.

61. Palacios, "Las restituciones," 131–132.

62. The term "primordial titles," referring to the land titles granted to Indian pueblos in the colonial period, achieved widespread use in the nineteenth century.

63. Carlos Ortiz Paniagua, "El servicio de copias certificadas en al AGN," in *VII Congreso Nacional de Archivos* 35 (Mexico City: AGN, 1996), 220–223.

64. Ibid., 222.

65. Ibid.

66. Ibid., 223.

67. Ibid.

68. *Diario oficial* (Mexico City), vol. 3, no. 123, December 1, 1854.

69. Palacios, "Las restituciones," 133.

70. AGN, Archivo de Buscas y Traslado de Tierras, exp. 57; Ortiz Paniagua, "El servicio," 220–221.

71. AGN, Archivo de Buscas y Traslado de Tierras, exp. 29.

72. Ibid., exp. 1, 1867–1869.

73. "[E]n sus colinas y montañas habitaban las tribus chichimecas, gente bárbara del gentilísimo; y que en cuyo puerto los caciques del pueblo de Xilotepec para evitar los daños y robos que hacía la gente chichimeca, a los caminantes que transitaban de los Zacatecas a México fundaron dicha población con licencia y aprobación del gobierno de España, y les concedieron por el monarca mercedes de no pagar tributo alguno por muchos años y otras muchas consideraciones y privilegios." Ibid.

74. Ibid., exp. 95.

75. From a photocopy in AGN, Títulos Primordiales, caja 17, exp. 5.

76. "[L]os viejos Miguel Axaxayacatzin . . . atlauhteco Pedro Maexochocotzin Bartolomé Cuauhxochitzin . . . señalaron límites para la congregación . . . se chocaron con violencia los viejos, se combatieron los pueblos de los cual se admiraron nuestros padres abuelos y abuelas, cuando reglamentaron las tierras." AGN, Tierras 2674, exp. 1. I have used my own transcription of the title, but another—taken from the nineteenth-century translation of the title into Spanish—is found in López Caballero, *Los títulos primordiales*, 341–349. A translation of other fragments of the document from the original Nahuatl to Spanish is in Ignacio Silva Cruz, *Transcripción traducción y dictamen de los títulos primordiales del pueblo de San Miguel Atlahutla. Siglo XVI*, paleography and trans. Ignacio Silva Cruz (Mexico City: AGN, 2002), 18–55.

77. "[O]s diréis a vuestros hijos quien sois a la vez padre, y al que en lo de adelante fuese así a los de Anahuac diréis a los que comienzan a pararse, los que ya gatean, a los que se arrastran, a los que empiezan a voltearse boca abajo a los del vientre que aún no nacen, a los que están por venir de vuestro linaje a los que hacía atrás vienen andando a gatas para que vean cómo han de aposesionarse." AGN, Tierras 2674, exp. 1.

78. "[E]sta gran Provincia del gran Pueblo de los Cuchilmingalad los Suchiilmingalas, chucalco, chitalpopocas, nombrados por nacimiento así del gran Pueblo de Tonala fundado en la tierra más rica que el Rey nuestro Señor tiene en su corona, pues toda la tierra es plata." My thanks to William B. Taylor for bringing this important title to my attention and for furnishing a copy of the transcription he and one of his students, Jessie J. Vidrio, made of it. Original in the Bancroft Library, M-M 1738, Berkeley, California.

79. The original map was stolen from Chiconquiaco in 1992, leaving only the 1870 copy in the pueblo.

80. Jesús Javier Bonilla Palmeros, *Códices de Chinconquiaco* (Veracruz: Gobierno del Estado de Veracruz, Ediciones Gernika, S.A., 2007), 183.

81. AGN, Archivo de Buscas y Traslado de Tierras 16, exp. 47.

82. Library of Congress, Washington, D.C., ms. 83089243, "Government Records of Puebla, Mexico, 1871." The manuscript consists of twelve records containing the 1871 litigation against the counterfeiters, among which are falsified titles and twenty-four color maps. The library accessioned the material in 1945. See *The Library of Congress Quarterly Journal of Current Acquisitions* 3, 3 (1946): 46.

83. The pueblos could not easily muster these sums of money. In 1868 an average-size municipality would have an annual revenue of 632 pesos. See the example of the Oaxacan municipality of Tamazulapan in Edgar Mendoza García, "Organización y funcionamiento del gobierno local: Los municipios de los distritos políticos de Teposcolula y Coxtlahuaca, 1857–1900," in Antonio Escobar Ohmstede, ed., *Los pueblos indios en los tiempos de Benito Juárez (1847–1872)* (Mexico City: Universidad Autónoma Metropolitana, 2007), 168.

84. Library of Congress, "Government Records of Puebla, Mexico, 1871."

85. "Por los fabores que meditabamos subsecuentes ante el respetable senado de esta sala titular para que quedase absuelto el presente dokumento primordial de kuanto en su partida de esta bista de posesión se diga y se mencione en meritoriosa y legal justicia de aprobación kategristika [*sic*] de este preliminar facultado en nombre del rey nuestro

señor Karlos V para que respektuosamente se esten protoko(ileg) da fe en este archivo principal." Ibid.

86. "El lugar de la infidelidad [donde] están las tierras del pueblo." From a photocopy in AGN, Títulos Primordiales, caja 17, exp. 5.

87. Carmen Aguilera, *Lienzos de Tepeticpac* (Tlaxcala: Gobierno del Estado de Tlaxcala, 1998), 101–108.

88. Archivo del Registro Agrario Nacional, San Salvador Chachapan, Amozoc, state of Puebla.

89. H. R. Harvey, "El lienzo de San Bartolomé Coatepec," *Boletín del Instituto Nacional de Antropología e Historia* 25 (1966): 1–5.

90. Ibid., 2.

91. Florencio Barrera, "La falsificación de títulos de tierras a principios al siglo XX," *Historias* 72 (January–April 2009): 41–63.

92. Mallon, *Peasant and Nation*, 23–133.

93. Escobar Ohmstede and Rojas Rabiela, *La presencia indígena*, 437, 440.

94. "Decree of Maximilian of Hapsburg, published in Spanish and Nahuatl, Regarding Pueblos' Sites and Land," in León-Portilla, *Tepuztlahcuilolli*, 289–291.

95. Miguel León-Portilla, *Ordenanzas de tema indígena en castellano y en náhuatl expedidas por Maximiliano de Habsburgo* (Querétaro, Mexico: Instituto de Estudios Constitucionales, 2003), 13.

96. Daniela Marino, "*Ahora que Dios nos ha dado padre* . . . El Segundo Imperio y la cultura jurídico político campesina en el Centro de Mexico," *Historia Mexicana* 55, 4 (2006): 1362.

97. Jean Meyer, "La junta protectora de las clases menesterosas, indigenismo y agrarismo en el Segundo Imperio," in Antonio Escobar Ohmstede, ed., *Indio, nación y comunidad. en el México del siglo XIX* (Mexico City: Centro Francés de Estudios Mexicanos Centroamericanos, Centro de Investigaciones, and Estudios Superiores en Antropología Social, 1993), 335.

98. Marino, "*Ahora que Dios*," 1373.

99. Ibid., 1386, 1389–1390.

100. Ibid., 1375.

101. Erica Pani, "¿'Verdaderas figuras de Cooper' o 'pobres inditos infelices'? La política indigenista de Maximiliano," *Historia Mexicana* 47, 3 (1998): 598.

102. "Era una novedad para ellos [los indios] verse invitados a tomar parte en la cosa pública," Zamacois cited in ibid., 598–599.

103. Fabila, *Cinco siglos*, vol. 1, 159–168.

104. Ibid., 183–189.

105. Interview with René Marneau Villavicencio, Puebla, December 3, 2006.

106. Fabila, *Cinco siglos*, vol. 1, 189–205.

107. Escobar Ohmstede and Gutiérrez Rivas, "El liberalismo," 272 (quote), 286.

108. Dana Markiewicz, *The Mexican Revolution and the Limits of Agrarian Reform 1915–1946* (Boulder: Lynne Rienner, 1993), 15.

109. Mendoza García, *Los bienes de comunidad*, 218–224.

110. AGN, Archivo de Buscas y Traslado de Tierras, exp. 97.

111. Ibid., exp. 104, 105.

112. My thanks to Lic. Lorenzo Martínez for allowing me to examine this record, located in the Tribunal Unitario Agrario (TUA), no. 47, city of Puebla, exp. 13/95 2761/887.

113. Markiewicz, *Mexican Revolution*, 16–17.

114. Arturo Warman, "The Political Project of Zapatismo," trans. Judith Brister, in Friedrich Katz, ed., *Riot, Rebellion, and Revolution: Rural Social Conflict in Mexico* (Princeton: Princeton University Press, 1988), 322 (quote), 326; Warman, *Y venimos a contradecir. Los campesinos de Morelos y el estado nacional* (Mexico City: Centro de Investigaciones Superiores del Instituto Nacional de Antropología e Historia, 1978), 104–109.

115. Warman, "Political Project of Zapatismo," 326–327.

116. See note 57 in this chapter.

117. Markiewicz, *Mexican Revolution*, 23–24.

118. Palacios, "Las restituciones," 125, 128–130, 135–136.

119. Circular 15, no. 11, "Constitution and Reforms," Mexico, January 24, 1917, in Fabila, *Cinco siglos*, vol. 1, 301–302.

120. AGN, Archivo de Buscas y Traslado de Tierras, exp. 89.

121. Ibid., exp. 108.

122. Ibid., exp. 54.

123. Ignacio Silva Cruz, *Transcripción y traducción del Códice Techialoyan de Cuajimalpa*, paleography and trans. Ignacio Silva Cruz (Mexico City: AGN, 2002), 18.

124. AGN, Archivo de Buscas y Traslado de Tierras, exp. 51.

125. The Indians' and peasants' practice of copying their maps and drawing territorial plans for the agrarian authorities was very widespread. In 1918, Circular no. 32 stated that the maps accompanying the records of land allocations were missing information or carried information furnished by the pueblos' inhabitants: "Ordenando a las Comisiones Locales Agrarias que los planos de los terrenos que deben obrar en los expedientes, sean formados por Ingenieros Técnicos y de acuerdo la Circular Núm. 15." Circular 32, "Constitution and Reforms," Mexico, May 30, 1918, in Fabila, *Cinco siglos*, vol. 1, 333–334.

126. All of the maps and genealogies to which I refer are found in the sacristy of Santa Inés's church. Through his archival research, Luis Reyes has verified that from the colonial period on, the majority of records documenting Tlaxcala's local history have been kept in the sacristies of village churches, where—fortunately—the stewards of the religious brotherhoods have carefully watched over native codices, chronicles, and maps. Personal communication with Luis Reyes, Mexico City, May 1999.

127. Regrettably, despite my entreaties, the community authorities would not grant me permission to reproduce the photograph I took of the two "maps" in question.

128. Alba González Jácome, "Ambiente y cultura en la agricultura tradicional de México: Casos y perspectivas," *Anales de Antropología* 37 (2003): 127, 132.

129. Ibid., 127.

130. Ibid.

131. Claude Morin, *Santa Inés Zacatelco (1646–1812): Contribución a la demografía histórica colonial* (Mexico City: INAH, 1973), 14.

132. Archivo General Agrario exp. 23/5013; Markiewicz, *Mexican Revolution*, 39.

133. Registro Agrario Nacional de Puebla, Atlixco, December 17, 1934, letter from the legal representative of the hacienda of Manatla to the delegate of the Departamento Agrario of Puebla, Atlixco, Puebla.

134. Archivo General Agrario, exp. 23/5013.

135. Th. J. Raymond Buve, "Neither Carranza nor Zapata! The Rise and Fall of a Peasant Movement That Tried to Challenge Both, Tlaxcala, 1910–1919," in Friedrich Katz, ed., *Riot, Rebellion, and Revolution: Rural Social Conflict in Mexico* (Princeton: Princeton University Press, 1988), 338–375.

136. "Lo de Domingo Arenas, la festividad la celebramos con el motivo que él lucho por las tierras que el campesino casi no tenía tierras, los hacendados acaparaban todas esas tierras y todo lo cosechaban y al campesino le regalaban lo que ellos querían, entonces Domingo Arenas se levanto en armas y les comunicó que pues tenían que pelear por esas tierras y ser repartidas a todas las personas que no tenían sus tierras y estaban trabajando, los hacían trabajar todo el día y les regalaban lo poco que querían de *maicito* para sustento de su hogar, entonces por eso este señor se levantó en Armas y se hizo una revolución aquí en Zacatelco y pues si, logró, recuperaron esas tierras." Interview with Toribio Morales Carvente, Santa Inés Zacatelco, Tlaxcala, August 30, 2006.

137. Palacios, "Las restituciones," 141.

138. Markiewicz, *Mexican Revolution*, 1–7.

139. Ibid., 37–38.

140. Ibid.

141. Ibid., 50, 63, 84. Presidential resolutions, in this context, refer to the official sanctioning by the serving president of a distribution of land to a pueblo or to the enlargement of its existing lands.

142. Ibid., 83, 87–88, 95.

143. Ibid., 88–90.

144. Ibid., 88–90, 167–168.

145. Ibid., 1.

146. Ramón Vera Herrera, "Procede-Procecom 'Las escrituraciones del diablo,'" *Ojarasca* 86 (June 2004): 1–4, at http://www.jornada.unam.mx/2004/06/14/oja86-procede .html. Accessed May 2008.

147. Guillermo de la Peña, "Sociedad civil y resistencia popular en el Mexico de final del siglo XX," in Leticia Reina and Elisa Servín, eds., *Crisis, reforma y Revolución México: Historias de fin de siglo* (Mexico City: Editorial Taurus Consejo Nacional para la Cultura y las Artes and INAH, 2002), 379.

148. Interview with René Marneau Villavicencio, Puebla, December 3, 2006.

149. "Cuando los representantes de los pueblos llegan al [AGN] los llevan al centro de referencia, ahí se registran, luego solicitan la búsqueda de sus documento, aún en el caso de que no haya información si encuentran la sentencia de un pleito que viene al caso de tierras esa sentencia se convierte en el título. Cuando hay mapas suelen identificar sus límites en estos mapas antiguos cuando los ven. En ocasiones hay documentos que encuentran pero que son apócrifos. Estos llevan sellos en ocasiones, y hay algunos elaborados con tinta de finales del siglo XIX." Interviews with Soledad Villafuerte, director

of the Department of Paleography, Diplomatics, and Document Certification, conducted in Mexico City in spring 2003, by which time Villafuerte had twenty-six years' experience in the department.

150. Ibid.

151. Peasant from Oaxaca, conversation in Mexico City, July 2005.

152. "[L]a señora culebra tierna, el señor tronco de Muchos, estos son los antiguos nombres que tenían antes de que viniera [Hernán] Cortés. No tengo padre ni madre que me crearon soy huérfano allí en [tachado] donde me hallaron tembló trece días y estaba un arco iris también a los tres días que me hallaron, vi que del pie del arco iris me cogió la gente con gran gusto de todos, me criaron con grande ánimo de mis sirvientes ya siendo yo grande, llegó el tiempo de medir mis tierras, tireles a muchos y maté a los Guapiz Zapotecos cuando yo los quería matar, salieron trueno del aire, con que murieron todas las gentes. Andando el tiempo me escapé fui a traer a mi mujer a Xuchitepeque y a su padre y madre y a todos sus sirvientes También. Andando el tiempo me nació un hijo se animó la Señora recibió el bautismo y se llama D[o]n Felipe Gregorio." Archivo General Agrario, map of San Miguel Ecatepec.

153. "[V]an y hacen una ceremonia con rezos y piden a la naturaleza permiso, rezan para que todo vaya bien y ofrendan gallos y gallinas, mezcal y tabaco. A los animales les cortan la cabeza, las alas y las patitas y lo entierran con el resto de las cosas abajo, encima hacen la mojonera." Interview with Sr. Medardo, Ayuk Indian (Mixe), Alotepec, February 11, 2006.

4

Defending Land

INDIAN PUEBLOS' CONTEMPORARY QUEST FOR THE
ORIGINS OF LOCAL COMMUNITY HISTORY

PUEBLOS THAT HOLD PRIMORDIAL TITLES: PRESENT-DAY CASES

As we have seen repeatedly, the primacy of land for the Indian pueblos and its interweaving with ancient documents, primordial titles, and local history form part of a complex process of negotiation the pueblos undertook in the face of state power as a way of defending their lands. Such negotiation implies that the Indians understood the official legal landscape, enabling them to interpret from their own cultural vantage point documents, programmatic statements, and agrarian legislation emanating from the state. In this process, moreover, the legalization of land claims, the stamp of official certification, and the primordial titles themselves constitute a kind of contemporary mythology elaborated by the pueblos.[1] The Indians' ability to incorporate—sometimes successfully—elements of their native culture into the most adverse legal contexts stems from their capacity for negotiation, which, in turn, is a function of their ideological flexibility.

The case of Ixcamilpa, a pueblo located in the state of Puebla, is instructive in this regard. In 1912, members of the pueblo went before the revolutionary leader Emiliano Zapata to request the restitution of their lands, which they asserted had been wrested from them long ago by local hacendados. In support of their claim, they produced the pueblo's colonial-era primordial titles. On this basis and within the framework of the Plan of Ayala, they achieved their objective. On April 30, 1912, Zapata granted the pueblo its lands through a specific decree of restitution. Nonetheless, six decades later many of the pueblo's campesinos still found themselves without land. Around 1976 they decided to band together and litigate their case in Mexico City, citing the lands affected by the "restitution" and—as documentary evidence—using the decree Zapata had issued in their favor in 1912. The Indians also directly confronted and fought against the local landlords, who reacted with force by having them jailed, using the judicial police and army to pursue and capture them. Undeterred, the Indian campesinos—in keeping with the substance of the 1912 decision—persevered and began to achieve the distribution of the lands that had been controlled by the hacendados, or "the rich," as the Indians liked to call them.[2]

In retaliation, the landlords threatened one of the elders of the pueblo, Don Joaquín Sánchez González, with death. Sánchez González kept the pueblo's primordial titles (Figure 4.1) in his personal care, titles the "rich" now also threatened to destroy. To prevent these outcomes, the Ixcamilpans maintained an armed guard in front of Sánchez González's house throughout the night for fifteen days. As a result of their militant stance and the notoriety of the case, these essentially humble Indians succeeded in gaining the support of both campesinos across the state of Puebla and the Socialist Workers Party. In addition, they mounted a campaign to win national recognition for their movement and secured an audience with the state's governor on April 20, 1982, so that the pueblo's lands could be handed back to them before April 30, which they planned to set aside to commemorate the seventieth anniversary of Zapata's official restitution of the lands to them.[3]

As we have seen, developments since the early 1980s have placed the interests of campesinos at great risk. As a result of Mexico's incorporation into the North American Free Trade Agreement (NAFTA) in 1994, the Mexican countryside fell into a deep recession, from which there are no signs of improvement. Unlike similar treaties or conventions (such as the one on which the European Union operates), NAFTA is purely a commercial mechanism, setting up a free trade zone among Canada, the United States, and Mexico. It lacks any central body for effecting social and political coordination; its only institutional face is a secretariat that exists to execute and fulfill the resolutions and mandates that derive from the treaty itself. Consequently, the 1992 reforms to Article 27 of the constitution, erasing the supports the government had long provided to the country's campesino population, exposed Mexico's countryside to the harsh vicissitudes of the market. Thus, U.S. agribusiness, strongly protected by Washington, has been able—without the burden of paying tariffs—to introduce numerous agricultural and livestock products into the Mexican market.[4] As a result, Mexico has lost its

4.1 Don Joaquín Sánchez González with his pueblo's titles. Photograph by Rentato Ravelo Lecuona. Courtesy, Sra. Judith, Ravelo's widow.

capacity for self-sufficiency in the production of foodstuffs; almost all of the food consumed in the country today is imported. Equally damaging is the fact that rural Mexico has become deserted, as every year hundreds of thousands of Indians and campesinos—unable to sustain themselves and their families economically—flee the country to find work in the United States.

The lead-up to implementation of the NAFTA treaty, in conjunction with neoliberal policies pursued in Mexico for almost thirty years, helped create the conditions that ignited the January 1, 1994, armed rebellion by the Ejército Zapatista de Liberación Nacional (EZLN), or Zapatista Army of National Liberation, in the state of Chiapas. This largely indigenous movement, strongly influenced by Zapata's revolutionary doctrines and ideology, captured worldwide attention and spotlighted the failure of the neoliberal project in Mexico.

From the beginning, the EZLN called attention to the depressed state of Mexico's indigenous population and to the grinding poverty in which the country's Indians, campesinos, and poor in general were forced to live. In its first declaration, issued on January 2, 1994, the movement's leadership expressed the anger and exasperation felt by elements in both urban and rural sectors who had been ruined by the neoliberal policies of recent years: "TODAY WE SAY ENOUGH!, we are the inheritors of the true authors of our nationhood, we, the dispossessed, in our millions and we call on all our brothers to respond to this summons as the only way to not die of hunger when faced with the insatiable graspings of a more than 70 year-old dictatorship headed by a circle of betrayers who represent the most conservative and traitorous groups."[5]

Although the EZLN uprising was initially led by the Maya, its representation has broadened to include a wide range of indigenous groups and organizations from throughout the country. Politically, the movement's greatest accomplishment has been its success in focusing both national and international attention on the problem of indigenous rights in Mexico. Since the uprising broke out in 1994, the print media, radio, and television have all provided substantial coverage of the problems the EZLN has addressed, as well as the remedies proposed to counteract them. This development has had a noticeable effect on many of Mexico's Indian communities, heightening their political awareness and giving them a sharper sense of their rights and obligations. They evidence a clear tendency to take pride in the group to which they belong and increasingly register the importance of their native language and culture. Indeed, for some years various Indian communities have stressed their rights as "native pueblos." This practice has helped energize a movement to preserve their languages, customs, and system of communal organization.[6]

Within this general environment, different Indian pueblos have continued to present their primordial titles before local land arbitration panels (Tribunales

Unitarios Agrarios), which were established in 1991 on the basis of Article 27 of the constitution. This development has had important legal ramifications, and it is worth digressing slightly to elucidate the context in which indigenous communities presented their colonial-era titles to these panels. The reforms enacted under President Carlos Salinas de Gortari ended the redistribution of land; in a word, the executive "reformed the constitution's Article 27 to wipe out the revolutionary promise of land."[7] Fifty years earlier, in tandem with the granting and restitution of land, the country's 1940 Agrarian Code had established a principle and guideline known as the Recognition and Entitlement of Communal Property (RTBC), aimed specifically at securing recognition for lands possessed by Indian pueblos. The RTBC stipulated that pueblos that had "maintained their lands since time immemorial" should present the titles the Spanish Crown had granted them to the agrarian authorities so the latter could replace them with new titles (consisting of a presidential resolution and a definitive map) issued by the Mexican government. To facilitate such exchanges, paleographic analyses would be done to ensure the authenticity of the colonial-period titles. Further, since the old titles reflected a totally antiquated system of measuring land, the RTBC also stipulated that new topographic surveys would need to be done, giving the measurement of land in square meters. These surveys would serve as the basis for legal recognition of Indian communal lands. Since only those lands the pueblos *actually* held at the time they submitted to this process could be recognized, however, some pueblos emerged with greater or lesser extensions of land than the colonial-era titles and documents might have allocated.[8]

Beginning with the adoption of the 1991 reform of Article 27, the land arbitration panels were to treat the primordial titles shown to them as no more than historical anecdotes, pointing circumstantially—and only circumstantially—to the age-old possession of particular land by Indian pueblos. Official legal title is contained in the presidential resolution emanating from completion of the RTBC process.[9] Nevertheless, depending on their political attitudes and leanings toward the pueblos, the judges serving on these panels might or might not take a pueblo's titles more directly into account in reaching a decision. One instance (of many) in which they did so involves the case of San Miguel Chignautla, in the state of Puebla. San Miguel's leaders presented their colonial primordial titles before land arbitration panel number 37 in the city of Puebla. The community's land issues are currently being resolved, with its primordial titles presumably finding a place in the chain of evidence.[10] A second example of the admission of primordial titles into the resolution of land claims occurred in 2006, when arbitration panel number 22 settled 40,076 hectares of communal property on the pueblo of Santiago Niltepec, in the state of Oaxaca, in part on the basis of its possession of primordial titles dating back to 1713.[11]

The pattern is not uniform, however—not every pueblo that retains its primordial titles is successful in maintaining its lands. The case of San Nicolás Totolapan (part of the local authority of Magdalena Contreras in the Federal District, Mexico City) illustrates this fact. The pueblo has preserved an exemplary Techialoyan-style codex, consisting of eleven folios with Nahuatl text and colored pictorial representations. Bound as a book in the nineteenth century, at the pueblo's request the codex—yet to be published in its totality—has been certified as an authentic colonial manuscript by various specialists.[12] In addition, the community still possesses a royal decree granted to it in 1563 by Viceroy Luis de Velasco. After the Mexican Revolution and with these documents serving as its primordial titles, the inhabitants of San Nicolás Totolapan requested, through the local agrarian commission of the Federal District, the restitution of 50,000 hectares of their communal lands. On December 15, 1921, the agrarian authorities hearing the case denied the claim, finding that the pueblo's primordial titles were illegitimate. As a result, the pueblo—through a presidential decree of April 29, 1924—was granted only 1,300 hectares of ejido lands. The latter came from the expropriation of a nearby estate, called "La Eslava," that had existed in the area since colonial times[13] and which, during the seventeenth century, formed the largest hacienda in the southern part of the Valley of Mexico. Throughout the nineteenth century and into the early twentieth century, the Indians of San Nicolás Totolapan had labored on the hacienda under harsh conditions. Indeed, its owners and administrators had been accustomed to treating the pueblo's inhabitants as virtual prisoners, depriving them of their land and committing a wide range of abuses against them. Not surprisingly, in 1912 many of San Nicolás's residents joined the forces led by Emiliano Zapata, and in 1913 the Zapatistas took revenge on the hacienda's owner, assassinating him.[14]

In 1935 the pueblo requested that its ejido lands be enlarged. Four years later it was granted an additional 1,404 hectares, far short of its original request.[15] For a number of years its inhabitants have continued to pursue their case through various legal channels, including appearing before the Mexican Supreme Court, in their effort to win recognition of their primordial titles. Although the national archive certified the authenticity of their titles in 2000,[16] the federal government has been unwilling to do the same. The colonial documents the pueblo possesses record that its lands cover several kilometers, extending into what has been developed into extremely valuable urban commercial property. The old community lands of San Nicolás now include a residential neighborhood with opulent homes owned by the wealthy and politically powerful, a massive structure that houses offices of the national oil company (PEMEX), a large, privately owned hospital that forms part of a multihospital system (Hospital Ángeles de México), and the installations of a private television station (Televisión Azteca). Arraigned against this phalanx of powerful state and private interests, the inhabitants of San Nicolás have met a wall of resistance in asserting their legal claims. Acknowledging the complicated tangle of interests, the pueblo has scaled down its request, indicating that it would like to be given part of the land as yet undeveloped so its younger members will have a site on which to construct homes and plant crops. Nonetheless, given the great historical and artistic value of San Nicolás's documents, in particular its Techialoyan codex, some government authorities have not settled for the status quo but have attempted to expropriate these documents as well.[17]

Although blocked thus far, the pueblo's inhabitants have continued the struggle to win government validation of their titles, just as they have passed down the task of preserving these documents from one generation to the next. Those presently entrusted with their care have declared that once the government has recognized the titles as legitimate and the land issue has been resolved, the pueblo is prepared to donate the documents to the Archivo General de la Nación to ensure their long-term preservation. Within San Nicolás, various tales are told about the titles; for example, that the codex is stained with blood because in Porfirio Díaz's time, the owner of the hacienda of La Eslava visited the home of the person then in charge of caring for the codex:

> [P]icture, then, that our ancestors, and the one who had the codex, our
> representative, did not have beds; they had mats, and he put it under his mat;
> the hacendados arrived and fired questions at him, they [wanted] to take the
> codex from him because they knew that it was original, he didn't tell them
> where it was, so they knifed him and his blood got transferred to the codex
> and the codex is stained with his blood.[18]

Despite the failure of their previous attempts to secure government validation of their titles, San Nicolás's leaders and residents are actively pursuing an interesting strategy that clearly links them to their colonial forebears. Several of those entrusted with the care of the codex are considering approaching the Spanish embassy to ask it to help fund a trip by them to Spain, where the Techialoyan codex could be examined and authenticated. The pueblo's representatives believe the documents, such as the 1563 royal decree issued to San Nicolás by Viceroy Velasco, contain seals that originated in Spain and that Spanish authorities thus can and should attest to their authenticity. The pueblo's representatives have noted: "Let us see, when the monarchs [of Spain] come here, if we can introduce ourselves, in order to tell them that here, these are the documents for which we are unable to win prompt and proper recognition, that we would like a hearing or would like you [the embassy] to pay our way over there so that our documents can be examined."[19]

Thus, just as the colonial indigenous authorities from different pueblos wrote to the king or occasionally even traveled overseas to see him to deal with particular matters of justice and governance that could not be resolved in New Spain, so the present-day inhabitants of San Nicolás—who identify themselves as descendants of the Nahua—would do likewise in the belief that in the place that was the center of power of the colonial order, they could logically secure recognition of their primordial titles. On this basis, they could subsequently obtain the land they desire for their children and future descendants. In following such a course, they would be calling upon a symbolic power that—in a return to the paternalistic world of the colony—they place above the Mexican national state, a power that would accord recognition to their titles as the Spanish imperial authorities had done hundreds of years before.

Broadly speaking, then, it can be generalized that the Indian pueblos continue to manifest their capacity for negotiation through their search for and preservation of titles and maps. As long as they maintain their indissoluble ties with the land, so will they continue—albeit under more complicated, less static conditions—to serve a tradition they have managed to uphold since the colonial period. At present, as noted, a large number of Indian pueblos have regained a sense of pride in their identity, partly on the strength of the EZLN uprising. This newfound, or rediscovered, element of pride has played a preponderant role in their negotiations with the state on different levels and over a variety of problems, such as the possession of land, social issues, and the provision of aid for building up their communities' infrastructure.

Given this line of action, it is important to delineate in greater detail concrete cases of Indians' negotiation with the current Mexican state and its apparatus of power. I will focus in particular on two cases in which the recovery of local history has been germane to the negotiation process. The first case involves the pueblo of Atliaca, in the state of Guerrero, and the second the pueblo of Santa María Cuquila, in the state of Oaxaca. Both cases, without claiming that they are archetypal, offer a clear idea of what the preservation of and quest for community history and primordial titles mean for Indian pueblos.

A NAHUA PUEBLO AND ITS TITLES

Atliaca is the first Nahua pueblo one reaches when ascending the mountainous region of Guerrero. I conducted several short fieldwork projects in the pueblo over a roughly two-year period, spanning 2003 and 2004. According to the 2005 census, Atliaca numbers 7,439 inhabitants,[20] of whom 70 percent said Spanish was their second language. The pueblo and its environs, which belong administratively to the mestizo municipality of Tixtla, lie within a zone in which the most

4.2 Brick plant in the pueblo of Atliaca. Date: 2004. Courtesy, Adolfo de Paz.

widely spoken language is Nahuatl. Physically small and featuring traditional architecture, Atliaca contains a school, electric lights, and a hostel that—although intended for children who live in the surrounding indigenous communities—is in fact used primarily by children from Atliaca proper. The pueblo suffers from serious water and drainage problems. Eight years ago, four small children died because their tap water was contaminated with fecal matter.[21]

While a majority of the adult population is engaged in agricultural work—farming crops, especially corn, on communal lands—a considerable number of Atliacans are employed in the brick works. The brick works is likewise located on the pueblo's community lands, where bricks are manufactured from the black clay found in the area (Figure 4.2). This local industry was begun in Atliaca around 1979, when representatives from the National Indian Institute taught pueblo members how to manufacture bricks. Those who work in Atliaca's brick plant are drawn from the local population, and the bricks are sold at a good price in different localities—including Guerrero's capital city, Chilpancingo. Although the reserves of clay are being exhausted at a rapid rate, the production of bricks has generated healthy revenue for the pueblo. This economic situation has relieved the working population from having to emigrate to other localities in Guerrero, such as Zumpango—where Atliacans had traditionally gone to harvest tomatoes—or Huitzuco, Iguala, Tepecua, and Tazmala, where they found seasonal work in the fields.

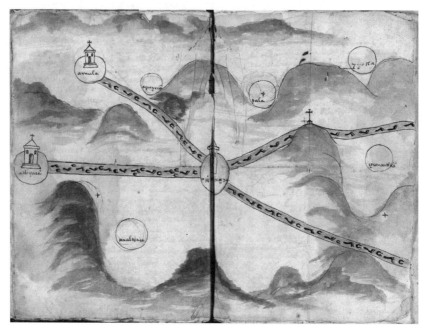

4.3 Reproduction, no. 1884. Date: 1619. Courtesy, Archivo General de la Nación, Mexico City.

Atliaca also has a spacious municipal government building for its authorities, who by local custom and tradition are named annually. The pueblo is highly traditional. For example, Atliaca is famous among surrounding communities for a deep well—called Ostotempan—found on its lands where every year, on the third day of May, Indians from more than thirty communities in the vicinity gather to appeal for rain by conducting an elaborate ceremony that lasts all night. During the ceremony they pitch huge offerings into the depths of the well, in addition to praying and sacrificing animals.[22] According to the story the Atliacans told me, giants live at the bottom of the well, which is why the offerings thrown into it are so large. Twelve pueblos in the region have each placed a cross at some distance around the well. The crosses represent an ancient tradition, analogous to the cult of the well of Ostotempan, which probably dates from the pre-Hispanic era. The pueblo of Atliaca, in fact, dates back to pre-Hispanic times and—as of the colonial period—was represented on an early–seventeenth-century map as a subdivision of the community of Tixtla (Figure 4.3).

Again, according to what I was told,[23] some years ago an unusual event occurred. A group of evangelical Nahuas from Atliaca appeared at the well one night and proceeded to pull up all the crosses on its periphery, in protest against

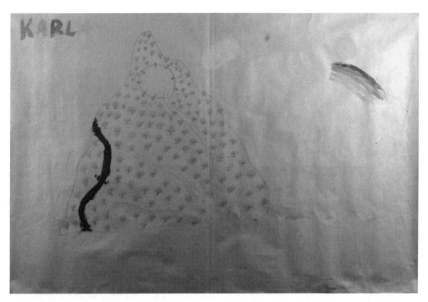

4.4 Drawing by Karla, a young Atliaca girl. Date: November 2003. Courtesy, Atliaca, Guerrero.

what they viewed as the practice of "idolatry." To the rest of the indigenous population, this action by the Protestant Indians amounted to sacrilege, and it nearly cost them their lives. For a period of time the evangelicals were forced to abandon the pueblo to avoid being lynched by the other Atliacans.

In November 2003, at the beginning of my fieldwork in Atliaca, I carried out an exercise with the Nahua children from the pueblo's hostel. The exercise called for them to choose a subject and, using colored pencils and crayons, to draw something about it on large index-style cards. I intended for these drawings to be framed and mounted to decorate the walls of the hostel's auditorium. As the afternoon came to an end, the children showed me their drawings. Among the pictures they had drawn were two scenes of the Ostotempan well, done by two young Nahua girls, from eight to ten years of age, named Karla and Miriam (Figures 4.4, 4.5).

Both drawings depict the crosses placed around the well, and one includes a band of text—evocative in tone—that explains the tradition of the Ostotempan festival. Furthermore, in their representations of the tepetl (hill) and of atl (water), the two drawings clearly recall the stylistic features of a codex. This similarity is substantiated by comparing the girls' drawings with a colonial-period pictorial manuscript from Tlalcosautitlán, an Indian pueblo relatively close to Atliaca (Figure 4.6). As we can observe, these images share much in common stylistically,

4.5 Drawing by Miriam, a young Atliaca girl. Date: November 2003. Courtesy, Atliaca, Guerrero.

especially in their depiction of the element of water. Even more interesting, however, is that shortly after first seeing the drawings, I learned that Karla and Miriam were daughters of two of the evangelicals who had uprooted the crosses some years earlier.

These associations and occurrences demonstrate that the Indians' adoption of a new religion did not carry with it a redefining or total displacing of their traditional culture. On the contrary, the two now coexisted with each other. In the routine of their daily lives, across realms both sacred and profane, the evangelical Indians' embrace of new religious beliefs was paralleled by their tacit invocation of traditional cultural practices and sensibilities.

On the issue of cultural traditions, the people of Atliaca believe caballeros or *caballeritos* (a kind of supernatural being) fly through the night sky. Glimpsed by the Atliacans in the form of comets, these figures are completely benign, indeed even helpful, defending them from evil beings that perpetually lie in wait to disturb their tranquility. Although such notions rest on a long tradition of oral history, there are instances in which their historical trajectory can be traced through documents.

A bridge is located at the town's edge. As with the tower of the pueblo's church, Atliacans say that the mortar that holds the bridge together is composed of human blood. This idea, which extends across many Mesoamerican pueblos,

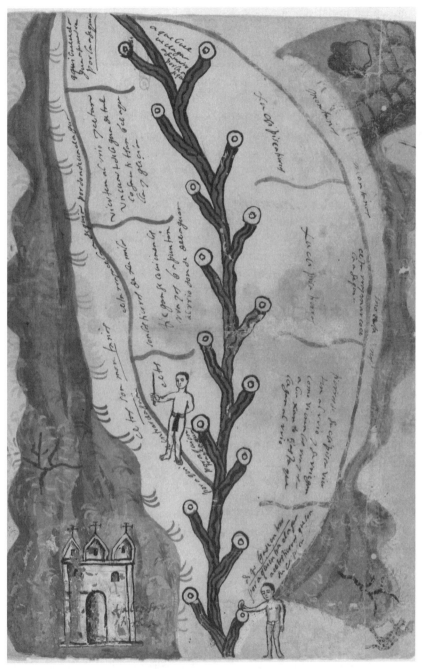

4.6 Reproduction, no. 1803. Date: 1587. Courtesy, Archivo General de la Nación, Mexico City.

is grounded in old stories which claim that the stones of which pre-Hispanic temples are made are held together by human blood. The *Relación Geográfica de Tlaxcala*, for example, states that the stones that form the pyramid of Cholula are fastened to one another with the blood of a child: "Children of two and three years of age were killed and with their blood, mixed with lime, in the form of zulaque,[24] they stopped up any water that flowed out."[25]

Not only is human blood present in the Atliaca bridge, but—it is also claimed—those who stroll over it at night are confronted by a supernatural being. This creature customarily appears in the form of an attractive woman who employs her charms to lure unwary men to her side. Once they are close to her, the woman begins to seduce them, and she succeeds in having sexual relations with the unwitting passersby. After completing the sex act, the seductress turns back into her previous disfigured form and takes her victim's semen, slaps some of it on his face, hurls it into the night sky, and then throws it into the fire. The terrified victim takes to his heels and, according to what I was told, pays for his unfortunate lack of judgment in having let himself be seduced by dying three days later.

When I asked the people who told me the story why this supernatural being propelled the semen up into the sky, they replied that it did so in worship of its "gods" and that this being was neither a man nor a woman but a species of witch that drew its energy from human semen. What is remarkable about this story—beyond the fact that it has elements that tie it to evil beings found in the western tradition, such as incubuses, thus suggesting that it may ultimately be derived from the tradition of European witchcraft (as, for example, in the witches' Sabbath)[26]—is the fact that a seventeenth-century document exists, stemming from the Mexican Inquisition, that not only relates the same story but sets it in the pueblo of Atliaca.

The circumstances are these: On February 19, 1663, the Inquisition's prosecuting attorney reviewed a letter sent to the tribunal from Tixtla, the capital town of the municipality to which Atliaca—situated 15 kilometers away—pertained. Scribblings in the margin of the letter indicated that "this information is vague and concerns Indians who are not subject to the tribunal." The report explained:

> There are some Indians who make themselves appear as women and—so
> transformed—lurk in the shadows to accost those of all ranks, and using
> seductive language [with the men] entice them, thinking they are women, into
> having carnal relations; and in this way [they] catch the semen in their hands
> and smear it on the man's face; they then resume the form of a man, and those
> to whom [illegible] die within three to four days, no remedy exists for them,
> seven or eight Spaniards, mestizos, and mulattos have died from this diabolical

intervention, and others, who have not succumbed to the final temptation, are still alive and have testified to these events.[27]

The Inquisition authorities, somewhat oddly, penned a note at the end of the denunciatory letter stating: "Like what precedes it, [this information] is also vague, it neither relates how it was learned nor who it was that heard it, and the person bringing the complaint is now deceased and therefore cannot be cross-examined."[28] Perhaps the complainant was himself a victim of these nocturnal witches who, as the people of Atliaca tell it, hang about their pueblo.

As we can see, the letter overlaps with the story told today in Atliaca, although there are differences between the two accounts. The most important difference is that in the contemporary story, people talk about a supernatural being that assumes a menacing form, whereas the seventeenth-century version refers to male Indians who disguise themselves as women to perpetrate a lethal offense against Spaniards, mestizos, and mulattos. Since this affair involved the native population, the Inquisition chose to ignore it. Moreover, the person who denounced these occurrences, a Spaniard, died soon thereafter, giving the Inquisition even less motivation to investigate the case.

In one respect, however, the Spaniard's denunciation left no room for doubt: the victims were Spaniards, mestizos, or mulattos. From the colonial period on, Atliaca was under the control of its neighboring city, Tixtla. Tixtla had been settled primarily by creole cattlemen, who in turn were served by mulattos, a racial subgroup that unquestionably struck terror among many Indians. A traditional dance, known as *tlacololeros*, is still performed in Tixtla. The dance features men with their faces painted black. They attach monkey pelts to their hats (symbolizing the traditional savage element) and carry whips with which they lash the ground as they dance frenetically. This ceremonial dance is a vivid reminder of the black foremen who served the white population and the fearsome whips they brandished. Without question, the creole and mestizo cattle ranchers visited considerable suffering on the population of Atliaca and its surrounding communities.

Indeed, Atliaca probably managed to survive as an independent pueblo—although one forced to contend with Tixtla's creole and mestizo population—because it was a way station and resting place for merchants and cattle runs plying the road between Mexico City and Acapulco. The pueblo sat at the side of the road. Perhaps even before the seventeenth century, as a kind of defense mechanism, some Indians from Atliaca and the settlements around it developed the custom of terrorizing creoles, mestizos, and mulattos in the region by dressing up as women, perhaps even coming to commit the acts of which they stood accused in the letter to the Inquisition. Over time, this custom was reworked in the oral transmission of the story so that the figure of the Indians turned into that of the supernatural being. In any case, whatever the fine points of the story, the account told in Atliaca today is remarkably similar to that contained in the seventeenth-century denunciation.

The denunciatory letter also mentions several traditional beliefs to which the inhabitants of Atliaca still subscribe, including that of the *naguales*. For example, the letter observes: "[T]he earth and the animals speak to each other and men turn themselves into animals and into birds of all sorts called naguales, and it is said that taking this form they have done great evil to many people of all ranks, be they men or women, though the priests have tried to set things right."[29] On this matter, the Atliacans have told me that many of their fellow townspeople are Nahuales. For example, Modesto Vázquez Salgado—with whom I have conversed about this subject at some length—described this incident: one day he went to a friend's house to pay a social visit. His host, he noticed, had nothing to offer him to eat but immediately went out and came back with a chicken. The next day his friend's neighbor complained that an animal had come into his corral and stolen one of his chickens. Upon hearing of this incident Vázquez Salgado broke into laughter, explaining that it was his friend who, by taking the form of an animal, had produced a meal for him.

In this same vein, in 2000 the pueblo instituted a prohibition preventing the church from opening before five o'clock in the morning because until shortly before then, it was filled with votive candles and offerings that, it seems, often signified that some of Atliaca's inhabitants were inflicting "harm" (performing witchcraft) on a neighboring resident. Consequently, the pueblo's authorities decided to keep both the church and its cemetery closed until the newly appointed hour. In fact, Atliaca's authorities occasionally fear that as the direct result of their special responsibilities, they will be the object of an evil act. A favorite and frequent means of visiting harm is to put worms, or *ocuilin*, in a person's food. I was told that this malign act often occurs at festivals and celebrations. As people sit down to eat, they are served a plate of hot beans. Suddenly the intended victim or victims—who are sometimes the pueblo's leaders—notice that something is moving on their plates, and the ocuilin emerge. The unfortunate target discovers that the guilty party is more often than not one of the guests, sitting calmly by, eating his meal. Issuing threats and insults, the rest of the group demands that the perpetrator use his power to eliminate the worms from the plate or the common bowl from which everyone will take food.

Atliaca, then, is home to a multitude of intersecting traditions and rituals, as well as a rich storehouse of tales about local caves and spells, not to speak of the giants who—its people insist—live at the bottom of the Ostotempan well. These creatures' size leads pueblo inhabitants to make equally huge offerings in their honor. These offerings consist of enormous baskets tossed into the well with live turkeys inside them. Hand in hand with their myths and legends, the Atliacans go about with cell phones and have cable television, and the pueblo's authorities wrestle with devising a proper means of regulating ownership of the community's principal sources of work: the brick plant and the family-run bus and trucking companies. They have likewise faced off against local caciques in the courts in defending their land and have recently had them ejected from that land.

The pueblo's inhabitants thus move in two worlds, combining—sometimes successfully—aspects of their traditional culture with new cultural elements introduced from without. Furthermore, they effect this combination dynamically but without amalgamating the traditional and the nontraditional. Rather, they weave back and forth between the two depending upon the circumstances. In 2006, on the eve of the Guerrero gubernatorial elections, we were strolling through the pueblo at dusk with our companion, Modesto Vásquez Salgado, when I noticed—next to the municipal government building with its large windows opened to the outside—a number of men passing out pickaxes, shovels, and sacks of cement. Vásquez Salgado began to laugh, and I asked him why. He told me that functionaries of the Institutional Revolutionary Party (Partido Revolucionario Institucional; PRI)[30] in Chilpancingo, in a naked electoral ploy, had brought the shovels and cement sacks to the government building and that "they're doing it so we vote for the PRI." I asked what he thought the townspeople were disposed to do, and he replied that in the opinion of those in the PRI, the people of Atliaca were "ignorant campesinos" whose votes would be bought with such things, but he added, "we shall see." A week later I learned that 98 percent of Atliaca's voters had given their ballots to the Partido de la Revolución Democrática (Democratic Revolutionary Party; PRD, a center-left–oriented party) and, further, that they had retained the pickaxes, shovels, and cement the PRI had given them as the way to buy their vote.

This sequence of events illustrates how Atliaca's Nahua population combines its own beliefs and traditions with the fluid situations imposed on it by the world beyond. In addition, the decision by the pueblo's voters to break with the politics of clientalism and their long tradition of supporting the PRI and to opt instead for another political party forms part of a new electoral autonomy through which they have ceased to be purely passive agents, automatically subject to co-optation when showered with a handful of small gifts. A lengthy struggle carried out against a local cacique who tried to wrest away their best land has also contributed to the Atliacans' more assertive posture by heightening their sense of political awareness. Their primordial titles played a key role in this legal tussle, as did the decision by a Nahua teacher and lawyer to use the pueblo's history as an instrument to defend its land.

4.7 Schoolteacher-lawyer Modesto Vázquez Salgado in Atliaca. Date: 2005. Courtesy, Adolfo de Paz.

Modesto Vázquez Salgado[31] (Figure 4.7) is a Nahua Indian, approximately sixty years old (in 2010), who hails from Atliaca. He was born in a palm-thatched house at 13 Abasolo Street. Modesto's father made a living producing mescal. He developed a fondness for the drink and often left his family for long periods, leaving the young Modesto to be raised mainly by his grandparents. From an early age, they sent the boy to work in the fields, so Modesto was much older than his classmates when he first went to school. One of his saddest recollections dates to when he was twelve and asked his father to buy him a pair of *huaraches* (sandals). Turned down by his father, he ran off with some men in the direction of Hueyapan, in the state of Veracruz. The men had told Modesto that he would earn money if he went with them to cut sugarcane on the local plantations. The boy, who knew how to wield a machete, went off to Hueyapan, although neither he nor his companions spoke Spanish, only Nahua.

For a month, the twelve-year-old Modesto labored at cutting sugarcane in primitive conditions. Meals generally consisted of only a few potatoes, and the workday lasted from early morning until nightfall. In payment for his work, the boy received a bit of clothing, a hat, the longed-for huaraches, and some money. As a result of the deplorable work conditions, some of the men with whom Modesto had come from Atliaca contemplated deserting Hueyapan and going to Mexico City. Overhearing them talk of the plan, he resolved to go with them "with the forty-nine pesos I had, and when they were ready to set off, well, I stuck with them, [and] since I was just a *chamaco* [kid], they planned to leave me behind, but when I came up to them with my clothes and my *mocha* [machete], telling them to take me with them, well, we were buddies."[32]

On the trip from Veracruz to Mexico City, Modesto ate sandwiches in Tehuacan, Puebla. They made him so sick and weakened his stomach to such an extent that to this day he eats only corn tortillas. Upon reaching Mexico City, the group made its way to the Zócalo (the main plaza), site of the cathedral and the National Palace, where Modesto wanted—like his companions—to be hired as a day laborer on construction projects. Given his youth, however, nobody took him on. He was out of money, and one of his traveling companions loaned him some pesos so he could return to Atliaca.

Once back in his pueblo, Modesto—naturally feeling somewhat fearful—came before his father, but luckily he was not castigated for having run away. A few months later a mestizo, Andrés de Loya, hired him to go to a place called Tepecua to take care of goats and hogs and also to work in the fields. One day, while drawing water from a well, he seriously injured his hand, leaving him unable to work. His boss, seeing that Modesto was no longer of use to him, threw him out of the house, accompanied by the insult "rotten Indian, you don't know how to work."

The boy's fortunes turned. He began working for an elderly woman who needed help caring for her goats. She healed Modesto's injured hand and, on Sundays, would wash his clothes. As a boy, he was highly imaginative and had hopes of studying, but he spoke no Spanish and had yet to set foot inside a school. The old woman sought help from one of her nieces, a teacher, so Modesto could attend primary school. Thus it was that he embarked upon a new routine: working during the day, helping in the fields, and studying by night. After completing primary school at fifteen, Modesto began his secondary-level curriculum at a workers' school in Tixtla, where he followed a roughly similar schedule: helping out in the teacher's house during the day and applying himself to his studies in the afternoons and evenings.

Ultimately, while working as a gardener at different homes in Tixtla, he succeeded in completing a program to become a bilingual teacher, with a specialty in the Nahuatl language. In between his studies and subsequently as a teacher, Modesto became interested in politics. He served for twenty years as a representative of the PRI in Atliaca but has disavowed the party. In the main, what he likes and what interests him is to be of service to the people, but without incurring any party-political obligations. On several occasions, others have invited him to join Atliaca's municipal government, versed as he is in the pueblo's customs and ways:

Even my childhood companions, who have gone beyond being mere authorities and served as president [of the municipal government], have said to me,
¡Come on, Modesto! Let's get to work, and I say to them, "we are working,"
but you ought to, well, yes, one should, but we have other concerns; the thing
is that now they all fight each other—it wasn't like that before, before we
all worked together, everyone united—now people don't know how to be
conciliatory.[33]

Modesto decided to be a PRI representative for practical reasons, as a way to
benefit the pueblo. After becoming a bilingual teacher, he realized that the government was not directing any resources to Atliaca. "There was no development,"
he says; consequently, he decided to exploit the election campaigns of different
candidates and secure what meager resources each one offered. To this end, he
linked up with others from the pueblo, telling them:

What we'll do now is spread ourselves around, this is the way the parties are
and they'll go at it tooth and nail, to gin up the interest of a party we have to
divide ourselves up, you represent the Partido de Acción Nacional [National
Action Party; PAN, a conservative-leaning party], you an opposition party,
and you still another party, and when these candidates come around we'll meet
them—but of course nothing was certain, it was only a put-on, done so that
those who represented the government at that time could see for themselves a
community in need of assistance.[34]

The tradition in Mexico was that candidates from the different parties tried
to buy the votes of the neediest by giving them basic foodstuffs and other useful
items. Modesto and some of his fellow Atliacans figured that to exploit this practice to the fullest, they needed to serve as local representatives of the most important political parties. Thus, each resident attached himself to a separate party;
since nobody wanted to represent the PRI, it fell to Modesto to do so. Whenever
a political candidate came to Atliaca, those in the know immediately asked him
his party affiliation and then guided him to the pueblo's corresponding "representative." Following this modus operandi, the group managed to secure essential
goods for Atliaca. The pragmatism and political maneuvering they demonstrated
were common among the Indian pueblos, long accustomed as they were to receiving little or no assistance from any of Mexico's political parties.

Modesto's initial years as a teacher, during the mid-1970s, passed unevent-
fully, although he tried to remain vigilant about the problems Atliaca faced.
Teaching indigenous pupils posed its own challenges. In addition to handling the
routine difficulties of the classroom, instructors often needed to intervene with
parents to be sure they sent their children to school rather than into the fields to
work. They also had to deal with the anti-Indian racist attitudes that prevailed
among the mestizo population of a city like Tixtla, Atliaca's capital town. Working

jointly with other teachers, Modesto helped establish the Chichipico school for bilingual education, near Tixtla. Tixtla's mestizos made a practice of mocking the school, commenting that it stood on a remote "little hill" and that the Indians in that vicinity were not "domesticated." These notions outraged Modesto and opened his eyes even further to the Indians' overriding need for education.

Atliaca's townsfolk believe Tixtla's mestizos look down on them because they speak Nahuatl. They also believe, however, that the racism Tixtla's inhabitants evidence toward them has declined in recent years for two reasons: first, because Atliaca's population now includes various professionals, and second, because the people as a whole have attained more education. In Modesto's view, the EZLN uprising in Chiapas has also had an impact by causing members of his pueblo to place new value on their native language and customs. The people of Atliaca distinctly recall that between thirty and fifty years ago, relations between mestizos and Indians were intolerable. For the most part, since the colonial period Tixtla has been identified with cattle ranching, its settlers enamored of bullfights and celebrations of horsemanship. As late as the 1950s, people from the town would ride into Atliaca on horseback, galloping through the pueblo and firing shots into the air to scare its inhabitants, who up until the 1960s spoke only Nahuatl, not Spanish: "they saw us as a lesser race." Modesto recalls that during his youth, there was segregation in Tixtla. In certain establishments, Nahuas were prohibited from taking seats or from eating at the main table during social gatherings and celebrations, "and that happened a lot, they looked down on us, [they said we were] ignorant people, Indian folk, 'cowardly types,' and so lots of people don't like our language and joke about it, they came down hard on us, but we've been seeing that those ways have now passed into history, things now are different."[35]

Like various other small cities in the Mexican hinterland, Tixtla was originally an Indian pueblo associated with a Spanish encomienda. The pueblo contained a group of important indigenous noblemen, and with both a source of water and fertile land, the region around it was highly coveted. Over time, Spanish ranchers settled in the area and began to raise cattle.[36] Slowly but surely, Tixtla's indigenous character faded, although not completely. During the nineteenth and early twentieth centuries, merchants and cattlemen endeavored to exert control over the Indian pueblos, such as Atliaca, in the surrounding area. For their part, when recounting the history of their pueblo, the inhabitants of Atliaca give it a higher status than Tixtla. The elders of the pueblo claim it is older than Tixtla, whose inhabitants, they also allege, dispossessed the Atliacans of their land. According to them, the entire Río Balsas, one of the largest rivers in the country, belonged to Atliaca. In their re-creation of the pueblo's history, the mestizos are portrayed as latecomers who have steadily usurped Atliaca's land; in that sense, apart from the precise number of hectares involved, they are right.

In 1977, when he was still working as a bilingual teacher, Atliaca's authorities commissioned Modesto to resolve a problem that affected a majority of the pueblo's inhabitants. Historically, the community has faced a water problem. Thus, it is not for nothing that its population conjures a past in which it was the master of all of the Río Balsas. In 1960, on the basis of collective labor, the pueblo's authorities managed to erect a water storage tank that would serve everyone in the community, and some years later they successfully lobbied the government for economic assistance so they could have the tank filled. The supply gradually dwindled, however. For a time the pueblo pursued a plan to bring water from a site known as Ixhuitlayocan, located behind a nearby hill called Amoltepetl. The plan had to be abandoned, however, because it turned out to be very costly to lay down pipes over this distance, and the authorities in both Tixtla and Chilpancingo (Guerrero's capital city) had failed to provide financial aid for the project. By 1977 the community was experiencing a severe water shortage. Only thirty of its families—those best positioned economically—had water running into their homes. Unlike the rest of the population, they had been able to lay down pipes and connect their houses to the storage tank. Thus, while all of the pueblo's inhabitants paid fees to the government for the use of water, most had to wait all night every night merely to obtain a bucketful. By contrast, families connected to the main supply not only enjoyed the privilege of taking daily baths but also exacerbated the general shortage by watering their patios and gardens. Modesto elected to confront these families and—with the backing of many in the community—had their water cut off. Not surprisingly, this action earned him the enmity of his pueblo's wealthier members, but it also enabled Atliaca's poorer families to have access to more water.[37]

Modesto's intervention in this affair marked the beginning of his more active involvement in problems the pueblo faced. In 1981, for example, a conflict broke out between Atliaca and a neighboring pueblo, Almolonga, whose inhabitants had taken over possession of a site that belonged to Atliaca, called Laguna Seca. Although the boundary lines were clearly demarcated, the Almolongans nonetheless brought a tractor onto the land Atliaca claimed as its own. The residents of Atliaca, mobilized by Modesto and other community leaders to confront the situation, reacted by going onto the disputed land at night and disabling the tractor, letting the air out of its tires and removing some of its parts. Almolonga sued Atliaca for damages and harm. Modesto, who was named in the suit, was arrested by the judicial police and taken to the jail in Tixtla. Both he and Atliaca's political leaders requested help from the staff of the National Indian Institute, which managed to have Modesto released within a few days for lack of evidence against him.

The 1981 confrontation over land was not the first of its kind for Modesto. He and others in the pueblo had faced a land-related problem in 1975. In contrast to the minor affair with Almolonga, the earlier conflict was more serious and far more protracted, calling for Atliaca to negotiate with the Mexican government for nearly three decades to avoid being dispossessed of part of its land. At present, the pueblo possesses 13,592 hectares of communal property. Until recently, however, and going back to 1975, a mestizo cattle rancher and mescal producer in the area, Félix Mier Peralta, laid claim to a parcel of Atliaca's communal land called Xicatepetl, amounting to 1,100 hectares. Mier Peralta was well placed; he enjoyed strong political support from the PRI, at that time the governing party in Guerrero, and, in addition, was related to one of the PRI's local representatives. The corruption that pervades all levels of government in Mexico, particularly in states like Guerrero, and the adversary's economic and political power made Atliaca's defense of its land a difficult proposition.

Between 1975 and 1995, in direct violation of Atliaca's rights and stated wishes, Mier Peralta turned his cattle loose to graze on the pueblo's land, which was fertile and had an abundance of forests and palm trees. His herd was substantial, approximately 200 head, and it caused extensive damage to fields on which the campesinos had sown crops. In addition, Mier Peralta induced several of his cattle rancher friends to release their own herds onto the pueblo's land. This provocation caused even greater damage, spelling total destruction of the corn that had been planted, and it led to serious confrontations between the pueblo and Mier Peralta: "It was impossible to sow the fields any more because the cattle were all over them. The dispute really heated up then and it was better [for Atliaca's campesinos] to just let the fields go."[38]

Mier Peralta mustered legal arguments to defend his land grab, arguing that historically Atliaca had never possessed much land and that he had purchased the property in question from its owners. The pueblo countered his claim, arguing that it possessed communal lands and held them legally by virtue of specific federal legislative action, but it lacked—or, rather, appeared at first to lack—supporting documentation. In previous decades, Atliaca had, in fact, made several attempts to receive its official distribution of ejido lands. In 1915 the national archive wrote a report on its search for the pueblo's primordial titles.[39] Two decades later, in 1935, the Agrarian Department asked the archive to conduct a search for Atliaca's historical documents,[40] and in 1940 the agrarian authorities prepared their own report—which contained a paleographic analysis—on the pueblo's titles.[41] These interventions demonstrate that beginning in 1915, Atliaca had taken concrete steps to legally retain its communal property through a formal ejido grant. All that remained was to complete the process.

In light of the situation, Modesto began actively to help Atliaca's political authorities rally in defense of the pueblo's land. On the opposing side, Mier Peralta intensified his efforts to install himself as the land's de facto owner. He succeeded in having state authorities draw up orders to apprehend Modesto and other members of the pueblo. When he heard about this latest tactic, Modesto decided to study law so he could defend both himself and the pueblo in the courts. He was admitted to the School of Law at the Autonomous University of Guerrero. Continuing his work as a bilingual teacher in the midst of his legal studies, Modesto traveled constantly between the school where he taught, near the city of Chilapa, and Chilpancingo, where the law school was located. To be able to afford to attend the school, he shared the rent for a small room with other students, "so I did my studies there at night, motivated to acquire the knowledge of how to defend myself on the appointed day. It didn't matter how tired I felt, I needed to put together the elements of a defense and to be able to respond because it's frightening to have an order to be seized hanging over one's head."[42]

Some members of Atliaca's population belonged to the PRI. These individuals took up the cattle rancher's position, arguing that the pueblo had no communal property, that all of the land was owned privately, and that Mier Peralta had purchased the contested land legally. The pueblo, however, had evidence to the contrary. In 1973 one of Atliaca's authorities, Severino Iglesias, had found the records documenting Atliaca's ejido grant in the house of a village elder. The records consisted of a presidential resolution along with the definitive map of the grant, dating to 1956. The resolution bore the signature of President Adolfo Ruiz Cortines (1952–1958). The papers had been wrapped in a nylon bag and placed in a gourd that was hung from the old man's ceiling. With these documents in hand, the pueblo's authorities, assisted by Modesto, began to look further into the case and to inform the rest of the community of their legal findings.

Persuaded of the strength of their case, the pueblo's inhabitants met collectively to decide how to proceed. One of their initial steps was to creep onto the land at night and remove the fencing Mier Peralta had installed on it. The cattleman reacted by suing them for damages, claiming they had vandalized and destroyed property that belonged to him. With the possibility of financial ruin hanging over them, the Atliacans began to doubt themselves. Modesto persisted in his arguments, however, explaining that the community's position was solid and that the suit would not proceed. He used his growing knowledge of the law to win over his compatriots:

> Because at some points the campesinos could have faced paying damages from 500,000 up to a million pesos, they all became terrified: how am I going to pay? I'll be hauled off to jail, but no, that's not going to happen, it's just empty slander we're facing, he [the cattleman] needs to look for a way of frightening people, but don't worry, we will set out, we will organize demonstrations, even before the judge, before the government, showing that he is wrong because we have the necessary elements [to do so]. Here in our hands are the records, the

resolution, the definitive map; we have the legal armament, don't worry, we are in the right, so they came out of it with confidence and we pushed ahead.[43]

Armed with placards and accompanied by a majority of the townsfolk, Atliaca's authorities began to demonstrate in the offices of the land arbitration panel in Chilpancingo. As many as 400 of the pueblo's inhabitants—men, women, children, and elders—demanded that the land the cattleman claimed be restored to them. The community retained lawyers to defend and present its case. The full process—from the time when Atliaca's authorities discovered the documents that validated the land's communal origins and status—would last almost thirty years.

Modesto acted as an adviser to the pueblo's political leaders for this entire period. At times, during community assemblies, he needed to explain the difference between communal lands and small landholdings and also to alleviate the fears various campesinos voiced about not wanting to be "communists." His reassurances, then, also involved explaining that communal lands were not synonymous with communism but rather—in Atliaca's context—that they signified community collaboration to cultivate and care for the land. It was an arduous task. Year after year, Modesto would reach home after a day in the classroom and at ten o'clock at night would visit the municipal offices to learn the pueblo's latest news from its leaders. He was used to pointing out that "you have to be persistent [with Atliaca's authorities]; they are never going to seek me out in my house."[44]

In the warm and quiet Atliaca nights, enjoying a cool drink in front of the church, the schoolteacher would try to learn how the pueblo's legal case to recover the land from Mier Peralta was proceeding. To keep people fully informed about its progress and to announce the convocation of special gatherings and meetings, he purchased—at his own expense—a sound-box and microphone. Although merchants in Atliaca had this equipment, they had no interest in loaning it out for community purposes; it was there purely to help them sell their products. Meanwhile, Modesto's simple apparatus became central to his efforts to mobilize and unite the pueblo behind its leaders' campaign to defend and recover community land.

In recording the history of their struggle, "thirty years" is only two words, but for Modesto and all the people of Atliaca, the road was long and rocky. Fortunately, near the end the pueblo gained the support of the regional branches of the PRD and the Partido del Trabajo (PT), both left-leaning political parties, and also of a major regional organization of indigenous pueblos sympathetic to the EZLN called the Consejo Guerrerense 500 Años de Resistencia Indígena, Negra y Popular (Guerrero Council: 500 Years of Indigenous, Black, and Popular Resistance).[45] In the final analysis, however, the heart of the pueblo's case rested on its possession of the documents issued in 1956, which made its grant of ejido land official. Atliaca's persistence and its long wait for justice were rewarded on December 27, 2004, when the government authorities ruled in its favor, enabling the pueblo to repossess its land. Although Mier Peralta was ordered to return the land and relinquish any claim over it, he was not—despite the tangible hardship he had caused to Atliaca's campesinos—obliged to pay any compensation. The community accepted this decision with equanimity. Modesto summed up its attitude: "[I]t is sufficient that he returns the land, everything else is over with, that is the most that can be asked for because in those circumstances nothing more can be done; since he is a farmer and is of that social class, that is the way to leave it."[46]

When Atliaca's authorities returned to the pueblo carrying the favorable court decision, everyone turned out, welcoming them by marching from the edge of the pueblo all the way to the municipal government building. Atliaca's leaders responded in kind by organizing a banquet, complete with music, to celebrate the victory. Later, assisted by a topographer from Mexico's Instituto de Geografía y Estadística, the pueblo's 13,592 hectares were again surveyed and marked off. Atliaca's oldest members helped guide the process, since they possessed the keenest knowledge of the community's limits and boundaries.

With both the official recognition of its community property and the recovery of that property an accomplished fact, the pueblo—operating communally—has taken steps to plant trees and maguey plants on the land. Modesto has urged the pueblo to adopt a set of rules that would spell out the rights and obligations of all the town's communal landholders, an idea that grew out of the National Agrarian Registry's initiative to register and certify Atliaca's campesinos as communal landholders. The proposed set of rules, drawn up using examples Modesto collected from other Indian pueblos, currently consists of eighty-six articles. Again deploying his sound-box, the schoolteacher has called the townsfolk to meetings so they can deliberate the rules themselves and receive reports as the final product—which they are crafting—takes shape.

Despite his sustained involvement in local political affairs, Modesto has never sought office. He believes he can be more effective serving in an advisory capacity and not participating directly, since politics inevitably generates resentment between governing officials and the governed: "I haven't been a municipal official myself, but I've always been involved here, from some distance, as an adviser because sometimes there are people who are 'wild cards,' with bad intentions, and we have to keep our eye on the ball. If we don't, you get 'burned,'[47] and if you keep to the 'sidelines' you can watch out for yourself."[48]

Modesto sees a distinct change in the attitude of Atliaca's inhabitants. Since taking up the struggle for their land, they have become aware that negotiating successfully with the state involves working collectively, as a unified group. The schoolteacher also thinks that from a political standpoint the pueblo's people are more attuned to holding their politicians to account, both on the state and local levels. He sees positive evidence of that and of their newfound conviction that their vote makes a difference in the results of the 2004 elections, when the PRI was defeated in Atliaca. He notes with satisfaction: "The movement to win back the land stopped with itself, but—as we immediately saw—the PRI had never lost here in Atliaca; now it has lost by 166 votes. The majority of people in Atliaca voted for the PRD, something which had never happened before."[49]

Today, Modesto continues to make a living as a bilingual teacher and also volunteers as an "adviser" to the pueblo's leaders, fraternizing with them at night in front of the church on the town square. On Saturdays he is accustomed to stopping by Atliaca's Office of Communal Properties (Comisaría de Bienes Comunales) where—recalling the historical model of a council of village elders—the pueblo's old men gather to converse. There, sifting through the pueblo's affairs, Modesto and the elders settle on which developments have been best for them, as well as for future generations of Atliacans.

Knowledge of their community history, allied with their common efforts, has unquestionably benefited the people of the pueblo. For many years, interests foreign to Atliaca exploited the fact that its residents had "forgotten" that they were a community that possessed communal land. As a result, parcels of their land had passed—wrongly—into private hands. Modesto's effort to make his fellow Atliacans aware of the importance of knowing their rights and educating themselves in how to negotiate more effectively with the state have proved successful. Modesto's professional formation, first as a teacher and later as a lawyer, stemmed from his awareness that to improve his own situation as well as that of the pueblo, he needed to reach beyond the community and find external resources. Over time, the techniques he employed in negotiating with the state became increasingly sophisticated. Finally, after many years of seeking redress in the courts, the schoolteacher-lawyer, together with the pueblo's authorities and ordinary citizens, succeeded in recovering Atliaca's land and in preserving its territorial integrity.

The second case study involves an Indian pueblo in Oaxaca, where sophisticated elements of negotiation with the state—such as the use of local history to advance community interest—also come into play.

SANTA MARÍA CUQUILA, OAXACA: POLITICS AND LOCAL HISTORY IN A MIXTEC COMMUNITY

Santa María Cuquila, whose Mixtec name is *ñuu kuiñi* (pueblo of the tiger) (Figure 4.8), is located in the southern part of Oaxaca's Sierra Madre, in the Mixteca Alta,

4.8 The pueblo of Santa María Cuquila as seen from the west. Date: 2004. Photograph by Martín Martínez.

at a coordinate of 17 degrees north latitude and 97 degrees east longitude. Sitting at 2,180 meters above sea level, the community is rimmed by eleven high peaks, which rise to an elevation of 3,360 meters. It enjoys a mild climate during most of the year, with an average temperature of 16.6° centigrade. The summer brings rain along with warmer, somewhat more humid weather; around Santa María are catchments and ponds formed by the diversion of water from the Río Atoyac.

Agriculture forms the main pillar of the pueblo's economy and revolves around the cultivation of corn and beans. Santa María's inhabitants also have considerable forestland, with stands of oak and different species of pine, as well as pastureland. Its population is Mixtec, and everyone in the pueblo speaks Mixtecan. Bilingualism is not uncommon, however; those age fifty and younger in particular often have a working or fluent knowledge of Spanish. The older segment of the population speaks only Mixtecan. As a result of the wave of people who have left Cuquila to find work in the United States, some members of the community are now trilingual, speaking Mixtecan, Spanish, and English. Younger members of the pueblo display a greater interest in learning English; although they speak Spanish well, they consider knowledge of English more prestigious.

Cuquila was relatively isolated until the mid-twentieth century, when in 1958 the government constructed a highway through the mountains in the direction of the coast. Running alongside Cuquila, the highway opened up communications, facilitating the pueblo's contact with Tlaxiaco and other nearby areas with mestizo populations and, as a by-product, jump-starting its children's acquisition of Spanish. Cuquila's population is small. The pueblo has 682 inhabitants,[50] dispersed among 139 houses. Of the latter, only 76 have piped water, and just 2 of those have drainage to the outside. Of the 139 homes, 108 have been hooked up to electricity.[51] The majority of Cuquilans are campesinos. The pueblo also has some skilled potters who produce very fine, but undecorated, work in clay. Indeed, until plastic made its appearance in the area, Cuquila supplied pots and jugs to all the pueblos scattered across the region, from the mountains to the coast. The potters even carried their wares to the market in Pinotepa Nacional, where they exchanged them for a variety of goods.[52] In recent years, however, the number of campesinos and potters has declined, while the number of Cuquilans who hire out as day laborers or bricklayers on construction projects—whether in other Mixtecan pueblos, Tlaxiaco, Oaxaca more widely, or the Federal District—has increased.[53]

Cuquila served as a seat of local municipal government until 1938, when—as we shall see—political difficulties seem to have played a strong role in causing what its inhabitants refer to as their "fall in status." The pueblo has seven dependent communities: San Isidro, Agua Zarca, Plan de Guadalupe, San Juan, Benito Juárez, San Pedro Llano Grande, and Cañada Candelaria.[54] At present, it pertains to the municipality of Tlaxiaco.

A SNAPSHOT OF LOCAL HISTORY

Within the boundaries of Santa María Cuquila is a large archaeological site dating from the Classic Period (400–850 AD). Still largely unexplored, the site is well preserved; among its ruins is a pre-Columbian ball court. The pueblo's community museum[55] houses a series of stelae, carved in the Ñuiñe style, that once stood on the site (Figure 4.9).[56] Moreover, according to archaeologist Ángel Iván Rivera, this site functioned as the seat of power and authority for the entire region during the Classic Period.[57]

The production of codices, furthermore, was a notable feature of the pueblo prior to the Spanish conquest. Four such documents, all dating to the end of the sixteenth century, have survived to the present; two of them are shown in Figures 4.10 and 4.11.[58] The research of two modern scholars has extended our knowledge of the pueblo's codex tradition. Mary Elizabeth Smith believed the *Codex López Ruiz* had its origin in Santa María Cuquila,[59] and Viola König noted that an important Mixtec genealogical codex, the *Codex Egerton*, was produced in Cuquila.[60] The *Codex Egerton* makes reference to local pre-Hispanic rulers and

4.9 *Ñuiñe*-style stelae, bearing the calendrical name of the figure 10 Monkey. Date: 2004. Courtesy, Santa María Cuquila Community Museum.

the alliances they formed through marriage. Smith, furthermore, found evidence that the pueblo depicted in the mountain jaguar (tiger) glyphs found on two colonial pictorial documents, the *Mapa de Ocotepec* and Mapa no. 2463 in the AGN, is also Cuquila—the pueblo of the jaguar (Figure 4.10).[61]

Some time ago I was able to reconstruct the family lineage of the caciques (*iya* in Mixtecan) who ruled Santa María Cuquila from the mid-sixteenth century until roughly 1809. Having done so, I noted that a strong tie existed between this lineage and that of the pueblo of Tepejillo (Tepexillo, Thepejillo), belonging to Acatlán in the lower Mixteca area (Table 4.1).[62]

We also know that at the beginning of the seventeenth century the local ruler went through the process of legally obtaining title from the monarchy to the lands that formed his cacicazgo. Thus it was that on July 28, 1707, Don Juan de la Cruz Mendoza y Terrazas completed the process of composición, under which it was verified that the cacicazgo comprised a number of pueblos in both the Mixteca Alta and the Mixteca Baja (Table 4.2).

This connection, tying a cacicazgo that originated in Cuquila[63] to pueblos in both the upper and lower Mixteca, demonstrates that intermarriage among the rulers helped create and consolidate a long-lasting cultural corridor between both parts of the Mixteca, an arrangement in which Cuquila clearly played a formative role. The fact that Indians from Cuquila had settled in Acatlán centuries

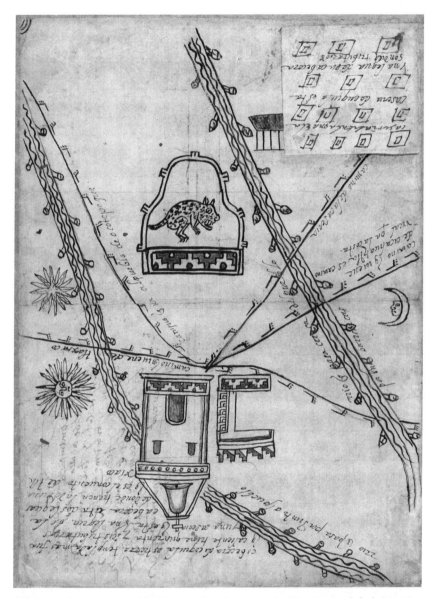

4.10 Reproduction, no. 2463. Date: 1599. Courtesy, Archivo General de la Nación, Mexico City.

earlier is evident from a dispute that occurred in 1733. The records of the case note that Acatlán, a half league (2.9 kilometers) from Tepejillo,[64] contained a district called Cuquila. Its inhabitants had lived there since time "immemorial,"

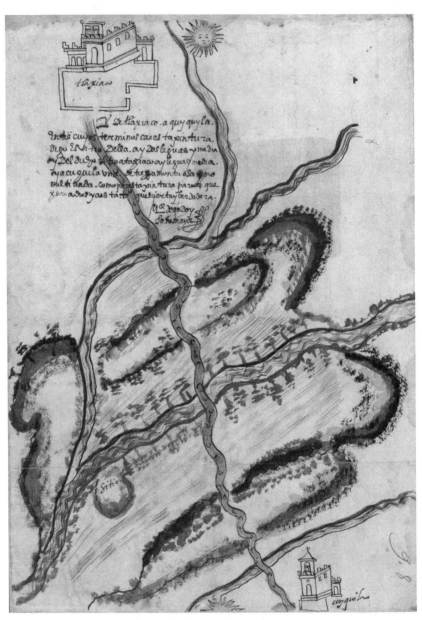

4.II Reproduction, no. 1692.9. Date: 1588. Courtesy, Archivo General de la Nación, Mexico City.

Table 4.1. Governors of the Ruling Line of Santa María de Cuquila, 1559–1800

1. Don Francisco de Austria: 1559–?

2. Don Pedro Castañeda: 1583–159?[1]

3. Don Raymundo de Velasco, married to Doña Inés de Velasco: ?

4. Don Juan de Velasco: ?

5. Doña María de Velasco (sister of Don Juan de Velasco), married to Don Antonio de Mendoza y Terrazas: ?

6. Don Juan de la Cruz Mendoza y Terrazas (son of Doña María de Velasco), married to Doña Andrea de Rojas: died in 1708 or 1709

7. Doña Catharina de Mendoza y Terrazas (the son of Don Juan de la Cruz), married to Don Diego de Miguel Mendoza Guzmán, cacique of the pueblos of San Francisco Juapanapa (in Huajuapan) and Tepejillo (Acatlán): died in 1708.

8. Doña Isidora de San Miguel (daughter of the latter-two caciques), married to Don Manuel de Santiago.[2]

9. At this juncture, the seat of the cacicazgo moved to Acatlán: Doña Theresa de Santiago (daughter of Doña Isidora and Manuel de Santiago) was orphaned at age nine. Her uncle on her mother's side, Don Fernando de Mendoza y Guzmán, cacique of Tepejillo, journeyed to Cuquila to bring her back to live in Tepejillo. After reaching adulthood, Doña Theresa married Don Severiano Antonio Ximenez Esquival, who had succeeded to the governorship of Tepejillo's cacicazgo.

10. Manuel de Esquivel Andrade (son of Doña Theresa and Don Severiano): 1766

11. Doña Clara Sebastiana Esquivel y Andrade (sister of Don Manuel Esquivel), married to Don Francisco de Jesús Velasco y Mendoza, cacique of Acatlán: 1772–1805

12. Don Narciso de Jesús Velasco y Esquivel (son of Doña Clara and Don Francisco)[3]

Notes:

1. AGN, Ramo Indios, vol. 2, exp. 374, f. 90v; AGN, Ramo de Mercedes, vol. 15, f. 130. Documents found in the AGN indicate that this cacique's dwelling place was Cuquila; hence it can be inferred that in this period Cuquila served as the seat of the cacicazgo: AGN, Ramo Mercedes, vol. 14, f. 130, 1590, and vol. 15, f. 130r; AGN, Ramo General de Parte, vol. 2, exp. 1087, f. 242v; AGN, Ramo Tierras 2692, exp. 17, and 2682, exp. 17. This lattermost document relates that Castañeda succeeded in preventing certain lands from being granted to a Spaniard.

2. AGN, Ramo de Tierras, vol. 876, exp. 1, and vol. 1285, exp. 1.

3. AGN, Ramo Indiferente Virreinal 5993, exp. 5.

dedicating themselves to growing corn, chile, and beans. The records also mention that the lands pertaining to the Cuquila district were adjacent to the land belonging to the ruler of San Pedro and San Pablo Tequistepec, with whom the residents of Cuquila had conflicts over boundaries.[65]

Two factors—the physical extension of the colonial cacicazgo that belonged to the ruling lineage of Cuquila and Iván Rivera's identification of the stylistic features of the pueblo's stelae as Ñuiñe—allied with Viola König's research findings, allow us to postulate that a westerly corridor existed linking Acatlán, Tonala, and Cuquila and that the corridor probably reached as far as the coastal community of Tututepec.[66] A late–sixteenth-century map from Santa María Cuquila (Figure

Table 4.2. Pueblos Forming the Cacicazgo of Cuquila, 1707

1.	San Francisco Huapanapan, Huajuapan (Mixteca Baja)
2.	Tepejillo, Acatlán (Mixteca Baja)
3.	Zochilazala [Zochiquilazala], Justlahuaca (Mixteca Baja)[1]
4.	Santa María Yodocohiio, Tonala, "in the Mixteca Baja"[2]
5.	"San Pablo Guaxolotitlan el Grande," Huajuapan (Mixteca Baja)[3]
6.	Santa María Cuquila (jurisdiction of Teposcolula)
7.	San Andrés de la Laguna Yocotno [Yodiotnoho] (jurisdiction of Teposcolula)
8.	San Miguel Tixaa [San Miguel Lucane, Nucani, Tixaa] (jurisdiction of Teposcolula)
9.	Santa María Magdalena [Magdalena Duayi, Nduahayihí, Cañadaltepec] (jurisdiction of Teposcolula)
10.	Santa Catarina Yutacuiñi (jurisdiction of Teposcolula)
11.	San Felipe Numihaha [Ixtapa, Salina] (jurisdiction of Teposcolula)
12.	Tamazulapa (jurisdiction of Teposcolula)
13.	Tejupan [Santiago Tejupan] (jurisdiction of Teposcolula)
14.	Chilapa [Santa María Chilapa de Díaz] (jurisdiction of Teposcolula)
15.	San Pedro Yucunama [Amoltepec][4]
16.	"San Francisco de los Chocho" (jurisdiction of Teposcolula)[5]

Notes:
1. AGN, Ramo de Tierras, vol. 1285, exp. 1. For the location of these communities, see Gerhard, *A Guide*, 42–44, 132, 166.
2. AGN, Ramo de Tierras, vol. 1285, exp. 1.
3. Ibid., vol. 2259, exp. 4. In 1751 Don Severiano Esquivel took the step of leasing his lands to members of his pueblo.
4. I am grateful to Itzel González Pérez for kindly furnishing me with the particulars of this record, from ibid., vol. 1285, exp. 1. For the location of specific sites, see Gerhard, *A Guide*, 289.
5. AGN, Ramo de Tierras, vol. 760, exp. 1.

4.10), bearing the words "the road that comes from Chicahuastla is the royal road to the coast,"[67] strengthens the likelihood of this connection. To all intents and purposes, Cuquila sits to this day along the same road that led to the coast.[68] Mary Elizabeth Smith pointed out still more evidence promoting the interconnection in the form of another map produced in Cuquila, dating to the end of the sixteenth century, that depicts vegetation in a manner highly similar to that found on a pictorial manuscript from the Oaxacan coast, the *Lienzo de Zacatepec 2* (Figure 4.12).[69]

As its significant archaeological site and surviving stelae attest, San María Cuquila was unquestionably a pueblo of some importance both before and after the Spanish conquest. Further testifying to this fact, in 1559 its cacique, Don Francisco de Austria, joined the most powerful caciques across the upper and lower Mixteca in granting authority to "Fray Jhoan de Cordova, of the order of Santo Domingo[,] and Alvaro Ruiz, an attorney for the Royal Audiencia, and Gaspar de la Torre, a resident of the city of Antequera," to defend their interests before King Philip II.[70]

4.12 Reproduction, no. 867. Date: 1595. Courtesy, Archivo General de la Nación, Mexico City.

As is seen in Table 4.1, shortly before the mid-eighteenth century the seat of Cuquila's cacicazgo was shifted to the region of Acatlán, in the lower Mixteca. As a result of this development, Cuquila began to lose some of its land to neighboring pueblos. The relocation came about fortuitously. At the beginning of the eighteenth century—as Table 4.1 also illustrates—Cuquila's rulers were Doña Isidora de San Miguel and Don Manuel de Santiago. The two died relatively young, causing their daughter to inherit the cacicazgo when she was only nine years old. Accordingly, her uncle on her mother's side, Don Fernando de Mendoza y Guzmán, the cacique of Tepejillo, journeyed to Cuquila to bring the orphaned girl to Tepejillo to live with him. Accompanied by a small entourage of servants, the young Theresa left Cuquila, never to return. When she attained adulthood she married Don Severiano Antonio Ximenez Esquivel, who had succeeded to the governorship of Tepejillo's cacicazgo.

As indicated previously, the inheritance of Cuquila's cacicazgo by a girl too young to exercise power had deleterious consequences for the pueblo. Deprived of its rulers, Cuquila's power passed into the hands of the local Indian cabildo. As a result, the community lost the shield of protection a cacique represented. The pueblos around Cuquila took note of this situation, and one in particular, Santo Tomás Ocotepec, decided to exploit Cuquila's vulnerability and make a grab for its best land, a parcel of territory known as Yutebaso. Ocotepec's cacique, Don Nicolás García de Roxas, was the hereditary ruler of both Santo Tomás Ocotepec and Nuyoo. He sought to carry out his design by having himself made the heir to the cacicazgo in 1726 and, on this basis, illegally folding into his possession the Yutebaso land that originally belonged to Cuquila.

Since Cuquila found itself without a ruler, it fell to the members of the cabildo to take action against the cacique of Ocotepec in defense of the seized land. The cabildo members were at a distinct disadvantage, however, because they were unable to read or write. Although they presented their claim in Teposcolula, the chief town of the jurisdiction to which they belonged, they were unsuccessful in recovering the Yutebaso land. The Spanish officials who considered the claim requested that Cuquila's authorities submit titles and other records verifying the pueblo's boundaries. Unfortunately, they had no such documentation. Many of the caciques in the Mixteca kept such material in their own hands, viewing it as their personal property. Such was the case with the caciques of Cuquila. Thus, when Doña Theresa departed for Tepejillo, the maps and other records documenting Cuquila's land were sent with her.[71] In this regard, the reverse side of a late–sixteenth-century map (Figure 4.12) from Cuquila pointedly reads: "These papers belong to doña Theresa de Andrade of Tepejillo, who is the granddaughter of Doña Catarina de la Cruz y Terrazas." The gloss clearly demonstrates that the pueblo's maps and other historical records were treated as the personal property of the young *cacica*.

Only later, in 1765, when Doña Theresa had reached full adulthood, did she, together with her husband, take up the complaint over the Yutebaso land that Cuquila's cabildo had initiated. However, they were not fighting the erstwhile cacique of Santo Tomás Ocotepec, Don Nicolás. During the interim, he had died. Now their adversary was his daughter and heir, the *yya* (ruler) Doña Pascuala Feliciana de Roxas. The litigation went on for years, and when the case was finally brought to an end in 1796, the audiencia ruled in favor of Ocotepec and against Cuquila. The fact that the Cuquilans had delayed for so many years in presenting the evidence for their case undoubtedly worked against them. Cuquila's community museum houses a document dating back to 1584 that notes that the parcel of Yutebaso land belonged to Cuquila and delimited the pueblo's boundaries with Santo Tomás Ocotepec.[72]

While the case was being litigated, the members of Cuquila's cabildo tried to prevent Ocotepec's caciques from taking possession of the land. At certain intervals, they encroached on it themselves. The conflict came to a violent head in the nineteenth century when several Cuquilans assassinated Cipriano Jiménez, the grandson of Feliciana de Roxas, in revenge for the loss of their land.[73]

As the case of Cuquila illustrates, the pueblo's rulers managed to extend their influence over a number of communities across a wide swath of territory in the upper and lower Mixteca. In various pueblos, furthermore, it was the caciques who frequently rose to the defense of pueblo lands. This was not surprising, since these rulers believed the lands belonged to them. In 1595, for example, the cacique of Cuquila, Pedro Castañeda (see Table 4.1), managed—accompanied by members of the Indian cabildo—to stop a wealthy Spaniard from gaining possession of some of Cuquila's land through a royal grant.[74]

When a pueblo found itself deprived of its rulers, the integrity of its communal lands—at least among the traditional communities of the Mixteca—was placed in serious jeopardy, as happened in the case of Santa María Cuquila. The cacicazgos in the Mixtec region were a vital pillar of indigenous society, and—in sharp contrast to what happened in Central Mexico—many of them remained intact through the eighteenth and even nineteenth centuries.[75] In parallel fashion, the Mixtec rulers continued to exert a forceful presence in their communities throughout the colonial period. Their role was more than honorific. As Kevin Terraciano has shown, the "noble houses subsumed many corporate landholding responsibilities in the Mixteca."[76]

This identification of the community with its rulers has persisted over the centuries in Cuquila. Many tales still abound about rulers who dwelled on what today is the archaeological site, a place the Cuquilans call "the Hill of the Cacica," or "the Tiger's Hill." The very oldest residents believe the site was originally a great "jungle" with a lagoon and was populated by fantastic animals, such as an eagle with "two beaks" that was probably two-headed[77] and a feathered serpent that brought water (*koosavi*), as well as tigers, lions, coyotes, and a plenitude of birds. The inhabitants of Cuquila stress that the double-beaked eagle wreaked havoc on people, snatching them up and carrying them off and also seizing hunters as they passed by with baskets full of animal skins. As the older Cuquilans tell it, many people lived on the hill before the Spanish arrived, "in the time when there was no sun, and when the sun came out all the people, all the animals died, then there was nothing, [and] God brought forth new life for us, so the people say."

In that primeval time a cacique and his sister also lived on the hill, and they possessed the power to summon stones and rock piles of varying sizes, to make them close in and come together one by one to build the hill the cacique wanted to reach to heaven. His sister was in charge of preparing the meals, and they were so tasty that the cacique wanted to know what she put in them. He decided one day to spy on her while she was cooking. Discovering to his great surprise that she put mucus from her nose in the food, he became enraged, upon which the top of the hill exploded into pieces and fell on a community 30 kilometers away, known as San Martín Huamelulpan, where—it is said—the remnants are still visible. When the summit of the hill flew off, so the story has it, it took both the lagoon and the feathered serpent with it.

As a result of this rage and destruction, the two caciques took leave of the Tiger's Hill, each by way of a different road. As they journeyed, the caciques founded various sites, causing water to gush forth and carrying out sacrifices. After he left the ruined hill, the brother in particular is credited with founding and naming different sites. During his journey a number of people approached him to ask for his help in constructing the church in Tlaxiaco. The cacique went to the people's aid, although he felt ashamed because he was clothed only in "a *capisayo*[78] sewn with coconut fiber." His misgivings notwithstanding, he arrived in Tlaxiaco, where he found gathered "many caciques [who] were laying the church's foundation. But the foundation did not hold fast [was not solid] because water flowed from the spot." With his walking stick the cacique pointed out the source of the water, thereby enabling the people to continue their work on the church. To facilitate the project, the cacique chose four other caciques, "nobles, and situated each in one of the four corners of the temple, and told them 'stay put until it is solid'[;] the masons worked the stone and mortar, such that the four [caciques] remained fixed there forever. Thus was Tlaxiaco's church completed."[79]

This story is illuminating because it demonstrates that the people of Cuquila—as carried down through their oral tradition—see their rulers as possessing supernatural powers, as being able to command stones to move through the air, to make water flow, to found dwelling sites, and to carry out ritual sacrifices. In addition, the story has several elements linking it to the Mixtecan pre-

Hispanic past; for example, when it mentions fantastic animals, wild animals—such as the double-beaked or double-headed eagle—living on the hill, it ushers us into the rich mythology surrounding the origins of the Mixtec, as they coexist with their gods and the animal kingdom. Furthermore, the fact that the two caciques, although they are brother and sister, are living together on the hill refers us to the *yuhitayu* (place for a bedroll or mat)—which forms the pre-Hispanic representation of the Mixtec ruling couple, man (*yya*) and woman (*yya dzehe*), and who, when paired together in the colonial period, represented a cacicazgo. The ruling couple is thus a symbol of elemental power.[80] In different Mesoamerican myths, however, both the ancient gods and kings lose their power after committing a transgression. In the story from Cuquila, the transgression that destroys the hill is the fact that the cacica mixed her mucous with the food, causing the destruction of their site and the subsequent exile of both rulers from their kingdom. I heard this story told many times; interestingly, the person narrating it sometimes felt ashamed to mention the part about the cacica using her mucous as an ingredient in the food. On those occasions he got around this incident either by telling me instead that the hill was destroyed because the cacique had licked a spoon or by simply jumping to the destruction of the hill, without trying to explain why it exploded into pieces or why the cacique had become so angry. In other tellings, however, this same person was so affected by the force of the story that he did not leave out the part about the cacica's transgression.

Once they had left this mythical kingdom, one by one the caciques went about founding sites and making water flow. As we have seen, the cacique from the Tiger's Hill is called to assist the people of Tlaxiaco. Although ashamed of his clothing, an ancient and traditional type made of coconut fiber, he nonetheless comes to the aid of the other caciques who are constructing Tlaxiaco's temple, which has been founded on a prestigious religious site. By means of his special powers, he is able to show the caciques the source of the water flow that has prevented them from laying the church's foundation. Moreover, in directing four of them to stand in the respective corners of the church to ensure its solidity, Cuquila's cacique goes to the extreme of carrying out human sacrifice. The four caciques will forever remain a part of the church, which—because of the offering of their blood—can safely stand into the future as a solid structure.[81]

Indeed, these caciques are still present in Cuquila's collective memory. The older members of the community in particular continue to tell stories about them, and they have even found their way into the pueblo's insignia. The Cuquilans believe these caciques are represented in a fragment of the *Mapa de Santo Tomás Ocotepec*,[82] a sixteenth-century manuscript they refer to as the pueblo's "coat of arms" and whose image has been reproduced on all of the community's official documents as well as on the doors of the small trucks used for

public transportation. The pueblo, or *ñuu*, of Cuquila is represented on this fragment as a hill, with the figure of a tiger appearing in its interior. Above this image
is a royal seat, or throne, on which a ruling couple, caciques who represent the
yuhitayu, are reclining.

In addition, a cacique named Pedro Castañeda turns up as a major figure
in stories recounted by people in the pueblo. He is attributed with having the
ability to move extremely large stones solely through the power of his will. The
stories also have it that he lived on the Tiger's Hill, and some say he was married
to the cacica of Santo Tomás Ocotepec, Doña Feliciana de Roxas, who—it will
be recalled—took up the legal case against Cuquila in the eighteenth century.
Castañeda, the cacique of Cuquila of these stories, was in fact an actual person,
and he probably ruled the pueblo during the second half of the sixteenth century (see Table 4.1). Various documents make clear that the Crown awarded him
several grants of land and in 1583 granted him a license to ride horseback.[83] On
this last point, some of the pueblo's elders relate that Castañeda rode a "horse
with two wings" and was vigilant in watching over the community's boundary
lines: "and on his winged horse he traveled to Yukuchiyo, which is the hill of
Tepalcate[,] and from there he traveled here, to this ruin [the archaeological site]
in Cacica, and so he traveled about everywhere, he went to Santo Domingo las
Nievas because that animal [his horse] is an animal that flies, it is like a two-
beaked eagle, and so it was, this is how it went with Pedro Castañeda."[84]

What makes this story particularly interesting is its reference to one of the
responsibilities traditional Mixtecan caciques carried out: that of maintaining a
steady and vigilant eye over the pueblo's land. This tradition was especially strong
in areas somewhat removed from the colony's cities, as was the case with the
pueblos of the Mixteca Alta. Their relative remoteness and the infrequent contact
between their inhabitants and the Spanish settler population protected and preserved a host of traditional indigenous social and political customs. In this regard,
Don Camilo told me that Pedro Castañeda was "like a commanding officer or a
policeman"[85] who watched over and took care of the land. One can surmise that
in a small domain like the Mixteca Alta, few Indians owned horses. The caciques
of Cuquila, however, were an exception to this probable rule because they had
enjoyed the privilege—conferred by royal edict—of riding horses since at least
the second half of the sixteenth century.[86] This privilege undoubtedly brought a
cacique considerable prestige in the eyes of his people. With the passage of time,
the inhabitants of Cuquila embellished the story by putting wings on the horse,
thereby enabling the cacique to fly on it so he could watch over both them and the
pueblo's land. The high stature accorded the caciques is also apparent in other elements of the stories the pueblo's elders told about Pedro Castañeda; for example,
that he came to Cuquila after the first men appeared in the world, announcing

to people what they needed to do and teaching them the arts of woodworking, sewing, and pottery. The elders are also given to say that the gods that existed in Castañeda's time were the sun, the moon, and the stars.

The memory of the caciques that has come down in this pueblo is undoubtedly bound up with the power they exercised over both the natural world and the people around them. As mentioned earlier, some studies draw attention to the fact that the *Codex Egerton*, a stylistically traditional genealogical codex from the first half of the sixteenth century, originated in Santa María Cuquila. For this reason, the inhabitants of Cuquila preserve a facsimile edition of this manuscript in their community museum, the original of which currently resides in the British Museum.[87] Two years ago a small contingent of Cuquilans showed this facsimile edition to one of the community's oldest native members, a Mixtec woman over eighty years old named Doña Paula Coronel. This event came about as we found ourselves chatting one day in the pueblo's small store, which sits along the side of the road that passes by the pueblo. Doña Paula, who speaks no Spanish, had come to the store to buy something. She saw the codex and stared intently at its striking images. Almost immediately, she started commenting in Mixtecan that her grandparents had told her that the yya of Cuquila were people with special, uncommon powers that enabled them to divert the course of mountain springs. She cited an example, telling us that in the direction of Tlaxiaco there had been a natural spring the caciques had diverted toward Chalcatongo and repeated that the "*yya* were people who possessed power." Doña Paula's comments took me aback. None of us had told her that the images on the codex represented the caciques of Cuquila, nor had she ever before laid eyes on a codex. Nevertheless, the facsimile reproductions immediately caused her to remember what her grandparents had related to her about the pueblo's yya.

Similarly, the location of the archaeological site, the Tiger's Hill, the ancient seat of the yya, is also a place where the people of Cuquila are accustomed to go at particular times—accompanied by their authorities and stewards of the pueblo's church—to ask for rainfall. They make a special point of visiting a spot called the "little house of the cacique," which is a pre-Hispanic tomb (tomb no. 1). They arrive at the tomb with candles and copal and set off fireworks to attract the rain, believing that if and when it rains it is thanks to the hill. Some years ago, they also brought musicians and people who recited prayers to ask for rain. They claim, too, that inside the hill is "something like a basement" and that those who enter it are cured of various illnesses, while those who offer supplications in this chamber can succeed in obtaining wealth.

The archaeological complex is very important to the Cuquilans. A great many rocks and stones are found around the site, quarry rocks that are not original to the pueblo. For centuries, the inhabitants of Cuquila have taken stones

4.13 Santa María Cuquila Community Museum. Date: 2004. Photograph by Martín Martínez.

from the site to use as *metates* for grinding corn. Several years ago, while looking for a stone to use for this purpose, an old campesino from the pueblo came across one of the stelae dating to the Classic Period. This piece, now housed in Cuquila's museum (Figures 4.13, 4.14), has the image of a monkey at its center (see Figure 4.9). Given the stela's size, he decided to leave it where it was and to return for it another day. That night the campesino "dreamed about a large man of great age with a white beard who thanked him for having been there at that moment and who told him: 'I give thanks to you for having visited me because when you visit me I feel alive.' Then the man took fright because of his ignorance of where the stone [the stela] came from, which held the key to its meaning."[88]

The next day the campesino (now deceased), whose name was Don José Hilario León, described his dream to a group of people who lived in an outlying settlement, called San Juan, that belonged to Santa María Cuquila. Upon hearing what José Hilario had to say, these campesinos "recalled that there had been a stela which their ancestors worshipped and in which they had placed their faith, so they had come and taken it to their community and placed it on display on the altar of the local church, they put candles around it, the stone [stela] was a sacred object for them, a saint."[89]

4.14 Interior view of Santa María Cuquila Community Museum. Date: 2004. Photograph by Martín Martínez.

Soon thereafter, word passed around Cuquila that the people of San Juan had the stela—surrounded by candles—in their church. They decided to collect it and bring it back; having done so, they placed it in the Office of Communal Properties, where they, too, surrounded it with candles and came before it to pray. When construction of Cuquila's community museum was completed in 2003, the pueblo decided to move the stela into it, where it would enjoy greater security. Since then, people from both San Juan and Cuquila maintain the practice of visiting the museum "to touch it [the stela], so that it will grant them some wish, because they have faith in it and so they ask it to give them what they want, whether their general well-being or something else, and some have come before it to ask for the power of possessing wisdom."[90] Significantly, Cuquila's campesinos believe the stela is

> like a rechargeable battery, well, the stone [the stela] acts like a rechargeable
> battery since it gets recharged by the energy coming from the rays of the sun
> and by the moon as well, that is . . . in the case of the moon every full moon is
> when this stone gets recharged, according to people who received this knowl-
> edge from their ancestors and still preserve it . . . so they say that when it has
> contact with the sun's rays, the stone is recharged and keeps its energy. People

have said that the stone betokens some primordial events of the community, exactly which ones they can't say, but they are definitely from this early time, according to people, the sufferings of the community are reflected on this stone.[91]

LAND AND PRIMORDIAL TITLES

As previously mentioned, not long before the mid-eighteenth century the pueblo of Cuquila stopped being the seat of a cacicazgo. This development was the principal reason the caciques of neighboring pueblos were able to wrest away some of its important land. Since the colonial period, the region of the Mixteca Alta has been populated by few non-indigenous people. This situation has permitted a broad range of traditional cultural elements to survive to the present day.[92] Furthermore, the widespread absence of Spanish settlers during the colonial period meant the native social and political structure could remain largely intact. Accordingly, the numerous conflicts over land that have flared in this region since colonial times have primarily involved the Indian pueblos themselves, not Indians versus Spaniards. For at least the last half millennium in the Mixteca Alta, when conflict has broken out it has almost always been pueblo fighting against pueblo, especially over boundaries. No pueblo in the region has experienced this phenomenon more strikingly than Cuquila.

Table 4.3 lays out the various conflicts the pueblo of Cuquila has had with neighboring communities and also illustrates that the majority of these conflicts took place in the twentieth century. From the records available, I have been able to identify and quantify twenty conflicts that have arisen between Cuquila and other pueblos, singly or otherwise, in the surrounding area. All of the disputes centered on land-related problems, and fourteen of them took place between 1941 and 1985. The year 1941 marks an important date for Cuquila because on June 26 of that year its authorities formally requested recognition of and legal title to their common lands.[93] Following this request, several neighboring pueblos contested the boundary lines Cuquila claimed as its own, whose origins were derived both from local oral tradition and from documents pertaining to the cacicazgo of Cuquila during the eighteenth century. Five pueblos in particular disputed Cuquila's land: to the north, San Juan Mixtepec; to the south, San Miguel del Progreso and Santo Tomás Ocotepec; and to the east, Tlaxiaco and Santa Cruz Nundaco. The Triquis inhabitants of San Andrés Chicahuastla, on their western side, were the only group with which the Cuquilans had no boundary conflicts during the twentieth century.

Although Cuquila had asserted legal claim in 1941 over an extensive territory that corresponded to the land historically possessed by its former caciques, it lacked sufficient social and political force to defend the claim over that much land. Three years earlier the Oaxacan state congress had in fact stripped Santa María Cuquila of its status as an independent municipality and placed it under the political jurisdiction of the mestizo municipality of Tlaxiaco.[94] Among the official reasons cited for this action was the fact that Cuquila lacked sufficient annual revenue to cover the costs of operating its municipal council.

The reasons, however, may have run deeper than the issue of revenue. Francisco López Barcenas has demonstrated that during the 1930s, regional poli-

Table 4.3. Conflicts over Land with Pueblos in the Region, 1584–1985

1. Year: 1584. Conflict with Chicahuastla[1]
2. Years: 1716–1801. Pascula Feliciana de Rojas, ruler of the pueblos of Santo Tomás Ocotepec and Santa Cruz Nundaco, against the native inhabitants of the pueblo of Santa María Cuquila, over the ownership of land[2]
3. Year: 1889. Conflict with Nundaco and San Esteban Atlalahuaca[3]
4. Year: 1897. Boundary conflict with Mixtepec, Justlahuaca[4]
5. Year: 1913. Conflict with San Juan Mixtepec[5]
6. Year: 1933. Boundary conflict with San Juan Mixtepec[6]
7. Year: 1941. Boundary conflict with San Juan Mixtepec[7]
8. Year: 1941. Settlement between Cuquila and Tlaxiaco, recording these boundaries: the site of Hayundutanasta, from where Tlaxiaco, San Pedro Yososcúa (jurisdiction of San Juan Mixtepec), and Santa María Cuquila intersect, one walks to the northwest where the site of Cavacúa is found, the point of intersection of Santa Cruz Nundaco, Tlaxiaco, and Santa María Cuquila[8]
9. Year: 1943. Boundary conflict with Tlaxiaco[9]
10. Year: 1944. Definitive agreement with the pueblos of Tlaxiaco, Vista Hermosa, Nundaco, Santo Tomás Ocotepec, and San José Chicahuastla[10]
11. Year: 1944. Conflict with San Miguel del Progreso, municipality of Tlaxiaco[11]
12. Year: 1945. Boundary conflict between Cuquila and the pueblo of San Pedro Yososcúa, Justlahuaca, whose municipal seat was San Juan Mixtepec. Mixtepec created this dependent community in 1938, with its boundaries jutting into those of Cuquila. The specific boundaries in conflict were Peña Colorada, Hondura de la Rana Prieta, Agua donde esta la Luna, and Loma del Pilar. Cuquila asserts that even though its titles, which are in the possession of the Department of Agrarian Reform, record the sites of Paredón Colorado, Cerro de San Benito, Sitio de la Estancia, Cueva del Panal or Cueva del Águila de Oro, and Loma de Laguna Seca, only four points—Hayunduntesata, Sitio de la Estancia, Cueva del Panal, and Loma de Laguna Seca—are indicated as constituting the boundary line between the dependent community of Yososcúa (municipality of Mixtepec) and these sites.[12]
13. Year: 1945. Land-related problems between Santa María Cuquila and the surrounding pueblos of San Pedro Yososcúa (municipality of San Juan Mixtepec), San Miguel del Progreso (municipality of San Juan Mixtepec), and San José Chicahuastla (municipality of San Martín Itunyoso)[13]
14. Year: 1960. Conflict over land with San Miguel del Progreso[14]

continued on next page

Table 4.3—*continued*

15. Year: 1968. Conflict over the felling of trees on Cuquila's land by San Pedro Yososcúa[15]
16. Year: 1968. Conflict with San Juan Mixtepec over its incursion onto Cuquila's communal land[16]
17. Year: 1975. Conflict over the fact that members of the pueblo of Santa María Cuquila residing in José Xochixtlán (municipality of San Martín Intunyoso, in the district of Tlaxiaco) have expressed the wish to come under José Xochixtlán's jurisdiction[17]
18. Year: 1980. Conflict with San Juan Mixtepec[18]
19. Years: 1982–1983. Conflict with San Juan Mixtepec[19]
20. Year: 1985. Conflict with Yucumí, San Pedro Yososcúa, San Juan Mixtepec, and Justlahuaca. Members of the community of Yucumí were taking possession of lands—which they contested—that belonged to Santa María Cuquila in a place known in the Mixtec language as *yoso yata yuca*. Problems had also arisen over this same area on April 16, 1984.[20]

Notes:
1. Litigation between Cuquila and Chicahuastla, Santa María Cuquila Community Museum.
2. AGN, Tierras, vol. 876, exp. 1.
3. Archivo General Agrario, Sección Bienes Comunales, exp. 276.1/236.
4. Archivo General del Poder Ejecutivo del Estado de Oaxaca (AGEPEO), legajo 61, exp. 15.
5. Archivo del Registro Agrario de Oaxaca, Santa María Cuquila, exp. 186.
6. Archivo General del Poder Ejecutivo del Estado de Oaxaca (AGEPEO), legajo 51, exp. 2.
7. Archivo General Agrario, Sección Bienes Comunales, exp. 276.1/236.
8. Archivo de Tlaxiaco, boundary settlement between Santa María Cuquila and Tlaxiaco. There is a sketch of the boundary lines in map form.
9. Archivo General del Poder Ejecutivo del Estado de Oaxaca (AGEPEO), legajo 51, exp. 23.
10. Archivo General Agrario, Sección Bienes Comunales, exp. 276.1/236.
11. Ibid.
12. Archivo del Registro Agrario de Oaxaca, Santa María Cuquila, exp. 186.
13. Ibid.
14. Ibid.
15. Ibid.
16. Ibid.
17. Ibid.
18. Ibid.
19. Ibid.
20. Ibid.

ticians managed to convince the Oaxacan state congress to take the same action against several Mixtec and Triquis municipalities in the region, bringing them under the control of mestizo power concentrated in communities such as Putla, Juxtlahuaca, and Tlaxiaco, among others.[95] In line with this occurrence, some older inhabitants of Cuquila recall that during this period a group of Mixtec and Triquis pueblos had joined together to demand recognition of their rights and that this development had "frightened," or at least caused concern to, the state government, which responded by depriving the pueblos of their status as independent municipalities and subordinating them to mestizo communities.[96] Undoubtedly, in the case of Cuquila both factors—the regional political dynamics and the pueblo's poverty—contributed to its "fall in status." While the loss of its standing as a separate municipality may have been accomplished in law, Cuquila's inhabitants nonetheless maintain the custom of meeting every third Sunday in June to name a municipal president. In addition, they still invest their officials with the positions and corresponding staffs of office of the old municipal council as a prelude to having these appointees fulfill their respective obligations beginning January 1 each year. As the Cuquilans see it, these are their legitimate authorities despite the lack of recognition by the Mexican state.[97]

Within this context of antagonistic interests, then, Cuquila sought recognition of, and legal title to, its communal land. Moreover, because several pueblos stubbornly fought the boundary issue, more than fifty years elapsed before the agrarian authorities granted Cuquila title to its ejido land. The legal process that began in 1941 lasted until February 27, 1995, when the pueblo received official title to common lands totaling 3,411 hectares. Three-and-a-half years later, on June 8, 1998, all of the land was finally distributed into the hands of the 484 eligible Cuquila campesinos. During the long struggle, Cuquila became entangled in fourteen disputes with its neighbors. Each dispute required that the pueblo's inhabitants reach a settlement with neighboring communities, hence the protracted nature of its battle to win legal recognition.[98]

The first incident in the national period relating to conflict over Cuquila's boundary lines occurred near the end of the nineteenth century. On May 16, 1889, Cuquila and two neighboring pueblos, San Esteban Atlalahuaca and Santa Cruz Nundaco, reached an amicable settlement in a hearing held before a notary public in the city of Tlaxiaco.[99]

Less than a decade later, on February 22, 1897, two of Cuquila's officials— its municipal president, Clemente Coronel, and its syndic, Germán Coronel— submitted an official request to the national archive, asking that a search be conducted for "the titles, and authentication of the same, relative to its [the pueblo's] land," since the community lacked these documents. The two leaders noted that the pueblo's boundaries were adjacent to Tlaxiaco on the east, on the west to San Miguel Chicahuastla, on the north to San Juan Mistepeque, and on the south to Santo Tomás Ocotepec.[100]

Subsequently, on April 5, 1897, the director of the archive, Justino Rubio, officially recorded that Cuquila's authorities had been shown a group of colonial-era documents, from which they selected several to be copied from the originals. They were sheets 42–44, 114–146, and 211–219, along with the "painting" (pictorial map) on sheet 122—all from record 1, number 876, in the set of volumes entitled Tierras. In addition, they requested copies of sheets 1, 2, 13–17 (both sides of the latter), and the "painting" on sheet 18 from record 40, number 2682, in the Tierras set. The archive officially noted that it had copied 89 "pertinent" sheets.[101]

More than four decades later, on November 8, 1940, the head of the Land Boundaries Office of Mexico's Department of Agrarian Reform sent these same documents—which he had received from Cuquila's authorities—to the department's Legal Affairs Office, requesting that the paleographic section analyze the documents and issue a report, with the intended objective that Cuquila obtain official recognition of its communal land. The documentation comprised 90 sheets as well as 2 maps (the aforementioned "paintings" [AGN nos. 867 and 1614]), assembled into a notebook with a leather cover. The head of the Land Boundaries Office, Arturo F. Sánchez, made it clear that the paleographer assigned to the task need only inform his office about the authenticity of the documents and the boundary lines vouched for in them.[102]

The process, however, had many more twists and turns. On June 28, 1941, Sánchez's office wrote to Cuquila's authorities to inform them that at the behest of the League of Agrarian Communities of the state of Oaxaca, an official complaint over common boundary lines had been lodged against Santa María Cuquila. The office also indicated that Cuquila needed to specify the pueblos with which it had legal disagreements over boundary lines and urgently to remit its titles and "any other documents which might serve to protect its common land" so they could be "subjected" to paleographic analysis. The pueblo was also asked to hold a community-wide meeting to invest its representatives with the authority to respond to the complaint filed by the league. Finally, the Land Boundaries Office required that Cuquila furnish all of the requested information in the form of official minutes and communiqués.[103]

On June 30, 1941, the National Confederation of Campesinos notified the Department of Agrarian Reform that the officials in charge of Cuquila's Common Lands Commission had asked it to intervene to help resolve a boundary dispute in which the pueblo was embroiled with the neighboring community of Mixtepec. The confederation took up the appeal, requesting that the Department of Agrarian Reform send an engineer to address the problem. The department responded with dispatch, since only two weeks later a specialist (with the surname Mondragón) was in the Mixteca Alta, surveying and measuring the land. Although they had prompted this initiative, the Cuquilans did not cooperate with the field project. In all likelihood, the engineer failed to get the inhabitants or the authorities of either pueblo to accept an agreement over boundary lines.[104]

In 1942, however, Cuquila resumed its efforts to settle the boundary dispute with Mixtepec, asking the Department of Agrarian Reform on four separate occasions to send an engineer to the pueblo for this purpose. In addition, Cuquila's authorities had managed to draw another federal agency, the Office of the Attorney General for Indian Affairs, into pushing their case. Despite these overtures, the department explained that since the Cuquilans had stood in the way of demarcating boundaries and thus of settling their conflict with Mixtepec in 1941, it would be another year before it could dispatch an engineer to the pueblo to resume the work. The promised engineer failed to show up in 1943. The picture was not entirely bleak, however. In 1944 the inhabitants of Cuquila succeeded in reaching agreements that settled boundary disputes with the neighboring pueblos of Tlaxiaco, Vista Hermosa, Nundaco, Santo Tomás Ocotepec, and San José Chicahuastla. Similar disputes, however, continued to bedevil its relations with the neighboring communities of San Pedro Yososcúa, attached to the municipality of San Juan Mixtepec, and San Miguel del Progreso, part of the municipality of Tlaxiaco. Channeling their requests through the Oaxacan branch of the National Confederation of Campesinos and the Office of the Attorney General for Indian Affairs, throughout 1943 Cuquila's authorities tried to secure from the Department of Agrarian Reform the return of the pueblo's primordial titles and the appointment of an engineer to survey and demarcate the boundaries of Cuquila's land and effect a settlement of its land-related disputes with other area pueblos.[105]

Cuquila received word, however, that no engineer could be sent until the paleographic section of the department's Legal Affairs Office had finished analyzing its titles. Finally, at the end of 1944 an engineer from the department, Samuel Sánchez, arrived in Cuquila to carry out the work of establishing the boundary line between Cuquila and Mixtepec. Sánchez fixed his starting point at the elevation of Yososcúa—the outlying settlement of Mixtepec—however, and the authorities of the latter community cried foul, insisting that this placement penalized its territorial holdings in favor of Santa María Cuquila's. On February 22, 1945, the engineer sent an urgent telegram to the head of the Department of Agrarian Reform reporting that a violent confrontation had broken out among the Mixtecans of Yososcúa, San Juan Mixtepec, and Cuquila. In protest against the boundary demarcation work carried out thus far, the inhabitants of the first two pueblos had forcibly detained seventeen Cuquilans. Sánchez noted that he had managed to protect them from the Mixtepecans' rage and had brought the disturbing events to the attention of the federal authorities. Not surprisingly, Sánchez, too, was unable to complete the boundary demarcation work. Thus once more, this time on March 14, 1945, Cuquila wrote to the Department of Agrarian Reform to request that it send an engineer to survey its land and delimit the pueblo's official boundaries.[106]

The dispute between Cuquila and Yososcúa arose from the latter's assertion that its boundary with Cuquila should be governed by descriptions recorded in the eighteenth-century primordial titles of San Juan Mixtepec, the pueblo to which it was subordinate. Tying the claim to this source made it all the more critical for Cuquila's inhabitants and leaders that the Department of Agrarian

Reform return their titles with the needed authentications. The department finally did so on March 21, 1945, having taken five years to complete the validation process. The paleographer who authenticated Cuquila's primordial titles was Juan Alarcón.[107]

Although Cuquila was now in possession of its titles, the pueblo's difficulties with Mixtepec had not ended. On April 21, 1945, the Department of Agrarian Reform—once again directing its attention to the dispute—requested that the Department of Defense send a military detachment to accompany Samuel Sánchez, who would return to the field to settle the boundary conflict between Cuquila and Mixtepec. The request went unanswered, and neither Sánchez nor any other engineer was prepared to carry out the boundary demarcation work without a military escort.[108]

Over the next three years, nothing was said or heard on the government level about the conflict between the two communities, nor was there any announcement regarding the progress of Cuquila's petition for official recognition of its communal land. On October 28, 1948, Cuquila's leaders wrote to the agrarian authority, requesting that the process leading to formal recognition of its land be accelerated. At this juncture, they again won the support of the Oaxacan branch of the National Confederation of Campesinos and the Office of the Attorney General for Indian Affairs—both of which wrote to the Department of Agrarian Reform, asking that it send an engineer to complete the work that would satisfy this objective. As we have seen, however, the department's dilatoriness in meeting Cuquila's goal resulted in part from the continuing boundary conflicts that marred the pueblo's relations with neighboring communities. In 1951, within a period of a little more than three weeks, Cuquila sought to remove this obstacle by coming to a formal agreement on boundaries with four pueblos: Santo Tomás Ocotepec (September 30), Santa Cruz Nundaco (October 4), Tlaxiaco (October 12), and San Miguel del Progreso (October 24).[109]

Despite this achievement, nearly a decade went by, and Cuquila had yet to find an engineer to complete the work that would allow the agrarian authorities to grant formal recognition of the pueblo's communal land. Moreover, in 1960 the Cuquilans disclosed that boundary conflicts had again broken out between themselves and the inhabitants of San Miguel del Progreso. The situation grew worse from one year to the next, and in 1968 Cuquila's authorities complained that not only had the state still failed to send an engineer but also that the residents and leaders of San Juan Mixtepec had illegally cut down trees on Cuquila's territory. On March 10, 1967, San Juan Mixtepec had evidently succeeded in obtaining what Cuquila thus far could not—a presidential decree certifying its communal land, along with the accompanying definitive map. Cuquila's failure to secure legal recognition of its land was costing it dearly by creating a situation in which Mixtepec felt free to take over some of its property. Clearly, the Department of Agrarian Reform's glacial pace was damaging to Cuquila's interests, and in 1971 the pueblo's authorities issued a demand—conveyed through the Oaxacan office of the National Confederation of Campesinos—that the department clarify the status of their long-standing petition for legal recognition of the pueblo's communal land. The department resisted the pressure. Cuquila's request continued to go nowhere, and its conflicts with San Juan Mixtepec showed no signs of abating.[110]

On October 3, 1972, the National Indian Institute informed the Department of Agrarian Affairs that it had overseen a technical-administrative project in Cuquila. The institute had taken a census and counted 466 inhabitants of the pueblo who participated in owning common land. It subsequently drew up plans for an area of ejido land covering 5,278 hectares, which bordered the communal lands, respectively, of San Juan Mixtepec to the north, San Miguel del Progreso and Santo Tomás Ocotepec to the south, Tlaxiaco and Santa Cruz Nundaco to the east, and San Andrés Chicahuastla to the west. The institute also noted that as part of the project an engineer, Enrique Gutiérrez, had accurately surveyed and measured Cuquila's territory. The latter, it could now be confirmed, covered a total of 5,317 hectares. Since Cuquila's appeal for recognition of its land dated back to 1940 and since (according to this report) it no longer had boundary conflicts with its neighbors, the institute requested that the Department of Agrarian Affairs furnish the pueblo with the official certification it lacked.[111]

Despite these recommendations, many more years transpired before significant progress was made toward fulfilling Cuquila's request. In 1993 the pueblo's authorities wrote to the governor of the state, Diodoro Carrasco, asking that he intervene on their behalf with the appropriate agrarian offices in Mexico City. They stressed that Cuquila had reached agreements on the boundary line issue with its neighboring pueblos. A new opening had been made. The following year a technical team confirmed, on the basis of its own observations, that Cuquila had indeed settled all of its boundary disputes. On February 27, 1995, Santa María Cuquila at last obtained official recognition of and title to an area of communal land amounting to 3,411 hectares, benefiting 484 campesinos. The disposition on Cuquila's behalf took full legal effect on June 8, 1998.[112] Thus, the pueblo waited more than half a century before the state took final action on its request. Three factors in particular help explain why this happened.

First, Cuquila was requesting in the mid-twentieth century the recognition of land it had controlled in the colonial period, when the pueblo still enjoyed the presence of its caciques. The area this territory covered had been whittled down through conflicts with neighboring pueblos, both in the eighteenth century—when Cuquila stopped being the seat of a cacicazgo—and in the twentieth century, when virtually all of the surrounding pueblos exerted further pressure on its land. The pueblo's landholdings in the twentieth century reflected its capacity for political negotiation, a capacity sharply diminished as a result of the economic impoverishment in which the pueblo found itself.

Second, as long as Cuquila was unable to reach "amicable" agreements with its neighboring pueblos, the national agrarian authorities were stymied in their efforts to complete a survey and demarcation of the pueblo's land, which needed to be done before formal recognition and title could be granted. The problem was convoluted and fed on itself. Because they were operating from a weak political position, Cuquila's leaders lacked the leverage to induce their counterparts from the other pueblos to negotiate and settle their differences. The latter, conversely, understood that the stalemated situation offered them the opportunity to try to expand their territorial limits at Cuquila's expense.

Third, the ponderously bureaucratic and chronically slow ways of the Department of Agrarian Reform virtually guaranteed that because they were caught up in boundary disputes with neighboring pueblos, pueblos that needed formal recognition of their land would experience long delays in obtaining such recognition. As we have seen in the case of Cuquila, which waited for years before an engineer materialized in the Mixteca Alta to survey and demarcate boundaries, this problem was especially acute with respect to small communities a considerable distance from Mexico City.

The symbolic meaning Cuquila's inhabitants attached to their primordial titles was also strongly influenced by their inheritance of a colonial past, as well as by the lengthy delay they endured in obtaining official recognition of their land. In my initial period of fieldwork in Cuquila, from January to May 2004, some of the pueblo's authorities told me that Cuquila's primordial titles had been lost for a long time and that they wanted to recover them. Soon thereafter, while conducting research in the Archivo General Agrario in Mexico City, I located the official document of recognition of Santa María Cuquila's communal lands, and there—along with it—were the pueblo's primordial titles, as described earlier in summary fashion. Two explanations are given in the community as to how its titles were lost. One of them, grounded in a mythical past, holds that

> there was a cacique, his personality was different from the rest because of a
> horn that he had [on his forehead]. He controlled everything in Cuquila,
> above all the records of its boundaries and other documents belonging to the
> village council; he knew all the workings of government[.] [I]n those days
> there were very few who understood how to read and write, but he had a flaw,
> above all in his mistreatment of everyone else, he stole their cattle, raped and
> kidnapped women[.] [T]hen a day came when the people themselves no longer tolerated these mistreatments, they banded together and before they killed

him he said, if you slay me your pueblo will be broken up into many parts and you will forever live having problems with other pueblos, since it is I who possesses the majority of them [the pueblo's documents], but the people, being so enraged, paid no heed and proceeded to kill him.[113]

From that time on, so I was told, Cuquila was plunged into fighting for its land with neighboring pueblos, and its primordial titles could not be found. As the other explanation has it, many years ago Cuquila's municipal president was out in the camp one night, consorting with his mistress from another pueblo. When out on these dalliances, he carried Cuquila's titles with him in a long "tube." The hour was late, and having imbibed a great deal, he fell asleep. The next morning the president forgot about the titles. A peasant from the pueblo of Yucuiti happened by. He saw the tube and took it home with him. After a number of years had passed, Cuquila's authorities made a trip to Yucuiti to repossess their titles. To their great surprise, when they reached the pueblo they discovered that the peasant had moved to Santa María Mixtequilla, on the Isthmus of Tehuantepec. Several more years went by, and a group of Cuquilans traveled to Santa María Mixtequilla to find the missing titles. When they reached the pueblo, they found out that the peasant and his family had moved again. The titles were lost for good, no longer recoverable.

In May 2004 I let Cuquila's authorities know that I had located their titles. Surprised and greatly pleased, they decided without delay to send the person in charge of administering the pueblo's common lands to Mexico City, accompanied by a small delegation of fellow Cuquilans. I went with them to the Archivo General Agrario and showed them the document the government had issued in granting official recognition of their land. Displaying an unexpected technical versatility, they spent the entire morning reviewing the bulky volume. Having found their titles, they requested a set of authenticated copies and designated me as the person to collect them when the process was complete. They called me incessantly over the next two months, wanting to know if the documents were ready to be picked up. Finally, on July 14, 2004, they were, and I notified Cuquila's authorities that I had their titles in my possession. The following day they were in Mexico City to collect them. The officials told me that when they received word that I had the authenticated titles, they rang the church bells to let the pueblo know that at long last its primordial titles were coming home. They were also greatly interested in the seals of authentication the agrarian authorities had stamped on the documents, expressing the opinion that the seals indicated that their titles were now truly legally valid. Needless to say, the completion of the process left them feeling both satisfied and appreciative.

In August 2004 I returned to Cuquila to visit friends. Still happy that I had been able to assist them in locating their titles, I brought the subject up with them. Their reply caused my jaw to drop. The Cuquilans told me that their titles had been lost a long time ago, and they again recounted the stories relating to their loss. On subsequent visits in recent years, when I have asked about the titles, without exception both Cuquila's authorities and its young and older inhabitants have told me that the pueblo's primordial titles were lost many years ago. On some occasions these authorities have even commented that as a historian, I should undertake a search for their primordial titles.

What took place to explain this mysterious turn of events? After pondering the question, I eventually managed to reconstruct what happened. In 2004 the Cuquilans once again fell into conflict over land with the neighboring pueblo of San Miguel del Progreso. San Miguel had been under the jurisdiction of Cuquila until 1938, when—like Santa María Cuquila—it became a dependent pueblo of Tlaxiaco. The people of San Miguel speak Mixtecan, although both modern linguistic analysis and the Triqui pueblo of Chicahuastla's oral tradition suggest that in ancient times its population was probably Triquis.[114]

San Miguel is notorious for being a bellicose community and for having a troubled relationship with surrounding pueblos. Many people in Cuquila have told me that its residents make a practice of going about armed. The problem between Cuquila and San Miguel can be traced back to events involving the land that lies at the point where the boundaries of the two communities converge and to the fact that the residents of San Miguel—claiming some of Cuquila's land as their own—cut a pipe that carried water to Cuquila. As a result of this provocation, in 2004, Cuquila's authorities initiated litigation against San Miguel in the federal agrarian court, the Tribunal Unitario Agrario, located in the town of Huajuapan. Furthermore, once I had "found" their primordial titles, they must have immediately submitted the documents as evidence before the court. Recall, however, that in November 1991 Carlos Salinas de Gortari's government had modified Article 27 of the Mexican constitution to allow the sale or rental of ejido land as a way of stimulating private investment and promoting the injection of foreign capital into the country's agricultural sector. In principle, this revision deprived traditional historical documents such as primordial titles of their validity as evidence in the resolution of conflicts over land, although in practice—as we have seen—the judges presiding over the agrarian courts might or might not take them into account in deciding the outcome of cases, depending upon their underlying political sympathies with respect to the Indian pueblos.[115]

I suspect that in Cuquila's case, the colonial documents that formed its primordial titles were of little value legally, since they made no reference to the point of land at which the boundaries of San Miguel and Cuquila met. Their focus instead was on Cuquila's boundaries with the pueblo of Santo Tomás Ocotepec.

In any event, the titles Cuquila had had authenticated in 2004 did not have the legal force its authorities had expected, and the pueblo's dispute with San Miguel remains unresolved to this day.

Initially, it may seem incredible that a community like Cuquila, which had presented its primordial titles to the Department of Agrarian Reform in the 1940s, would not know where they were and, moreover, would fabricate colorful stories about how they had been lost. In my judgment, this situation evolved out of Cuquila's conflicts with Santo Tomás Ocotepec in the colonial period, when for a number of years Cuquila no longer maintained possession of its titles and other legal documents. As we saw earlier, they had been carried off by the child cacica, Doña Theresa. A second contributing factor was the overly long wait—fifty years—Cuquila endured before the agrarian authorities granted the pueblo legal title to its land. This delay, caused in part by the continuing disputes with neighboring pueblos, created a belief among Cuquila's authorities that the pueblo's titles were of no use. In their eyes, if the titles were not useful to them in negotiating with the state, if they failed on a legal level to secure Cuquila's protection of its colonial territory, then it must mean they were not the pueblo's true, authentic titles. Whenever the titles are presented and fail to yield the expected results, they are declared lost and a drawn-out search is undertaken for them, a search intertwined with rumor and legend: that the horned cacique made them disappear, that another of the pueblo's caciques lost them, that they will be found in Tuxtla Gutiérrez (Chiapas), and so on.

The indigenous communities of Mesoamerica, like peasant societies everywhere, have long exhibited a resolute pragmatism. Mesoamerican mythical narratives typically incorporate "some elements of a tradition which includes events that really happened."[116] With respect to Cuquila's primordial titles, the notion that they were held by a cacique with a strange personality points up a situation common to the Mixteca Alta, whereby rulers were the ones who safeguarded the pueblo's important historical documents. Similarly, the fact that this cacique's death at the hands of the pueblo's inhabitants would bring with it the loss of their titles serves as a metaphor for their guilt over having committed a crime. The pueblo transgressed in assassinating the cacique and is punished by losing its titles. The danger the continuing absence of its caciques poses to a pueblo is also highlighted in Cuquila's case by the double loss it suffered, of both portions of its communal land and its titles. The second story told by Cuquilans, of how the pueblo's titles were lost as a result of the carelessness of their municipal president, who got drunk and fell asleep, likewise calls up the idea of transgression followed by penance. Here the pueblo loses its primordial titles as punishment for its authority's waywardness in getting drunk and seeking out his mistress. Yet another element that came into play and handicapped the authorities of smaller, often impoverished Indian communities was their illiteracy. Not knowing how to read or write placed them at a serious disadvantage.

Since Cuquila's inhabitants have been unable to make effective legal use of their primordial titles, they have resumed believing that their true titles are still lost. In their minds, the titles will remain lost until such time as their appearance translates into the successful protection of their land. This interpretation of events has its own logic. Why should documents that fail to aid in the protection and recovery of land be viewed as legitimate, despite assurances that they indeed constitute the sought-after primordial titles?

The case of Cuquila and its titles is illuminating. For Indian pueblos, as long as ancient and modern documents—such as primordial titles—serve to protect the integrity of their land, they are honored and safeguarded. When they fail to accomplish this purpose, they are spurned, discarded, relegated to some place where they are forgotten. In these cases, whether they date to the pre-Hispanic or the colonial period and whether they are traditional codices or lienzos simply does not matter. On the social, political, and symbolic levels the primordial titles are certainly important, but only insofar as they actually benefit a pueblo in preserving its territory. This attitude helps clarify and explain why a number of codices and lienzos have been and continue to be removed from pueblos. They may be important for various reasons, but to the pueblos their greatest worth is measured by their effectiveness in enabling them to protect their communal land and life in the face of a conflict. Thus, if no conflict exists or if they prove not to be useful in dealing with a conflict, these documents become nothing more than artifacts or "objects," the memory of which can fade rapidly for the indigenous population.

This outcome does not occur because the Indians are ignorant or unmindful of their cultural patrimony. On the contrary, as mentioned in Chapter 2, the issue of their cultural survival as a collectivity is of paramount importance to Indian communities. They place an inordinate value on passing down their cultural inheritance from one generation to the next, an inheritance that rests not just on pictorial and written manuscripts but on a variety of resources, including a vibrant oral tradition.

THE PAST IN THE PRESENT IN SANTA MARÍA CUQUILA

As we have seen, Cuquila was the seat of a political domain in both the pre-Hispanic and Spanish colonial eras. Little is directly known, however, about its history in the nineteenth century, and the paucity of the archival record makes attempts to fill in the picture hazardous at best. Nonetheless, we can infer that in line with other pueblos in the Mixteca Alta, Cuquila managed to counteract the effect of the laws of disentailment and retain portions of its communal land thanks largely to the poor quality of its soil. The Cuquilans stress that for the most part their land is cultivable only with the use of chemical fertilizers. These fertilizers did not appear in the pueblo until the 1960s, when—until shortly before the advent of the Salinas de Gortari government (1988–1994)—the Mexican state provided direct financial aid to help campesinos purchase fertilizers. The subsidies were later withdrawn, so the villagers now bear the entire burden. Those who suffer most are the pueblo's oldest members who cannot afford to buy fertilizer, which costs between 150 and 200 pesos to cover a harvest, and who no longer have extended family to help them.

In the face of this situation, some Cuquilan families supplement their income by making clay pots. Indeed, until around 1970, virtually the entire pueblo earned a living this way. The appearance of plastic containers in the region obviated the need for clay, however, and so most of Cuquila's population abandoned the cottage industry of pottery. Prior to this development, Cuquila had been the sole pottery-making pueblo in the region, selling its wares in markets throughout the Mixteca Alta and as far away as the Oaxacan coast. Before 1957, the year construction of the highway through the region was completed, it was a familiar sight to see men, women, and children methodically trudging for days—with loads of clay pots slung over their backs—to pueblos across the Mixteca Alta and along the coast. In some markets, such as that of Pinotepa Nacional, Cuquilans maintained the practice of bartering their pots for dry fish and salt.

The opening of the highway improved communications and made it possible for people to get around by bus, but it also introduced new products into the region, one of which—plastic containers—caused the sale of clay to spiral downward. Cuquila's inhabitants, like many campesinos in the region, found temporary work in construction of the highway, earning a small fixed income while the project lasted. During the twentieth century, however, the picture of the pueblo was that of a community afflicted by deep and chronic poverty. Its land was not fertile, forcing almost everyone to live off the sale of clay pots. Under these constrained economic circumstances, some of Cuquila's male population began to immigrate to Mexico City in the 1980s and to the United States in the next decade. Following a well-established pattern, those who found work in the United States remitted money to their relatives. The remittances were frequently used to help the family put up a new house; thus, among Cuquila's traditional houses made of wood and adobe, one now sees houses of two or more stories, made of concrete and built in the contemporary urban style. Although most of these new structures amount to little more than shells, the pueblo's vehicular traffic now includes automobiles and small trucks purchased in the United States.

The majority of people with whom I have conversed in Cuquila have told me that despite losing its status as an independent municipality in 1938, the pueblo has continued to maintain the same slate of officials who served the former municipality. As custom dictates, these officials are elected in the third week of June. The people first march in procession carrying the Virgin of Cuquila, which is otherwise kept in the church. Everyone then comes together to name the new municipal president and the fourteen officials who serve on the municipal council. None of these positions carries a salary, and each is filled by a new person every year. As noted earlier, the Mexican state recognizes Cuquila only as a dependent community of Tlaxiaco, so the only officially recognized authorities are its communal land commissioners. As a result, both the municipal president and members of the council must fall back on personal savings to serve the pueblo for a year, during which time they have no salary, as mentioned, and also give up most of the time needed to plant corn or to work in some other capacity to earn an income. Serving the community thus imposes a heavy economic burden on them. Many of the campesinos have to sell cattle (bulls in particular) or a piece of land to sustain themselves and their families during this year of service. Members of the council are obligated to complete the full term of office. If a person who is elected is living outside the pueblo, in Mexico City, say, or as a U.S. immigrant, he is contacted and is expected to return to Cuquila to fulfill the charge of serving its people. The social and cultural cohesion that binds Cuquilans together is such that few members of the community—even those living thousands of miles away—opt out of their obligation to serve. While this form of service is unrecognized by the state, its association with the cult of the Virgin of Cuquila, who presides over the annual election, endows it with a supernatural sanction.[117]

Consider, for example, the case of Genaro Sánchez Rojas. This Mixtec native of Cuquila moved to Mexico City with his parents at age seven. He grew up in the capital, eventually finding work in the construction industry as a bricklayer. Early in his career he immigrated to the United States, where he continued to work laying bricks. In 2006 he was called back to the pueblo after being elected to serve in its municipal government. Despite having left Cuquila as a young child, he responded to the call immediately. Genaro believes that although he did not reach maturity in Cuquila, he is above all of Mixtecan blood and has a duty to his pueblo. He therefore entertained no doubts about returning to take up his position. At present, he is serving as an assistant in the community museum and is completing the construction of a house for himself and his family. He evinces pride in being from Cuquila and in having the opportunity to help operate the museum.

Prior to the construction of the highway, there was no proper school in Cuquila, although a teacher in the community did provide lessons up to the fourth-grade level. It is scarcely surprising, then, that until the 1970s the pueblo's leaders barely knew how to read or write. Their meetings took place in a small adobe house, and when they traveled to Tlaxiaco to ask for government assistance they went on foot, journeying a day and a half to reach the city. In Tlaxiaco they slept under the portico that went around the main plaza and, as a rule, were treated badly by the city's mestizo authorities because of their fragmentary grasp of Spanish.

In those years a large number of Cuquila's municipal leaders consumed a substantial quantity of regionally produced *aguardiente* and were accustomed to taking shots of the drink during council meetings. This situation was emblematic of, and contributed to, the persistent social and economic backwardness of the pueblo. Even more striking was the fact that the few mestizo schoolteachers the government sent sporadically to instruct the pueblo's children were generally the same people who sold the aguardiente to the local population. These entrepreneurs even sent Cuquila's authorities to Tlaxiaco to buy the alcohol. The majority of the schoolteachers who sold aguardiente were natives of Tlaxiaco; while they had the lion's share of the business, others from Tlaxiaco also cashed in on the opportunity to sell the drink to the Cuquilans. According to what I have been told, alcoholism was fairly widespread in the pueblo, and women as well as men had a drinking habit. Today, in sharp contrast, only a handful of the pueblo's oldest members consume alcohol, and those under age sixty avoid drinking even beer.

The 1970s gave rise to a new generation of teachers in Cuquila, teachers who were native to the pueblo. These educators, including Tobías Diego López Ortiz, began to hold conversations with children, parents, and the pueblo's leaders to convince them that not only was alcohol injurious to one's health but that if, according to Tobías Diego López Ortiz, "you drank and got drunk the mestizos would deceive you more easily." Over time, these teachers succeeded in eradicating Cuquila's alcohol problem, to the point that when I began fieldwork in the pueblo in 2004, I thought its inhabitants must be Protestant. They barely drink anything during festival celebrations and even less on regular workdays. The pueblo's authorities are particularly observant of this standard. I gradually came to understand that through their diligence, Cuquila's indigenous schoolteachers had managed to persuade people that the consumption of alcohol was inextricably linked to their inability to improve conditions in the community.

During the 1970s, a second condition impressed itself on the residents of Santa María Cuquila. By then, the area around the pueblo had become completely deforested. The production of clay utensils, which reached back centuries, was associated with the use of wood-burning ovens. Hundreds of years of this artisanal production had left the countryside around Cuquila bereft of its forests.

The pueblo's Indian schoolteachers, with López Ortiz assuming a lead role, managed to convince their fellow Cuquilans of the critical importance of reforestation. With assistance provided by the State Forestry Department, they planted thousands of saplings that eventually succeeded in arresting further serious erosion of the soil. Moreover, they have kept up the reforestation project. Every year, in coordination with the state agencies and through a community effort to which the men of the pueblo freely contribute for the benefit of all (the so-called *tequio*, or traditional communal labor, of communities), they plant new pine and other varieties of trees.

These changes in Cuquila's social and cultural landscape vividly demonstrate how valuable it has been for the pueblo to have generated its own cadre of educated, enlightened citizens—in this case, schoolteachers.[118] With respect to education, the community fought for more than thirty years to have its own schools. In the 1980s it managed by sheer effort to wrest an agreement from the Oaxacan Department of Public Education that it would provide the permits, teachers, and material to allow a secondary-level school to be built and established in Cuquila. More recently, community authorities succeeded in obtaining support for the establishment of a pre-university-level school of technical studies. Moreover, the way they secured this support illustrates their capacity for negotiating with the state at an opportune moment.

In 2007, Tlaxiaco's municipal government was controlled by the Partido de la Revolución Democrática, while Oaxaca's state government was under the control of the Partido Revolucionario Institucional. Traditionally, the relationship between the two political parties has been adversarial. That year the governor of the state made an official visit to the Tlaxiaco region. Cleverly taking advantage of the conflict between the two parties, Cuquila's leaders managed to insinuate themselves with the governor's delegation, in place of their counterparts in Tlaxiaco. They lost no time explaining to the governor that the community needed a roof for its auditorium as well as a technical school. The governor approved the proposals and—going over the heads of the municipal authorities in Tlaxiaco—found the money in the state's budget to implement both projects, with the manpower supplied by Cuquila's residents. None of Mexico's political parties has a presence in Santa María Cuquila; its authorities simply seized the opportunity to exploit the rivalries that exist between parties on the state and national levels to realize practical benefits for the pueblo.

These and other benefits Cuquila has obtained since the early 1980s, especially in the area of education, are directly attributable to the community's high level of organization and its internal unity. In this connection, the creation of a community museum stands out as one of pueblo's most compelling initiatives, one that has at its core the attempt to recover local history.

Community museums began to appear in some of Oaxaca's Indian pueblos in 1986. The movement to establish museums in the pueblos evolved out of a proposal by the wife-husband anthropologist team Teresa Morales Lersch and Cuauhtémoc Camarena Ocampo, to offer an alternative to the official presentation of indigenous culture and history. Aware of the growing interest of several Oaxacan pueblos to have their own museums, the two researchers took concrete steps to flesh out the idea. After holding conversations with various community authorities, they began to design and organize workshops in which people could acquire the basic skills needed to carry out museum and historical society work.

Communities interested in having a museum make the decision to do so on a popular basis, through their municipal assembly. If community members decide to go forward, they form a committee whose membership is entirely local to steer and take charge of the museum's operations. The initiative is locally inspired and driven, realized through the interest and organization of people in the pueblo, as opposed to following plans devised by outside bureaucrats or academic specialists. A central function of these community museums is to house the pueblos' cultural patrimony. Some have collected and preserved a wide range of artifacts and objects, including painted manuscripts from the colonial period, ancient documents, archaeological pieces, textiles, ceramics, and more. All of the museums incorporate an interpretive function, offering insight into local legends and history as compiled and recorded by the townsfolk. Each pueblo, too, uses collective labor to remodel an old building or construct a new one to house its museum. Thus, at their core the projects are community-based efforts. Morales Lersch and Camarena Ocampo do no more than point out broad goals and strategies; the rest is done by the pueblo. As of 2005, Santa María Cuquila's community museum was one of seventeen operating in the state of Oaxaca.[119]

In Cuquila's case, the chain of events leading up to the founding of its museum started with the discovery of a pre-Hispanic stela. This carved object, now part of the museum's holdings, was found—as noted earlier—in one of the pueblo's small peripheral communities, whose inhabitants by custom kept it surrounded with candles. Subsequently, some Cuquila residents brought it back to the pueblo, where they placed it behind the municipal government building. López Ortiz recalls that in 1987, while serving as Cuquila's municipal president, he noticed the stela and was moved to ask about its origins and about the significance of the symbols carved on it. Apparently, nothing came of that initial expression of interest, but in 1992, the director of Cuquila's elementary school, López Ortiz, refocused his attention on the stela, commenting to the municipal president, Camilo Coronel:

> [W]e have to get that stone [the stela] moved; it has to have some special significance; it's important to take care of it however you look at it, it doesn't

have to be moved because it's a pretty object—we lifted it and moved it to different places, then we brought it back up here. [T]here was a small house here attached to the government building, we kept the object here but then we got the idea of washing it, washing the stone with a broom, and none of us knew what importance it really had, but we more or less cleaned it up, then stood it up here in its place.[120]

In early 1993, his curiosity aroused to find out more about the stela's origins, López Ortiz persuaded Coronel to go with him to the Oaxacan offices of the National Institute of Anthropology and History to ask how to care for the object properly. The two men were connected with the anthropological team of Camarena Ocampo and Morales Lersch, who, a few months later, made their first trip to Cuquila. After examining the stela, they informed López Ortiz and Coronel that the specimen was ancient—more than 2,000 years old—and that if the pueblo were so disposed, it could establish its own museum in which to house, preserve, and exhibit the stela. In December 1993, Cuquila's citizens held an assembly and approved the idea of creating a community museum. They formed a museum committee and selected its members, who included López Ortiz. Following these actions, they quickly received input and advice from Camarena Ocampo on developing plans for the museum.

Every weekend, López Ortiz and the other members of the museum committee visited the homes of campesino families in Cuquila in search of ancient artifacts and old manuscripts and to build up their store of local legends and history. To their considerable surprise, they discovered that some of these homes harbored other carved stelae, which they immediately moved to the pueblo's school for safekeeping, to await future display in the museum:

On Saturday[s] and Sunday[s] we went from house to house, asking where other fine little specimens of stelae might be found, and lots of people came up to us; that's how we managed to find the objects that are here. [S]ome people had already wrecked them, some wanted to use them for their stone horse trough, others as a stopper for the pot in which they stored their beans; and so that's how they had them but [we said] no, you are to give me this object; I'll take it with me. [W]hy do you want it, [they asked me]? [D]on't ask, you'll see, it's going to be in a pretty little place, you'll see it there.[121]

The plan to establish a museum in Cuquila was accompanied by a burst of energy and activity. Based on the workshops Camarena Ocampo had organized, some of the pueblo's inhabitants were taking photographs of Cuquila's artisans: the old women who still wove beautiful textiles (blouses, or *huipiles,* and jackets made of lamb's wool) and the older members who still manufactured clay bricks. In addition, some residents donated old photographs they had saved as well as old manuscripts, among which were two short colonial-period documents dating to the end of the sixteenth century.[122]

With a modest amount of funding from nongovernmental sources, Cuquila's authorities bought the building materials to construct the museum—a simple structure of brick and concrete. It took the pueblo many years to complete the project, since all the work was volunteered by the community. The museum opened its doors in 2003. The objects on display are arranged according to four broad themes: daily life, traditional handicrafts, pre-Hispanic history, and history of the colonial period. In the middle of the museum is a small exhibit case containing bones and pre-Hispanic pottery. Someone in the community has gone to considerable effort to craft a border around it, made of small slabs of stone. The enthusiasm the museum has engendered led another person to have a copy made in wood of the pueblo's "shield" or "seal," which as mentioned earlier contains the same images as those depicted on the *Lienzo of Ocotepec*—a pre-Hispanic temple with the caciques seated above it and the figure of a jaguar in its interior (Figure 4.14).

The museum has been instrumental in elevating the Cuquilans' knowledge about the history of their pueblo and in strengthening their identification with a rich indigenous past. The general perception is that the pueblo's antiquity and onetime status as a minor kingdom make its political subordination to Tlaxiaco misplaced and unjust. The community, as Cuquila's inhabitants see it, should be raised—or, properly speaking, restored—to the category of a separate municipality. Everything in its history, they assert, underscores this fact. When the pueblo voices its concerns on this matter to officials in the state government, it tries to make the case that the authorities in Tlaxiaco are withholding its share of federal resources. At the heart of the pueblo's complaint, however, is its belief that it deserves to be a full-blown municipality. The person currently in charge of Cuquila's community museum is Emiliano Melchor Ayala, who enthusiastically notes that the museum has several projects under way that are centered on promoting both the Mixtec language and the production of local handicrafts, such as clay pottery and woven jackets.

Although Cuquila's hope of regaining its previous status as a freestanding municipality is definitely quixotic, the feeling is nonetheless widespread among its people that the Mexican state should rightly take such action, given the pueblo's deep historical roots. Their lack of success in lobbying this issue with members of the Oaxacan state legislature has not caused them to stop trying. By giving the Cuquilans the opportunity to create a new civic space in which the principal theme is their own past, the museum has reinforced a sense of community pride.

In this chapter I have tried to show how the contemporary Indian pueblo attempts to defend its communal land and territory by employing historical documents, such as the primordial titles, and by resorting as well to more indirect devices, such as the representation of its history in the exhibits of a small community museum. Furthermore, I believe this approach demonstrates the pueblo's effective capacity for negotiation, since it relies on using materials and resources that have no prima facie relevance for the Mexican state. For the pueblo, however, local history is of the highest importance, since it demonstrates as nothing else can the pueblo's antiquity as a community and its concomitant right to possess its communal lands. The logic behind these sometimes subtle connections is not always apparent to the state, even less so to a state whose leaders are increasingly insensitive to the claims lodged by Indian pueblos. All the same, many pueblos are keenly aware of the importance of their history and attempt to bring its documentary evidence to the government's attention. Moreover, neither the disinterest nor the puzzlement this type of evidence and argument evokes among state bureaucrats has led the pueblos to stop presenting it. The sense of connection to a rich historical past undoubtedly reinforces community identity and inspires the defense of communally worked land.

Of course, the indigenous population is not always successful in recovering local community history; many pueblos undoubtedly lack a clear awareness of their historical past. Yet just as many pueblos have an interest in reconstituting and knowing their history as a way of both strengthening their sense of identity and meeting the challenge of maintaining themselves as indigenous communities in a rapidly changing world. Finally, this strategy of recovering and deepening historical consciousness evidences great cultural vitality on the part of many pueblos. They realize that knowing their past helps equip them to build a better present and future for themselves and their children.

NOTES

1. Monique Nuijten, "Between Fear and Fantasy: Governmentality and the Working of Power in Mexico," *Critique of Anthropology* 24, 2 (2004): 209–230.

2. *Testimonio sobre la lucha agraria de Ixcamilpa. Desde el tiempo de las haciendas hasta nuestros días* (Puebla: Unión Regional de Ejidos y Comunidades del Sur del Estado de Puebla, 1982), 11, 15, 21, 26–27, 31–32. I thank Laura Espejel for giving me a copy of this book.

3. Ibid.

4. Guillermo de la Peña, *Herederos de promesas agricultura, política y ritual en los altos de Morelos* (México: Centro de Investigaciones Superiores del Instituto Nacional de Antropología e Historia, 1980), 329.

5. "[N]osotros HOY DECIMOS ¡BASTA!, somos los herederos de los verdaderos forjadores de nuestra nacionalidad, los desposeídos somos millones y llamamos a todos nuestros hermanos a que se sumen a este llamado como el único camino para no morir

de hambre ante la ambición insaciable de una dictadura de más de 70 años encabezada por una camarilla de traidores que representan a los grupos más conservadores y vendepatrias." "Declaración de la Selva Lacandona, 2 de enero, hoy decimos ¡Basta!," in *EZLN Documentos y comunicados 1° de enero/8 de agosto de 1994*, prologue by Antonio García de León Crónicas, Elena Poniatowska, and Carlos Monsiváis (México: Ediciones Era, Colección Problemas de México, 1996), vol. 1, third impression, 33.

6. Lynn Stephen, *Zapata Lives! Histories and Cultural Politics in Southern Mexico* (Berkeley: University of California Press, 2002).

7. Interview with René Marneau Villavicencio, Puebla, August 29, 2008.

8. Ibid.

9. Ibid.

10. Interview with René Marneau Villavicencio, Puebla, December 3, 2006.

11. Verdict pronounced in agrarian case 449/2000 concerning recognition of the communal properties claimed by the community of Santiago Niltepec and outlying settlements, Municipality of Santiago Niltepec, Oaxaca, May 23, 2006. I am indebted to Sebastián van Doesburg for providing me with a copy of this document.

12. Three pictorial scenes from the manuscript have been reproduced and published, at a reduced scale, in Gerardo Camacho de la Rosa, *Raíz y razón de Totolapan: El drama de la Guerra Zapatista* (México: Centro de Estudios Antropológicos Científicos, Artísticos, Tradicionales y Lingüísticos "Ce-Acatl," A.C., Gobierno del Distrito Federal, 2007). The scenes depict armed jaguar warriors, friars evangelizing Indians, and a man at the side of a house, along with cactuses, trees, and other vegetation. I am indebted to Laura Espejel for giving me a copy of this book.

13. Ibid., 7; http://www.mcontreras.df.gob.mx/historia/rep_agrario.html, accessed May 2008.

14. Camacho de la Rosa, *Raíz y razón de Totolapan*, 17–43.

15. Http://www.mcontreras.df.gob.mx/historia/rep_agrario.html, accessed May 2008.

16. Interview with Roque Nava, Ángela Nava, José Ruiz, and Miguel Ruiz, San Nicolás Totolapan, spring 2003, who as representatives of San Nicolás Totolapan currently have the pueblo's primordial titles under their care; Camacho de la Rosa, *Raíz y razón de Totolapan*, 7–8.

17. Interview cited in note 16.

18. "[E]ntonces imagínese usted que nuestros antepasados el que tuvo el códice que fue representante no tenían camas tenían petate y lo puso debajo se su petate llegaron y lo acribillaron los hacendados y que le [querían] quitar el códice porque sabían ellos que sí es original y él no les dijo donde estaba y lo acuchillaron y pasó la sangre al libro esta manchado el libro de su sangre." Interview with Ángela Nava, San Nicolás Totolapan, spring 2003, whose family, as the representative of San Nicolás Totolapan, is in charge of preserving the pueblo's primordial titles. Nava pointed out that her father has safeguarded the codex since approximately 1963.

19. "[Q]ue fuéramos cuando vienen los reyes [de España] vamos a ver si nos podemos introducirnos y decirles miren aquí traemos los documentos que no nos reconocen así rápido y queremos una audiencia o queremos que ustedes nos pague el pasaporte para irnos allá para que estudien nuestros documentos." Ibid.

20. Instituto Nacional de Geografía y Estadística, 2005 census.

21. Misael Habana, "Mueren cuatro niños en Guerrero por ingerir agua contaminada," *La Jornada* (Mexico City), Saturday, April 6, 2002.

22. This ceremony of appealing for rain has been little documented, but a very good description of the ritual is found in María Teresa Sepúlveda y Herrera, "Petición de lluvias en Ostotempa," *Boletín del Instituto Nacional de Antropología e Historia,* Second Epoch, no. 4 (1973): 9–20.

23. The information in this part of the chapter, which is derived from my fieldwork, was given to me principally by Modesto Vázquez Salgado. I am indebted to him for all the time he spent with me in 2003 and 2004.

24. Zulaque: a bituminous paste made with fiber, lime, oil, and slag, or bits of ground-up glass, used for plugging the joints of tubes that carried water and for other hydraulic works.

25. "Mataban niños de dos y tres años y de la sangre dellos mezclada con cal a manera de zulaque, tapiaban las fuentes que manaban." *Relaciones geográficas del siglo XVI: Tlaxcala*, vol. 1, ed. René Acuña (Mexico City: Instituto de Investigaciones Antropológicas and UNAM, 1984), 250.

26. Carlo Ginzburg, *Ecstasies: Deciphering the Witches' Sabbath* (Chicago: University of Chicago Press, 2004).

27. "Son algunos indios de tomar forma de mujeres y en ella buscan en la sombra de todos estados, y hablando con ellos [con los hombres pretextándolos?] de amores les obliga a tener exceso carnal con ellos, pensando ser mujeres, y en este acto cogen el semen en la mano y le dan con él en el rostro, y se vuelven a la forma de varones y estos a quien [illegible] mueren dentro de tres a cuatro días sin remedio alguno, y han muerto con esta diabólica invención siete u ocho españoles, mestizos y mulatos, y otros que no han tenido el tal exceso lo testifican y han quedado vivos." AGN, Ramo de Inquisición, 513, exp. 5.

28. Ibid.

29. "[Q]ue habla la tierra los animales y se vuelven los hombres animales y pájaros de todas suertes que llaman naguales, y en que estas formas dicen que se han hecho muchos males a muchas personas de todos estados y en todos ellos, dicen se valen de estas formas mujeres y hombres; y aunque los ministros han procurado remediarlo." Ibid.

30. The PRI is the party that governed Mexico for more than seventy years. For almost thirty years it has hewed to a conservative line, advocating neoliberal policies.

31. Modesto without doubt is a Nahua leader who has served as a cultural intermediary and political broker for his community. For more examples see Yanna Yannakakis, *The Art of Being In-Between: Native Intermediaries, Indian Identity, and Local Rule in Colonial Oaxaca* (Durham, N.C.: Duke University Press, 2008).

32. "[C]on cuarenta y nueve pesos que yo tenía y cuando ya se iban pues me les pegué porque como era chamaco [niño] pensaron en dejarme pero cuando llegue con ellos con mi ropa y mi mocha [machete] les dije que me llevaran pues éramos compañeros." Interview with Modesto Vázquez Salgado, Atliaca, Guerrero, fall 2003.

33. "[I]ncluso mis compañeros de niñez ya pasaron de autoridades fueron presidentes y me decían ¡órale Modesto! Vamos trabajando y yo les digo 'estamos trabajando' pero

tu deberías, pues si debería pero tenemos otros asuntos, el caso es que ahora se pelean—antes no era así, antes trabajábamos todos juntos, todos unidos—ahora no saben conciliar." Ibid.

34. "[L]o que vamos a hacer ahora es repartirnos, los partidos están así y van a contender muy feamente para poner en celos a un partido tenemos que repartirnos, tu representas al Partido de Acción Nacional [PAN un partido conservador] tu de oposición y tu representas otro partido y nos vamos a presentar cuando lleguen esos candidatos, pero no era cierto nada más era simulación, era para que los representantes del gobierno de aquél entonces pudieran ver a una comunidad que necesita apoyo." Ibid.

35. "[Y] eso sucedía en muchos casos, se veía pues como despecho [nos decían que éramos] gente ignorante, gente india, 'pata rajada' por eso mucha gente nuestra lengua no la quiere porque se burlan mucho, aquí nos bombardeaban feo pero hemos estado difundiendo que eso ya paso a la historia, ahora es diferente." Interview with Modesto Vázquez Salgado, Tixtla, Guerrero, spring 2004.

36. AGI, Justicia 127: "Don Martín Indian governor of the pueblo of Tixtlan versus Diego Jaramillo, resident of Mexico, over the right to a ranch."

37. Interview with Modesto Vázquez Salgado, Atliaca, Guerrero, summer 2004.

38. Interview with Modesto Vázquez Salgado, Atliaca, Guerrero, fall 2003.

39. AGN, Archivo de Buscas y Traslado de Tierras 45, exp. 10, 1915.

40. Ibid., 65, exp. 101, 1935.

41. Archivo General Agrario, exp. 9777, 1940.

42. "[E]ntonces ahí hacía mis trabajos en la noche y con ánimo que tenía para saber como defenderme el día de la cita, no importaba el cansancio y necesitaba buscar elementos para hacer la defensa para poder responder porque es un temor el tener una orden de aprensión." Interview with Modesto Vázquez Salgado, Atliaca, Guerrero, summer 2004.

43. "Porque a veces se les acumulaba [a los campesinos] daños [al ganadero] de 500 mil o inclusive millones pues todos espantados ¿dónde voy a pagar? Voy a ir a la cárcel pero eso no va suceder eso van a querer hacer inclusive como son calumnias, él [ganadero] tiene que buscar la forma de atemorizar la gente pero no se preocupen ahí vamos a ir vamos a manifestaciones, inclusive ante el juez, ante el gobierno que eso no es cierto porque tenemos los elementos, aquí están los papeles, resolución, el plano definitivo tenemos las armas, no se preocupen estamos en nuestro derecho, entonces ellos con confianza salen y no los dejábamos." Ibid.

44. Ibid.

45. The reference to "500 years" in the organization's name alludes to the 1992 quincentenary of Columbus's landfall in the Bahamas.

46. Interview with Modesto Vázquez Salgado, Atliaca, Guerrero, spring 2005.

47. Colloquialism meaning to incur ill will or come out on the short end.

48. "Yo no he sido autoridad, pero siempre he estado ahí metido de lejitos de asesor porque a veces hay gente 'malilla' con malas intenciones y tenemos que estar atentos y si no estamos atentos pues te 'quemas' y si estas de 'lejitos' te cuidas." Interview with Modesto Vázquez Salgado, Tixtla, Guerrero, spring 2005.

49. "[A]hora que se ganaron las tierras no se difundió eso a nivel político pero, automáticamente se vio, nunca había perdido el PRI aquí en Atliaca, ahora perdió por

166 votos, en Atliaca la mayoría votó por el PRD, nunca en la historia había sucedido esto." Ibid.

50. According to the 2000 census, conducted by the Instituto Nacional de Geografía y Estadística, 302 are men and 380 are women.

51. Instituto Nacional de Geografía y Estadística, 2000 census.

52. Interviews with Emiliano Melchor and Sixto Melchor, Santa María Cuquila, January and May 2004.

53. Interview with authorities, Santa María Cuquila, August 2005.

54. Interviews with authorities, Santa María Cuquila, August 2004 and August 2005.

55. Iván Rivera, "La iconografía de las Piedras grabadas de Cuquila y la distribución de la escritura ñuiñe en la Mixteca Alta," in Sebastián van Doesburg, ed., *Pictografía y escritura alfabetica en Oaxaca* (Oaxaca: Instituto Estatal de Educación Publica de Oaxaca, 2008), 53–72.

56. This style, which corresponds chronologically to the period 400–800 AD and geographically to the lower Mixteca region of northeastern Oaxaca and the area south of Puebla, is highly eclectic, drawing not only on Zapotecan elements but on those from Teotihuacan and the coast of the Gulf of Mexico as well.

57. Personal communication, Ángel Iván Rivera, 2008.

58. AGN, Mapas nos. 1692.9, 2463, 876, and 1614.

59. Mary Elizabeth Smith, *The Codex López Ruiz: A Lost Mixtec Pictorial Manuscript* (Nashville: Vanderbilt University Publications in Anthropology, 1998), 210.

60. Viola König, *Inhaltliche, Analyse und Interpretation von Codex Egerton* (Hamburgo: Museo de Hamburgo, 1979).

61. Viola König, "Mary E. Smith's Interpretation of the *Codex Tulane*, in the *Codex López Ruiz* and Other Documents. Some Conclusions on the Role of Tlaxiaco in the Western Part of the Mixteca Alta," *Mexicon* 27, 6 (December 2005): 112–115; Smith, *Codex López Ruiz*, 84. For a brief study and photograph of the *Lienzo de Ocotepec*, see Alfonso Caso, "Mapa de Santo Tomás Ocotepeque, Oaxaca," in *Summa Antropológica en Homenaje a Roberto J. Weitlaner* (Mexico City: INAH, 1966), 131–137.

62. Located in the southern part of the state of Puebla, Acatlán (Ciudad Acatlán de Osorio Mixtecos) adjoins Oaxaca on the north. Peter Gerhard mentions these sites in its area: Tuzantla, Tehuicingo, Totoltepec, Piastla, Tecomatlan, Guapanapa, Petlalcingo, Tepexillo, Ixitlan, and Chila. It lies within the Mixtec-populated region and geographically forms part of the Mixteca Baja. Gerhard's reference is to a Santa Ana Tepexillo, which appears as a pueblo in the eighteenth century. Gerhard, *A Guide*, 42–44.

63. The AGN contains documents that reveal that this cacique resided in Cuquila, for which reason it is logical to conclude that in this period the seat of the cacicazgo was Cuquila: AGN, Ramo Mercedes, 14, f. 130, 1590, and 15, f. 139r; AGN, Ramo General de Parte, 2, exp. 1087, f. 242v; AGN, Ramo Tierras 2692, exp. 17.

64. A league is 5,000 varas, or 4.18 kilometers.

65. AGN, Ramo de Tierras, 525, exp. 1.

66. König, *Inhaltliche*, 114.

67. AGN, Mapa no. 2463.

68. König, "Mary E. Smith's Interpretation."

69. Mary Elizabeth Smith, *Picture Writing from Ancient Southern México: Mixtec Place Signs and Maps* (Norman: University of Oklahoma Press, 1973), 96. The map from Cuquila is AGN, Mapa no. 867.

70. Archivo General de Indias, Justicia 160, no. 2.

71. AGN, Ramo de Tierras, 876, exp. 1. For more on how the Mixtecan caciques were accustomed to carrying maps, codices, and other documents with them when they moved about, treating them as personal material, see Smith, *Codex López Ruiz*, 209; König, "Mary E. Smith's Interpretation," 112.

72. "De Cuquila, número 42," document dated 1584, preserved in the Santa María Cuquila community museum.

73. Trial and civil proceedings over the dispossession of land committed by citizens of the pueblo of Cuquila against Doña Pascuala Feliciana de Roxas, cacique of the pueblos of Santo Tomás Ocotepec, Santa Cruz Nundaco, and others, 1724–1827, Archivo Histórico Municipal of Tlaxiaco, Oaxaca.

74. AGN, Ramo de Tierras, no. 2682, exp. 17.

75. Monaghan, "Mixtec Caciques."

76. Kevin Terraciano, *The Mixtecs of Colonial Oaxaca* (Stanford: Stanford University Press, 2001), 206.

77. In the Mixteca, two-headed or bicephelous eagles have been associated with the ancient Mixtec kings since pre-Hispanic times. Ferdinand Anders, Maarten Jansen, and Gabina Aurora Pérez-Jiménez, *Crónica Mixteca el rey 8 venado, Garra de Jaguar, y la dinastía de Teozacualco-Zaachila. Libro explicativo del llamado Códice Zouche-Nuttall* (México: Sociedad Estatal Quinto Centenario, Academische Druck- und Verlagsanstalt, and Fondo de Cultura Económica, 1992), facsimile ed., plate 19. A wooden sculpture from the colonial period, on which a two-headed eagle is carved, can also be seen in the church of Cuquila.

78. *Capisayo* is the antiquated term for a short piece of clothing that consists of both a cape and a smock. The smock is a long, buttonless jacket.

79. Interviews with Camilo Coronel Sánchez, Santa María Cuquila, 2007 and 2008, and Emiliano Melchor Ayala and Sixto Melchor Ayala, Santa María Cuquila, 2004.

80. Terraciano, *The Mixtecs*, 158; Stephanie Wood, "Power Differentials in Early Mesoamerican Gender Ideology: The Founding Couple," in Guilhem Olivier, ed., *Símbolos de poder en Mesoamérica* (México: UNAM, 2008), 517–531.

81. For other modern stories of human sacrifice carried out prior to the construction of important buildings, see Helios Pujol Figuerola, "De sacrificio y sacrificios en la comunidad tzeltal de San Juan Evangelista Cancuc en las Altas Tierras de Chiapas," in Leonardo López Luján and Guilhem Olivier, eds., *El sacrificio humano en la tradición religiosa mesoamericana* (México: INAH, Instituto de Investigaciones Históricas, and UNAM, 2010), 519–546.

82. Caso, "Mapa de Santo Tomás Ocotepeque."

83. AGN, Ramo de Indios, 2, exp. 374, f. 90v.

84. "[Y] pasaba [en su caballo con alas] a Yukuchiyo que es Loma Tepalcate y de ahí pasaba a esta ruina aquí en Cacica [el sitio arqueológico] y así viajaba si por todos lados,

iba a Santo Domingo las Nievas porque ese animal [su caballo] es un animal que vuela es como águila de dos picos, así fue, eso es de Pedro Castañeda." Interview with Camilo Coronel Sánchez, Santa María Cuquila, March 2007.

85. "[C]omo un comandante o como un policía." Ibid.

86. As cacique of Cuquila, in 1583 Don Francisco de Austria, the father of Don Pedro Castañeda, had received a license allowing him to ride horseback. AGN, Ramo General de Parte, 2, exp. 1087, f. 242v.

87. Maarten Jansen, *La gran familia de los reyes mixtecos libro explicativo de los códices llamados Egerton y Becker II* (México: Akademische Druck- und Verlagsanstalt and Fondo de Cultura Económica, 1994), facsimile ed.

88. "[S]oñó a un señor mayor de mucha edad con barbas blancas y le dijo que le agradeció por haber estado ahí en ese momento y que le dijo: 'te agradezco por haberme visitado porque cuando tu me visitas me siento vivo.' Entonces este señor se espantó porque desconocía la procedencia de esta piedra [la estela] qué era lo que significaba." Interviews with Emiliano Melchor Ayala, Santa María Cuquila, summer 2005, and Felipe Cortes López, Santa María Cuquila, November 2007.

89. "[R]ecordaron de que había una estela que los antepasados lo adoraban le tenían fe a esta piedra entonces lo que hicieron fue venir por ella lo trasladaron hacia la comunidad, lo exhibieron en el templo de la comunidad en el altar, le pusieron veladoras, velas, para ellos era sagrado era un santo para ellos esta piedra [la estela]." Interview with Felipe Cortes López, Santa María Cuquila, November 2007.

90. Ibid.

91. "[C]omo una pila recargable, bueno esa piedra [la estela] funciona como pila recargable ya que se recarga por la energía de los rayos solares y de la luna también, o sea... por ejemplo de la luna es cada luna llena es cuando se recarga esta piedra [la estela] según la gente que le trasmitieron su antepasados ese conocimiento y aún lo conservan ... entonces dicen que esa piedra al tener contacto con los rayos solares se recarga y conserva la energía. La gente ha comentado de que la piedra [la estela] muestra algunos antecedentes de la comunidad, exactamente no podría decirlo pero son antecedentes, los sufrimientos de la comunidad lo refleja en esta piedra según la gente." Ibid.

92. Terraciano, *The Mixtecs*, 5.

93. Registro Agrario de Oaxaca, Santa María Cuquila, exp. 186, Report of the Nationalist Indigenist Institute, the Situation of Cuquila, October 3, 1972.

94. Periódico Oficial del Gobierno del Estado de Oaxaca, October 19, 1938, 3. "The argument that emerged from the overall account was that Santa María Cuquila was abolished as a municipality because of its economic insufficiency; its annual intake of revenue was 216.00 pesos, an amount not even remotely adequate to cover the most urgent expenses of its municipal council." Germán Ortiz Coronel, "*Ñuu Kuini*: Un territorio en disputa, conflictos agrarios y negociación en la Mixteca" (master's thesis, Universidad Autónoma Metropolitana, Mexico City, 2007), 110n117.

95. Francisco López Bárcenas, "La autonomía entre los triquis. Para que haya paz y tranquilidad," *Ojarasca* 118 (February 2007), at http://www.jornada.unam.mx/2007/02/12/oja118-lopbarcenas.html, accessed May 2008.

96. Interview with Germán Ortiz Coronel, Cuquila, July 2008.

97. By custom and practice, Cuquila's municipal government has fourteen positions. In 2008 they and the persons filling them were the municipal president, Odilón Pedro Melchor Hilario; alternate municipal president, Juan Gregoio López Reyes; secretary, Alfonso Cruz Hilario; treasurer, Tomás Rojas Reyes; first municipal trustee, Germán Ortíz Coronel; alternate municipal trustee, Daniel Pascual Reyes Melchor; education councilor, Atalo Sánchez Ortiz; treasury councilor, Pedro Sánchez Coronel; public works councilor, Rubén León Reyes; burial grounds councilor, Pedro Manuel Ayala Coronel; constitutional overseer, Bonifacio López Coronel; alternate constitutional overseer, Cupertino Maurilio López Reyes; chief judge, Félix López Reyes; sergeant at arms, Víctor Hilario Santiago.

98. Archivo General Agrario, exp. 276.1/236.

99. Ibid.

100. Ibid.

101. Ibid.

102. Ibid.

103. Ibid.

104. Ibid.

105. Ibid.

106. Ibid.

107. Cuquila's primordial titles consisted of these colonial-period documents: a royal grant of June 16, 1595, by Viceroy Luis de Velasco, awarding the pueblo's Indians the right to a cattle ranch, and the authentication, dated January 7, 1707, and made by the alcalde mayor of Tonala to the cabildo of Cuquila, of a set of historical records, probably in connection with the ongoing process of land title legalization. The records authenticated by Tonala's alcalde, to which he gave the collective name "titles," were two grants for raising cattle—one made to the community of Cuquila as a whole and concerning which no further information exists and the other to the cacique Pedro Castañeda, which bears the date January 12, 1590. Another document among Cuquila's primordial titles is the record, dated June 3, 1793, of an official inspection made of the boundary lines separating Cuquila and Santo Tomás Ocotepec. The inspection occurred in connection with Cuquila's defense of its land against the claims made by the cacica Feliciana de Rojas. The last document pertains to the efforts made at the end of the sixteenth century by a Spaniard, Joseph de Bravo, to obtain a royal grant to establish a cattle ranch on land along the boundary line between Cuquila and Mixtepec. Both Cuquila's cacique, Pedro Castañeda, and its other authorities intervened and succeeded in thwarting the Spaniard's plan.

108. Archivo General Agrario, exp. 276.1/236.

109. Ibid.

110. Ibid.

111. Ibid.

112. Ibid.

113. "[H]ubo un señor cacique, tenia una personalidad diferente a los demás por el cuerno que tenia [en la frente] que controlaba todo Cuquila sobre todo los linderos y otros documentos del ayuntamiento, el conocía todas las dependencias de gobierno, en aquel entonces eran pocos los que sabían leer y escribir, pero el tenia un defecto sobre

todo el maltrato a los demás, les robaba sus ganados, violaba y robaba mujeres, entonces llego un día que la misma población ya no soportó estos maltratos y se reunieron y antes de que lo mataran dijo si me matan su pueblo se partirá en muchos pedazos y siempre vivirán en problemas con otros pueblos ya que yo cuento con la mayor parte de ellos [de los papeles del pueblo], pero la población de tan enojados que estaban no le hicieron caso y procedieron en matarlo." Interview with Sixto Melchor Ayala, Santa María Cuquila, October 14, 2006.

114. Personal communication with the linguist Michel Swanton, 2009.

115. Interview with René Marneau Villavicencio, Puebla, December 3, 2006.

116. Alfredo López Austin, "El texto Sahaguntino sobre los mexicas," *Anales de Antropología* (México) (1985): 328.

117. One can say that the election of Cuquila's municipal government goes beyond the power of the national state and derives its legitimacy from God. In this sense, what takes place in Cuquila is similar to what happens in many other indigenous pueblos in Latin America, where the election of authorities carries a divine legitimacy. Abercrombie, *Pathways of Memory*, 58–59.

118. To understand the role schoolteachers played in post-revolutionary Mexico, see Mary Kay Vaughan, *Cultural Politics in Revolution* (Tucson: University of Arizona Press, 1997).

119. Cuauhtémoc Camarena Ocampo and Teresa Morales Lersch, "Museos Comunitarios de Oaxaca memoria comunal para combatir el olvido," *Arqueología Mexicana* 72 (2005): 72–77.

120. "[E]sa piedra [la estela] lo tenemos que levantar algo ha de tener de importante, es importante cuidar esa pieza si lo creen así o cómo lo ven ustedes, no hay que levantar porque ha de ser una cosa bonita bueno, lo levantamos entre varios otra vez lo volvimos a llevar acá arriba estaba una casita ahí pegado anexo al palacio [municipal] ahí lo fuimos a guardar esa pieza pero entonces ya se nos ocurrió a nosotros lavarlo, lavar la pieza con escoba, y todo no sabíamos qué importancia tenía, mas o menos ya se limpio la pieza ya lo paramos y ahí estuvo." Interview with Tobías Diego López Ortiz, Santa María Cuquila, November 2007.

121. "Anduvimos sábado y domingo de casa en casa aquí andábamos preguntando donde hay más piedritas de esas que se vean bonitas y mucha gente se acercaba, fue como logramos encontrar las piezas que están ahí, unos ya estaban destruyendo, unos ya querían utilizar para su camellón otro para atranque de la olla de fríjol y así las tenían pero no, esta piedra me lo dan y esta me la llevo, ¿para qué la quieras? [me decían] no pregunten ya que vean ya que este ahí en un lugarcito bonito ahí lo van a ver." Ibid.

122. One is a royal grant of land, made to Cuquila in 1584, for cattle and livestock purposes, and the other is a copy of a legal dispute, dated 1590, between Cuquila and Chicahusatla (a Triqui pueblo bordering Cuquila) over a small piece of land.

Conclusion

In this work I have attempted to demonstrate the singular importance a particular range of historical documents holds for many Indian pueblos in Mexico and also to show how pueblos have used these same documents—produced by the Indians themselves—and the local history they record to negotiate the defense of their lands and communal way of life with Spanish colonial authorities and the Mexican national state. To do so, I have taken the perspective of the *longue durée*, analyzing these developments from the sixteenth century to the present. The originality of this study, I believe, lies precisely in taking this perspective and breaking with the artificially truncated and compressed cycles characteristic of the current historiographical approach.

To manage the problem of analyzing how Indian pueblos actually used local history over such an extended period—five centuries—I chose to focus on a series of individual cases that illustrate the central ideas underlying and guiding the study. The analysis is thus grounded more in the empirical than in the theoretical. It concentrates on examining a number of specific examples that fall within successive historical epochs. To the extent that works dealing with the social memory of Indian pueblos, or what I prefer to call local history, already exist, they are generally restricted to the colonial period. In contrast, we know much less about this subject with respect to the nineteenth and twentieth centuries, the contemporary period. This work represents an attempt to respond to and overcome that lack of knowledge.

To preserve the record of their own history and carry it down to the present as a living tradition, Indian pueblos have had to resist the maneuvers of both the colonial and the national states, for which shaping and blurring the indigenous past have been central to their strategies of domination and colonization. Although the Indians have valorized, and continue to valorize, both oral tradition and books and written legal codes, it is the former—as a continuing, dynamic process of creative and collective transformation—that enables them successfully to retell the story of their past.

The art of memory requires not only remembering but also what has been called "structured forgetting." Both Frank Salomon and Thomas Abercrombie have argued that the contradiction inherent in seeking to reduce or reformulate oral narrative into a written version lies in the irreconcilable notions of time and history. The western perception of historical time as a linear progression and a chain of non-repeating events prevents non-Indians from recognizing and comprehending the different perception of historical time held by the Indian pueblos, in which the validity of a sequence of episodes in a narrative is not dependent on its fitting into a single master narrative.

Although the recovery of local history by Indian pueblos became widespread beginning in the seventeenth century, an important precedent for this phenomenon had been set during the previous century, when the Spanish Crown and its agents in New Spain sought to incorporate the native population into the colonial justice system. This concern was bound up with the Crown's justification of its rightful title to Spanish America; as vassals of the empire, the Indians required royal protection and assistance so they could be integrated into the new imperial order. The creation of special legal protections for the indigenous population—however effective they actually were—significantly buttressed the Crown's assertion of rights over its New World territories. At the same time, however, the Spanish monarchs not only had to make their dominion legitimate; they had to ensure that it was profitable as well.

The Crown's need to legitimize its rule permitted the Indians to enjoy a relative degree of official protection and, as an adjunct, to incorporate some of their own customs and practices into the system of colonial justice, as long as they were shorn of any traces of idolatry and did not pose any threats to the primacy of royal jurisdiction. The cloak of special legal protection also meant that the appointment of high-level colonial officials in this period followed a carefully delineated set of protocols. Those selected to be viceroys and audiencia judges upheld the Crown's juridical and political disposition to afford protection to the Indians.

In 1531, many pueblos as well as individual Indian nobles and commoners began to present traditional codices and maps to the audiencia as evidence in legal claims and lawsuits—a practice they later continued with the viceroys. For the most part, these documents—or juridical codices, as I choose to call them—lacked the richness and complexity of their pre-Hispanic counterparts. Nevertheless, they were a clear expression of the Indians' willingness and determination to capitalize on the opportunity the Crown gave them for negotiation. Throughout the sixteenth century, New Spain's viceroys emended the justice system, as it applied to the native population, to achieve more effective social and political control over the pueblos. For the Indians, on the other hand, the courts served as something of an escape valve, an arena for deliberation and dialogue, allowing for the release of numerous social tensions that built up between themselves and the Spanish colonizers.

However, while the justice system in this period may have taken indigenous cultural elements into account when dealing with the Indians, the Spanish authorities still considered the Indians to be minors, incapable of defending themselves juridically because of their innate deficiencies of character and station. As of 1563, therefore, their condition was officially described as one of wretchedness; in light of this fact, it became the duty of the Crown to shield, defend, and protect its Indian vassals. The native lords and nobles (tlatoque and pipiltin) were exempted from belonging to this category of miserables (wretches), since in the eyes of the Crown and royal officials the Indian nobility enjoyed a status similar to that of the Castilian nobility.

The end of the sixteenth century brought a clear shift in the colonial justice system with respect to the native population. The willingness to entertain the use of indigenous customs and practices in the courts was substantially curtailed. The last years of the sixteenth century and the beginning of the seventeenth century witnessed a hardening in the Crown's policies toward its Indian vassals and a corresponding surge of interest in maximizing the flow of revenue into the royal treasury.

If, on the one hand, the colonial authorities drew back at this time from encouraging or allowing the Indians to introduce elements of their traditional culture into the colonial justice system—indeed, starting at the end of the sixteenth century the Crown promoted legislation that forbade Indians from recalling their pre-Hispanic past—on the other, both the pueblos through their representatives and Indians on their own authority displayed a marked interest in narrating their pre-Hispanic and colonial-period history to the colonial officials. They did so orally, visually in "painted manuscripts," or in writing, all in an effort to preserve their lands. A range of specialized documents—including land titles (or primordial titles as they were generally known starting in the nineteenth century), pictorial maps, Techialoyan-style codices, and various records emanating from legal disputes—reveal this pattern and process of negotiation.

Interestingly, however, the pueblos produced titles and Techialoyan codices in the seventeenth and eighteenth centuries even though they were under no apparent formal obligation to do so. In offering up such documents, they were probably motivated by the desire to prevent Spaniards from appropriating either their communal land or land belonging to Indian caciques. Unlike the Indians, Spaniards were required at this time, as part of the Crown's program of composición, to legalize their ownership of land and purchase title to it. Elements of the Spanish population took advantage of this process to seize Indian lands by filing lawsuits, occupying surplus property, or conniving with corrupt officials—jueces privativos and alcaldes mayores—who in return for accepting bribes could effect the "legal" transfer of Indians' lands into the hands of individual Spaniards.

During the seventeenth and eighteenth centuries, then, the pueblos generally produced maps and pictorial documents as a way of laying claim to their rights over land and water. Some pueblos found themselves out in the cold, however, either because no one in the community had the skill—rudimentary as it might be—to produce such documents or because they lacked the funds with which to pay someone to produce them. Under these circumstances, some pueblos—confronting the urgent need to defend their communal land—took ancient pictorial documents that had been created for different purposes into their possession and tried to pass them off before the colonial courts as their primordial titles. Other pueblos adopted the strategy of altering and retouching their ancient painted manuscripts or pictorial maps to make the depictions on them consonant with the legal exigencies of the moment. I have termed this latter type of action the *refunctionalization* of a pictorial document.

When appearing in judicial proceedings during the seventeenth and eighteenth centuries, the colony's Indians thus called upon historical arguments to validate the ancient possession of their land. As such, all of the information concerning their past, the very image of their history that Mexico's Indians rendered pictorially and in writing, is unquestionably part of a dynamic process of negotiation they maintained with the colonial power—a process that, to be fully grasped, must be studied within these particular social, political, and historical terms.

After the colonial period and well into the nineteenth century, the Indian pueblos continued to manifest a notable ideological flexibility in which their traditional customs and cultural practices played an important role. Moreover, the pueblos succeeded in doing so within a complex and problematic environment, since as a result of legislation passed first by the Cadiz Cortes government and then by successive liberal and conservative national governments, they lost the protection the monarchy had given them by virtue of their special juridical status. With the abolition of a separate Indian court, the Indians were henceforth placed on the same legal footing as other social and ethnic groups, divested of the protection of a "paternalistic" monarchy—however much such protection may have been confined to the realm of legislation.

In theory, under the new regime the Indians enjoyed the same rights as other groups. In reality, though, the ground had shifted and the pueblos quickly had to learn the new rules imposed by a succession of governments that—although they may have differed ideologically—were united in viewing the Indians as a roadblock to the creation and consolidation of a modern state.

This obstacle notwithstanding, their new status as Mexican citizens enabled the Indians to negotiate certain benefits for themselves, in particular that of retaining elements of their traditional rights and practices. They also developed strategies to preserve the colonial order in various corners of their local world, notably on the level of pueblo government organization and activity. Their success in this regard was reflected in the Indian pueblos' response to the aggressions they suffered and to the changes that impinged on them from without during the nineteenth century, a response marked by the presence of important traditional cultural elements.

This responsiveness by the Indians demonstrates above all their consistent capacity for negotiation, especially in the face of threats mounted in this period against the preservation of pueblo communal lands. Beginning in the mid-nineteenth century, they further refined this capacity by requesting through the offices of the state official searches for their primordial titles. The laws of disentailment gave particular impetus to the efforts by many Indian authorities or their representatives to locate primordial titles and fend off the annexation and loss of pueblo land. Although this strategic initiative was an essential feature of the Indians' experience and of Indian-Hispanic relations, it has received little study to date.

As the initiative gained force, numerous pueblos across Mexico began to request land titles and other historical documents from the Archivo General de la Nación. The copies of documents furnished to Indian pueblos during the nineteenth century generally came out of the archive's Tierras branch and consisted of such colonial-period records as royal grants, fragments of lawsuits and litigation, and maps—some of which were of great antiquity. This development enables us to observe how in the nineteenth century, oral narratives and local history, as set down in various colonial titles, continued to have legal relevance for the Indian pueblos and were copied and occasionally translated by archive staff so the Indians could use them as legal instruments in the defense of their lands.

During this period, other pueblos that possessed long-held maps and documents updated their maps, adding specific details concerning the boundary lines that marked off the community's land, prior to introducing them in the courts as a way of protecting the land from outside encroachment and exploitation. In still other cases, some pueblos tried to deceive the authorities by fabricating "ancient" documents and passing them off as authentic, thus repeating a colonial-period practice that affected the treatment of primordial titles and Techialoyan-style codices.

As the nineteenth century wore on, the situation with respect to the survival of Indian communal lands was mixed. Yet because the environment in which the Indians operated was so antagonistic to their interests, some scholars who have studied the issue in recent years subscribe to the idea that the loss of land by Indians, and campesinos more generally, was universal during the Porfiriato. While many pueblos indeed lost their land during this period, others—following specific regional dynamics—succeeded in rebuffing outside threats and holding on to their communal land. Their success in doing so reflects several factors: the Indians' capacity for negotiation—one of their signal cultural traits—as well as the poor quality and outlying location of some of their land, which lessened its appeal for cattlemen, agriculturalists, and businessmen looking for viable commercial sites.

During the Mexican Revolution and after, the Indians continued to ask the national archive to search for historical documents validating their possession of communal land. Moreover, the creation of the National Agrarian Commission (1915) and the Agrarian Department (1934) abrogated the mid–nineteenth-century Laws of the Reform as they affected Indian pueblos. The pueblos regained their earlier juridical status, and an effort was launched to resolve indigenous land issues on this basis. One of the first actions taken in 1915 was to "restitute" to the pueblos those lands they had lost after 1856. This action sparked a fervent attempt by the pueblos to reconstruct the foundations of their history, the core evidence for which lay in the primordial titles. The national archive thus received and acted upon numerous search requests. Some pueblos also called upon the oral testimony of older community members to document their pre-1856 possession of lands and secure their restitution. The search for primordial titles was reinforced and accelerated by the terms of Article 27 of the 1917 Mexican constitution. To facilitate this work, the National Agrarian Commission contracted paleographers to transcribe the colonial documents the Indian communities used to prove the antiquity of their original landholdings.

The restitution program, however, was thoroughly inadequate to the task of resolving Indians' land problems because many pueblos came up empty in the search for documents to support their claims of lost territory. The government's response to this situation was to propose the formation of new agrarian units and the provision of new grants of land. Yet this step, too, tied the pueblos' hands because it required that they either produce their primordial titles (something they patently lacked) or furnish documentation that fixed their founding date.

As I have tried to demonstrate throughout this work, the Indian pueblos invested their historical documents with great importance whenever they found themselves in negotiations to preserve or augment their land. Moreover, when they lacked these documents, they invoked other strategies to negotiate the preservation of their land with the state. For Indian communities, the importance of land and its connection to ancient documents, primordial titles, and local history is part of a complex process of negotiation they undertake with the state to defend their communal lands. This process implies a true understanding of official legal norms and the Indians' interpretive reading—from their own cultural perspective—of declarations, programmatic statements, documents, and agrarian legislation emanating from and issued by the state, in which the official seals of government, land title legalizations, and the primordial titles themselves meld into a modern mythology created by the pueblos. The Indians' practiced capacity for negotiation, resting in turn on their impressive ideological flexibility, enables them to incorporate—sometimes to a successful end—elements of their native culture into the most adverse legal circumstances.

I have further tried to show, by considering contemporary cases, how Indian pueblos maintain the tradition of using local history to negotiate the protection of their land and native culture with the Mexican state. This process is especially evident in the case of Atliaca and its recovery of its land and historical documents after a long struggle championed and led by the schoolteacher-lawyer Modesto Vázquez Salgado. Similarly, the inhabitants of Santa María Cuquila, by calling up and celebrating their rich historical past, are intent—as we have seen—on proving their pueblo's importance and providing the justification for its reconstitution as an independent municipality. Santa María Cuquila's efforts have failed to bear fruit in its negotiations with the state. The community museum the Cuquilans established, however, has made them more aware of their origins, given them a stronger sense of group identity, and reinforced their feelings of belonging to a particular locale.

Beyond that, the community museum has given Cuquila's men and women a greater stake in things, a greater say in their own welfare, by fostering projects that strengthen such cottage industries as the production of textiles, clay objects, and dolls clothed in traditional dress. In addition, the Mixtec campesinos who help run the museum have drawn on the enriched cultural environment to which they are exposed, adding features to the museum that interest them and discarding others they consider less useful. It seems instructive to isolate and highlight just what history, or which elements of its history, each of these communities has chosen to recover.[1] In the case of Atliaca, the history that is recovered or resurrected is one in which the pueblo maintains communal lands, whereas for Santa María Cuquila it is a history in which ancient caciques play the lead role. In the territory of Guerrero, the cacicazgos did not endure as long as they did in the Mixteca Alta, a contrast revealed in the simple fact of what each pueblo chooses to recover and make its own. The two communities identify and select certain elements from their past that give them cohesion. For Atliaca, the emphasis is placed on communally worked land; for Cuquila, it falls on the local cacicazgo as a central symbol of regional power.

Through the intercession of Guilhem Olivier, in 2006 I was able to have Javier Urcid—a noted epigrapher at Brandeis University—decipher the inscriptions on, and compose the wall text and explanatory labels for, the stelae housed in Cuquila's museum. Urcid pointed out that the central image on one of the stelae is the figure of a monkey (see Figure 4.9). This identification caused the museum's director, Emiliano Melchor Ayala, to become uneasy. He explained that the figure represented in the center of the stela was a jaguar (*kuiñi*), the symbol of the pueblo. Over time, I noticed that the museum did not display the explanatory text Urcid produced for this stela. I asked the reason and was given evasive answers by Emiliano. I realized, of course, that the museum was not going to mount text that interpreted the central figure on the stela as anything other than a jaguar or tiger. After all, the Cuquilans' history is being set down, and they are the ones who decide what to highlight and what to exclude.

The Indians' cultural dynamism and ideological flexibility have played a crucial role in their survival across five centuries of unmistakable marginalization and injustice. These characteristics have helped the indigenous population define and craft cultural, political, and—in particular—ethical alternatives against the dominating power of both the colonial state and its national successor. The Indians have responded to this challenge in multiple ways, and the recovery of their local history is just one of many strategies they have devised in their effort to survive as indigenous communities. In the way it has created and goes on creating a wide-ranging cultural dynamism, this particular strategy, I think, counts as one of the most imaginative. Moreover, while the Indians have not always managed to protect their lands—a fact that dogs them even today—this history is not a history of defeats. On the contrary, in rediscovering their own history they rediscover themselves and, through this process, acquire the strength and resolve to cultivate and re-create the distinctive ethnic, political, and ethical characteristics of their own culture.[2]

Without question, a successful element in their struggle has been access to education. The intellectually minded Indians I have met in my fieldwork play a prominent role in the development of their communities. They display several interrelated qualities: a new sense of being rooted in and belonging to their communities, an interest in forging a unity among Indian pueblos that goes beyond their own community, and a synthesis of both native and external cultural elements in their actions. These individuals are manifestly a valuable resource for the pueblos; they personify the way Indian communities organize themselves and fight in determined fashion to save their rich cultural and material patrimony.

As a final note, I wish to underscore Gary Gossen's observation that Mexico, as a multiethnic and multicultural nation, "can do no less than recognize that it has a number of different histories, each of which gives meaning to the society to which it corresponds and a useful perspective on its existential situation."[3]

Over the course of this work, I have tried to recover some of these histories, local histories imaginatively and dynamically reconstructed by Indian pueblos with the purpose of preserving their territory—their community—together with their past, present, and future. To recognize this multiplicity of histories makes us all, as Gossen points out, "wiser, richer, and more penetrating with respect to human understanding."[4]

NOTES

1. I am grateful to William Taylor for bringing this point to my attention.

2. Concerning the Indians and utopia, see Federico Navarrete, "La tierra sin mal, una utopia anti-estatal americana," in Guilhem Olivier, ed., *Símbolos de poder en Mesoamérica* (México: UNAM, 2008), 475–492.

3. Gossen, "Cuatro mundos," 189.

4. Ibid., 190.

Maps

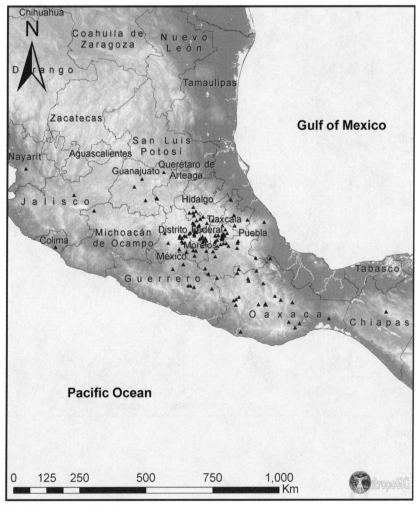

Map 1 Overview of Study Area

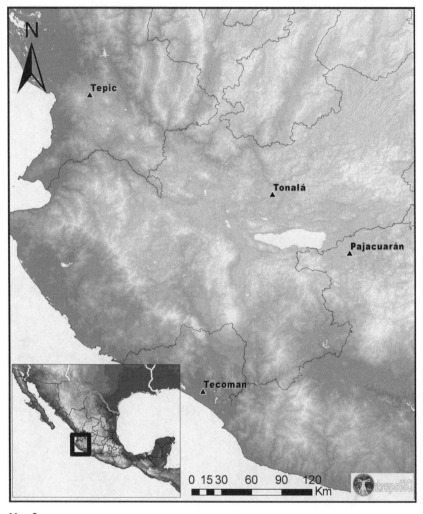

0 15 30   60   90   120
                              Km

Map 2

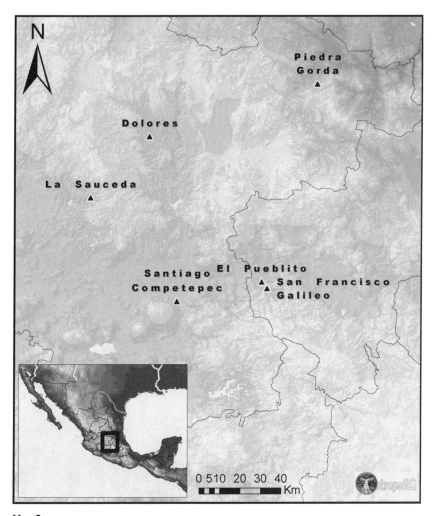

Map 3

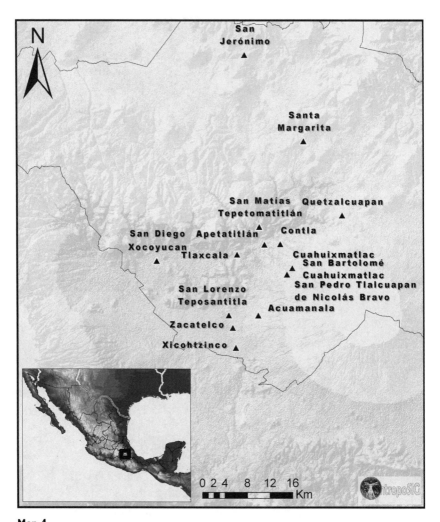

N

San
Jerónimo

Santa
Margarita

San Matías   Quetzalcuapan
Tepetomatitlán

San Diego   Apetatitlán   Contla
Xocoyucan
          Tlaxcala   Cuahuixmatlac
                               San Bartolomé
                               Cuahuixmatlac
San Lorenzo   San Pedro Tlalcuapan
Teposantitla   de Nicolás Bravo
                     Acuamanala
Zacatelco

Xicohtzinco

0 2 4   8   12 16
                      Km

tropoSIG

Map 4

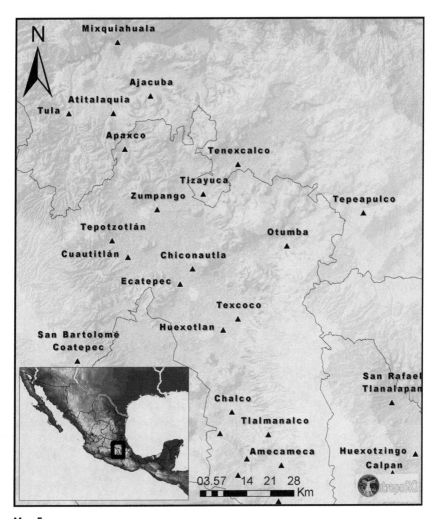

N

Mixquiahuala

Ajacuba
Atitalaquia
Tula

Apaxco

Tenexcalco

Tizayuca
Zumpango

Tepeapulco

Tepotzotlán

Otumba
Cuautitlán
Chiconautla

Ecatepec

Texcoco
Huexotlan

San Bartolomé
Coatepec

San Rafael
Tlanalapan

Chalco
Tlalmanalco

Amecameca

Huexotzingo
Calpan

0 3.57   14   21   28
                        Km

Map 5

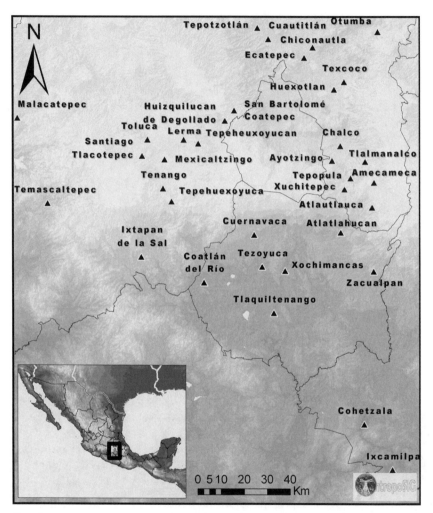

Map 6

Map 7

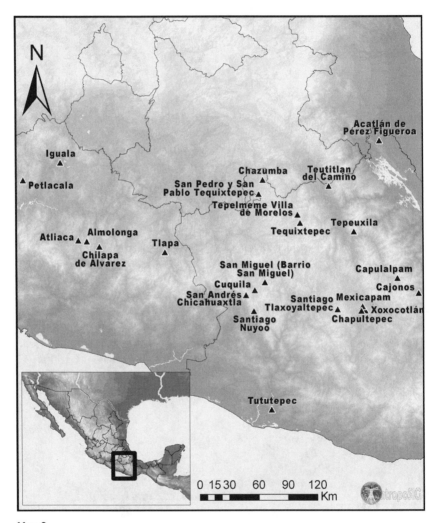

Map 8

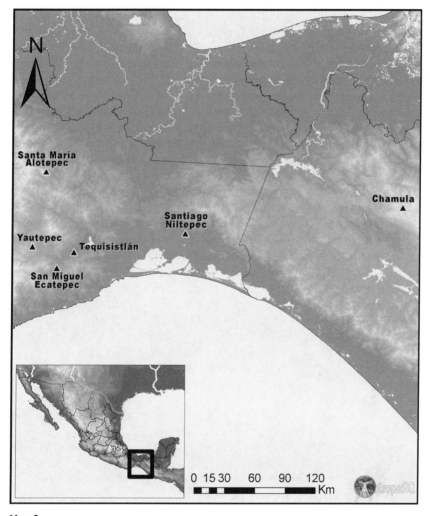

Map 9

List of Libraries and Archives Consulted

Archivo General Agrario, México, DF
Archivo General Agrario, Puebla, Puebla
Archivo General de Indias, Seville, Spain (AGI)
Archivo General de la Nación, México, DF (AGN)
Archivo Sacristía Acuitlapilco, Tlaxcala, Tlaxcala
Archivo Sacristía de Santa Inés Zacatelco, Tlaxcala, Tlaxcala
Biblioteca Nacional del Museo Nacional de Antropología e Historia, México, DF
Library of Congress, Washington, D.C., USA
National Library of France, Mexican Section, Paris, France

List of Significant Towns Mentioned in the Book

1. Ajacuba, Mexico City
2. Alotepec (Mixes), state of Oaxaca
3. Amecameca, state of Mexico
4. Apasco, state of Hidalgo
5. Atitalaquia, state of Hidalgo
6. Atliaca, Tixtla municipality, state of Guerrero
7. Ayotzingo, Chalco, state of México
8. Barrio de San Pablo, Mexico City
9. Bartolomé Cuahuaxmatl, state of Tlaxcala
10. Calpan, state of Puebla
11. Calpulalpan, Sierra Juárez, state of Oaxaca
12. Chalco, state of México
13. Chazumba, Mixteca, state of Oaxaca
14. Chiconautla, state of México
15. Chiconquiaco, state of Veracruz
16. Chilapa, state of Guerrero
17. Chinacamitlan, state of México
18. Ciudad de Puebla, state of Puebla
19. Coatlán del Río, state of Morelos
20. Contla, state of Tlaxcala
21. Coyoacan, Mexico City
22. Cuajimalpa, Mexico City
23. Cuauhquechollan, state of Puebla
24. Cuauhtinchan, state of Puebla
25. Cuautitlan, state of México
26. Cuernavaca, state of Morelos
27. Cuetzalan (Chiutla de la Sal), state of Puebla
28. Dolores, state of Guanajuato

29. Ecatepec, state of México
30. El Pueblito, state of Querétaro
31. Huexotzinco, state of Puebla
32. Huizquilucan, state of México
33. Iguala, state of Guerrero
34. Ixcamilpa, state of Puebla (limit with the state of Guerrero)
35. Iztapan, state of México
36. Iztaquimaxtitlan, state of Puebla
37. Izucar, state of Puebla
38. Lerma, state of México
39. Malacatepec, state of México
40. Mexicalcingo, state of México
41. Mizquihuala, state of Hidalgo
42. Otumba, state of México
43. Petlaca, state of Guerrero
44. Pueblito, state of Querétaro
45. San Antonio Acuamanala, state of Tlaxcala
46. San Antonio Cacalotepec, San Andrés Cholula municipality, state of Puebla
47. San Bartola Yautepec, Zapotecos, state of Oaxaca
48. San Bartolomé Coatepec, state of México
49. San Bartolomé Cuahuixmatlac, state of Tlaxcala
50. San Bartolomé Cuayxmantla, doctrine of Santa Ana Chautempan, state of Tlaxcala
51. San Cristóbal Pajacuaran, Zamora, state of Michoacán
52. San Diego Acapulco, San Francisco Acapetlahuacan jurisdiction, state of Tlaxcala?
53. San Diego Xocollocan, state of Tlaxcala
54. San Francisco Caxonos, Zapotecs from the Sierra, state of Oaxaca

55. San Francisco Galilelo, state of Querétaro
56. San Hipólito Tepetzoltic, state of Tlaxcala?
57. San Jerónimo Acapulco and Santa María de la Asunción Tepehuexoyuca, Tenango del Valle, state of México
58. San Jerónimo Tenextlatlatylolla, state of Tlaxcala?
59. San Juan Chamula, state of Chiapas
60. San Juan Chapultepec, subject of Cuilapan, state of Oaxaca
61. San Juan Cuauhtla in the Sierra Negra, state of Puebla
62. San Juan Quetzalcuapan, state of Tlaxcala
63. San Lorenzo Teposantitlan, state of Tlaxcala
64. San Lucas Xochimanca, Xochimilco jurisdiction, Mexico City
65. San Luis Huexotlan, state of México
66. San Martín Mexicapan, state of Oaxaca
67. San Martín Tepetomatitla, doctrine of San Pablo Apetlatitla, state of Tlaxcala
68. San Mateo and Santiago Tepopula, Chalco, state of México
69. San Mateo Ocotlán, state of Tlaxcala
70. San Matías Tepetomatitlan, state of Tlaxcala
71. San Miguel Atlatlauca, Chalco, state of México
72. San Miguel Atlautlauca, formerly attached to the Tlalmanalco jurisdiction, southern part of the Valley of Mexico
73. San Miguel Chignautla, state of Puebla

74. San Miguel Ecatepec, Tequicistlán, Tehuantepec district, state of Oaxaca
75. San Miguel Tequistepec in the Valley of Coixtlahuaca, state of Oaxaca
76. San Nicolás Tetitzintla, Tehuacan district, state of Puebla
77. San Nicolás Totolapan, Mexico City
78. San Pablo Apetatitla, Santa Ana Chautempan, state of Tlaxcala
79. San Pedro Piedra Gorda, state of Guanajuato
80. San Pedro Tlalauapan, Santa Ana Chautempan, state of Tlaxcala
81. San Pedro y San Pablo Tequistepec, Mixteca Baja, state of Oaxaca
82. San Rafael Tlanamilolpan, doctrine of San Martín Texmelucan
83. San Salvador Chachapan, state of Puebla
84. San Sebastian Tepatlachico, Tepeaca, state of Puebla
85. Santa Ana Chautempan, state of Tlaxcala
86. Santa Ana Tlacotenco, Mexico City
87. Santa Cruz Xoxocotlan, state of Oaxaca
88. Santa Inés Zacatelco, state of Tlaxcala
89. Santa Margarita Maapiltepexco, state of Tlaxcala?
90. Santa Margarita Mazapyltepehco, state of Tlaxcala?
91. Santa María Acuitlapilco, state of Tlaxcala
92. Santa María Cuquila, Tlaxiaco district, Mixteca Alta, state of Oaxaca
93. Santa María de Jesús Acapetlahuayan, Acapetlahuacan, Atlixco, state of Puebla

94. Santa María de la Asunción Tepehuexoyuta, Valle de Tenango, state of México
95. Santa María Magdalena Mixuca, Mexico City
96. Santa María Sauceda, state of Guanajuato
97. Santiago Competepec, Celaya, state of Guanajuato
98. Santiago Niltepec, state of Oaxaca
99. Santiago Nuyoo, Mixteca Alta, state of Oaxaca
100. Santiago Tecoman, state of Colima
101. Santiago Tenexcalco, state of Hidalgo
102. Santiago Tlaxoyaltepec, Etla, state of Oaxaca
103. Santiago Yauhnahuac, state of Puebla
104. Santísima Trinidad Tetatsi Tenellecac de Techalollan, state of Tlaxcala?
105. Santo Domingo Tlaquiltenango, state of Morelos
106. Santo Tomás Ocotepec, Mixteca Alta, state of Oaxaca
107. Santo Toribio Xicotzinco, state of Tlaxcala
108. Tacuba, Mexico City
109. Tecamachalco, state of Puebla
110. Temazcaltepec, state of México
111. Tenango del Valle, state of México
112. Tenochtitlan, Mexico City
113. Tepeapulco, state of Hidalgo
114. Tepehuexoyucan, Asunción Tepezoyuca, state of México
115. Tepenene, Mixteca Alta, state of Oaxaca
116. Tepeticpac, state of Tlaxcala

117. Tepeucila, Cuicatlan, state of Oaxaca
118. Tepezintla, Sierra Norte, state of Puebla
119. Tepic, state of Nayarit
120. Tepozatlán, state of México
121. Tequixtlatec, state of Oaxaca
122. Teutilan del Camino, state of Oaxaca
123. Texcoco, state of México
124. Tezoyuca, state of Morelos
125. Tizayuca, state of Hidalgo
126. Tlacotepec, state of México
127. Tlalmanalco, state of México
128. Tlapa, state of Guerrero
129. Tlalpan, Mexico City
130. Tlatelolco, Mexico City
131. Tlaxcala, state of Tlaxcala
132. Toluca, state of México
133. Tonalá, state of Jalisco
134. Tula, state of Hidalgo
135. Tututepec, coast of Oaxaca, state of Oaxaca
136. Xalpantepec (now Jalpan), state of Puebla
137. Xixingo, state of Puebla
138. Xuchitepec, Chalco, state of México
139. Zacualpan perteneciente, Cuautla Amilpas jurisdiction, state of Morelos
140. Zumpango, state of México

Bibliography

ACRONYMS FOR SOME PUBLISHERS

AGN	Archivo General de la Nación
CEHAM	Centro de Estudios Históricos del Agrarismo en México
CIESAS	Centro de Investigaciones y Estudios Superiores en Antropología Social
CONACULTA	Consejo Nacional para la Cultura y las Artes
INAH	Instituto Nacional de Antropología e Historia
UNAM	Universidad Nacional Autónoma de México

SOURCES

Abercrombie, Thomas A. *Pathways of Memory and Power: Ethnography and History among an Andean People.* Madison: University of Wisconsin Press, 1998.

Aguilera, Carmen. *Lienzos de Tepeticpac.* Tlaxcala: Gobierno del Estado de Tlaxcala, 1998.

Aiton, Arthur Scott. *Antonio de Mendoza, First Viceroy of New Spain.* Durham, N.C.: Duke University Press, 1927.

Alejos García, José. *Mosojäntel: Etnografía del discurso agrarista entre kis ch'oles de Chiapas.* Mexico City: Instituto de Investigaciones Filológicas and UNAM, 1994.

Bibliography

Alvarado, Fray de Francisco. *Vocabulario en lengua mixteca*. Mexico City: Instituto Nacional Indigenista and INAH, 1962.

Anders, Ferdinand, Maarten Jansen, and Gabina Aurora Pérez-Jiménez. *Crónica Mixteca El rey 8 venado, Garra de Jaguar, y la dinastía de Teozacualco-Zaachila. Libro explicativo del llamado Códice Zouche-Nuttall*. México: Sociedad Estatal Quinto Centenario, Academische Druck- und Verlagsanstalt, and Fondo de Cultura Económica, 1992, facsimile ed.

Apuntes históricos por el ilustrísimo y Reverendísimo Sr. Dr. Dn. Eulogio G. Gillow Obispo de Antequera, Diócesis de Oaxaca. Facsimilar de la edición de 1889 realizada por la Imprenta del Sagrado Corazón de Jesús, Mexico, Mexico. Oaxaca: Ediciones Toledo, 1990, first facsimile ed.

Assadourian, Carlos Sempat. "La despoblación indígena en Perú y Nueva España durante el siglo XVI y la formación de la economía colonial." *Historia Mexicana* 38, 3 (1989): 419–454.

———. "Memoriales de fray Gerónimo de Mendieta." *Historia Mexicana* 37, 3 (1988): 357–422.

Barlow, Robert. "[N47:III:1] El Códice de Coetzalan, Puebla." *Tlalocan: A Journal of Source Materials on the Native Cultures of Mexico* 3, 1 (1949): 91–92.

———. "Las joyas de Martín Ocelotl." *Revista Yan* 3 (1954): 56–59.

Bataillon, Marcel. *Erasmo y España, estudios sobre la historia espiritual del siglo xvi*. Mexico City: Fondo de Cultura Económica, 1996, 2nd ed.

Baudot, George. *Utopia and History in Mexico: The First Chroniclers of Mexican Civilization (1520–1569)*. Niwot: University Press of Colorado, 1995.

Bautista, Juan. *¿Cómo te confundes? ¿Acaso no somos conquistados? Anales de Juan Bautista*, introduction, study, trans., and ed. from the Nahua text by Luis Reyes García. Mexico: CIESAS and Biblioteca Lorenzo Boturini y Nacional Basílica de Guadalupe, 2001.

Becerra Mora, Rodolfo. "La tira de Tepetzintla (Un estudio regional)." Master's thesis, Estudios Mesoamericanos, UNAM, Mexico City, 2002.

Beleña, Eusebio Buenaventura. *Recopilación sumaria de todos los autos acordados de la Real Audiencia y Sala del Crimen de esta Nueva España*, introduction by María del Refugio González. Mexico City: UNAM and Instituto de Investigaciones Jurídicas, 1991, facsimile ed., 11 vols.

Benavente, Fray Toribio de [Motolinía]. *Memoriales o libros de las cosas de la Nueva España y de los naturales de ella*, ed. Edmundo O'Gorman. Mexico City: UNAM, 1971.

Berdan, Frances F., and Patricia Rieff Anawalt, eds. *The Essential Codex Mendoza*. Berkeley: University of California Press, 1997.

Bonilla Palmeros, Jesús Javier. *Códices de Chiconquiaco*. Veracruz: Gobierno del Estado de Veracruz, Ediciones Gernika, S.A., 2007.

Borah, Woodrow Wilson. "El status jurídico de los indios en Nueva España." *América Indígena* 45, 2 (April–June 1985): 257–276.

———. *Justice by Insurance: The General Indian Court of Colonial Mexico and the Legal Aides of the Half-Real*. Berkeley: University of California Press, 1983.

Burrus S.J., Ernest J., ed. *The Writings of Alonso de la Veracruz: V. The Original Texts with English Translation. Spanish Writings: II Letters and Reports.* Rome: Jesuit Historical Institute, 1972.

Buve, Raymond J. "'Neither Carranza nor Zapata!': The Rise and Fall of a Peasant Movement That Tried to Challenge Both, Tlaxcala, 1910–1919," in Friedrich Katz, ed., *Riot, Rebellion, and Revolution: Rural Social Conflict in Mexico,* 338–375. Princeton: Princeton University Press, 1988.

Camacho de la Rosa, Gerardo. *Raíz y razón de Totolapan: El drama de la guerra Zapatista.* México: Centro de Estudios Antropológicos Científicos, Artisticos, Tradicionales y Lingüísticos "Ce-Acatl," A.C., Gobierno del Distrito Federal, 2007.

Camarena Ocampo, Cuauhtémoc, and Teresa Morales Lersch. "Museos comunitarios de Oaxaca memoria comunal para combatir el olvido." *Arqueología Mexicana* 72 (2005): 72–77.

Carrasco Pizano, Pedro. *Pagan Rituals and Beliefs among the Chontal Indians of Oaxaca, Mexico.* Berkeley: University of California Press, 1960.

———. "Rango de Tecuhtli entre los nahuas trasmontanos." *Tlalocan* 5, 2 (1966): 133–160.

———. "Sobre mito e historia en las tradiciones nahuas." *Historia Mexicana* 39, 3 (1990): 677–686.

———. *The Tenochca Empire of Ancient Mexico: The Triple Alliance of Tenochtitlan, Tetzcoco and Tlacopan.* Norman: University of Oklahoma Press, 1999.

Carrillo y Gariel, Abelardo. *El Cristo de Mexicaltzing: Técnicas de las esculturas en caña.* Mexico City: Dirección de Monumentos Coloniales, 1949.

Caso, Alfonso. "Mapa de Santo Tomás Ocotepeque, Oaxaca," in *Summa antropológica en homenaje a Roberto J. Weitlaner,* 131–137. Mexico City: INAH, 1966.

Castañeda, Paulino. "La condición miserable del indio y sus privilegios." *Anuario de Estudios Americanos* 23 (1971): 245–335.

Castro Gutiérrez, Felipe. *La rebelión de los indios y la paz de los españoles.* Mexico City: CIESAS and Instituto Nacional Indigenista, 1996.

Celestino Solís, Eustaquio, Valencia R. Armando, and Constantino Medina Lima. *Actas del cabildo de Tlaxcala, 1547–1567.* Mexico City: AGN and CIESAS, 1985.

Chance, John K. "Indian Elites in Late Colonial Mesoamerica," in Joyce Marcus and Judith Francis Zeitlin, eds., *Caciques and Their People: A Volume in Honor of Ronald Spores,* 45–65. Ann Arbor: Museum of Anthropology, University of Michigan, 1994.

———. "Mesoamerican Ethnographic Past." *Ethnohistory* 43, 3 (Summer 1996): 379–403.

Chevalier, François. *La formación de los latifundios en México.* Mexico City: Fondo de Cultura Económica, 1976.

Chuchiak, John F. "Papal Bulls, Extirpators, and the *Madrid Codex*: The Content and Probable Provenience of the M.56 Patch," in Gabrielle Vail and Anthony Aveni, eds., *The Madrid Codex: New Approaches to Understanding an Ancient Maya Manuscript,* 57–88. Boulder: University Press of Colorado, 2004.

Bibliography

Coatsworth, John H. *El impacto económico de los ferrocarriles en el porfiriato II*. Mexico City: Sep-Setentas, 1976, 2 vols.

Códice Osuna. Reproducción facsimilar de la obra del mismo título editada en Madrid, 1878. Acompañada de 158 páginas inéditas encontradas en el Archivo General de la Nación (México) por el profesor Luis Chávez Orozco. Mexico City: Ediciones del Instituto Indigenista Interamericano, 1947.

Códices indígenas de algunos pueblos del Marquesado del Valle de Oaxaca publicados por el Archivo General de la Nación para el Primer Congreso Mexicano de Historia celebrado en la Ciudad de Oaxaca. Mexico City: Talleres Gráficos de la Nación, 1933.

Cordova, Fray Juan de. *Vocabulario en lengua zapoteca*. Oaxaca: Ediciones Toledo, 1987.

"Declaración de la Selva Lacandona, 2 de enero, hoy decimos ¡Basta!" in *EZLN Documentos y comunicados 1° de enero/8 de agosto de 1994*, prologue by Antonio García de León Crónicas, Elena Poniatowska, and Carlos Monsiváis, 33–35. México: Ediciones Era, Colección Problemas de México, 1996, vol. 1, 3rd ed.

"Decree of Maximilian of Habsburg, Published in Spanish and Nahuatl, Regarding Pueblos' Sites and Land," in Ascensión H. de León-Portilla, *Tepuztlahcuilolli. Impresos en náhuatl. Historia y bibliografía*, 289–291. Mexico City: UNAM, 1988, vol. 1.

Diario oficial. Vol. 3, 123, December 1, 1854.

Ducey, Michael T. "Hijos del pueblo y ciudadanos: Identidades políticas entre los rebeldes indios del siglo XIX," in Brian Connaughton, Carlos Illanes, and Sonia Pérez Toledo, eds., *Construcción de la legitimidad política en México*, 127–151. Mexico City: El Colegio de Michoacán, Universidad Autónoma Metropolitana, UNAM, and El Colegio de México, 1999.

———. "Viven sin ley ni rey: Rebeliones coloniales en Papantla, 1760–1790," in Victoria Chenaut, ed., *Procesos rurales e historia regional (sierra y costa totonacas de Veracruz)*, 15–49. Mexico City: CIESAS, 1996.

Durán, Fray Diego. *Historia de las indias de nueva España e islas de la tierra firme*, paleography, ed., and notes by Angel Ma. Garibay K. Mexico City: Editorial Porrúa, 1984, 2 vols.

Dyckerhoff, Ursula. "Forged Village Documents from Huejotzingo and Calpan," in *Actes du XLII e. Congrès International des Américanistes. Congrès du Centenaire, Paris, 2–9 Septembre 1976*, 52–63. Paris: Société des Américanistes, Musée de l'Homme, 1979, vol. 7.

Earle, Rebecca. "Creole Patriotism and the Myth of the 'Loyal Indian.'" *Past and Present* (Oxford) 172 (2001): 125–145.

Edmonson, Munro S., trans. *Heaven-Born Merida and Its Destiny: The Book of Chilam Balam of Chumayel*. Austin: University of Texas Press, 1986.

Escalante Gonzalbo, Pablo. "Pintar la historia tras la crisis de la conquista," in *Los pinceles de la historia. El origen del reino de la Nueva España*, 24–49. Mexico City: Museo Nacional de Arte and UNAM, 1999.

Escobar Ohmstede, Antonio. "Introduction, La 'modernización' de México a través del liberalismo. Los pueblos indios durante el juarismo," in Antonio Escobar Ohmstede, ed., *Los pueblos indios en los tiempos de Benito Juárez (1847–1872)*, 11–29. Mexico City: Universidad Autónoma Metropolitana, 2007.

———, ed. *Indio, nación y comunidad en el México del siglo XIX*. Mexico City: Centro de Estudios Mexicanos Centroamericanos and CIESAS, 1993.

———, ed. *Los pueblos indios en los tiempos de Benito Juárez (1847–1872)*. Mexico City: Universidad Autónoma Metropolitana, 2007.

Escobar Ohmstede, Antonio, and Teresa Rojas Rabiela, eds. *La presencia indígena en la prensa capitalina del siglo XIX. Catálogo de noticias I*. Mexico City: Instituto Nacional Indigenista and CIESAS, 1992.

Escobar Ohmstede, Antonio, and Ana María Gutiérrez Rivas. "El liberalismo y los pueblos indígenas en las Hustecas, 1856–1885," in Antonio Escobar Ohmstede, ed., *Los pueblos indios en los tiempos de Benito Juárez (1847–1872)*, 253–297. Mexico City: Universidad Autónoma Metropolitana, 2007.

Fabila, Manuel. *Cinco siglos de legislación agraria [1493–1940]*. Mexico City: Secretaría de la Reforma Agraria and CEHAM, 1981, 2 vols.

Falcón, Romana, ed. *Culturas de pobreza y resistencia. Estudios de marginados, proscritos y descontentos México, 1804–1910*. Mexico City: El Colegio de Mexico and Universidad Autónoma de Querétaro, 2005.

Figuerola Pujol, Helios. "De sacrificio y sacrificios en la comunidad tzeltal de San Juan Evangelista Cancuc en las altas tierras de Chiapas," in Leonardo López Luján and Guilhem Olivier, eds., *El sacrificio humano en la tradición religiosa mesoamericana*, 519–546. Mexico City: INAH, Instituto de Investigaciones Históricas, and UNAM, 2010.

Florentine Codex, General History of the Things of New Spain, Fray Bernardino de Sahagún, ed. and trans. Charles E. Dibble and Arthur J.O. Anderson. Santa Fe, N.M.: School of American Research and the University of Utah, 1950–1982, 13 vols.

Fraser, Donald J. "La política de desamortización en las comunidades indígenas, 1856–1872," *Historia Mexicana* 21, 4 (1972): 615–652.

García-Abásolo, Antonio F. *Martín Enríquez y la Reforma de 1568 en Nueva España*. Seville: Excelentísima Diputación Provincial de Sevilla, 1983.

García González, Oscar. "Memoria colectiva de un éxodo. Los nuevos poblados zapatistas en la selva." *Anales de Antropología* 39, 2 (2005): 51–87.

García Martínez, Bernardo. *Los pueblos de la Sierra. El poder y el espacio entre los indios del norte de Puebla hasta 1700*. Mexico City: El Colegio de México and CEHAM, 1987.

Gerhard, Peter. "Congregaciones de indios en la Nueva España antes de 1570." *Historia Mexicana* 26, 3 (1977): 347–395.

———. *A Guide to the Historical Geography of New Spain*. Cambridge: Cambridge University Press, 1972.

Gibson, Charles. *The Aztec under Spanish Rule: A History of the Indians of the Valley of Mexico*. Stanford: Stanford University Press, 1964.

————. "Llamamiento general, Repartimiento, and the Empire of Acolhuacán." *Hispanic American Historical Review* 36 (1956): 1–27.

Ginzburg, Carlo. *Ecstasies: Deciphering the Witches' Sabbath*. Chicago: University of Chicago Press, 2004.

Glass, John B., and Donald Robertson. "A Census of Native Middle American Pictorial Manuscripts," in Robert Wauchope, ed., *Handbook of Middle American Indians: Guide to Ethnohistorical Sources*, 81–252. Austin: University of Texas Press, 1975, vol. 14, part 3.

Góngora, Mario. *Studies in the Colonial History of Spanish America*. Cambridge: Cambridge University Press, 1975.

González Jácome, Alba. "Ambiente y cultura en la agricultura tradicional de México: Casos y perspectivas." *Anales de Antropología* 37 (2003): 117–140.

Gossen, Gary H. "Cuatro mundos del hombre: Tiempo e historia entre los Chamulas." *Estudios de Cultura Maya* 12 (1979): 179–190.

Gruzinski, Serge. *The Conquest of Mexico: The Incorporation of Indian Societies into the Western World, 16th–18th Centuries*. Cambridge, U.K.: Polity, 1993.

Guardino, Peter F. *Peasants, Politics, and the Formation of Mexico's National State: Guerrero, 1800–1857*. Stanford: Stanford University Press, 1996.

Habana, Misael. "Mueren cuatro niños en Guerrero por ingerir agua contaminada." *La Jornada* (México City), April 6, 2002.

Hanke, Lewis. *The Spanish Struggle for Justice in the Conquest of America*. Philadelphia: University of Pennsylvania Press, 1949.

Hanke, Lewis, and Celso Rodríguez. *Los Virreyes españoles en América durante el gobierno de la Casa de Austria, México I,* Biblioteca de Autores Españoles desde la Formación del Lenguaje hasta nuestros días, continuación de la Colección Rivadeneira, Tomo CCLXXIII. Madrid: Real Academia Española, 1976.

Harvey, H. R. "El lienzo de San Bartolomé Coatepec." *Boletín del Instituto Nacional de Antropología e Historia* 25 (1966): 1–5.

Haskett, Robert. "Visions of Municipal Glory Undimmed: The Nahuatl Town Histories of Colonial Cuernavaca." *Colonial Latin American Historical Review* 1, 1 (1992): 1–36.

————. *Visions of Paradise: Primordial Titles and Mesoamerican History in Cuernavaca*. Norman: University of Oklahoma Press, 2005.

Herrera, Carmen, and Ethelia Ruiz Medrano. *El entintado mundo de la fijeza imaginaria, el Códice de Tepeucila*. Mexico City: INAH, 1997.

Herrera de la Rosa, Santos, and Ignacio Silva Cruz. *Transcripción y traducción del plano de San Agustín de las Cuevas, hoy Tlalpan*. Mexico City: AGN, 2002.

Hill, Jonathan D. *Rethinking History and Myth: Indigenous South American Perspectives on the Past*. Urbana: University of Illinois Press, 1988.

Historia tolteca-chichimeca, ed. Paul Kirchhoff, Lina Odena Güemes, and Luis Reyes García. Mexico City: CIESAS and Fondo de Cultura Económica, 1989, 2nd ed.

Howard-Malverde, Rosaleen. "Talking about the Past: Tense and Testimonials in Quechua Narrative Discourse." *Amerindia* 13 (1988): 125–155.

Inoue, Yukitaka. "Fundación de pueblos indígenas novohispanos según algunos *Títulos primordiales* del Valle de Mexico." *Institute of International Relations and Area Studies* 5 (Ritsumeikan University) (2007): 107–131.

Instituto Nacional de Geografía y Estadística. 2000 census.

———. 2005 census.

Israel, Jonathan I. *Race, Class and Politics in Colonial Mexico.* London: Oxford University Press, 1975.

Jago, Charles. "Philip II and the Cortes of Castile: The Case of the Cortes of 1578." *Past and Present* 109 (1985): 24–43.

Jansen, Maarten. *La gran familia de los reyes mixtecos libro explicativo de los códices llamados Egerton y Becker II.* Mexico City: Akademische Druck- und Verlagsanstalt and Fondo de Cultura Económica, 1994, facsimile ed.

Kellogg, Susan. *Law and the Transformation of Aztec Culture, 1500–1700.* Norman: University of Oklahoma Press, 1995.

Knowlton, Robert J. "El ejido mexicano en el siglo XIX." *Historia Mexicana* 48, 1 (1998): 71–96.

König, Viola. *Inhaltliche, Analyse und Interpretation von Codex Egerton.* Hamburgo: Museo de Hamburgo, 1979.

———. "Mary E. Smith's Interpretation of the *Codex Tulane,* in the *Codex López Ruiz,* and Other Documents: Some Conclusions on the Role of Tlaxiaco in the Western Part of the Mixteca Alta." *Mexicon* 27, 6 (December 2005): 112–115.

Krippner-Martínez, James. "The Vision of the Victors: Power and Colonial Justice." *Colonial Latin American Review* 4, 1 (1995): 3–28.

Kyle, Chris. "Land, Labor and the Chilapa Market: A New Look at the 1840s' Peasant Wars in Central Guerrero." *Ethnohistory* 50, 1 (Winter 2003): 89–130.

León-Portilla, Miguel. *Ordenanzas de tema indígena en castellano y en náhuatl expedidas por Maximiliano de Habsburgo.* Querétaro, Mexico: Instituto de Estudios Constitucionales, 2003.

The Library of Congress Quarterly Journal of Current Acquisitions. Washington, D.C., 3, 3 (1946).

Lipsett-Rivera, Sonia. *To Defend Our Water with the Blood of Our Veins: The Struggle for Resources in Colonial Puebla.* Albuquerque: University of New Mexico Press, 1999.

Lockhart, James. *The Nahuas after the Conquest: A Social and Cultural History of the Indians of Central Mexico, Sixteenth through Eighteenth Centuries.* Palo Alto: Stanford University Press, 1992.

Lockhart, James, Frances Berdan, and Arthur J.O. Anderson. *The Tlaxcalan Actas: A Compendium of Records of the Cabildo of Tlaxcala (1545–1627).* Salt Lake City: University of Utah Press, 1986.

López Austin, Alfredo. "Del origen de los mexicas: ¿Nomadismo o migración?" *Historia Mexicana* 39, 3 (1990): 663–675.

———. "El texto Sahaguntino sobre los mexicas." *Anales de Antropología* (1985): 287–335.

————. *La Constitución Real de México-Tenochtitlan*. Mexico City: UNAM, 1961.

López Bárcenas, Francisco. "La autonomía entre los triquis. Para que haya paz y tranquilidad." *Ojarasca* 118 (February 2007), at http://www.jornada.unam.mx/2007/02/12/oja118-lopbarcenas.html.

López Caballero, Paula, ed. *Los títulos primordiales del Centro de México*. Mexico City: CONACULTA, 2003.

Lupo, Alessandro. "Los cuentos de los abuelos. Un ejemplo de construcción de la memoria entre los nahuas de la Sierra Norte de Puebla, México." *Anales de la Fundación Joaquín Costa* 15 (Huesca) (1997): 263–283.

MacLachlan, Colin M. *Criminal Justice in Eighteenth Century Mexico: A Study of the Tribunal of the Acordada*. Berkeley: University of California Press, 1974.

Mallon, Florencia E. *Peasant and Nation: The Making of Postcolonial Mexico and Peru*. Berkeley: University of California Press, 1995.

Marino, Daniela. "Ahora que Dios nos ha dado padre . . . El Segundo Imperio y la cultura jurídico político campesina en el Centro de Mexico." *Historia Mexicana* 55, 4 (2006): 1353–1410.

————. "La modernidad a juicio: Pleitos por la tierra y la identidad comunal en el Estado de Mexico [Municipalidad de Huixquilucan, 1856–1900]," in Romana Falcón, ed., *Culturas de pobreza y resistencia. Estudios de marginados, proscritos y descontentos México, 1804–1910*, 237–264. Mexico City: El Colegio de México and Universidad Autónoma de Querétaro, 2005.

Markiewicz, Dana. *The Mexican Revolution and the Limits of Agrarian Reform, 1915–1946*. Boulder: Lynne Rienner, 1993.

Markov, Gretchen Koch. "The Legal Status of Indians under Spanish Rule." PhD diss., University of Rochester, Rochester, N.Y., 1983.

Martín, Mónica Patricia. *El indio y los sacramentos en Hispanamerica colonial. Circunstancias adversas y malas interpretaciones*. Buenos Aires: PRHISCO-CONICET, 1993.

Martínez, José Luis. *Documentos Cortesianos*. Mexico City: UNAM and Fondo de Cultura Económica, 1990, 4 vols.

Medina Lima, Constantino, paleography, introduction, and notes. *Libro de los guardianes y gobernadores de Cuauhtinchan [1519–1640]*. Mexico City: CIESAS, 1995.

Megged, Amos. "Poverty and Welfare in Mesoamérica during the Sixteenth and Seventeenth Centuries: European Archetypes and Colonial Translations." *Colonial Latin American Historical Review* 6, 1 (1997): 1–29.

Mendoza García, Edgar. "Distrito político y desamortización: Resistencia y reparto de la propiedad comunal en los pueblos de Cuicatlán y Coixtlahuaca, 1856–1900," in Romana Falcón, ed., *Culturas de pobreza y resistencia. Estudios de marginados, proscritos y descontentos México, 1804–1910*, 209–235. Mexico City: El Colegio de México and Universidad Autónoma de Querétaro, 2005.

————. *Los bienes de comunidad y la defensa de las tierras en la Mixteca oaxaqueña. Cohesión y autonomía del municipio de Santo Domingo Tepenene, 1856–1912*. Mexico City: Senado de la República, 2004.

———. "Organización y funcionamiento del gobierno local: Los municipios de los distritos políticos de Teposcolula y Coxtlahuaca, 1857–1900," in Antonio Escobar Ohmstede, ed., *Los pueblos indios en los tiempos de Benito Juárez (1847–1872)*, 151–170. Mexico City: Universidad Autónoma Metropolitana, 2007.

Menegus Bornemann, Margarita. "Los bienes de comunidad y las Reformas Borbónicas (1786–1814)," in Antonio Miguel Bernard Rodríguez, ed., *Estructuras agrarias y reformismo ilustrado en la España del siglo XVIII*, 383–389. Madrid: Ministerio de Agricultura Pesca y Alimentación, 1989.

Meyer, Jean. "La junta protectora de las clases menesterosas, indigenismo y agrarismo en el Segundo Imperio," in Antonio Escobar Ohmstede, ed., *Indio, nación y comunidad. En el México del siglo XIX*, 329–364. Mexico City: Centro Francés de Estudios Mexicanos Centroamericanos, Centro de Investigaciones, and Estudios Superiores en Antropología Social, 1993.

Miranda, Francisco. *Don Vasco de Quiroga y su Colegio de San Nicolás*. Morelia, Mexico: Fimax Publicitas, 1972.

Miranda, José. *El tributo indígena en la Nueva España*. Mexico City: El Colegio de México, 1980.

Molina, Alonso de. *Vocabulario en lengua castellana y mexicana y mexicana y castellana*. Miguel León Portilla, preliminary study. Mexico City: Editorial Porrúa, S.A., 1992, 3rd ed.

Monaghan, John. "Mixtec Caciques in the Nineteenth and Twentieth Centuries." *Cuadernos de Historia Latinoamericana* (Special number of *Códices, Caciques and Communities* 5) (1997): 265–281.

Monaghan, John, and Byron Harmann. "La construcción cultural de la lectura en Mesoamérica," in Constanza Vega Sosa, ed., *Códices y documentos sobre Mexico. Tercer Simposio Internacional*, 485–505. Mexico City: INAH, 2000.

Monaghan, John, Arthur Joyce, and Ronald Spores. "Transformations of the Indigenous Cacicazgo in the Nineteenth Century." *Ethnohistory* 50, 1 (Winter 2003): 131–150.

Moreno Valle, Lucina. *Catálogo de la Colección Lafragua, 1821–1853*. Mexico City: UNAM and Instituto de Investigaciones Bibliográficas, 1975.

Morera, Jaime. *Pinturas coloniales de animas del purgatorio*. Mexico City: Instituto de Investigaciones Estéticas and UNAM, 2001.

Morin, Claude. *Santa Inés Zacatelco (1646–1812): Contribución a la demografía histórica colonial*. Mexico City: INAH, 1973.

Muro Orejón, Antonio, studies and notes. *Las Leyes Nuevas de 1542–1543. Ordenanzas para la gobernación de las Indias y buen tratamiento y conservación de los indios*. Seville: Escuela de Estudios Hispano-Americanos, 1961, facsimile ed.

Nash, June. *Bajo la mirada de los antepasados. Creencias y comportamiento en una comunidad maya*. Mexico City: Instituto Indigenista Interamericano, special ed., 1975.

Navarrete, Federico. "La tierra sin mal, una utopía anti-estatal Americana," in Guilhem Olivier, ed., *Símbolos de poder en Mesoamérica*, 475–492. Mexico City: UNAM, 2008.

————. *Las relaciones interétnicas en México*. Mexico City: UNAM, 2004.

————. "Los libros quemados y los nuevos libros. Paradojas de la autenticidad en la tradición mesoamericana," in Alberto Dallad, ed., *La abolición del arte. El Coloquio Internacional de Historia del Arte*, 53–71. Mexico City: Instituto de Investigaciones Estéticas and UNAM, 1998.

————. "Medio siglo de explorar el universo de las fuentes nahuas: Entre la historia, la literatura y el nacionalismo." *Estudios de Cultura Náhuatl* 27 (1997): 156–179.

Nuijten, Monique. "Between Fear and Fantasy: Governmentality and the Working of Power in Mexico." *Critique of Anthropology* 24, 2 (2004): 209–230.

Nygren, Anja. "Struggle over Meanings: Reconstruction of Indigenous Mythology, Cultural Identity, and Social Representation." *Ethnohistory* 45, 1 (1998): 31–61.

Offner, Jerome. *Law and Politics in Aztec Texcoco*. New York: Cambridge University Press, 1983.

Olivier, Guilhem. *Mockeries and Metamorphoses of an Aztec God: Tezcatlipoca, "Lord of the Smoking Mirror."* Boulder: University Press of Colorado, 2003.

————. "The Sacred Bundles and the Coronation of the Aztec King in Mexico-Tenochtitlan," in Julia Guernsey and F. Kent Reilley, eds., *Sacred Bundles: Ritual Acts of Wrapping and Binding in Mesoamérica*, 199–225. Barnardsville, N.C.: Boundary and Archeology Research Center, 2006.

Ortiz Coronel, Germán. "*Ñúu Kuini:* Un territorio en disputa, conflictos agrarios y negociación en la Mixteca." Master's thesis, Universidad Autónoma Metropolitana, Mexico City, 2007.

Ortiz Paniagua, Carlos. "El servicio de copias certificadas en el AGN," in *VII Congreso Nacional de Archivos* 35, 220–223. Mexico City: AGN, 1996.

Osborn, Wayne Smyth. "A Community Study of Meztitlán, New Spain, 1520–1810." PhD diss., University of Iowa, Iowa City, 1970.

Oudijk, Michel. *Historiography of the Bènizàa. The Postclassic and Early Colonial Periods [1000–1600 AD]*. Leiden: Research School of Asian, African, and Amerindian Studies, Universiteit Leiden, 2000.

Padgen, Anthony. *Spanish Imperialism and the Political Imagination*. New Haven: Yale University Press, 1990.

Palacios, Guillermo. "Las restituciones de la Revolución," in Ismael Maldonado Salazar, Guillermo Palacios, and Reyna María Silva Chacón, eds., *Estudios campesinos en el Archivo General Agrario*, 119–161. Mexico City: Registro Agrario Nacional and CIESAS (Colección Agraria), 2001, vol. 3.

Pani, Erica. "¿'Verdaderas figuras de Cooper' o 'pobres inditos infelices'? La política indigenista de Maximiliano." *Historia Mexicana* 47, 3 (1998): 571–604.

Parmenter, Ross. *Four Lienzos of the Coixtlahuaca Valley*. Washington D.C.: Dumbarton Oaks, Trustees for Harvard University, 1982.

Peña, Guillermo de la. *Herederos de promesas agricultura, política y ritual en los altos de Morelos*. Mexico City: Centro de Investigaciones Superiores del INAH, 1980.

———. "Sociedad civil y resistencia popular en el Mexico de final del siglo XX," in Leticia Reina and Elisa Servin, eds., *Crisis, reforma y Revolución México: Historias de fin de siglo,* 371–425. Mexico City: Editorial Taurus, CONACULTA, and INAH, 2002.

Pla Brugat, Dolores. "Indios, mestizos y blancos, según algunas estadísticas elaboradas en México en el siglo XIX," in *Diario de Campo* 43, 106–111. Mexico City: Coordinación Nacional de Antropología and INAH, 2007.

Rappaport, Joanne. *The Politics of Memory: Native Historical Interpretation in the Colombian Andes.* New York: Cambridge University Press, 1990.

Recopilación de leyes, de los reinos de las Indias, prologue by Ramón Menéndez y Pidal, introduction by Juan Manzano Manzano. Madrid: Cultura Hispánica, 1973, 4 vols.

Relaciones geográficas del siglo XVI: Tlaxcala, ed. René Acuña. Mexico City: Instituto de Investigaciones Antropológicas and UNAM, 1984, vol. 1.

Reyes García, Luis. *Documentos sobre tierras y señoríos en Cuauhtinchan.* Mexico City: INAH, Colección Fuentes, 1978.

Reyes García, Luis, and Eustaquio Celestino Solís. *Documentos históricos Cuauhuixmatlac Atetecochco.* Mexico City: Departamento de Filosofía y Letras de la Universidad Autónoma de Tlaxcala, Instituto Tlaxcalteca de la Cultura, and Comisión para escribir la historia de Cuauhuixmatlac, 2001.

———. *Documentos nahuas de la Ciudad de Mexico del siglo XVI.* Mexico City: CIESAS and AGN, 1996.

———. "Ordenanzas para el gobierno de Cuauhtinchan, año 1559." *Estudios de Cultura Náhuatl* 10 (1972): 245–313.

Ricard, Robert. *La conquista espiritual de México.* Mexico City: Fondo de Cultura Económica, 1986.

Robertson, Donald. *Mexican Manuscript Painting of the Early Colonial Period: The Metropolitan Schools.* Norman: University of Oklahoma Press, 1994, 2nd ed.

———. "Techialoyan Manuscripts and Paintings, with a Catalog," in Howard F. Cline, ed., *Handbook of Middle American Indians,* vol. 14: *Guide to Ethnohistorical Sources,* part 3, 253–280. Austin: University of Texas Press, 1975.

Roland Dealy, Ross. "Vasco de Quiroga's Thought on War: Its Erasmian and Utopian Roots." PhD diss., Indiana University, Bloomington, 1975.

Roskamp, Hans. *La historiografía indígena de Michoacán: El lienzo de Jucutácato y los títulos de Carapan.* Leiden: Research School of Asian, African, and Amerindian Studies, Universiteit Leiden, 1998.

Ruiz Medrano, Carlos Rubén. "Los rebeldes de Colotlán en 1780 y la llegada del rey Mariano a Tepic en 1801: Episodios de la resistencia indígena en las postrimerías del período colonial mexicano." Unpublished manuscript, 2008.

Ruiz Medrano, Ethelia. "El espejo y su reflejo: Títulos primordiales de los pueblos indios utilizados por españoles en Tlaxcala, siglo XVIII," in Danna Levin and Federico Navarrete, eds., *Indios, mestizos y españoles. Interculturalidad e historiografía en la Nueva España,* 167–202. Mexico City: Universidad Autónoma Metropolitana, Instituto de Investigaciones Históricas, and UNAM, 2007.

―――. "En el cerro y la iglesia: La figura cosmológica *atl-tépetl-oztotl.*" *Relaciones* (El Colegio de Michoacán) 22, 86 (Spring 2001): 143–183.

―――. "La compra de la encomienda por parte de los indios de Nueva España," in Nora Jiménez Hernández, Águeda Jiménez, and José Román Gutiérrez, eds., *Felipe II y el oficio del Rey: La fragua de un imperio*, 835–869. Mexico City: INAH, Universidad Autónoma de Zacatecas, Universidad de Guadalajara, and Sociedad Estatal para la Conmemoración de los Centenarios de Felipe II y Carlos V, Madrid, 2001.

―――. "Las primeras instituciones del poder colonial," in Bernardo García Martínez, ed., *Gran historia de México ilustrada*, 41–60. Mexico City: Planeta DeAgostini and INAH, 2002, vol. 2.

―――. "The Lords of the Earth: Historical Context of the Mapa de Cuauhtinchan No. 2," in David Carrasco and Scott Sessions, eds., *Cave, City, and Eagle's Nest: An Interpretive Journey through the Mapa de Cuauhtinchan No. 2*, foreword by John H. Coatsworth, 91–119. Albuquerque: University of New Mexico Press, 2007.

―――. "Poder e iglesia en Nueva España: La disputa por el diezmo," in Francisco González Hermosillo Adams, ed., *Gobierno y economía en los pueblos indios de la Nueva España*, 97–112. Mexico City: INAH, 2002.

―――. *Reshaping New Spain: Government and Private Interests in the Colonial Bureaucracy, 1535–1550.* Boulder: University Press of Colorado, 2005.

―――. "Símbolos de poder en códices y textos nahuas y mixtecos colonials," in Guilhem Olivier, ed., *Símbolos de poder en Mesoamérica*, 443–474. Mexico City: Instituto de Investigaciones Históricas and Instituto de Investigaciones Antropológicas–UNAM, 2008.

Ruiz Medrano, Ethelia, and Susan Kellogg. "Fighting Destiny: Nahua Nobles and the Friars in the Sixteenth-Century Revolt of the Encomenderos against the King," in Ethelia Ruiz Medrano and Susan Kellogg, eds., *Negotiation with Domination: Colonial New Spain's Indian Pueblos Confront the Spanish State*, 45–78. Boulder: University Press of Colorado, 2010.

―――, eds. *Negotiation with Domination: Colonial New Spain's Indian Pueblos Confront the Spanish State.* Boulder: University Press of Colorado, 2010.

Ruiz Medrano, Ethelia, and Xavier Noguez. *Dos pictografías del estado de México: El Códice de Tlacotepec.* Zinacantepec: El Colegio Mexiquense, 2004.

Ruiz Medrano, Ethelia, and Perla Valle. "Los colores de la Justicia. Códices jurídicos del siglo XVI en la Biblioteca Nacional de Francia." *Journal de la Société des Américanistes de Paris* 84, 2 (1998): 227–241.

Sahagún, Fray Bernardino de. *Códice Florentino* (facsimile edition of manuscript 218-20, Palatina Collection, Medicea Laurenziana Library). Mexico City: Gobierno de la República and AGN, 1982, 3 vols.

Salomon, Frank. "Chronicles of the Impossible: Notes on Three Peruvian Indigenous Historians," in Rolena Adorno, ed., *From Oral to Written Expressions: Native Andean Chronicles of the Early Colonial Period*, 9–39. Latin American Series, Foreign and

Comparative Studies Program 4. Syracuse, N.Y.: Maxwell School of Citizenship and Public Affairs, Syracuse University, 1982.

Sarabia Viejo, María Justina. *Don Luis de Velasco virrey de Nueva España, 1550–1564*. Seville: Escuela de Estudios Hispano-Americanos, 1978.

Scholes, France V., and Eleanor B. Adams. *Documentos para la historia del México colonial [Cartas del licenciado Jerónimo de Valderrama y otros documentos sobre su visita al gobierno de Nueva España, 1563–1565]*, vol. 7. Mexico City: José Porrúa e Hijos, 1961.

Scholes, Walter Vinton. *The Diego Ramirez Visita*, no. 4. Columbia: University of Missouri, 1946.

Scott, James. *Weapons of the Weak: Everyday Forms of Peasant Resistance*. New Haven: Yale University Press, 1985.

Sell, Barry B., and Susan Kellogg. "We Want to Give Them Laws: Royal Ordinances in a Mid-Sixteenth Century Náhuatl Text." *Estudios de Cultura Náhuatl* 27 (1997): 325–367.

Sepúlveda y Herrera, María Teresa. *Los lienzos de San Juan Cuauhtla, Puebla*. Mexico City: INAH and Miguel Angel Porrúa, 2005.

———. "Petición de lluvias en Ostotempa." *Boletín del Instituto Nacional de Antropología e Historia*, Second Epoch, 4 (1973): 9–20.

Silva Cruz, Ignacio. *Transcripción y traducción del Códice Techialoyan de Cuajimalpa*, paleography and trans. Ignacio Silva Cruz. Mexico City: AGN, 2002.

———. *Transcripción, traducción y dictamen de los títulos primordiales del pueblo de San Miguel Atlahutla. Siglo XVI*, paleography and trans. Ignacio Silva Cruz. Mexico City: AGN, 2002.

Silva Prada, Natalia. *La política de una rebelión: Los indígenas frente al tumulto de 1692 en la Ciudad de México*. Mexico City: El Colegio de México and CEHAM, 2007.

Simpson, Lesley Byrd. *The Encomienda in New Spain: The Beginning of Spanish Mexico*. Berkeley: University of California Press, 1982.

Smith, Mary Elizabeth. *The Codex López Ruiz: A Lost Mixtec Pictorial Manuscript*. Nashville: Vanderbilt University Publications in Anthropology, 1998.

———. *Picture Writing from Ancient Southern México: Mixtec Place Signs and Maps*. Norman: University of Oklahoma Press, 1973.

Solórzano y Pereyra, Juan de. *Política Indiana. Edición facsimilar tomada de la de 1776 (Madrid)*. Mexico City: Secretaría de Programación y Presupuesto, 1979, 2 vols.

Stavig, Ward. "Ambiguous Visions: Nature, Law and Culture in Indigenous-Spanish Land Relations in Colonial Peru." *Hispanic American Historical Review* 80, 1 (2000): 77–111.

Stephen, Lynn. *Zapata Lives! Histories and Cultural Politics in Southern Mexico*. Berkeley: University of California Press, 2002.

Swanton, Michael W. "El texto popoloca de la *Historia Tolteca-Chichimeca*." *Revista Relaciones* (El Colegio de Michoacán) 22, 86 (Spring 2001): 115–140.

Tavárez, David Eduardo. "La idolatría letrada: Un análisis comparativo de textos clandestinos rituales y devocionales en comunidades nahuas y zapotecas, 1613–1654." *Historia Mexicana* 49, 2 (October–December 1999): 197–251.

Taylor, William. "Conflict and Balance in District Politics: Tecali and the *Sierra Norte de Puebla* in the Eighteenth Century," in Arij Oweneel and Simon Miller, eds., *The Indian Community of Colonial Mexico: Fifteen Essays on Land Tenure, Corporate Organizations, Ideology and Village Politics*, 270–294. Amsterdam: CEDLA, 1990.

———. *Magistrates of the Sacred: Priests and Parishioners in Eighteenth-Century Mexico.* Stanford: Stanford University Press, 1996.

Tecuanhuey Sandoval, Alicia. "La resistencia del subdelegado de Atlixco a los ayuntamientos en los pueblos del partido, 1812–1814," in *Memorias de la Academia Mexicana de la Historia correspondiente de la Real de Madrid*, 15–36. Mexico: n.p., 2002.

Terraciano, Kevin. *The Mixtecs of Colonial Oaxaca.* Stanford: Stanford University Press, 2001.

Terraciano, Kevin, and Lisa Sousa. "The 'Original Conquest' of Oaxaca: Late Colonial Nahuatl and Mixtec Accounts of the Spanish Conquest." *Ethnohistory* 50, 2 (2003): 349–400.

Testimonio sobre la lucha agraria de Ixcamilpa. Desde el tiempo de las haciendas hasta nuestros días. Puebla: Unión Regional de Ejidos y Comunidades del Sur del Estado de Puebla, 1982.

Torales Pacheco, María Cristina. "A Note on the Composiciones de Tierras in the Jurisdiction of Cholula, Puebla [1591–1757]," in Simon Miller and Arij Ouweneel, eds., *The Indian Community of Colonial Mexico: Fifteen Essays on Land Tenure, Corporate Organizations, Ideology and Village Politics*, 87–102. Amsterdam: CEDLA, 1990.

Torre Villar, Ernesto de la. *Las congregaciones de los pueblos de indios.* Mexico City: UNAM, 1995.

Tutino, John. *From Insurrection to Revolution in Mexico: Social Bases of Agrarian Violence, 1750–1940.* Princeton: Princeton University Press, 1986.

———. "Globalizaciones, autonomías y revoluciones: Poder y participación popular en la historia de México," in Leticia Reina and Elisa Servín, eds., *Crisis, reforma y Revolución México: Historias de fin de siglo*, 25–85. Mexico City: Taurus, CONACULTA, and INAH, 2002.

van Doesburg, Sebastián. *Documentos Antiguos de San Miguel Tequixtepec, Oaxaca. Los primeros cien años de la colonia [1533–1617].* Leiden: Research School of Asian, African and Amerindian Studies, University of Leiden, 2002.

———. "The Prehispanic History of the Valley of Coixtlahuaca, Oaxaca," in Maarten Jansen and Luis Reyes García, eds., *Códices, caciques y comunidades*, 103–160. Cuadernos de Historia Latinoamericana no. 5. Ridderkerk: Asociación de Historiadores Latinoamericanist, 1997.

Van Young, Eric. *The Other Rebellion: Popular Violence, Ideology, and the Mexican Struggle for Independence 1810–1821.* Stanford: Stanford University Press, 2001.

Vera Herrera, Ramón. "Procede-Procecom 'Las escrituraciones del diablo.'" *Ojarasca* 86 (June 2004): 1–4, at http://www.jornada.unam.mx/2004/06/14/oja86-procede.html.

Vigil Batista, Alejandra. *Catálogo del Archivo de Tenencia de la Tierra en la provincia de Puebla. Sección de manuscritos Fondo Reservado, Biblioteca Nacional.* Puebla: Gobierno del Estado de Puebla and Comisión Puebla V Centenario, 1992.

Wachtel, Natan. *La vision des vaincus: Les Indiens du Pérou devant la conquête espagnole.* Paris: Gallimard, 1971.

Wagner, Henry Raup. *The Life and Writings of Bartolomé de las Casas.* Albuquerque: University of New Mexico Press, 1967.

Warman, Arturo. *Y venimos a contradecir. Los campesinos de Morelos y el estado nacional.* Mexico City: Centro de Investigaciones Superiores del INAH, 1978, 2nd ed.

———, trans. Judith Brister. "The Political Project of Zapatismo," in Friedrich Katz, ed., *Riot, Rebellion, and Revolution: Rural Social Conflict in Mexico,* 321–337. Princeton: Princeton University Press, 1988.

Whited Norman, Anne. "*Testerian* Codices: Hieroglyphic Catechisms for Native Conversion in New Spain." PhD diss., Tulane University, New Orleans, 1985.

Wood, Stephanie Gail. "The Cosmic Conquest: Late Colonial Views of the Sword and the Cross in Central Mexican Títulos." *Ethnohistory* 38, 29 (1991): 176–195.

———. "Don Diego García de Mendoza Moctezuma: A Techialoyan Mastermind?" *Estudios de Cultura Náhuatl* 19 (1989): 215–259.

———. "El problema de la historicidad de los títulos y los códices Techialoyan," in Xavier Noguez and Stephanie Wood, eds., *De Tlacuilos a escribanos,* 167–221. Mexico City: El Colegio de Michoacán and El Colegio Mexiquense, 1998.

———. "Power Differentials in Early Mesoamerican Gender Ideology: The Founding Couple," in Guilhem Olivier, ed., *Símbolos de poder en Mesoamérica,* 517–531. México: UNAM, 2008.

———. "The Social vs. Legal Context of Nahuatl *Títulos*," in Elizabeth Hill Boone and Tom Cummins, eds., *Native Traditions in the Postconquest World,* 201–231. Washington, D.C.: Dumbarton Oaks Research Library and Collection, 1998.

———. *Transcending Conquest: Nahua Views of Spanish Colonial Mexico.* Norman: University of Oklahoma Press, 2003.

Wright, David. *Conquistadores otomíes en la Guerra Chichimeca.* Querétaro, Mexico: Secretaría de Cultura Bienestar Social and Gobierno del Estado de Querétaro, 1988.

Zavala, Silvio. *El servicio personal de los indios en la Nueva España 1600–1635,* vol. 5, part 1. Mexico City: El Colegio de México and El Colegio Nacional, 1990.

———. *La encomienda Indiana.* Mexico City: Editorial Porrúa, 1973.

Zeitlin, Francis Judith, and Lillian Thomas. "Spanish Justice and the Indian Cacique: Disjunctive Political Systems in Sixteenth-Century Tehuantepec." *Ethnohistory* 39, 3 (Summer 1992): 285–314.

Zorita, Alonso de. *Relación de la Nueva España,* ed. and paleography Ethelia Ruiz Medrano, José Mariano Leyva, and Wiebke Arhndt. Mexico City: CONACULTA and Colección Cien de México, 1999, 2 vols.

Zuazo, Alonso de. *Cartas y memoriales [1511–1539],* ed. Rodrigo Martínez Baracs. Mexico City: CONACULTA and Colección Cien de México, 2000.

Index

Page numbers in *italics* indicate illustrations.

Index

Cano, Martín, 48
Cano Moctezuma family, 119
Capultitlán, 44
Cárdenas, Lázaro, 193, 195
Caro, Juan, 48
Carranza, Venustiano, 185, 186, 194
Carranza de Miranda, Bartolomé de, 27, 129
Carrasco, Diodoro, 261
Carrasco, Pedro, 136
Carrillo, Gaspar, 57
Casas, Bartolomé de las, 129; on Indian rights, 26–28
Castañeda, Pedro, 247, 250–51, 280(nn86, 88), 281(n107)
Castilblanco. *See* Iztaquimaxtitlan
Castile, and rights to America, 25–26, 73(n79)
Catholic Church: as protector, 21–22; secularization and, 85–86
Caves, 54, 107, 132–33, 136, 147(n176)
Caxonos, 134–35, 136
Cazalla, Dr. Agustin, 129
Cazonzi, 17
Centralist government, rebellion against, 163–64
Ceremonies: pre-Hispanic, 220–22; traditional, 159, 276(n22)
Ceynos, Francisco, justice system, 24, 47
Chachapan, 118; forged map of, 179, *180*
Chalco, 38, 100; community histories, 114–16, 170, 171
Chamula Indians, 109–10
Charles V, 17, 18, 26, 28, 29, 124, 126, 129, 145(n130), 155; in primordial titles, 112, 117
Chautempan, 174
Chazumba, 167
Chiapas, 109, 132, 214
Chicahuastla, 254, 257, 259
Chichimeca region, 88, 162, 204(n73)
Chichimeca Tequeytli, Felipe, 116
Chichimequillas (Santa María Sauceda), 170–71
Chichipico school, 231
Chicnauztepetl, 107
Chiconquiaco, 172, 205(n79)
Chignautla, 107, 143(n95), 215
Chilam Balam de Chumayel, 134
Chilapa, rebellion in, 163–64
Chilpancingo, 219
Chiltern, Jon, 134

Chimaltzin family, 57
Chinacamitlan, 83–84
Chiptalpopoca, Mascaron, 172
Ch'oles, 110, 132
Cholotecas, 129
Cholula, 187, 224
Chontatl, Cebrian, 45–46
Christian humanism, 28–29
Christianity, 108; conversion to, 26, 27, 34; native sacred objects and, 137–38; papal bulls and, 133–34; and primordial titles, 112–13; and traditional customs, 220–21
Cipac, Martín, 48
"Ciprianillo," 136–37
Citizenship, 4; indigenous, 153–54, 157
Clergy, secular, 62, 86
Coata, Martín, 57
Coatepec, 179
Coatlán del Río (Morelos), 187
Coca, Francisco, 173–74
Codex Colombino, 105
Codex Egerton, 239–40, 251
Codex López Ruiz, 239
Codex Mendoza, 13
Codex of Yucumana, 119
Codex Tulane, 105
Codíce Madrid, 134
Codices, 1, 5, *33,* 45, 68–69, 73(n72), 119, 130, 149(n212); from Concepción, 104–5; conquest depictions in, 17, 18, *19*; from Cuquila, 239–40; indigenous uses of, 31–32, 138; interpretation of, 45–46; as land histories, 97–103; as legal documents, 11–12, *38,* 38–39, 45–46, 55–56, *56,* 216, 275(n18), 285; papal bulls in, 134, 135–36; Techialoyan-style, 96–97, 105–6, 111, 171, 286; Tepeucila, 35–36; in Totolapan, 216, 217, 275(n18)
Coixtlahuaca, Valle de, 129
Colegio de Santa Cruz (Tlatelolco), 35
Committee to Protect the Needy Classes, 181
Commoners, 13, 75(n106), 94
Common Lands Commission (Cuquila), 258
Communities, 4, 85, 153, 165, 218, 291; codices produced for, 31–32; congregación, 91–96; expenses imposed on, 62, 81–82; formation of, 88–89; history, 3, 247–48, 283–84, 289–90; Mixteca Alta, 237–39
Comonfort, Ignacio, 164

Index

Index

Slavery, Indian, 23–24
Socialist Workers Party, 212
Socoyuca, 90
Spain, fiscal crisis under Philip II, 61–62
Spaniards, 87, 93–94, 151
Spanish, 5; historical administrative records, 98–99; inclusion in traditional history, 108–9
State Forestry Department, 270
Stela, 278(n56); Cuquila's, 239, *240*, 243, 252–54, 271–72, 280(n91), 282(n120), 290
Suchitepeque, 37

Tacuba, 38; and Triple Alliance, 43–44
Tamaulipas, 164
Tapia, Andrés de, 35
Tapia, Hernando de, 60
Tapia, Isabel de, 35
Tarascans, 17
Tasmalaca, 84
Taxation, 62, 157. *See also* Tribute
Teachers, 82
Tecali, 125
Tecamachalco, 80
Techialoyan codices, 96–97, 103, 105–6, 111, 171, 286
Tecuytlatoque, 15
Tejada, Lorenzo de, 38–39, 60
Tello, José Manuel, forgeries of, 173, 175, 177–79, 187
Temazcaltepec, Malacatepec attacks on, 54–56
Templo mayor, 17
Temyluca, Pedro, 48
Tenango, codices in, 45–46
Tenango del Valle, sacred objects in, 132–33
Tenexcalco, dispute with Tizayuca, 58–60
Tenextlatlatylolla, 174
Tenochtitlán, 17, 43
Tepan, Antón, 48
Tepatlachico (Tepatlasco), 116–17, *118*, 145(n130)
Tepeapulco, 58, 59
Tepehuexoyuca, 171, 177
Tepehuexoyucan (Asunción Tepezoyuca). *See* Santa María de la Asunción Tepehuexoyuca
Tepejillo (Tepexillo, Thepejillo), *240*, 246
Tepenene, 183
Tepeticpac, 178
Tepetomatitla, 174

Tepetomatitlan (Tepotomatytlan), 174, 177, *178*
Tepetzoltic, 175
Tepeucila Indians, 35–36
Tepezintla, 135
Tepic, 161
Tepopula, 170
Teposantitlan, 174, 175
Tepozotlán, lawsuits, 40–41
Tepuxaco, 40
Tequistepec, 243; history of, 129–31, *131*
Tequiscistlán (Ecatepec), 1; title documentation, 197–99
Tequixtlatec, 136
Testerian codex, 135–36
Tetatsi Tenellecac de Techalollan, 175
Tetepango, 66
Tetitzintla, 187
Texcoco, 13, 14, 15, 44, 45–46
Texinca: history of, 122–23, *123*; land rights, 121–22
Texmelucan, 174
Textile industry, 85
Teyacapa, Magdalena, 39–40
Tezcacoacatl, Diego, 48
Tezoyuca, 37
Third Creation, 110
Tierra Aldentro, 162
Tiger's Hill (Cuquila), 247–48, 249, 250, 251–52
Titles, 98–99, 100, 142(nn88, 90), 217–18; codices and, 104–5; Cuquila's, 262–66, 281–82(nn107, 113); forged/counterfeit, 124–25, 173–79; hacienda, 101–2, 107–8; Ixcamilpa, 211–12, *213*; noble lineages and, 119–21, *117*; migration histories in, 106–7; in National Archive, 167–71; in Oaxaca, 127–28, 130; obtaining copies of, 168–69, 170–71; primordial, 106–7, 111–13, 114–16, 142(nn88, 90), 143(nn95, 96), 144(n124), 205–6(n85), 214–15, 216, 227, 281(n107), 286; to pueblos, 102–3, 113–14, 167–68; searches for, 167–68, 208–9(n149); traditional culture in, 171–72
Tixtla, 224, 225, 231
Tizayuca, conflict with Santiago Tenexcalco, 58–60
Tlacololeros, 225
Tlacopan, 15